MULTIPLE PATHS OF MIDLIFE DEVELOPMENT

STUDIES ON SUCCESSFUL MIDLIFE DEVELOPMENT

*The John D. and Catherine T. MacArthur Foundation Series
on Mental Health and Development*

Other titles in the series

SEXUALITY ACROSS THE LIFE COURSE
Edited by Alice S. Rossi

THE PARENTAL EXPERIENCE IN MIDLIFE
Edited by Carol D. Ryff and Marsha Mailick Seltzer

MULTIPLE PATHS OF MIDLIFE DEVELOPMENT

Edited by

Margie E. Lachman

and

Jacquelyn Boone James

The University of Chicago Press

Chicago and London

HQ
1059.4
M85
1997

MARGIE E. LACHMAN is professor of psychology at Brandeis University.
JACQUELYN BOONE JAMES is assistant director of the Henry Murray Research
Center of Radcliffe College.

THE UNIVERSITY OF CHICAGO PRESS, CHICAGO 60637
THE UNIVERSITY OF CHICAGO PRESS, LTD., LONDON

© 1997 by The University of Chicago
All rights reserved. Published 1997
Printed in the United States of America

06 05 04 03 02 01 00 99 98 97   1 2 3 4 5
ISBN: 0-226-46758-9 (cloth)

The University of Chicago Press gratefully acknowledges a subvention from the
John D. and Catherine T. MacArthur Foundation in partial support of the costs of
production of this volume.

Library of Congress Cataloging-in-Publication Data

Multiple paths of midlife development / edited by Margie E. Lachman
and Jacquelyn Boone James.
       p.   cm. — (Studies on successful midlife development)
    Includes bibliographical references and index.
    ISBN 0-226-46758-9 (cloth)
    1. Middle age.   2. Middle age—Psychological aspects.   3. Middle
aged persons.   I. Lachman, Margie E.   II. James, Jacquelyn Boone.
III. Series: John D. and Catherine T. MacArthur Foundation series on
mental health and development.   Studies on successful midlife
development.
HQ1059.4.M85   1997
305.24′4—dc20   96-29289
                                                          CIP

⊗ *The paper used in this publication meets the minimum requirements of the
American National Standard for Information Sciences—Permanence of Paper for
Printed Library Materials, ANSI Z39.48-1984.*

In memory of my mother, Joyce R. Lachman (MEL),
and my father, Jerry B. Boone (JBJ),
whose paths through midlife were cut short.

CONTENTS

Anne Colby

This book is the product of a collaborative program of research on middle adulthood cosponsored by the MacArthur Foundation Research Network on Successful Midlife Development (MIDMAC) and the Henry A. Murray Research Center of Radcliffe College. The purpose of the program was to support the use of data from the Murray Center's social science data archive for the study of a broad range of issues relating to midlife development and adaptation.

Beginning in 1982, the John D. and Catherine T. MacArthur Foundation's Program in Mental Health and Human Development established a number of research networks. These networks brought together distinguished researchers from many disciplines to address issues of normal and deviant development across the life course. Among these networks is the MacArthur Foundation Research Network on Successful Midlife Development, established in 1989 and chaired by Gilbert Brim. The major objective is to identify the main biomedical, social, and psychological factors that contribute to good health, personal well-being, and social responsibility during midlife.

Like MIDMAC, many of the other MacArthur networks have a developmental orientation and stress positive adaptation and successful development. They also study maladaptive development and psychopathology. In addition to pursuing these substantive research goals, the networks constitute "an experiment in scientific organization" based on sustained collaboration across disciplines and institutions. Along with this cross-disciplinary focus, the networks represent an effort to shift the research climate toward greater openness in the scientific process, including the sharing of data as well as conclusions of research (Kahn, 1993).

The Murray Research Center institutionalizes a related set of substantive concerns with human development across the life span, the sharing of research data, scientific openness, and a spirit of collaboration, including collaboration across disciplines. The Henry A. Murray

Research Center of Radcliffe College was established in 1976 as a national repository for social and behavioral science data, focusing especially on studies from psychology, psychiatry, sociology, and education, with some additional data sets from criminology, political science, and economics.

The Murray Center's approach to the study of human development is informed by the belief that longitudinal designs are a necessary tool if we are to understand patterns of developmental change and the relation of early experiences and conditions to later outcomes. There is wide agreement among social scientists about the value of studies that follow the same people over long periods of time. But long-term longitudinal studies are very costly in terms of both funding and the time commitment needed for the research team. Because of their value and cost, it is especially important that extensive, high-quality longitudinal data sets be made available for use by other investigators. For this reason, the preservation and promotion of data from longitudinal studies is central to the mission of the Murray Center.

The Murray Center's approach to this task is unique in several ways. First, the Murray Center is the only archive that preserves the original subject records as well as coded, machine-readable data. These raw data, such as transcripts of in-depth interviews, behavioral observations, and responses to projective tests, are especially valuable for secondary analysis, allowing the application of different perspectives and new scoring procedures to the original data. This makes possible the radical restructuring of the subject records and mitigates the degree to which one is locked into the theoretical assumptions under which the data were collected. Restructuring the data set in this way depends upon the availability of qualitative materials, such as transcribed interviews and observations.

In spite of the clear advantages of making raw data available, most data banks offer only coded computer data. Some major longitudinal studies are achieved in a manner that allows access to the records by outside investigators, but in general each of these studies is housed separately. The Murray Research Center is the only repository that is designed to offer a wide range of data sets with original, qualitative records, many of which are longitudinal. The Murray Center is also unique in that samples from many of the studies it holds are available for further follow-up by the new investigator. This is, of course, very valuable in that it allows a new investigator to design the outcome measures used. Use of archival data also allows for the addition of a new cohort to a single-cohort longitudinal study or the integration of two data sets into a single multicohort study.

The Murray Center currently holds 216 data sets, 73 of which are longitudinal. The center adds new studies to the archive each year and has recently developed a major collection of longitudinal studies of mental health. Funding from the National Institute of Mental Health and the MacArthur Foundation supported the acquisition of many key longitudinal studies for this collection, including, for example, Baumrind's Family Socialization and Developmental Competence Project, Brunswick's Harlem Longitudinal Study, Glueck and Glueck's Crime Causation Study, the Institute of Human Development's Intergenerational Studies, Terman's Life Cycle Study of Children of High Ability, and Vaillant's Study of Adult Development (the Grant Study).

The issue of underuse (or waste) of data has been a concern of funders and research administrators for some time and has recently received renewed attention. As Kozlowski (1993) has pointed out, "The further one gets from a project, the greater is the chance of loss. Those details which once seemed too obvious to note become fragmented or lost." For this reason and because grants tend not to fully cover thorough and complete analyses of complex data sets, projects are often abandoned with a great deal of valuable data unanalyzed. A central purpose of the Murray Center is to turn data that might otherwise be wasted into a rich and accessible resource for new research. In order for data to be an effective resource for new research and thus contribute to minimizing the waste of data, it is important not only to preserve and document data but also to let the research community know about the availability of the data and to provide some training in how to use archival data. The latter is especially important, because methods for secondary analysis, especially secondary analysis of qualitative data, are unfamiliar to many researchers and not taught in many graduate study programs.

In order to ensure the maximum usefulness of its archival data for new research, the Murray Center has offered a number of programs to support the use of the data and a series of conferences on techniques for productively reanalyzing longitudinal archival data. These conferences have resulted in several books, including *Working with Archival Data* (Elder, Pavalko, & Clipp, 1993), which outlines this research team's very useful approach to the secondary analysis of qualitative data.

In 1991 MIDMAC and the Murray Research Center began a collaborative research program that was designed to serve the goals of both organizations. It would generate new knowledge about the relatively understudied era of midlife, and it would do so through the reanalysis of data in the Murray Center's archive. In some ways the program was rather like a mininetwork, in that it involved researchers from several disciplines and many institutions working together over time on a related set of studies. From among those who submitted proposals, 14 researchers, from the fields of psychology, sociology, nursing, and human development, were selected to participate in the program. These participants met for two days in June 1991, along with members of MIDMAC and the staff of the Murray Center. Participants worked together to hone their research questions and methods and discussed theoretical and conceptual issues that cut across related projects. Over the next year, the group kept in touch by means of a newsletter that was circulated several times. Through the newsletter they shared the problems they had encountered and the ingenious solutions they had devised to solve those problems. In September 1992, they met again to discuss the results of their research and their interpretations of what they had found. Through this process, participants gained an intensive and well-supported experience in the reanalysis of archival data, and they also generated a substantial body of empirical work on experiences in the middle years of adulthood. This book is a compilation of that work. The studies reported here demonstrate in a concrete way a number of approaches to using archival data for new research. Therefore, the volume can be used as a sourcebook for researchers seeking to learn more about the secondary analysis of longitudinal data, including qualitative data, as well as a sourcebook of current research on midlife development.

REFERENCES

Elder, G. H., Jr., Pavalko, E. K., & Clipp, E. C. (1993). *Working with archival data: Studying lives.* (Series: Quantitative applications in the social sciences; 88.) Newbury Park, CA: Sage Publications.

Kahn, R. (1993). *An experiment in scientific organization.* MacArthur Foundation Occasional Paper.

Kozlowski, L. T. (1993, July/August). Data-waste: The ethical challenge of the underdone and unfinished. *APA Observer,* 26–29.

Margie E. Lachman and Jacquelyn Boone James

This volume is the culmination of an 18-month collaborative re-search project cosponsored by the John D. and Catherine T. MacAr-thur Research Network on Successful Midlife Development and the Murray Research Center at Radcliffe College. Scholars were selected in a competitive call for proposals to conduct research on successful mid-life development. Small research grants were provided to support sec-ondary analysis of data sets housed in the Murray Research Center, a national archive of behavioral and social sciences data sets for the study of lives.

All participants attended a workshop in Cambridge, Massachusetts, to establish a common set of goals and to obtain necessary research materials. Research was conducted at the researchers' home institu-tions. A research conference at which researchers presented their find-ings was held a year and a half later in Cape Cod. Manuscripts were written with the benefit of feedback from others in the program. They were then sent out for peer review and revised accordingly.

The volume is organized around four themes that represent differ-ent facets of adult development: (1) psychological (the self), (2) social/interpersonal, (3) physical health, and (4) work. These major life do-mains are covered in four parts, which provide the overall structural framework for the book. The first chapter provides an overview of theory and research and outlines the key themes and the goals. The major goal is to investigate the biopsychosocial contributors to success-ful development in midlife. Each of the four parts contains an intro-duction chapter and two or more empirical chapters. The introductory chapters provide brief state-of-the-art reviews of the topic and an inte-grative analysis of the studies reported in that part, with an eye toward directions for future research in the field.

The volume promises to contribute to the developmental literature on the topic of midlife. The chapters are a blend of conceptual and empirical analyses. Many of them draw on existing theories of adult development, providing support as well as challenges. The empirical findings are exciting and in many cases novel. In addition, this is one of the few books devoted to secondary analysis and organized around a central theme, thereby providing a useful model for similar enterprises in the future.

Much of the past work on midlife has been limited by its use of cross-sectional data, its focus on clinical populations, and its analysis of only one target group. Given the diversity of data sets included, this book has the added advantage of providing a broader perspective on midlife. The chapters speak to similarities and differences in the midlife experience as a function of gender, social class, and birth cohort. It is also noteworthy that all of the data sets are longitudinal. This enables the researchers to take a true developmental perspective and to pay attention to historical trends. And the book as a whole asserts the importance of taking a multidisciplinary, life-span approach to the study of midlife development. It is only through consideration of the psychological and health-related aspects of the self in the context of work and family that we can understand the multiple paths to successful development in midlife.

We would like to express our gratitude to a number of people for supporting this project. First, we appreciate the financial and collegial support from the John D. and Catherine T. MacArthur Foundation Research Network on Successful Midlife Development, chaired by Gilbert Brim, and the Murray Research Center, directed by Anne Colby. Second, we thank the many reviewers, who provided us with invaluable feedback on the chapters: Toni Antonucci, Nancy Avis, Rosalind Barnett, Rosemary Blieszner, Nia Chester, Faye Crosby, Ravenna Helson, Regula Herzog, James Jackson, John Kotre, Joan Liem, Dan McAdams, Alice Rossi, Carol Ryff, George Vaillant, Ilene Siegler, Joseph Speisman, Joseph Veroff, Allan Waterman, and Susan Whitborne. There were also three anonymous reviewers who critiqued the book and provided us with a number of useful suggestions. David Brent and his staff at the University of Chicago Press were especially helpful to us throughout the editorial and review processes. The authors were extremely responsive to our suggestions and were patient during the lengthy publication process. We thank them for their excellent contributions. Finally, we wish to thank our families for helping to make our own midlife paths both challenging and fulfilling.

ONE

Charting the Course of Midlife Development: An Overview

Margie E. Lachman and Jacquelyn Boone James

Over the past three decades, research and theory on the adult years has helped to expand our concept of development beyond childcentric views toward a life-span perspective (Baltes, 1987; Featherman & Lerner, 1985; Lachman & Baltes, 1994; Lerner, 1976). Although much attention has been given to the later years of the life cycle, the middle years of adulthood have often been overlooked. In developmental theory and research, the midlife period has received less emphasis when compared to other age periods. This is perhaps best illustrated by the fact that there are handbooks and journals devoted specifically to other parts of the life course (infancy, childhood, adolescence, old age), but none for midlife. This state of affairs led to Brim's (1992) observation that "midlife is the last uncharted territory of the life course" (p. 171). This book contributes to the growing body of work that is focused on understanding the middle years.

There are a number of possible reasons for the historically limited research on midlife. First, there has been a widespread assumption that little happens in midlife, that is, it is a relatively quiet period between the turmoil of adolescence and early adulthood and the storm of old age. The one exception is the midlife crisis, which has indeed been the focus of attention in popular books and the press. But it has seldom been subjected to systematic scientific inquiry. Second, it is well known that it is difficult to get middle-aged adults to participate in research, because they are busy and have little time, especially for coming into a laboratory. The vast majority of studies published on adulthood include two age groups, a young group (typically 20-year-olds) and an older group (aged 60 and above), with a large gap in the middle, even though this design is both methodologically and statistically unsound. Third, midlife is not a clearly demarcated time period. Unlike childhood or old age, which have clear age-graded markers tied to school or the work cycle, it is difficult to define midlife. Midlife may be more aptly characterized by key events (e.g., menopause, empty nest) than by a particular age period. What midlife is also varies as a function of cohort, culture, and context (Lerner, 1983). To illustrate, consider that in cultures in which the life span is shorter and key life course events take place earlier, midlife is typically not a recognized phenomenon (Shweder, forthcoming).

In addition, another factor may explain the lack of progress in understanding midlife. There are glimmers of evidence from existing research suggesting that the course of midlife is extremely diverse and varied. Charting the course of midlife is difficult because there are so many different paths. Developmental theory and research, however, have been dominated by universal, stage-oriented models (see Lerner, 1976; Reese & Overton, 1970). Although these approaches have been relatively useful for studying child development, they are not widely applicable to middle adulthood and beyond. Some have tried to borrow stage model conceptions to apply to the study of midlife (Gould, 1978; Levinson, 1978). However, there is little documentation of the utility of these approaches. In midlife, paths diverge as a function of experience and choices as well as genetic makeup. There is enormous variation in career tracks and family forms. Until recently, we have not had models of development available to study such varied patterns.

These are some of the challenges that faced us as we set out to study the midlife period. Thus our aim is to present multiple paths of midlife development. A life-span developmental perspective (Baltes, 1987; Featherman & Lerner, 1985) considers the sociohistorical context and recognizes the sources of diversity and variation in the midlife experience. Using this framework and building on work from early theorists (e.g., Erikson, 1968; Jung, 1933) and researchers (e.g., Eichorn, Clausen, Haan, Honzik, & Mussen, 1981; Neugarten & Gutmann, 1968; Vaillant, 1977) the authors in this book engaged in empirical studies of midlife with the goal of expanding our knowledge about midlife development. We begin with a brief review of past work and key issues to set a context for the chapters that follow.

When Is Midlife?

There is much variability in the age delimiters of the midlife period, in terms both of people's perceptions of midlife and of how it is defined in different studies. If we think of midlife as the middle period of adulthood, our understanding of the boundaries depends on how long we expect to live at a given time and place in a given setting. Longevity has changed dramatically over this century and varies across cultures.

Thus, in the United States and other Western nations, what used to be considered old age is now the realm of midlife.

As for perceptions, there is evidence that what defines midlife depends on whom you ask. In a recent study of adults, the perceived age of the onset and end of midlife was positively correlated with the age of the respondent (Lachman, Lewkowicz, Marcus, & Peng, 1994). Younger adults in their 20s typically reported that middle age begins at around 30 and ends at 55. Older adults, in their 60s and 70s, perceived middle age as starting at 40 and extending into the 70s. Across all adult respondents the average ages typically reported for midlife are 35 to 65. But there is much variability in the perceived ages of onset and exit (American Board of Family Practice 1990). This suggests that chronological age may not be the best indicator of midlife. Neugarten (1968) points out that it may be more useful to define midlife in terms of status or roles. Thus, midlife may be better understood if it is tied to specific events (e.g., having grandchildren). Indeed, today it is commonplace for two people of the same age to be at very different phases in the event-based cycles (Bumpass & Aquilino, 1995). One 45-year-old, for example, might have school-age children while another has grandchildren. Others might be at the stage of launching their children. However, there is a caveat for this event-based approach as well. Familial experiences are likely to intereact with age and have different effects as a function of when they occur in the life course. Thus, the impact of events may vary depending on whether they are "on-time" or "off-time" in the life cycle (see Chap. 11; Neugarten & Hagestad, 1976).

SUBJECTIVE VIEWS OF MIDLIFE

Although it is not possible to know exactly what the midpoint is for one's own life, people seem to have a sense of when they are middle-aged. This may be based on normative longevity data, the age of death of family members, or one's social position (e.g., taking on responsibilities for others who are younger or older). We believe there are certain properties associated with this middle position in the lifespan. According to our research, midlife appears to be a time to look back and a time to look ahead, a time to ask how are things going and what is left to do. We propose that time perspectives vary across adulthood, with young adults most likely to focus on the future, whereas elderly adults turn their attention primarily to the past (reminiscence, ego integrity). In contrast, we expect that in midlife the vantage point includes both past and future perspectives along with the present focus. In midlife there may be a sense of urgency that time is running out, yet there is so much more to do, and the options are diminishing; so it is now or never, but it is not too late.

As one middle-aged woman told us when we interviewed her about her midlife experiences, "one suddenly realizes that half your life is over; it is a last chance time before old age creeps up." An older man reflecting on midlife said, "it is a period of stress because of all one is trying to accomplish. When you are young you don't feel pressured to get things accomplished. What is involved is a growing sense of mortality, of little accomplished and limited time to accomplish anything." (Lachman et al., 1994).

Being in the middle of something may engender these characteristic feelings. Being in the middle of one's life may not be that different from being in the middle of a semester, the middle of a big project, or the middle of the summer. You are inclined to think about what you had hoped to do within a given time frame, what you have actually done, and what you still have to do. In our culture, midlife appears to be a time for reassessment, with possibilities for making changes. The perception seems to be that there is still time left, although there may be a sense that your choices are becoming more limited and that time will eventually run out. You may turn your attention to the next generation, in terms of what they can bring to fruition and what you can leave for their legacy (Erikson, 1968). These realizations may lead to changing aspirations, changing timetables, giving up goals, or taking on new goals (Brim, 1992). One interesting question is whether these perspectives would differ by gender or by socioeconomic stratum, as suggested by several of the authors in this book (see Chaps. 2, 6, & 12).

The theme of middle is also illustrated by position in the interpersonal realm. Midlife adults are situated between the younger and the older generations, usually with some responsibilities for both children and parents, and possibly grandchildren or grandparents as well. This may be true not only in the family but also in the workplace (see Chap. 8). One may become a mentor or supervisor at work and have a sense of a future investment. Thus, the well-being of those younger and older often rests on the shoulders of midlife adults. The stress that is often felt in work and family roles may reflect this pressure from many sides on those who are in the middle (see Chaps. 6, 9, 10, & 11).

Many of our current impressions of midlife are based on generalizations from clinical samples. Thus, our images are biased toward negative experiences and problems because clinicians typically encounter those who are having difficulties (Hunter & Sundel, 1989). However, those who have extreme difficulty in midlife are few in number, although they may be highly visible (Kessler, Foster, Webster, & House, 1992). Traditional trait psychologists hold the view that having difficulties or a crisis in midlife is the result of a lifelong characteristic style of coping rather than a midlife phenomenon per se. Thus, those who have crises in midlife tend to be neurotic and more prone to having crises at many transition points (McCrae & Costa, 1990; Whitbourne, 1986). As some recent work has shown, many people do think there is a midlife crisis. But their conception is not necessarily that it is a period of difficulties; rather it may be an opportunity for growth and development (Lachman et al., 1994).

None of these propositions has been fully investigated, however, and the need to extend the empirical base of our accounts of midlife provided fertile ground for the studies in this book. In order to describe the experiences that are especially characteristic of middle age, we must compare middle-aged people with those who are younger and older and place midlife in the context of the adult life span.

EARLY THEORIES

Perhaps the two best-known theories of psychological health in middle age are those of Carl Jung and Erik Erikson. We provide a brief description of these theories to set the stage for the research studies. According to Jung (1971), the goals of successful midlife development are twofold: the first involves the completion of "individuation"; the realization of the first then makes possible the rare achievement of the second, which he referred to as "transcendence."

Theory

The first goal, individuation, involves the realization, integration, or balancing of all systems of the psyche (animus/anima, conscious/unconscious, mind/body, shadow/persona) to their fullest expression. If, for example, introversion had been more salient than extraversion, or anima (the internalized notion of femininity) had been overdeveloped while animus (masculinity) was neglected, then energy must be directed toward bringing out the neglected (unconscious) part. Balance then makes possible the emergence of the true self. Jung's view of successful development did not stop with the realization of the self. Instead he believed that individuation makes possible the achievement of transcendence, whereby a more evolved self moves beyond the preoccupation with bodily concerns and other pursuits of youth and acquires the capacity to live in harmony (oneness) with all of humanity and the laws of nature.

Jung saw many obstacles on the path to individuation, however, and some of his propositions may have provided the ground for further thinking (in some cases mythmaking) about midlife development. He viewed the transition to midlife as a developmental hurdle quite vulnerable to poor outcomes. This supposed precariousness of the midlife period may have provided the foundation for beliefs about the inevitability of a midlife crisis (see also Jacques, 1965).

Jung (1933) referred to midlife as the afternoon of life and believed few were prepared for this phase. He warned that one needed to navigate midlife with a different set of goals from earlier in life. If people misinterpreted the changes in the middle years and considered them not a normative part of development but pathologies and crises, they would miss the potential for growth and change. Midlife, according to Jung (1933), involves changes not only in the psyche but also in the physique. "One can observe that older women develop rough and deep voices, incipient moustaches, hard facial expressions and other masculine traits. On the other hand, the masculine physique is toned down by feminine features, as for instance adiposity and softer facial expressions. Man's values and even his body tend to undergo a reversal into the opposite" (p. 107).

As a life span theory, Erik Erikson's (1968) theoretical framework posits that the middle years are but one part of the steadily developing person's journey through the "eight ages" (p. 247). In Erikson's view, the tasks of middle adulthood rest upon successful resolution of earlier tasks. The midlife adult who has proceeded "normatively" through earlier stages is usually faced with the "crisis" of generativity versus stagnation.

Erikson's (1968) use of the term *crisis* has little to do with the general understanding of the word as some disaster or tragedy. Rather, the term refers to a transition, a turning point—"a crucial moment when development must move one way or another" (p. 16). This distinction is important, especially since *midlife crisis* has become a household word (Rosenberg & Stark, 1987) and generated much debate regarding whether such a crisis actually occurs (see Costa, McCrae, & Norris, 1981; McCrae & Costa, 1990; Rosenberg & Stark, 1987; Schlossberg, 1987; Whitbourne & Weinstock, 1986).

Generativity versus stagnation, then, is Erikson's representation of what the healthy developing adult seeks to resolve during the middle years. It refers to the propensity among midlife adults to be concerned with producing, nurturing, and guiding the next generation, perhaps in relation to one's own progeny, but as Erikson makes clear, extending to other realms as well, one's world of work, for example, the political arena, and the worlds of art, culture, and the like (see Chap. 8).

A concern about the legacy that one will leave, generativity involves "a preoccupation with caring for others, productivity, and an inner awareness of one's need to be needed" (Stewart, Franz, & Layton, 1988, p. 50). Although the term *generativity* is specific to Erikson's theoretical model, the idea of generativity is a part of many other theorists' propositions about the developmental tasks associated with the middle years. Both Jung (1933) and Jacques (1965) emphasized the importance of coming to terms with one's creative potential as a necessary task involved in the successful transition to midlife. Levinson (1978) pointed out the frequency with which midlife men became mentors to younger professionals. Becker (1973) wrote eloquently of a midlife phase of "heroism" during which adults seek immortality by creating products that will survive them. And Vaillant and Milofsky (1980), in a major longitudinal study, found that midlife men saw themselves as "keepers of the meaning."

Research Derivations

Although Jungian and Eriksonian theories have had important heuristic value, the key propositions and constructs have been elusive and difficult to test. Both theories attempt to deal with development in terms of increasing integration (Jung) or the resolution of certain life tasks (Erikson). Yet both are also limited in their insensitivity to variation across gender, ethnicity and culture, social class, and historical time. Recent developments in operationalizing constructs such as generativity have led to empirical studies of Erikson's theoretical constructs (Ryff & Heincke, 1983; Vaillant & Milofsky 1980; Whitbourne, Zuschlag, Elliot, & Waterman, 1992). Much of the research about generativity has examined whether a concern with generativity is an age-related phenomenon (Darling-Fisher & Leidy, 1988; Ryff, 1982; Ryff & Heincke, 1983; Vaillant & Milofsky, 1980; Viney, 1987) and whether it can only come into ascendancy after the preoccupation with intimacy is less pressing (Acklin, 1986; Hannah & George, 1989; Vaillant & Milofsky, 1980). Recent research has moved far beyond Erikson's conceptions and has begun to focus on the qualities of generativity (see, for example, McAdams, 1993; McAdams, Reutzel, & Foley, 1986; McAdams & St. Aubin, 1992); including the individual desire or need to be generative, the demand from the culture, concern for the next generation, "belief in the species," commitment, action, and a narrative model for the generative script. There is still much to be learned about the qualities of generativity within different domains, as MacDermid, Heilbrun, and DeHaan (chap. 8) point out, and about the extent to which the resolution of this crisis of stagnation and generativity is essential for psychological wellness (see Peterson & Stewart, 1993).

Exploration of the psychosocial qualities of middle age was begun in the late 1950s and early 1960s by Neugarten (1968) and her colleagues. They suggested that the middle-age period was better defined in terms of status in different domains rather than by chronological age. They also found evidence for gender differences in the defining events, with women focusing on the family and men more on the work domain. Middle age was seen as the "period of maximum capacity and ability to handle a highly complex environment and a highly differentiated self" (Neugarten, 1968, p. 97). Much of their work centered on the gender role crossover, which was derived from Jungian theory. Numerous studies have been devoted to the investigation of this aspect of Jung's theory, with substantial confirmation provided by Gutmann and his colleagues (Neugarten & Gutmann, 1968), but with mixed results from other studies.

The question of whether men develop more communal characteristics and women develop more agentic characteristics with aging still remains a puzzle today (James, Lewkowicz, Libhaber, & Lachman, 1995). This issue is considered in Chapters 4 and 5. They cannot completely settle the question, but they suggest new directions for this line of research.

Some of our researchers searched for the adequacy of the theoretical map: Is there evidence of normative concern or preoccupation with, for example, generativity (Chap. 8) or with changes in the balance of personality attributes in midlife (Chaps. 4 & 5)? Are these normative concerns sensitive to variations in cultural and historical settings, especially changing expectations about gender roles during different time periods?

Others asked whether there is any evidence to suggest that certain processes specified by theory (identity, intimacy, finding creative outlets in terms of work, dealing with stress) turn out to predict psychological well-being or physical health (see Chap. 10). Paul, for example, extends Erikson's definition of intimacy beyond the bounds of couples and examines psychological well-being in relation to qualities within and between multiple relationships (Chap. 7). Vandewater and Stewart (Chap. 14) provide an interesting portrait of the ways in which different career identities, an extension of Erikson's notion of identity development, are revealed in personality structures in the lives of women followed over 25 years. Tomlinson-Keasey and Gomel (Chap. 13) document atypical career patterns for women of a particular cohort to reveal both predictors of and consequences for women of courage who went against the social norms of their day. In these ways, the authors use both the charting of the life course and constructions of maturity to describe and predict healthy functioning within the context of the time and place specified by the data. Even though we are a long way from being able to predict healthy functioning in midlife, the studies presented here extend previous research by focusing on a few important processes, goals, and markers.

The Midlife Research Program

Many widespread ideas about midlife have come from the popular press, without empirical basis, from studies based on small samples using clinical observations, from studies with a view of only one point in time, or from a one-cohort longitudinal database. The chapters in this book provide data on a range of questions relating to psychosocial development at midlife. All are theory guided and engage in deductive and inductive hypothesis generation. These studies are unlike previous research reports in that they use a wide variety of data sets (different samples, designs, cohorts, periods, and to some extent different social classes), use multivariate designs, offer different perspectives on the same question (especially with respect to changes in the self in midlife), and report on multiple dimensions. In addition to the variety of data sources, the studies are based on longitudinal data sets. From these data we can see how midlife emerges and takes form over time. Collectively, across studies, we begin to get a picture of the consistency as well as the variations in the midlife story. The chapters are grouped into four parts focused on the self, relations with others, health and stress, and work. Each part begins with an introductory chapter to provide background for the set of studies as well as to suggest future directions for new research in the area.

We can also see the power of exploiting archival data for a focused research effort. Especially valuable for the research reported here were the data from the archives of the Murray Research Center. In addition to data on computer files, the Center makes raw records available for reanalysis, and several of the chapters draw on these qualitative data to add interpretive power to the results or to illuminate counterintuitive findings (see Chaps. 5, 7, 11, & 14).

Indeed, many of these chapters provide models of the creative potential of secondary analysis using a life course perspective (see also Elder, 1985). All of the studies presented here provide extensive detail about the effort involved in readying existing data sets for reuse. Tomlinson-Keasey and Gomel (Chap. 13) and Leong and Boyle (Chap. 15) provide outstanding examples of the amount of reworking, culling, and dealing with tricky issues such as missing data that is involved in using large existing data sets (see also Elder, Pavalko, & Clipp, 1993).

Several investigators demonstrated the capacity of existing data to enable recoding of measures or items originally designed to assess different constructs. Thomas (Chap. 10), for example, created social ties and health indices from various items within different sections of the questionnaire completed by the women of her sample. MacDermid, Heilbrun, and DeHaan (Chap. 8) used the rewards and concerns reported by midlife women to assess several components of generativity of employed mothers in different roles.

Several studies made use of elaborate coding schemes developed for use with qualitative material. Some developed coding schemes particular to their research questions and theoretical concerns. One such coding strategy was developed by Paul (Chap. 7). She assessed various components or qualities of relationships among different members of the individual's social network (both family and friends). Another was developed by Franz (Chap. 3) to assess age-related changes in thoughts as expressed in Thematic Apperception Tests at ages 30 and 41. And Parker and Aldwin (Chap. 4) used a content analysis approach to assess life values from an open-ended question, asking, "What is the main purpose or task in life?" Some of these coding schemes were theoretically derived; others were empirically generated.

Other authors used well-validated techniques and constructs that, with a little thought and ingenuity, could be applied to materials found within existing data sets. Vandewater and Stewart (Chap. 14), for example, applied the Q-sort method to assess personality within the 39 pages of data from one wave of a longitudinal study of educated women. Similarly, James and Lewkowicz (Chap. 5) assessed motives (usually derived from Thematic Apperception Tests) using in-depth interviews from a longitudinal data set by applying Winter's (1982) coding scheme for assessing motives from open-ended text materials. And Franz (Chap. 3) used Stewart's (1982, 1992) measure of stances of adaptation to assess increasing maturity with time over ten years during midlife. Other coding strategies for use in secondary analysis have been described elsewhere (see James & Paul, 1993).

From wrestling with theory, from analyzing longitudinal data with in-depth interviews, from using multiple perspectives and innovative methods, the authors take a view that moves us beyond the hackneyed debate about whether there is stability or change in different areas of development. The findings illustrate that the picture is complex. Consistent with past work on personality (Costa & McCrae, 1980), the authors find stability for the traditional traitlike measures. But they also find evidence for change in dimensions such as interests and values (see Chap. 3). It is clear that a more fruitful approach is to ask for whom, under what conditions, and for what aspects of the individual and society there is change and for which stability (Lachman, 1989).

This book focuses on different *paths* in midlife, that is, different dimensions of functioning: the psychological aspects of the self, relationships with friends and family, physical health, and work life. These paths often cross in the course of midlife. Middle-aged adults experience changes in their social world (e.g., children moving in and out, parents becoming sick or dying), while experiencing physical changes (e.g., menopause, heart disease, weight gain) and perhaps changes in the work world (e.g., going back to work, promotions, firing, topping out). One preeminent concern in midlife is to find a way to integrate the different tracks, even if this means making choices and giving priority to some areas over others. Baltes and Baltes (1990) have suggested it is adaptive to be selective and to specialize in later life. It is unclear whether this process of selective optimization applies to midlife as well. Midlife may instead be a period when a person must expand and manage multiple responsibilities before the selectivity of later life. In midlife the demands are high relative to those of young adulthood and old age, whereas the capacity to handle them remains steady or begins to decline (Brim, 1992). This set of conditions may lead to increased stress during the midlife period (see Chaps. 9 & 11).

This conceptual view is consistent with perceptions of what midlife is like. In a study of beliefs about the middle years, adults of all ages agreed that in contrast to other age periods, midlife involves many more responsibilities, increased stress in several different domains, and little time for leisure (Lachman et al., 1994). At the same time it was seen as the peak period for competence, ability to handle stress, sense of control, purpose in life, productivity, social responsibility, and other agentic qualities (self-reliant, leader, assertive, authoritative). Thus the midlife adult is potentially well equipped with psychosocial resources to handle role overload. These findings are remarkably similar to those found for earlier cohorts (Neugarten, 1968). Neugarten reported a "central importance of what might be called the executive processes of personality in middle age: self-awareness, selectivity, manipulation, control of the environment, mastery, competence, and wide array of cognitive strategies" (p. 98). In a similar vein, Brändtstadter and Renner (1990) found that assimilative tendencies (tenacious goal pursuit) were at their peak in early midlife, while accommodative processes (flexible goal adjustment) began to increase toward the end of midlife. Thus, midlife appears to be a transition point in goal orientation, with a move toward more willingness to change goals and levels of aspiration when faced with obstacles (Brim, 1992).

In keeping with this view, the chapters in this book address the need to consider the multiplicity of factors involved in midlife development, including intrapsychic changes, hormonal changes, changes in roles, and surely, period effects. Some people may be able to achieve success across multiple domains, but others will shine in some areas at the expense of others. And the preeminence of different components of life is likely to vary over time during the extended period of midlife. Thus, there are multiple paths that can be taken and revisited again and again en route to the individual's goals at midlife, which may also undergo revision and reformulation.

It is clear that we have made progress in understanding midlife since Jung's (1933) call for education about this period of life over six decades ago. For example, Eichorn, Clausen, Haan, Honzik, and Mussen (1981), Baruch and Brooks-Gunn (1984), Giele (1982), Levinson (1978), and Vaillant (1977) all have started to tell the story. We hope this book, with its research focus, brings us closer to an understanding of this important and relatively long period of life. Our findings can be used to educate adults about the enormous potential and promise amid the gains and losses of the middle years.

Multiple Paths

Readers may ask, what is the path to success in midlife? It no doubt helps to have had a successful past. But that is by no means the only route: see Chapters 13, 14, and 15. This work suggests that life history variables do not necessarily play a large role in predicting such midlife outcomes as well-being and career success. Surely one is not guaranteed a successful midlife because of success at earlier periods. There are many examples of privileged children and young adults who go astray in their middle years (Vaillant, 1977). One can also find examples of success stories among those who had difficult early lives (Elder, 1985). The answer, of necessity, must be one of complexity. The pictures that emerge from the research reports are diverse and varied. The keys to success vary in the expected ways, by time period, gender, culture, and ethnic background. This also suggests that there are multiple roads one can take. There is more than one route to reach a particular outcome. What is considered successful midlife may also vary by person. Ratings of subjective well-being seem to be somewhat independent of objective circumstances involving health or wealth (Brim, 1992).

This book contains different accounts of midlife. It focuses on different paths in midlife, involving the psychological aspects of the self, relationships with friends and family, physical health, and the workplace. How these different aspects of the person interrelate is one important focus. The intersection of different components of the individual's life is a major theme in midlife because there are potentially so many paths open and operating simultaneously. We have only just begun the journey to see how these processes play out.

REFERENCES

Acklin, M. W. (1986). Adult maturational processes and the facilitating environment. *Journal of Religion and Health 25*(3), 198–205.

American Board of Family Practice. (1990). *Perspectives on middle age: The vintage years.* Princeton, NJ: New World Decisions.

Baltes, P. B. (1987). Theoretical propositions of life-span developmental psychology: On the dynamics between growth and decline. *Developmental Psychology, 23,* 611–626.

Baltes, P. B., & Baltes, M. M. (1990). Psychological perspectives on successful aging: The model of selective optimization with compensation. In P. B. Baltes & M. M. Baltes (Eds.), *Successful aging: Perspectives from the behavioral sciences* (pp. 1–34). New York: Cambridge University Press.

Baruch, G., & Brooks-Gunn, J. (1984). *Women in midlife.* New York: Plenum.

Becker, E. (1973). *The denial of death.* New York: Free Press.

Brändtstadter, J., & Renner, G. (1990). Tenacious goal pursuit and flexible goal adjustment: Explication and age-related analysis of assimilative and accommodative strategies of coping. *Psychology and Aging, 5,* 58–67.

Brim, G. (1992). *Ambition: How we manage success and failure throughout our lives.* New York: Basic Books.

Bumpass, L. L., & Aquilino, W. S. (1995). *A social map of midlife: Family and work over the middle life course.* Vero Beach, FL: MacArthur Foundation Research Network on Successful Midlife Development.

Costa, P. T., Jr., & McCrae, R. R. (1980). Still stable after all these years: Personality as a key to some issues in adulthood and old age. In P. B. Baltes & O. G. Brim, Jr. (Eds.), *Life-span development and behavior* (Vol. 3, pp. 65–102). New York: Academic Press.

Costa, P. T., Jr., McCrae, R. R., & Norris, A. H. (1981). Personal adjustment to aging: Longitudinal prediction from neuroticism and extraversion. *Journal of Gerontology, 36,* 78–85.

Darling-Fisher, C. S., & Leidy, N. K. (1988). Measuring Eriksonian development in the adult: The modified Erikson psychosocial stage inventory. *Psychological Reports, 62,* 747–754.

Eichorn, D. H., Clausen, J. A., Haan, N., Honzik, M. P., and Mussen, P. H. (Eds.), (1981). *Past and present in middle life.* New York: Academic Press.

Elder, G. H., Jr. (Ed.). (1985). *Life course dynamics: Trajectories and transitions, 1968–1980.* Ithaca, NY: Cornell University Press.

Elder, G. H., Pavalko, E. K., & Clipp, E. C. (1993). *Working with archival data: Studying lives.* Newbury Park, CA: Sage.

Erikson, E. (1968). *Identity: Youth and crisis.* New York: W. W. Norton.

Featherman, D. L., & Lerner, R. M. (1985). Ontogenesis and sociogenesis: Problematics for theory and research about development and socialization across the lifespan. *American Sociological Review, 50,* 659–676.

Giele, J. (Ed.). (1982). Women in the middle years: Current knowledge and directions for research policy. New York: John Wiley.

Gould, R. L. (1978). *Transformations: Growth and change in adult life.* NY: Simon & Schuster.

Hannah, M. T., & George, D. (1989). Measuring effective functioning in the elderly: An application of Erikson's theory. *Journal of Personality Assessment, 53*(2), 319–328.

Helson, R., & Wink, P. (1987). Two conceptions of maturity examined in the findings of a longitudinal study. *Journal of Personality and Social Psychology, 53,* 531–541.

Hunter, S., & Sundel, M. (Eds.). (1989). *Midlife myths: Issues, findings, and practice implications.* Newbury Park, CA: Sage.

Jacques, E. (1965). Death and the midlife crisis. *International Journal of Psychoanalysis, 46*(4), 502–513.

James, J. B., Lewkowicz, C., Libhaber, J., & Lachman, M. E. (1995). Rethinking the gender identity crossover hypothesis: A test of a new model. *Sex Roles, 32,* 185–207.

James, J. B., & Paul, E. L. (1993). The value of archival data for new perspectives on personality. In D. C. Funder, R. D. Parke, C. Tomlinson-Keasey, and K. Widaman (Eds.), *Studying lives through time: Personality and development* (pp. 45–63). Washington, DC: American Psychological Association.

Jung, C. G. (1933). *Modern man in search of a soul.* New York: Harcourt Press & World.

Jung, C. G. (1971). Aion: Phenomenology of the self (the ego, the shadow, the syzgy:Anima/animus). In J. Campbell (Ed.), *The Portable Jung.* New York: Viking Penguin Books.

Kessler, R. C., Foster, C., Webster, P. S., & House, J. S. (1992). The relationship between age and depressive symptoms in two national surveys. *Psychology and Aging, 7,* 119–126.

Lachman, M. E. (1989). Personality and aging at the crossroads: Beyond stability versus change. In K. W. Schaie & C. Schooler (Eds.), *Social structure and aging: Psychological processes* (pp. 167–189). Hillsdale, NJ: Erlbaum.

Lachman, M. E., & Baltes, P. B. (1994). Psychological aging in lifespan perspective. In M. Rutter & D. F. Hay (Eds.), *Development through life: A handbook for clinicians* (pp. 583–606). London: Blackwell Scientific.

Lachman, M. E., Lewkowicz, C., Marcus, A., & Peng, Y. (1994). Images of midlife development among young, middle-aged, and elderly adults. *Journal of Adult Development, 1,* 201–211.

Lerner, R. M. (1976). *Concepts and theories of human development.* Reading, MA: Addison-Wesley.

Lerner, R. M. (1983). A "goodness of fit" model of person-context interaction. In D. Magnusson & V. L. Allen (Eds.), *Human Development: An interactional perspective* (pp. 279–294). New York: Academic Press.

Levinson, D. J., with Darrow, C. N., Klein, E. B., Levinson, M. H., & Braxton, M. (1978). *The seasons of a man's life.* New York: Ballantine Books.

McAdams, D. P. (1993). *The stories we live by: Personal myths and the making of the self.* New York: William Morrow.

McAdams, D. P., Reutzel, K., & Foley, J. M. (1986). Complexity and generativity at mid-life: Relations among social motives, ego development, and adults' plans for the future. *Journal of Personality and Social Psychology, 50*(4), 800–807.

McAdams, D. P., & St. Aubin, E. de. (1992). A theory of generativity and its assessment through self-report, behavioral acts, and narrative themes in autobiography. *Journal of Personality and Social Psychology, 62*(6), 1003–1015.

McCrae, R. R., & Costa, P. T., Jr. (1990). *Personality in adulthood.* New York: Guilford Press.

Neugarten, B. L. (1968). The awareness of middle age. In B. L. Neugarten (Ed.), *Middle age and aging* (pp. 93–98). Chicago: University of Chicago Press.

Neugarten, B. L., & Gutmann, D. L. (1968). Age-sex roles and personality in middle age: A thematic apperception study. In B. L. Neugarten (Ed.), *Middle age and aging* (pp. 58–76). Chicago: University of Chicago Press.

Neugarten, B. L., & Hagestad, G. O. (1976). Age and the life course. In R. H. Binstock & E. Shanas (Eds.), *Handbook of aging and the social sciences* (pp. 35–55). New York: Van Nostrand Reinhold.

Peterson, B. E., & Stewart, A. J. (1993). Generativity and social motives in young adults. *Journal of Personality and Social Psychology, 65,* 186–198.

Reese, H. W., & Overton, W. F. (1970). Models of development and theories of development. In L. R. Goulet & P. B. Baltes (Eds.), *Life-span developmental psychology: Research and theory* (pp. 115–145). New York: Academic Press.

Rosenberg, A., & Stark, E. (1987, May). The prime of our lives. *Psychology Today, 21*(5), 62–71.

Ryff, C. D. (1982). Self-perceived personality change in adulthood and aging. *Journal of Personality and Social Psychology, 42*(1), 108–115.

Ryff, C. D., & Heincke, S. G. (1983). Subjective organization of personality in adulthood and aging. *Journal of Personality and Social Psychology, 44*(4), 807–816.

Schlossberg, N. K. (1987, May). Taking the mystery out of change: By recognizing our strengths and building on them we can learn how to master transitions. *Psychology Today 21*(5), 74–76.

Shweder, R. (Ed.). (forthcoming). *Midlife and other cultural fictions.* Chicago: University of Chicago Press.

Stewart, A. J. (1982). The course of individual adaptation to life changes. *Journal of Personality and Social Psychology, 42,* 1100–1113.

Stewart, A. J. (1992). Scoring manual for psychological stances toward the environment. In C. P. Smith, J. W. Atkinson, D. C. McClelland, & J. Veroff (Eds.), *Motivation and personality: Handbook of thematic analysis* (pp. 451–480). Cambridge, England: Cambridge University Press.

Stewart, A. J., Franz, C., & Layton, L. (1988). The changing self: Using personal documents to study lives. In D. McAdams & R. Ochbert (Eds.) *Psychobiography and life narratives* (pp. 41–74). Durham: Duke University Press.

Stewart, A. J., Lykes, M. B., & LaFrance, M. (1982). Educated women's career patterns: Separating social and developmental changes. *Journal of Social Issues, 38*(1), 97–117.

Vaillant, G. E. (1977). *Adaptation to life.* Boston: Little, Brown.

Vaillant, G. E., & Milofsky, E. (1980). The natural history of male psychological health: IX. Empirical evidence for Eriksons' model of the life cycle. *American Journal of Psychiatry, 137,* 1348–1359.

Viney, L. L. (1987). A sociophenomenological approach to life-span development complementing Erikson's sociodynamic approach. *Human Development, 30*(3), 125–136.

Whitbourne, S. K. (1986). *The me I know: A study of adult identity.* New York: Springer-Verlag.

Whitbourne, S. K., & Weinstock, C. S. (1986). *Adult development.* New York: Praeger.

Whitbourne, S. K., Zuschlag, M. K., Elliot, L. B., & Waterman, K. (1992). Psychosocial development in adulthood: A 22-year sequential study. *Journal of Personality and Social Psychology, 63,* 260–271.

Winter, D. G. (1982). *Manual for scoring motive imagery in running text.* Unpublished scoring manual, University of Michigan, Ann Arbor.

I Changes in the Self

The Self in Middle Age

Ravenna Helson

Human life in society has gradients built into it. We enter the adult world with abundant energy but little experience; we approach our exit with abundant experience but little energy. Middle age is a long stretch with an initial fuzzy boundary during which we make a transition from being novices who need to prove themselves to being carriers and transmitters of the culture. The emphasis in young adulthood and early middle age is on separating from one's family of origin (though still remaining in connection), becoming intimate with a partner, developing skills in work, and rearing children. The emphasis in later middle age is on facilitation of others and the responsible use of power. Then there is another fuzzy boundary between middle age and old age, during which a reduction in physical power tends to be accompanied by loss of social centrality.

A person in the middle feels safe. Middle age is sometimes described as a time of feeling settled and secure, or perhaps bored and in a rut. There are no major adjustments to make. A person in the middle can see the point of view of those on either side, and indeed, people in middle age are often responsible for those both older and younger. This is a source of the busyness of the middle-aged. It is also one source of their complexity of outlook. Another source is experience. The middle-aged are said to have expertise and to integrate cognitive and affective or nonlogical considerations more successfully than younger people. A third source of complexity comes from their particular vantage point at the peak of their powers in the middle of their journey through life, able to see where they have been but now newly aware of the descent ahead. For those in early middle age, the emergence of this view will fill some with a sense of urgency: they must seize their last chance to realize their hopes and ambitions. Middle age has the reputation of being a time of excitement and dangerous turns. For those in later middle age, the view from the peak will lead some to tighten their grip on the power they know they will lose.

These are various aspects of what might be called the archetypal situation of being in the middle of life, when the metaphor of the life journey involves the ascent of a mountain, a plateau, and descent. Even in the metaphor one recognizes that middle age has no one meaning because of the multiple aspects of middleness, the difference between early and late middle age, differences in the elevation attained by different individuals, and the greater impact of the archetypal situation in some times and places than others. When one turns to empirical studies, the complexities and ambiguities are evident. For example, studies often show that the middle-aged are perceived by others and perceive themselves to be the most competent, powerful, and complex of age groups, but gender, cultural context, social class, and domain of functioning can affect the findings (Cameron, 1970, 1973; Gatz & Karel, 1993; Lachman, 1986; Ryff, 1982).

There are few subjects that have elicited such passionate and sometimes profound discussion as middle age. The first major theorist of adult development, C. G. Jung, divided psychological development into two phases (1969). In the first, from childhood to about age 40, he said that the ego gains increasing mastery. During the early adult years most people focus on meeting the obligations of society and establishing their place in it. At midlife, people begin to question their commitments. They become increasingly receptive to previously suppressed or neglected aspects of personality and more spiritually attuned. There may come to be a "reconciliation of opposites" (such as masculine and feminine) and a broader and less ego-centered personality (Jung, 1996). Although Jung observed that modern restrictive cultures often made personality change in midlife dramatic, urgent, and problematical, he thought that most people made the transition without much difficulty or awareness. Jung's discussion of external influences was not much elaborated. He concentrated his attention on intrapsychic experience, such as encounters with one's anima or animus (Jung, 1966).

Whereas Jung was most interested in midlife processes of separating oneself from one's social roles or *persona*, Erikson (1950, 1968) gave particular attention to the late adolescent process of building up a persona or *identity* in society. Intimacy was the task of young adulthood. The critical task of midlife was the avoidance of self-preoccupied stagnation and the achievement of generativity, that is, a concern for guiding and nurturing the next generation, or advancing causes that benefit society and for which one cares. To some extent this idea is an extraverted version of Jung's conceptualization of inner focus at midlife followed by the restructuring of personality in a less ego-centered way.

Both Jung and Erikson believed that the processes they described were important for the continuity of culture.

Some of the inner life that interested Jung and the prosocial concern represented in Erikson's concept of generativity are to be found among characteristics of middle-aged individuals described by Bernice Neugarten (1968). She established a social psychology of adulthood and middle age. She discussed the influence of social change, social norms, and social status on the rhythms and proportions of the life cycle, suggesting, for example, that increased longevity had contributed to the delineation of middle age as a stage in the life cycle. Studying interviews with 100 successful men and women between ages 45 and 55, she was impressed with the central importance of their executive processes of personality, such as self-awareness, selectivity, and strategies for manipulation and control of the environment. The middle-aged are no longer the socialized, she said, but the socializers. She described the reflectiveness of the middle-aged and their empathy with people younger and older. One of her central ideas was that one's time perspective changes in middle age: life between structured in terms of life left to live rather than time since birth.

Quite a few other theorists have contributed interesting conceptualizations of middle age or various of its aspects. However, theorists of adult development have many critics. Some say that there is no personality change after age 30, or that the personality changes gradually from adolescence through adulthood without punctuation in middle age, or that the concept of middle age is too vague to have meaning, or that the self changes in different ways in every individual. One encounters the idea that little is known about middle age.

We have to be reasonable in our expectations of what we can know. Very few theorists think of life stages as invariant sequences of qualitatively different motivations and self-conceptions, or as marked by abrupt transitions or crises in the usual sense of that word. Rather, "the motivational, cognitive, emotional, or behavior structures that characterize adult life change over the years, and . . . the structures developed at one period are gradually replaced by the structures typical of the next phase" (Stevens-Long, 1990, p. 153). The phenomena of middle age are the result of recurrent but not inevitable complexes of intersecting physiological, psychological, social, cultural, and historical factors. Thus middle age will have different meanings in different times and places and for different individuals. Furthermore, time keeps changing and new cohorts of individuals (such as the baby boomers) want theories to describe *their* middle age. Though we can hope to accumulate studies of enough samples to build more differentiated theories, insufficient data are a persistent problem. Even if one confines one's attention to longitudinal studies, many investigators do not contextualize their findings sufficiently for us to understand why they obtained the results they report. In addition, different studies have asked different questions, used different measures, and tested people of different backgrounds with different temporal boundaries to distinguish the periods of life. Nevertheless, middle age is no unexplored continent, and the research findings are not entirely chaotic. Let us review some of what is known about the personality of the middle-aged in the United States over the last several generations.

Let us begin with a brief look at evidence about how personality and self-descriptions change from adolescence to late adulthood. Then we will discuss evidence about change from age 30 to age 60, the period over which we should expect to find evidence of processes particular to middle age.

CHANGES IN THE SELF FROM ADOLESCENCE TO THE LATER YEARS

A number of studies have reported self-descriptions of individuals over a wide age range. Participants in *Four Stages of Life* (Lowenthal, Thurnher, & Chiriboga, 1975), studied in the late 1960s, were four groups of predominantly working-class men and women in San Francisco: high school seniors, newlyweds, a group in middle age, and a group in the preretirement years. They described themselves in terms of 70 adjectives. Summarizing the differences in self-description that were associated with age and stage, Chiriboga and Thurnher (1975) reported a steady increase in positive and socially desirable adjectives that reflected what Neugarten called the "executive" functions of the ego.

In a large cross-sectional Hawaiian sample of Caucasians, Chinese, and Japanese with considerable variety in their social histories, both males and females described themselves with adjectives indicating increases in work orientation, less abrasiveness, and more socially desirable characteristics (kind, warm, pleasant) from adolescence to the later years (Johnson, Nagoshi, Ahern, Wilson, McClearn & Vandenberg, 1983).

In a longitudinal study of men and women at four times of testing from adolescence to late middle age, Haan, Millsap, & Hartka (1986) found substantial increases in the direction of dependability, cognitive commitment, outgoingness, self-confidence, and warmth. Participants in this study, conducted by the Institute of Human Development (IHD), were born in Berkeley or Oakland in the 1920s. Measures were factors from the California Q Sort (Block, 1978); hence, they were based not on self-report but on descriptions of the individuals by interviewers and other psychologists who had read their files.

Participants in all of these studies were found to increase in competence, assurance, and self-control from adolescence through late middle age. Beyond middle age, there may be a lessening of dynamic complexity in self-representation (Labouvie-Vief, Chiodo, Goguen, Diehl, & Orwell, 1995) and in sense of growth and purpose (Ryff, 1991).

Changes from Late Young Adulthood through Middle Age

By looking at the period of life between age 30 and age 60, we may hope to find out how much change and what kind of change occurs during middle age. However, there is less convergence of findings over this period. Conspicuous in young adulthood and middle age are the growth and expansionist motivations of achievement, intimacy, power, and self-actualization (Kuhlen, 1964). These motivations are influenced by factors affecting the opportunity for growth and self-expansion, such as social class, gender, and cohort. They also combine in many ways, and different measuring instruments assess different blends of motives, values, and traits.

Nevertheless, Gould (1972) and Levinson, Darrow, Klein, Levinson, & McKee (1978) proposed, with some evidence, something like this: people show a period of industriousness in their 30s, accentuated striving and readjustments of various sorts between their late 30s and late 40s, and responsibility and stability in their 50s. Findings of several longitudinal studies are at least roughly consistent with this schema. Vaillant and MacArthur (1972) reported that the Grant sample of Harvard men from the classes of 1942–1944 worked in "compulsive calm" in their 30s during their occupational apprenticeships, then became more inner-directed, more accepting of disappointment, and less instinctually inhibited in their 40s. In their 50s the men showed generative behavior and preoccupations (Vaillant & Milofsky, 1980).

Some of the same trends were found for the IHD samples (described above), even though they were not homogeneous in social background or educational level. Haan et al. (1986) reported significant increases for both men and women in dependability in young adulthood, outgoingness over early middle age, and warmth over later middle age. Changes that were similar for men and women, but significant only for women, were increases in cognitive commitment and self-confidence over early middle age and a decrease in rebellious asser-tiveness over later middle age.

Rossi (1980) argued persuasively that the stage theories of Gould and Levinson were reflecting the life experience of cohorts born in the 1920s and early 1930s. Participants in the Grant and IHD studies, as she pointed out, were born in this era. However, participants in the Mills Longitudinal Study were born in the late 1930s. They graduated from this private women's college in 1958 or 1960. Between age 27, when most were mothers of young children, and age 43, when most were parents of adolescents and working at least part-time, these women showed a shift on the Adjective Check List (ACL) (Gough & Heilbrun, 1983) to a more favorable self-concept, with gains in perse-verance, organization, achievement orientation, self-esteem, reflec-tiveness, autonomy, and the ability to engage pleasantly, considerately, and constructively with others (Helson & Moane, 1987). Because the roles of the women changed sharply over their 30s and because they described themselves (retrospectively) as more helpless and unhappy in their early 30s than their early 40s, much of their personality change appears to have come after age 30. Helson and Wink (1992) studied personality change in these same Mills women between their early 40s and early 50s. They found evidence of turmoil in their early 40s fol-lowed by an increase of stability by age 52. Over this period, the women had decreased in negative emotionality and increased in decisiveness and in comfort and stability attained through adherence to personal and social standards. This study provides contextual information to show that the women's life structures were different at average ages 43 and 52. For example, at age 52 their mothering responsibilities had declined sharply and their care for parents had increased. Three-fourths of the sample were menopausal or postmenopausal. Normative personality change was not attributable to any of these individual life changes, however; it seemed to reflect a more global pattern of influ-ence.

Though most individuals in the Grant, IHD, and Mills samples were found to expand or grow, other studies report a more mixed pattern. In *Managerial Lives in Transition* (Howard & Bray, 1988) the subjects were White male managerial candidates at AT&T, born in the early 1930s and studied between the late '50s to the late 1970s at approximate ages 25, 33, and 45. Some had attended college, while others had not. In general the changes from ages 33 to 45 were continuations of changes between 25 and 33, usually somewhat less pronounced. The largest change was a drop in ambition over both of these periods, interpreted by the authors as a realistic evaluation of the chances of promotion in the company. Noncollege men declined in advancement motivation over the first eight years, whereas college men showed more decline between ages 33 and 45. The men showed increases in autonomy over both periods. They increased in feelings of hostility and decreased in a need for friendships or the understanding of others. "It was as if their years of living from youth to middle age had propped them up for the assumption of individual responsibilities, but at the same time had hardened them into willful independence" (Howard & Bray, 1988, p. 150).

Social Class and Middle Age

Chronological age is a risky indicator of stage of life unless a sample is homogeneous. Even people's ideas about when middle age occurs are related to their social class, gender, and cohort. In a study by Neugarten and Peterson (described in Neugarten & Datan, 1974), upper-middle-class men described young adulthood as a period of exploration, the period from 30 to 40 as a time of progressive achievement and increasing autonomy; and middle age in their minds began at 50 and was the period of greatest productivity and major rewards. For the women, middle age required some adjustments as children departed but was a period of mellowness and serenity. For blue-collar workers, male and female, young adulthood was a time of settling down and facing inescapable responsibilities. Middle age began at 40 and was described in terms of decline.

Middle Age and the Environment

The environment presents different demands and opportunities in different times and places. The class differences in the characterization of middle age reported by Neugarten and Peterson, as well as the difference in personality changes over early middle age between the AT&T managerial candidates and the Grant, IHD, and Mills samples, may be understood in terms of the different relation between the individual and the opportunity structure of the environment. Howard and Bray give an interesting account of the adjustments that the Bell System had to make in the late 1960s and 1970s to the decreased value of stocks, consent decrees to facilitate the hiring of women and minorities, and the beginning of antitrust suits (1988, pp. 136–142). These factors would have influenced the careers of the White male AT&T sample adversely. The Mills women, in contrast, were supported by new work opportunities and the women's movement over this same period.

The nature of occupational experience contributes not only to one's ambitions and self-esteem but also to ego development (Helson & Roberts, 1994) and wisdom. Staudinger, Smith, and Baltes (1992) offer evidence that clinical psychologists increase in wisdom more than people in other occupations.

The environment is thought to play an important role in moving individuals to a new life stage. For a 40-year-old, the death of a sibling or friend may begin a heightened awareness of life's finitude. Karp (1988) describes the 50s as a "decade of reminders," in which one's everyday encounters convey the information that one is considered an old-timer, someone to call "mister" and ask for advice, and that death is becoming "less of a stranger."

The properties of a life stage depend on both personality and environment. Mitchell and Helson (1990) described the *prime of life* of women in their early 50s in terms of a convergence between augmented resources of personality, the sense of accomplishment from the launching of children, and a new and freer life style. McAdams and St. Aubin (1992) conceptualize generativity motivation as involving inner desire and cultural demand which tend to converge in middle adulthood, but do not do so necessarily.

Gender Differences in the Experience of Middle Age

Men and women arrive at middle age with difference resources and life circumstances. They make self-evaluations according to different standards. They face different challenges and different threats. Are these differences large enough to require different developmental theories?

Erikson, Kohlberg, and Levinson have been criticized for their emphasis on the masculine values of autonomy, rationality, and career achievement and for paying insufficient attention to the caring, being-in-relationship, and family responsibilities that are important to women (Franz & White, 1985; Gilligan, 1982; Miller, 1976; Reinke, Ellicott, Harris, & Hancock, 1985). Gilligan (1982) advanced a theory of women's development in relationships. For earlier cohorts of women, the middle stage that she describes, characterized by responsibility for others with suppression of self-interest, can be associated with women's early parental period; and the move to the next stage, in which a woman comes to accord her own interests as much respect as those of others, can be considered a task of middle age. In several studies, women showed increases in achievement motivation and independence as children got older (Baruch, 1967; Helson & Moane, 1987; Livson, 1981; and others). One can imagine that in the era from 1955 to 1975, for many women it took courage to go to work. It might have been a support to them to feel that in so doing they were making a transition to a higher moral stage, which may well have been the case. However, Gilligan's theory has met with sharp criticism on the grounds that it accepts exploitative gender roles (Mednick, 1989). It may still fit the experience and meet the needs of many women, but its applicability seems narrower today than a decade ago.

Some feminists say that the linear progression of stage theories fits the lives of men better than those of women (Bateson, 1989; Gergen, 1990). Women's lives, they say, are discontinuous and variable in pattern. Roles wax and wane, and flexibility and adaptability are important virtues (Tomlinson-Keasey, in press). As in the case of Gilligan's theory, however, other feminists would see these characteristics in terms of the lack of control that women have had over their lives. They would not want to elevate make-do strategies into a developmental model.

Such controversy over developmental theories illustrates why many social scientists advocate a social contructivist paradigm. For those interested in life-span issues, for example, the question is not the objective truth about development, considered by constructivists as unascertainable, but how theories can be constructed that encourage the expression of the theorist's value system (Gergen, 1990). We will return to this issue.

Several feminists have objected to overemphasis on physiological factors in treatments of women's middle age and to the treatment of menopause and the empty nest in terms of loss (Barnett & Baruch, 1978; Gergen, 1990). Cross-sectional and longitudinal studies find that most women do not regret the end of fertility, do not find the symptoms of the menopause severe, feel buoyant when their children are successfully launched, and continue to feel satisfied as long as they keep in touch (Datan, 1986; Mitchell & Helson, 1990; Neugarten, Wood, Kraines, & Loomis, 1968; White & Edwards, 1990). Thus the experience of middle age does not seem to be more closely or negatively related to physiology and social roles in women than in men.

On the other side of the issue of emphasis on physiology, Rossi (1980) recommended that the span defined as middle age be reduced to a narrow age range within which known biological changes are taking place. She believed that there was strong evidence for the waning of gender differentiation in the middle years and that it might be attributable to change in endocrine functioning. Because the three chapters in Part 1 all address the issue of gender differences in personality change, I will return to it in discussing their findings.

We know little about how gender differences in personality change are affected by occupational roles. In a longitudinal study of women physicians at ages 31 and 46, Cartwright and Wink (1994) report some of the same changes that have been found for professional men, such as increased leadership potential and better judgment in impulse expression. However, the women physicians increased markedly in seriousness and decreased markedly in concern with validation from others. The authors attribute the magnitude of these changes in part to professional demands on physicians over recent medical history but also to the women's difficult experiences as marginal pioneers in the field.

Subjective Experiences in Middle Age

Important claims about middle age concern subjective experience. Neugarten's (1968) memorable essay on the subjective experience of middle age was based on excerpts and insightful interpretation of interviews. Karp (1988) provided a similar kind of essay about the decade of the 50s. Gould (1972) quantified subjective experience over different periods of life by administering questionnaire items to individuals over a wide age span. For example, the item "There's still plenty of time to do most of the things I want to do" showed a drop in endorsement between ages 35 and 40, then remained level until the late 50s. Helson and her colleagues (Helson & Moane, 1987; Helson & Wink, 1992) used some of Gould's items and made up others from the work of Levinson and Neugarten. They asked participants in the Mills Longitudinal Study to rate these "feelings about life." The data were obtained when the women were age 43 and again when they were age 52, though the items were not entirely the same. The contemporaneous descriptions supported the earlier study of Neugarten (1968) in showing that the women in their early 50s saw themselves as assured, oriented to the present rather than the future, cognitively broad and complex, well-adjusted and smooth in relationships, and aware of aging. Comparisons of ratings at ages 43 and 52 supported the hypothesis that the early 40s were experienced as a period of more turmoil (Helson & Wink, 1992). Stewart (1996) used these items to show change in generativity and power across middle age in three cohorts of women.

The subjective experience of middle age has also been studied through coding of personal accounts, narratives, and personal documents. For example, Peterson and Stewart (1990) coded the published writings and private documents of Vera Brittain to document the shift in her experience from preoccupation with identity and intimacy in young adulthood to a concern with generativity in middle age. New points of view based on narrative psychology (Cohler, 1982; McAdams, 1985; and others) lend themselves to evaluation with the help of subjective accounts. For example, Cohler (1982) believes that people construct life stories to give meaning to their lives and that they need to reorganize their perceptions at certain points to give more coherence to these stories. In middle age a recognition of the finitude of life and increased interiority lead to one of the major revisions.

Labouvie-Vief and her associates studied changes in emotional experience from adolescence to middle age by taping interviews with men and women. They asked them to describe a recent incident that aroused a particular emotion. Younger people used a language of emotions almost devoid of feeling and described feelings in terms of how one should feel and with a concern for how to control feeling. Those in middle adulthood showed a reorganized emotion language. They described their feelings more vividly and differentiated an inner realm of emotional experience from an outer realm of convention. They acknowledged the conflict between these realms and were concerned to acknowledge the inner (Labouvie-Vief & Hakim-Larson, 1989).

Midlife Crisis and Midlife Transition

The subjective experience most controversially associated with middle age is the midlife crisis. The term *crisis* comes from Eriksonian theory and is not associated with breakdown or with any particular time of life. It means that there is heightened concern and a need to make a choice. Jung attributed breakdown in middle age to oppressive cultures and rigid personalities. Neugarten explicitly disavowed the idea of a midlife crisis or of abrupt change, emphasizing that the personality changes in small increments over a long time. Of major theorists, Levinson comes closest to subscribing to a common experience of agitation during the midlife transition. (See Levinson, Darrow, Klein,

Levinson, & McKee, 1978.) He described several major polarities that men in their 40s may be concerned with, the turbulence commonly associated with them, and the dangers in delaying a confrontation. Like Jung, he believed that the personality organization of young adulthood is not adaptive in older people, that changes are necessary. The change considered desirable by these theorists is in the direction of giving up the values, prerogatives, and crutches of youth and moving to greater breadth and less egocentrism.

Midlife transition is a term less likely to cause misunderstanding than *midlife crisis.* The issues associated with the idea of a midlife transition seem to me to be whether young adults are narrower, more self-concerned, and so forth than 50-year-olds, and if so, what kinds of difficulties people have in moving in the age-appropriate direction.

Young people are expected to be concerned about their identities, their careers and families, their place in the world. We have seen evidence that ambitions rise and fall in young adulthood and early middle age. We have seen evidence that people in late middle age are more settled and socially facilitative than younger adults. In the Mills Study, women in their early 40s were quite aware of the extent to which they had conformed to the *social clock* (social norms about what should be expected of people at different ages) and were concerned to take action to maximize socially desirable life outcomes. In their early 50s, however, the sense of meeting expectations or furthering themselves was almost entirely absent. They were pillars of society. One woman said, "I can't imagine that anyone would devote any thought to what I should be doing in my 50s!" (Helson & McCabe, 1993).

In their early 50s the Mills women were asked to describe and date the onset and duration of their most difficult time since college, the one that had most affected their lives and values (Helson, 1992). Women without children were more likely than women with children to report such a time as having occurred in young adulthood. Women with superior resources of personality usually reported difficult times between ages 36 and 46, whereas women with less adequate resources reported experiences that occurred earlier or later. For women who reported their most difficult and influential time at midlife, the most common themes were a search for independent identity and abandonment. The search for an independent identity would seem to be a version of the urge to realize one's suppressed or undeveloped potential. Abandonment (by partners) was usually reported by career women and was interpreted as the consequence of the independent identity that the women had already developed without undue difficulty. Rigidity in the culture or in the partner contributed to the abandonment experiences of these women. Even so, the difficult times led to reappraisal of self and values. This study offers support for the idea of important turning points at midlife but shows some of the contextual factors that influence the nature and timing of such experiences.

What about the relation between the conscious and the unconscious at midlife? Stein and Stein (1987) believe that midlife involves a transition similar to that of adolescence, the psychological purpose of which is the transformation of consciousness. Whereas so-called primitive peoples have initiation rituals to facilitate transitions, our society does not, and psychotherapy, they say, is increasingly performing this function. The Steins describe three phases of the midlife transition: destructuring, liminality, and restructuring. The period of liminality is marked by moods expressed as being lost in a deep wood, wandering alone in the desert, and so forth. The unconscious is active and produces vivid and powerful dream images that may ultimately be useful in bringing about a restructuring. Although the Steins give a very interesting account of the midlife transition, the processes they describe may not be pronounced in most people. Jung did not expect many individuals to be aware of the shifts between conscious and unconscious that he believed began around midlife.

Because artists have the talent to express subtle and only partly conscious phenomena, some of the relatively unselfconscious genres of art may be a good place to find evidence of what Jung called the individuation process. Maduro (1974) studied a community of folk artists in India, ranging in age from the 30s to over 50. Creativity and age were strongly correlated. He showed that the cognitive processes of the most creative (older) artists were freer and their egos more permeable than those of the less creative, younger artists.

Many of the best books for children, at least until the current era, were written by people active in other fields who turned aside from their areas of specialization to write something for children. What they wrote seems always to have been fantasy, which of course lends itself to the expression of the unconscious. They usually wrote these books in middle age. For example, Tolkien, the linguist, was 45 when he wrote *The Hobbit;* and Frank Baum was 43 when he wrote *The Wizard of Oz,* two years after retiring from his work as a salesman because of a serious heart condition. I have interpreted the classic fantasies of E. Nesbit, written in her early 40s, in the context of the individuation process (Helson, 1984).

Critics of theories of adult development often focus on discrediting the existence of a normative midlife crisis. For example, in a questionnaire study of a large sample of men, Costa and McCrae (1980) found no evidence that psychological disturbance was more common at midlife than at other periods. Other critics say that midlife is quite the opposite of a period of turmoil; it is a time of productivity and altruism (Gallagher, 1993). I think it is time to move on from debating this point. No major theorist argues for a normative midlife crisis in the sense of psychological disturbance. The evidence supports theories of adult development in showing that personality often changes across middle age toward increasing complexity, productivity, and altruism, and that there are often difficulties in making these changes. The nature of the difficulties and the way change is experienced have recurring features, though they also vary with the individual's psychological problems and resources and with social and cultural circumstances.

Individual Differences in the Transaction of Middle Age

In keeping with the title of this book, a number of studies show that there are multiple paths of midlife development. For example, Livson (1981) identified men and women of the Oakland Growth Study (born in the early 1920s) who were all particularly well adjusted at age 50 and divided them according to whether they had scored above or below the sample median for improvement in adjustment from ages 40 to 50. Her analyses led her to the conclusion that women and men with a traditional gender-role orientation showed relatively uninterrupted personality growth from adolescence to age 50. The women steadily developed their affiliative side and the men their instrumental side. In contrast, nontraditional men and women interrupted their development in early adulthood and showed various signs of constriction at age 40. However, they recovered by age 50, reviving and expanding ego functions that they were developing in adolescence. The women repossessed their intellectuality and achievement orientation, and the men rediscovered their expressiveness. Livson's study shows that the lifting of conformity to gender roles in midlife may lead some individuals more than others in the direction of androgyny (Gutmann, 1987). Of course, the magnitude of these effects may have been particularly large in the cohort of the Oakland Growth Study sample, who were 40 in the early 1960s.

Arguing against Havighurst's idea (1948) that middle age involves the negotiation of a standard set of developmental tasks, Helson and McCabe (1993) examined the lives of three subgroups of women in the Mills longitudinal sample between their late 30s and early 50s: never-married women, traditional homemakers, and women who divorced around age 40. About half of the single women were actively advancing their careers, while the others were not. But whatever their ideas about work, most of the singles around age 40 thought it was time to establish a stable relationship. There were both failures and successes. Of the traditional homemakers, some were productive and happy in their early 40s, but a majority were not. Most felt pressure to enter the labor force but resisted. Some felt a need to establish a more egalitarian relationship with their husbands. But in most of these cases they divorced in their late 40s (when their children left home) and remarried within a year or two. Of the third group, women who divorced around age 40, some were careerists and others not, but in middle age all were working hard to establish a new life structure in which they could support themselves and their children. These three groups of midlife women were all much involved in efforts to improve their lives, but their efforts were of very different kinds. Across groups, women with superior personality resources were more likely to effect the desired change. See also the evidence of Klohnen, Vandewater, and Young (1996) that individual differences in ego resilience substantially affect whether midlife is a time of deterioration or of increasing confidence and adjustment.

In *Men at Midlife* (1981), Farrell and Rosenberg studied the experiences of 500 men in dealing with the tasks of middle age, such as being a source of financial and emotional stability for the older and younger generations. The largest group (32%) were open to stresses but had a positive outlook and the resources to deal with their problems. The smallest group (12%) openly discussed their problems (in interviews) but had feelings of alienation and no sense of the future. More than half of the men were classified by the authors as denying their stress; some of them were punitive authoritarians while others were "pseudo-developed" (expressing platitudes about the gratifications of middle age but lacking hopefulness and the ability to make decisions about their problems). Most of the men who dealt with the stresses of middle age successfully came from the affluent middle class, and most of the punitive authoritarians were sons of unskilled or semi-skilled laborers. Farrell and Rosenberg believe that for men vocational failure is likely to be accompanied by alienation and loss of self-esteem, and that failure is related to social class. Because more than half of the sample denied their stress, it is unlikely, they say, that questionnaires detect the level of psychological discomfort among middle-aged men.

Conclusions and Comments

There is much evidence for change in self-descriptions as well as personality as measured by inventories and observer ratings from the 30s to 60s. Critics who dispute this evidence (such as McCrae & Costa, 1990) use a narrow conception of personality and research designs that are intended to show stability rather than change (Helson, 1993; Helson & Stewart, 1994).

The general trend is toward increased competence. However, the particular ways and amounts that personality changes over middle age are very much affected by one's resources for expansion and growth, the cultural restrictions that one needs to overcome, and the opportunities available. Generalist theories such as those of Jung, Erikson, and Neugarten offer intuitive abstractions that attempt to surmount these particularities. These theories may be improved, but there is considerable evidence to support them. However, more specific theories and bodies of findings are necessary to document the specific meanings of middle age for various subgroups in society and for different cohorts. The social constructivist paradigm explains how the motivation is generated to produce special-interest theories: we want theories to express our own needs and values. An alternative or supplement to this paradigm is the concept of bandwidth/fidelity trade-off (Cronbach & Gleser, 1957). General theories of middle age have a wide bandwidth but cannot give a close fit to any individual or group. They cannot provide the detail of specific theories developed under particular conditions for portraying the middle age of individuals under these conditions. On the other hand, they are not as wrong as specific theories in portraying the middle age of individuals under other particular conditions.

CONTRIBUTIONS OF PART 1

Chapter 3, by Carol Franz, is a study of personality stability and change over the transition to midlife, the period from age 30 to age

40. Both Chapter 3 and Chapter 4 help to fill in our knowledge of this decade between young adulthood and middle age. Franz analyses TAT data from the Sears, Maccoby, and Levin sample, who were originally studied as five-year-olds in 1951 and then again in 1978 and 1987. Perhaps the jewel of Franz's chapter is the idea of looking for TAT (Thematic Apperception Test) indices for the changing state of mind between ages 30 and 40. She finds that grandiosity and youthful worry and uncertainty were more evident at age 31 than at age 41, and that "grounded realism" and a measure of maturity and complexity were more evident at age 41. The findings are consistent with the literature and convey the thought contents of these individuals with a vividness that most measures do not convey. I hope that Franz will be able to test these indices in comparisons of other samples and to develop indices over other age ranges. Her finding that need achievement decreases and need affiliation increases in her sample from ages 31 to 41 is interesting and will find support and perhaps clarification in the next study.

Rebecca Parker and Carolyn Aldwin (Chap. 4) present findings from a longitudinal study that consists of three cohorts of students who attended the University of California at Davis in the mid-60s, 1979, and 1989. Parker and Aldwin are interested in how and why gender identity changes in adulthood. The confusion about these questions in the literature, they say, may be attributable to difference in measures, age ranges of subjects, differences in cohort and social period, or more than one of these. They hypothesize that personality traits (such as masculinity and femininity) will show more relation to age than values (such as family vs. career priority), and that values will show more relation to period than to age. Using their three cohorts to advantage, they find that both men and women across cohort increase in masculinity (vs. feminity) from ages 20 to 30 and remain stable from 30 to 40. Value attached to family decreased for all cohorts over the period 1969–1979 and increased over the period of 1979–1991. Value attached to career showed the opposite pattern. In addition to the three Davis cohorts, this study brings in additional subjects from *The Four Stages of Life* (Lowenthal, Thurnher, & Chiriboga, 1975). Though results from these small samples of older and less-educated men and women muddy the waters a little, the overall findings are impressive. Some may think that the literature review was a bit of a bulldozer. For example, it classifies values and TAT motivational patterns together. But it is hard to make progress through this jungle without bruising any vines.

Jacqueline James and Corinne Lewkowicz (Chap. 5) also address the question of gender-related personality change with age. Their subjects are from three of Lowenthal et al.'s Four Stages of Life, restudied at several intervals over the 1970s. Needs for power and affiliation were scored from responses to open-ended questions about goals. This is a relatively untried procedure and may have risks. At any rate, the quantitative findings do not show the hypothesized results. However, the authors describe believable life histories of several women who increased in their need for power in middle age. One of the strengths of this chapter is its thoughtful theoretical and methodological discussion.

All three of these chapters investigate gender-related personality change with age, but none of them finds support for increasing androgyny in both men and women. The samples in the first two studies are too young. I also agree with James and Lewkowicz that a multifaceted or multidimensional approach is advantageous for studying this issue. As they observe, longitudinal studies, where there is ample information about the participants, often give positive findings. The changes are found on inventories and adjective check lists, so I do not share the concerns of some of the authors that such instruments are unsuitable for the task.

In the Mills sample, Paul Wink and I (Wink & Helson, 1993) expected both women and their partners to become more competent ("masculine") and affiliative ("feminine") from the early parental to the postparental periods of life, because much literature supports the idea that across gender people increase in integrative cognitive and social skills (Neugarten, 1968; Schaie, 1977; Stevens-Long, 1990). In addition, we tested the hypothesis, derived particularly from work of Gutmann (1987), that wives would increase more in competence, confidence, and independence than their partners, and that husbands would increase more in affiliation. Our measures were cluster scales and supplementary scales from the Adjective Check List (ACL; Gough & Heilbrun, 1983). Although the results generally supported these hypotheses, another finding was that the women changed much more than the men. This was also the case in the study of personality change in the IHD samples (Haan et al., 1986). Part of the explanation may be that over the last generation, at least, women's lives have changed more than men's as children grew up. The Mills women were encouraged by the women's movement and by the new availability of career opportunities. We were able to show that a sample of mothers of the Mills women had scored as less competent and independent than their husbands in their early 50s, the same age by which differences in personality had disappeared between their daughters and sons-in-law. So these personality changes do not seem to be inevitable, though they have been reported for many samples in many cultures and historical periods.

*

Social climate and cohort are just beginning to receive their proper attention in the study of middle age. We need not only to document their influence but to understand the nature of the influence and how and when it is exerted. It is a major contribution of these chapters that they add to the literature the experience of several new longitudinal samples of men and women entering middle age. Two of the studies systematically compare longitudinal samples. This is all too seldom done, but it is necessary for the evaluation of social climate and cohort. Is the idea of the androgyny of later life an example of a general theory that will continue to be useful or of one that will soon cease to apply? We don't know quite yet, but the authors in Part 1 prepare the way, and we will look to them for further contributions.

REFERENCES

Barnett, R. C., & Baruch, G. K. (1978). Women in the middle years: A critique of research and theory. *Psychology of Women Quarterly, 3,* 187–197.

Baruch, R. (1967). The achievement motive in women: Implications for career development. *Journal of Personality and Social Psychology, 5,* 260–267.

Bateson, M. C. (1989). *Composing a life.* New York: Atlantic Monthly Press.

Block, J. (1978). *The Q-sort method in personality assessment and psychiatric research.* Palo Alto, CA: Consulting Psychologists Press.

Cameron, P. (1970). The generation gap: Which generation is believed powerful vs. generational members' self-appraisal of power? *Developmental Psychology, 3,* 403.

Cameron, P. (1973). Which generation is believed to be intellectually superior and which generation believes itself intellectually superior? *International Journal of Aging and Human Development, 7,* 143.

Cartwright, L. K., & Wink, P. (1994). Personality change in women physicians from medical student years to mid 40s. *Psychology of Women Quarterly, 18,* 291–308.

Chiriboga, D., & Thurner, M. (1975). Concept of self. In M. F. Lowenthal, M. Thurner, & D. Chiriboga, *Four stages of life.* San Francisco: Jossey-Bass.

Cohler, B. (1982). Personal narrative and life course. In P. B. Baltes & O. G. Brim (Eds.), *Life-span development and behavior* (Vol. 4, pp. 205–241). San Diego, CA: Academic Press.

Costa, P. T., & McCrae, R. R. (1980). Still stable after all these years: Personality as a key to some issues in adulthood and old age. In P. B. Baltes & O. G. Brim, Jr. (Eds), *Life-span development and behavior,* Vol. 3 (pp. 65–102). New York: Academic Press.

Cronbach, L. J., & Gleser, G. C. (1957). *Psychological tests and personnel decisions.* Urbana: University of Illinois Press.

Datan, N. (1986). Corpses, lepers, and menstruating women: Tradition, transition, and the sociology of knowledge. *Sex Roles, 14,* 693–703.

Erikson, E. (1950). *Childhood and society.* New York: Norton.

Erikson, E. (1968). *Identity: Youth and crisis.* New York: Norton.

Farrell, M. P., & Rosenberg, S. D. (1981). *Men at midlife.* Dover, MA: Auburn House.

Franz, C. E., & White, K. M. (1985). Individuation and attachment in personality development: Extending Erikson's theory. *Journal of Personality, 53,* 136–168.

Gallagher, W. (1993). Midlife myths. *Atlantic Monthly,* May, 51–68.

Gatz, M., & Karel, M. J. (1993). Individual change in perceived control over 20 years. *International Journal of Behavioral Development, 16,* 305–322.

Gergen, M. M. (1990). Finished at 40: Women's development within the patriarchy. *Psychology of Women Quarterly, 14,* 471–493.

Gilligan, C. (1982). *In a different voice: Psychological theory and women's development.* Cambridge: Harvard University Press.

Gough, H. G., & Heilbrun, A. B., Jr. (1983). *The Adjective Check List manual: 1980 edition.* Palo Alto, CA: Consulting Psychologists Press.

Gould, R. (1972). The phases of adult life: A study in developmental psychology. *American Journal of Psychiatry, 129,* 521–531.

Gutmann, D. L. (1987). *Reclaimed powers: Toward a new psychology of men and women in later life.* New York: Basic Books.

Haan, N., Millsap, R., & Hartka, E. (1986). As time goes by: Change and stability in personality over fifty years. *Psychology and Aging, 1,* 220–232.

Havighurst, R. J. (1948). *Developmental tasks and education.* New York: David McKay.

Helson, R. (1984). E. Nesbit's 41st year: Her life, times, and symbols of personality growth. *Imagination, Cognition, and Personality,* 4 (1), 53–68.

Helson, R. (1992). Women's difficult times and the rewriting of the life story. *Psychology of Women Quarterly, 16,* 331–347.

Helson, R. (1993). Comparing longitudinal samples: Towards a paradigm of tension between stability and change. In D. C. Funder, R. D. Parke, C. Tomlinson-Keasey, & K. Widaman (Eds.), *Studying lives through time* (pp. 93–119). Washington, DC: American Psychological Association.

Helson, R., & McCabe, L. (1993). The social clock in middle age. In B. F. Turner & L. E. Troll (Eds.), *Women growing older* (pp. 68–93). Newbury Park, CA: Sage.

Helson, R., & Moane, G. (1987). Personality change in women from college to midlife. *Journal of Personality and Social Psychology, 53,* 176–186.

Helson, R., & Roberts, B. W. (1994). Ego development and personality change in adulthood. *Journal of Personality and Social Psychology, 66,* 911–920.

Helson, R., & Stewart, A. J. (1994). Personality change in adulthood. In T. Heatherton & J. Weinberger (Eds.), *Can personality change?* Washington, DC: American Psychological Association.

Helson, R., & Wink, P. (1992). Personality change in women from the early 40s to early 50s. *Psychology and Aging, 7,* 46–55.

Howard, A., & Bray, D. (1988). *Managerial lives in transition: Advancing age and changing times.* New York: Guilford.

Johnson, R. C., Nagoshi, C. T., Ahern, F. M., Wilson, J. R., McClearn, G. E., & Vandenberg, S. G. (1983). Age and cohort effects on personality factor scores across sexes and racial/ethnic groups. *Personality and Individual Differences, 4,* 709–713.

Jung, C. G. (1966). Two essays on analytical psychology (*Collected Works, 7*). Princeton: Princeton University Press.

Jung, C. G. (1969). The stages of life. In *The structure and dynamics of the psyche* (*Collected Works, 8*): Princeton: Princeton University Press.

Karp, D. A. (1988). A decade of reminders: Changing age consciousness between fifty and sixty years old. *The Gerontologist, 28,* 727–738.

Klohnen, E., Vandewater, E. A., & Young, A. (1996). Negotiating the middle years: Ego-resiliency and successful midlife adjustment in women. *Psychology and Aging, 11, 3.*

Kuhlen, R. G. (1964). Developmental changes in motivation during the adult years. In J. E. Birren (Ed.), *Relations of development and aging* (pp. 209–246). Springfield, IL: Charles C. Thomas.

Labouvie-Vief, G., Chiodo, L. M., Goguen, L. A., Diehl, M., & Orwell, L. (1995). Representations of self across the life span. *Psychology and Aging, 10,* 404–415.

Labouvie-Vief, G., & Hakim-Larson, J. (1989). Developmental shifts in adult thought. In S. Hunter & M. Sundel (Eds.), *Midlife myths: Issues, findings, and practice implications* (pp. 69–96). Newbury Park, CA: Sage.

Lachman, M. E. (1986). Locus of control in aging research: A case for multidimensional and domain-specific assessment. *Psychology and Aging, 1,* 34–40.

Levinson, D., Darrow, C. N., Klein, E. B., Levinson, M. H., & McKee, B. (1978). *The seasons of a man's life.* New York: Knopf.

Livson, F. B. (1981). Paths to psychological health in the middle years: Sex differences. In D. H. Eichorn, J. A. Clausen, N. Haan, M. P. Honzik, & P. Mussen (Eds.), *Present and past in middle life* (pp. 195–221). San Diego, CA: Academic Press.

Lowenthal, M. F., Thurnher, M., & Chiriboga, D. (1975). *Four stages of life.* San Francisco: Jossey-Bass.

Maduro, R. (1974). Artistic creativity and aging in India. *International Journal of Aging and Human Development, 5,* 303–329.

McAdams, D. P. (1985). *Power, intimacy, and the life story: Personological inquiries into identity.* Homewood, IL: Dow Jones-Irwin.

McAdams, D. P., & St. Aubin, E. de. (1992). A theory of generativity and its assessment through self-report, behavioral acts, and narrative themes in autobiography. *Journal of Personality and Social Psychology, 62,* 1003–1015.

McCrae, R. R., & Costa, P. T., Jr. (1990). *Personality and adulthood.* New York: Guilford Press.

Mednick, M. T. (1989). On the politics of psychological constructs: Stop the bandwagon, I want to get off. *American Psychologist, 44,* 1118–1123.

Miller, J. B. (1976). *Toward a new psychology of women.* Boston: Beacon.

Mitchell, V., & Helson, R. (1990). Women's prime of life. *Psychology of Women Quarterly, 14,* 451–470.

Neugarten, B. L. (1968). The awareness of middle age. In B. L. Neugarten (Ed.), *Middle age and aging* (pp. 93–98). Chicago: University of Chicago Press.

Neugarten, B. L., & Datan, N. (1974). The middle years. In S. Arieti (Ed.), *The foundations of psychiatry* (pp. 592–608). New York: Basic Books.

Neugarten, B. L., Wood, V., Kraines, R. J., & Loomis, B. (1968). Women's attitudes towards the menopause. In B. L. Neugarten (Ed.), *Middle age and aging* (pp. 195–200). Chicago: University of Chicago Press.

Peterson, B., & Stewart, A. J. (1990). Using personal and fictional documents to assess psychological development: A case study of Vera Britain's generativity. *Psychology and Aging, 5,* 400–411.

Reinke, B. J., Ellicott, A. M., Harris, R. L., & Hancock, E. (1985). Timing of psychosocial changes in women's lives. *Human Development, 28,* 259–280.

Rossi, A. S. (1980). Life-span theories and women's lives. *Signs, 6,* 4–32.

Ryff, C. D. (1982). Self-perceived personality change in adulthood and aging. *Journal of Personality and Social Psychology, 42,* 108–115.

Ryff, C. D. (1991). Possible selves in adulthood and old age: A tale of shifting horizons. *Psychology and Aging, 6,* 286–295.

Schaie, K. W. (1977). Toward a stage theory of adults cognitive development. *International Journal of Aging and Adult Development, 8,* 129–138.

Staudinger, U. M., Smith, J., & Baltes, P. B. (1992). Wisdom-related knowledge in a life-review task: Age differences and the role of professional specialization. *Psychology and Aging, 7,* 271–281.

Stein, J. O., & Stein, M. (1987). Psychotherapy, initiation, and the midlife transition. In L. C. Mahdi, S. Foster, & M. Little (Eds.), *Betwixt and between: Patterns of masculine and feminine initiation* (pp. 287–303). LaSalle, IL: Open Court.

Stevens-Long, J. (1990). Adult development: Theories past and future. In R. A. Nemiroff & C. A. Colarusso (Eds.), *New dimensions in adult development* (pp. 125–165). New York: Basic Books.

Stewart, A. J. (1996). Personality in middle age: Gender, history, and mid-course corrections. Murray Award lecture, Division 8, American Psychological Association, Toronto, Canada.

Tomlinson-Keasey, C. (in press). Tracing the lives of gifted women. In R. Jenkins-Friedman & F. D. Horowitz (Eds.), *Life-span research on gifted and talented children and youth.* Washington, DC: American Psychological Association.

Vaillant, G. E., & MacArthur, C. C. (1972). Natural history of male psychological health I: The adult life cycle from 18–50. *Seminars in Psychiatry, 4,* 417–429.

Vaillant, G. E., & Milofsky, E. (1980). The natural history of male psychological health IX: Empirical evidence for Erikson's model of the life cycle. *American Journal of Psychiatry, 137,* 1348–1359.

White, L., & Edwards, J. N. (1990). Emptying the nest and parental well-being: An analysis of national panel data. *American Sociological Review, 55,* 235–242.

Wink, P., & Helson, R. (1993). Personality change in women and their partners. *Journal of Personality and Social Psychology, 65,* 597–605.

THREE

Stability and Change in the Transition to Midlife:
A Longitudinal Study of Midlife Adults
Carol E. Franz

Perceptions of middle age vary widely. To some people it heralds the beginnings of decline and a period of midlife crisis. To others it is the prime of life (Mitchell & Helson, 1990) or a time of consolidation and balance (Vaillant & Milofsky, 1980). That midlife is commonly viewed as a transition period encourages those psychologists interested in the phenomenon of stability and change in personality across the life course to examine this period more closely. Although normative changes in personality during adulthood are proposed by some theorists and researchers, and vigorously denied by others (e.g., McCrae & Costa, 1990), the dearth of systematic efforts to discover what qualities change over time suggests that life course psychologists have not yet tested the boundaries of stability and change, especially in midlife adults.

The question of where change can be found is in part a measurement issue. In a review of the literature on stability and change in personality, Lachman (1989) found considerable stability in studies of five major personality traits: neuroticism, extraversion, openness to experience, agreeableness, and conscientiousness. Intrapsychic variables (e.g., motives, coping styles, defenses, and self-concept) that tended to be assessed using more open-ended measures and projective techniques such as the Thematic Apperception Test (TAT) were more subject to change. It may be that projective tests are more sensitive to nuances of change than measures requiring conscious averaging and evaluation of one's characteristics. In addition, stability was most evident in short-term studies using questionnaires; change was most evident in longer term studies using open-ended measures. Much of the research, though, has been cross-sectional, and Lachman urges more longitudinal studies. Few studies cover transitions to midlife, a period when some specific changes might be anticipated.

Another element contributing to the problems in delineating stability and change is the researcher's bias—in particular, the way in which personality has often been conceptualized as being typified by consistency over time. According to McCall (1977):

> I detect a tendency for our discipline to emphasize information on the stability of individual differences at the expense of data on the developmental functions . . . I am appealing for an equally as rigorous attempt to describe and explain developmental change. (pp. 338–339)

Helson (1993) argues that personality needs to be defined in a way that sanctions the search for both stability and changes, that

> encourages one to consider a variety of fairly stable motivational and resource patterns, to take into account the social world through which the individual moves, and to try to show when and why the organization of motivations and resource changes. (p. 97)

The issue, then, is to not foreclose the theoretical/empirical question but to develop more sensitive models for *how* one looks for change or stability, with *what* tools, *who* is more likely to change, and *what* kinds of stability or change it makes sense to look for at what points (*when*) during the life cycle. Lachman's work emphasized the issues of *how* with her discussion of assessment techniques and cross-sectional rather than longitudinal approaches. Transition periods—such as the transition to midlife—appear to be reasonable times when change can be anticipated. The focus of this chapter is on what kinds of change might be examined in the transition to midlife. Follow-ups of the now-adult Sears, Maccoby, and Levin (1957) sample at age 31 and age 41 provide an opportunity to examine stability and change in personality and maturity in one group's transition to midlife. These White subjects were born into lower-middle- and middle-class families in 1946, in the Northeast.

Studies of these midlife adults have yielded some evidence for stability, both in "parallel continuities" (that is, continuity with parental characteristics: Caspi & Bem, 1990), and in some personality characteristics. For instance, experiencing warm loving parents at age 5 was associated with the ability to sustain warm, long-lasting relationships 36 years later at age 41 (Franz, McClelland, & Weinberger, 1991). Parenting that encouraged and allowed taking action in the world was associated with greater agency (socialized power) in children's personality at age 31 and in their work life at 41 (McClelland & Franz, 1992; McClelland & Pilon, 1983). Parents who set high standards for their young children in terms of early impulse control—early weaning and toilet training practices—were more likely to have their children grow up to also set high standards for excellence (high need for achievement) 26 years later (McClelland & Pilon, 1983). Parents who in 1951 were extremely permissive and set few limits on children's behavior had children who were more likely to break limits by being 1960s activists. Activists were more assertive than other subjects at both age 31 and age 41 (Franz & McClelland, 1994). Preliminary analyses of traits as reported on the adjective checklist suggests stability in the extent to which subjects were more or less extraverted, emotionally labile, conscientious, and agreeable than other subjects from age 31 to age 41 (Franz, 1992). Finally, low self-esteem at age 12 was strongly associated with greater depression (r (28) = .68) at age 41 (Franz & Weinberger, 1993). In spite of this evidence for stability, the kinds of changes suggested by much of the theoretical literature are more subtle than these broad dimensions and have more to do with thought content than global characteristics.

THEORETICAL OVERVIEW

What kinds of changes are expected or normative for middle-aged adults? We can look to theory for guidelines concerning age-related and normative change. No theorists, however, see personality development as entirely discontinuous. The view tends rather to be one of change and continuity. In the words of James (1910):

> The Me, like every other aggregate, changes as it grows. . . . The identity which we recognize as we survey the long procession can only be the relative identity of a slow shifting in which there is always some common ingredient retained. The commonest element of all, the most uniform, is the possession of some common memories. However different the man may look from the youth, both look back on the same childhood and call it their own. (p. 48)

In the transition to midlife, at least three types of change can be anticipated: universalistic (age-related/maturational), normative or typical change in response to predictable events or change in one's social context, and idiosyncratic change.

Universalistic/Maturational Models of Change

Universalistic theories propose general patterns associated with the process of aging or increased maturity. Several theorists propose change in midlife. In Erikson's (1963) view of psychosocial change, regardless of culture or cohort, the midlife adult becomes concerned with issues of generativity such as caring about the well-being of others, productivity, and concern for the next generation. This process of change, according to Erikson, is relatively unconscious. The midlife adult's move toward more interdependent ways of thinking and being—and becoming less self-assertive and more involved with the well-being of others—is also reflected in the theories of Kegan (1982), Levinson, Darrow, Klein, Levinson, and McKee (1978), Schaie (1977–1978), and White (1966).

Several theorists also suggest that adults in their forties become more realistic and pragmatic about themselves and their strivings (Buhler, 1968; Buhler & Goldenberg, 1968; Gould, 1980; Levinson et al., 1978). Grandiosity and creative expansion are viewed as healthy aspects of adolescence and early adulthood; at midlife adults become more realistic regarding their own omnipotence and invulnerability (Buhler, 1968; Buhler & Goldenberg, 1968). According to other theorists, the midlife adult's cognitions and emotions become less black and white and more contextualized, differentiated, and complex (Jung, 1972; Labouvie-Vief, Hakim-Larson, & Hobart, 1987; Loevinger, 1976), and more introspective (Lubin, 1964; Neugarten, 1970; Rosen & Neugarten, 1964). Finally, maturity—broadly defined depending on the theorist or researcher—is assumed to increase with age and to change in quality (Erikson, 1963; Franz & White, 1985; Helson & Wink, 1992; Vaillant, 1977). Thus it can be seen that to assess these kinds of changes, we need measures that are fairly sensitive to subtle qualities in how one thinks about oneself.

Normative Change

Other researchers and theorists propose that normative life events, not age, are related to change. Sequences of development and typical concerns or responses, then, may be specific to gender, social roles, culture, or cohort. For instance, Gutmann proposed that men move from an active, assertive mode to a more dependent, passive one at midlife; women become more assertive (Gutmann, 1975; Neugarten, 1970). These changes occur because of predictable shifts in parenting roles for men and women; men and women function in line with different biological demands. The timing of these changes, though, will depend on the timing of the empty nest in a culture or group.

Helson and Wink (1992) suggest that common social contexts may differ by cohort. Although changes may occur in a particular cohort in response to expectable changes in roles, even the definition of roles may be specific to a cohort. For instance, the role definition of being a young mother in middle-class White America in the 1950s, when the majority of mothers did not work, is likely to differ substantially from that of a young mother in the 1990s, when the majority of young mothers are working at least part-time.

Other researchers have suggested that the life path or personality of a cohort may change because of commonly experienced major historical events. Elder (1979), for instance, has examined the way in which the Great Depression differentially affected development depending on age, gender, and social class. Stewart (Stewart & Healy, 1989; Stewart, Lykes, & LaFrance, 1983) has shown how educated women's life courses have varied in relation to historical events such as the women's movement and age. She has proposed a model that accounts for both age and the timing of a major cohort-specific historical event in predicting how an event causes change (Stewart & Healy, 1989).

Veroff (1982, 1986) also argues that the context of the individual needs to be incorporated into an understanding of motives (as measured by the Thematic Apperception Test: TAT) in the life course. *N* Achievement, he has found, peaks earlier in adulthood for men. Similarly, Veroff attributes increases in the need for power in two different cohorts of men between 1957 and 1978 to the rise of impact-oriented jobs in the workplace (Veroff, Depner, Kulka, & Douvan, 1980; Veroff, Reuman, & Feld, 1984). Thus, depending on sex, social context, and life cycle, the meaning and strength of a motive may vary. Without multiple cohorts in a study, however, universalistic/maturational and normative changes cannot be delineated.

Idiosyncratic Change

Finally, idiosyncratic change can occur in response to factors such as stress (Fiske & Chiriboga, 1990), life events, or low-probability events for a midlife transition age group such as major health problems or the death of a spouse (Brim & Ryff, 1980). In some samples, subgroups experiencing a stress may be large enough that typical change specific to the timing of that stress can be identified. For instance, in this sample, the more individuals increased their work status between age 31 and age 41, the more their need for achievement also increased (Franz, 1992). The largest changes in work status occurred among women reentering the workplace.

Fiske and Chiriboga (1990) concluded that health, work, and family stability maintain continuity in personality; stress in these realms is associated with discontinuity. In general, though, the adults in their sample reported becoming more patient, tolerant, and mature with age and valuing work and achievement less. There is little theory, however, to guide predictions concerning the type or direction of change. Although it is important to understand idiosyncratic change, this chapter focuses on more general maturational or normative changes.

In summary, what kinds of changes in thought content can be predicted during the midlife transition? The theories reviewed can be collapsed to make a few predictions: midlife adults are likely to decrease in assertion, increase in affiliation (suggesting a move toward interdependence), and show higher levels of complexity and maturity, lessened grandiosity, and greater realism. These changes may occur differentially even within a single cohort; in particular, as Gutmann, noted, by sex.

To investigate the question of continuity and change in thought content during the midlife transition, I assessed three types of characteristics with the research version of the TAT given to the same sample of adults at age 31 and age 41. The qualities assessed included: (1) a content analysis of themes prominent in the stories at different ages; (2) social motives such as *n* Achievement, *n* Power, *n* Affiliation, and the need for Intimacy; and (3) Psychological Stance (an indicator of psychosocial maturity). The TAT was chosen as a measure because it has been shown to be sensitive to change (Lachman, 1989). According to DeCharms (1992):

> Although the thought sampling (that is, TAT-based) technique has roots in the concepts of the unconscious and projection, we avoid these terms in favor of construing the thought sample as a nonself-conscious description of the way a person experiences her world. (p. 326)

Thus, the TAT appears to be a more sensitive measure of the types of personality qualities—thoughts, motives, maturity—hypothesized to change during these years.

THE STUDY

The midlife adults I report on in this study were part of a longitudinal study started in 1951 by Sears, Maccoby, and Levin (1957). The five-year-old child about whom the mother was interviewed became the subject of follow-up efforts. Of particular interest are the data collected at age 31 and age 41. The sample was all White, American-born, with an intact family in 1951. Details of the sample selection, interview procedure, coding, and reliabilities may be found in Sears et al. (1957).

In 1978 McClelland followed up a subsample of the Sears et al. children (then age 31) who were still living in the Boston area. Of the 130 subjects located, 118 were interviewed. Seventy-eight of these subjects came to a second session in which they were administered a variety of personality measures, including a six-picture TAT. The pictures included the captain, the draftsman at his desk, two women scientists, the trapeze picture, a couple by a river, and a couple at a café. Details of this sample have been reported elsewhere. T-tests of parenting and demographic measures indicate that the 1978 sample was representative of the 1951 sample (Koestner, Franz, & Weinberger, 1990; McClelland & Pilon, 1983).

The subsample studied at age 41 (followed up by McClelland and Franz)[1] comprised subjects from the earlier wave of data collection (1978). Individuals were followed up by mail if they had moved beyond driving distance of Boston. Details concerning the sample can be found in Franz et al., 1991, and McClelland and Franz, 1992. Checks on the sampling indicated that the sample was representative of the 1978 sample and the original 1951 sample. Comparison of the smaller group of 49 subjects (18 men, 31 women) for whom there was TAT data at both times also revealed no significant differences, with the exception that women were more likely to participate than men. Because of the sample size, the results reported here are considered preliminary.

The majority of these adults were married (85%) at age 41; most came from middle-class, white-collar backgrounds (65%), and the remainder from lower-middle-class, blue-collar families. They all had at least finished high school. Only 8% sought no further education; 50% had at least some college education and 42% had pursued more education after college. Nearly all (91%) of the adults who were married or divorced had children (range 0–6 children; Mean = 1.92). No one was yet experiencing the empty nest. At the time of the follow-up, most of the men and women (92%) were working at least part-time outside the home. As is typically found (Rix, 1988), men were more highly educated, worked at higher status jobs, and earned more income than the women (Franz et al., 1991).

At both age 31 and age 41, 18 men and 31 women completed TATs; the TAT at age 41 differed from that at age 31 by one picture—the picture of the couple at the café was replaced by a picture of a man and woman walking through a field with a horse and a dog ("Singapore"). Subjects tended to assign intimacy and affiliative images to both pictures (McClelland, personal communication, May 1992).

Social Motives

Stories were scored for n Power (n Pow; Winter 1992); n Achievement (n Ach; McClelland, Atkinson, Clark, & Lowell, 1992), n Affiliation (n Aff; Heyns, Veroff, & Atkinson, 1992) and Intimacy motivation (n Int; McAdams, 1992). The needs for power (n Pow) and achievement (n Ach) can be thought of as assertive, self-oriented motives; n Affiliation and Intimacy motivation can be thought of as affiliative or communal needs. In brief, n Pow has been described as a desire to have impact on other people; n Ach as a desire for excellence or doing things better. N Affiliation was conceptualized as the motive to establish, maintain, or restore close relationships. McAdams (1985) constructed his measure of Intimacy motivation in order to get at more positive, warm, approach tendencies to close relationships that he believed were not assessed by the n Affiliation scoring system. The reliability of the TAT has been addressed in detail in other sources (Lundy, 1985, 1988; Smith, 1992).

Maturity

Maturity was assessed using Stewart's (1982, 1992) measure of psychological stance (stances of adaptation). Four developmental stances, indicating increasing maturity or adaptation, were assessed: dependency (receptivity), autonomy, assertiveness, and integration. These stances are on a continuum "at one end of which the individual is perceived as at risk of being entirely submerged in the enviroment, at the other end of which the individual is depicted as in some stable and neutral relation to the environment" (Smith, p. 13). Because theoretically people mature over time and become more complex and differentiated, psychological stance will increase over time.

Age-related Thoughts (ARTs)

No empirically based scoring system was available for assessing how a person's thoughts changed with age, so a new content-analytic coding system was derived for this study from two samples of adult subjects.[2] Using a standard criterion group approach in deriving scoring systems, TATs of 5 adults in their early 30s were compared with TATs of 5 adults in their early 40s from this sample by three different groups of psychologists. Any themes present in one age group but absent in the other formed the initial scoring system.

Three *young* and three *old* themes were identified. Themes evident in the younger subjects were (1) worry (someone in the story is concerned that something might go wrong or anticipates bad things happening unrelated to interpersonal issues); (2) conflict and instability in affiliative relationships (e.g., divorce, affairs, quarrels); and (3) idealizations or grandiosity (e.g., imagining a cure for an incurable disease, attempting to save the world or perform impossible feats). Stories by older subjects were distinguished by themes of (1) realism, planning, and moderation at work; (2) helping or teaching that was not role related; and (3) finding both support *and* enjoyment (not *or* enjoyment) in being with other people. The rudimentary coding system was then applied to a second set of TATs from adults from a different sample (ages 32 to 75, so TATs from 10 persons under age 39 and 10 persons age 41 to age 50 were scored). Scores successfully categorized 18 out of 20 subjects as young or old.

Themes were then carefully operationalized and a scoring manual was created (Franz & McClelland, 1992). Scoring rules were finalized. These included the decision to score a theme no more than once in a story. Coders attained a high level of reliability (above 87% agreement on *presence* of imagery). All of the TAT pictures in common (that is, 5 pictures at each time) were coded for both time periods for *age-related thoughts* (ARTs). Duplicate subject numbers and any cues to date were removed; protocols were randomly placed in sets so as to minimize coder bias. In order to maximize coder reliability, the coder scored all stories written to a single picture—by all the subjects—at the same time.

Initial analyses indicated that very few subjects were scored for *non-role-related helping* (no subjects at age 31; 6 at 41); as a result, that category was dropped from these analyses. Two measures of age-related

TABLE 3.1 Paired *t*-test Comparisons of Age-related Thoughts from Ages 31 and 41

| | Age 31 | | Age 41 | | |
	Mean	SD	Mean	SD	t test
Youthful uncertainty	4.36	2.09	1.35	.97	10.16***
Grounded realism	1.22	.99	3.71	1.38	11.63***
Idealizations	1.22	1.25	.18	.39	5.45***

N = 49 (18 men, 31 women)
***p < .001

thoughts were created at each age: *youthful uncertainty* (the sum of worry and relational conflict) and *grounded realism* (the sum of realism and warm, supportive relatedness). Because of the specific mention of grandiosity in several theories, scores for *idealizations* were kept separate. No sex differences occurred in any of the TAT-based measures at either time. All TAT-based measures were corrected for correlation with text length (Winter, 1992). Because the same subjects were studied at both times, changes in thought content were evaluated using paired *t*-tests.

RESULTS

Age-related Thoughts

The tendency to write worrisome, conflicted stories (*youthful uncertainty*) and stories with idealistic or grandiose themes (*idealization*) decreased significantly in these adults in the ten years from age 31 to 41. At the same time, as can be seen in Table 3.1, these adults significantly increased their use of themes of planning, realistic strivings, and warm, refreshing relationships.

For instance, at age 31, a subject looking at the TAT of a man at his desk with a picture of his family was more likely to write about the disappointments and strain in the man's work or that "his family have become like strangers to him." At 41, in response to the same picture cue, the story by the same subject is more likely to read "Looking at the picture of his wife provides him with an opportunity to experience warm thoughts and feelings. He goes back to work feeling refreshed." Similarly, one 31-year-old fantasizes to the trapeze picture that

> Two wealthy lovers are breaking in new equipment they
> have installed in their bedroom . . . after various flips and

TABLE 3.2 Paired *t*-test Comparisons of Motives and
Psychological Stance at Ages 31 and 41

	Age 31		Age 41		
	Mean	*SD*	Mean	*SD*	*t* test
n Power	6.06	4.11	5.17	3.13	1.39 *ns*
n Achievement	3.60	3.56	1.75	4.13	2.95 $p < .01$
n Affiliation	9.45	3.14	11.56	3.58	−3.56 $p < .01$
n Intimacy	6.33	2.91	6.70	3.63	−.65 *ns*
Psychological stance	2.22	.46	2.54	.24	−5.10 $p < .001$

$N = 49$

flops, they will tumble from the net below to their waterbed and realize their fantasies of making love in the center ring under the bigtop.

At 41, the trapeze artists are "performing their circus routine. They are at the height of their career." The decrease in idealizations indicates, perhaps, less need for grandiosity when the realistic achievements of adulthood materialize as "realistic self-esteem" (Kohut, 1985, p. 128). Kohut's view is supported by the fact that high idealization at 31 is correlated $r(46) = .45$ ($p < .01$) with greater psychological stance at 41 and with lower depression as measured by the Zung (1965) depression scale ($r(40) = -.31, p < .05$).

Motive and Maturity Change

On the basis of theory, I predicted that assertive motives would decline in the transition to midlife and communal motives would increase as adults moved toward greater interdependence. Men's and women's stories at age 41 contained fewer themes concerning personal standards of excellence (*n* Ach) than at 31 (Table 3.2). By age 41 men also wrote stories significantly lower in themes concerning having an impact on others (*n* Pow). Both men and women increased in concern about entering or maintaining positive relationships with others (*n* Aff), though no changes were evident in Intimacy motivation. Psychological stance, an indicator of greater maturity, complexity, and adaptation to the environment, was significantly higher at age 41 than at age 31. At the highest levels of emotional stance, people wrote cognitively complex stories that allowed for ambivalence in and integration of emotions and relationships.

It appears that considerable change occurs in this sample, much of it in the directions suggested by the universalistic theorists reviewed earlier in this chapter. *N* Ach and *n* Pow can be viewed as self-assertive motives, and *n* Affiliation as a communal orientation toward other persons (Veroff, 1982). The decreases in self-assertion and increases in communion in this sample support the notion that in midlife there is movement away from a self-focused assertiveness and toward a more interpersonal focus. The results do not support Gutmann's (1975) hypothesis that women become less communal and more assertive, though the women in this sample have not yet reached the postparental stage.

Another way of evaluating Gutmann's theory is to examine whether personality change might be specific to men with particularly agentic qualities and women with high communal qualities. Among men, being high in *n* Power at age 31 was significantly associated with high *n* Affiliation at age 41 (r [16] = .61; $p < .01$). The needs for power and affiliation had been negatively correlated at age 31 (r [16] = −.32). No such relationship existed between *n* Achievement at 31 and the affiliative motives at 41. Among the women, communal motives at age 31 are not associated with assertive motives at 41. Interestingly enough, in support of Veroff, Reuman, & Feld's (1984) view that men and women experience the need for achievement differently, women's *n* Achievement at age 31 was correlated −.50 ($df = 29$, $p < .01$) with the need for power at 41. The same relationship for the men was $r = .07$. Because of the small sample size, these relationships need to be examined in other groups; however, the results indicating both decreased assertion in men and the somewhat different meaning of achievement for women supported those of other researchers.

Differential Stability

Changes in thought content do not rule out the possibility of differential stability: that is, "the retention of an individual's relative placement in a group" (Caspi & Bem, p. 550). In Table 3.3, the degree to which scores on each measure were correlated over ten years can be seen. N Achievement, *n* Intimacy, and Psychological Stance were significantly correlated with the corresponding measure over these ten years. Trends were apparent for *n* Affiliation and *n* Power ($p < .10$, two-tailed). None of the ARTs categories were correlated over time, with the exception of *uncertainty* imagery among women. Of some

TABLE 3.3 Stability of Age-related Thoughts, Motives,
and Psychological Stance: Correlations between
Age 31 and Age 41 Measures

	Men (18)	Women (31)	Total (49)
Youthful uncertainty	−.20	.37*	.19
Grounded realism	−.06	.17	.11
Idealizations	.04	−.15	−.06
n Achievement	.33	.33*t*	.36*
n Power	−.09	.35*t*	.26*t*
n Affiliation	.17	.28	.24*t*
n Intimacy	−.18	.48**	.29*
Psychological stance	.65**	.36*	.50**

t $p < .10$; *$p < .05$; **$p < .01$ (two-tailed)

interest is the greater level of stability of motives in general among the women.

Change and some stability, then, are both apparent in this sample; levels of *n* Ach and psychological maturity changed significantly over time, but from these analyses it can be seen that individuals retained their relative placement within the group. Greater consistency appears for Intimacy motivation: subjects tended to write as many Intimacy motivation themes at age 31 as at age 41 and maintained their relative placement in the group.

CONCLUSIONS

An undergraduate student's pithy summary of the difference between the 41- and 31-year-old adults was: "These guys (pointing to the 41-year-old pile) are more *boring*." A middle-aged adult protested: "Is this all there is to life?" In a way, yes, the 41-year-old adults could seem more boring; they wrote fewer assertive themes, portrayed their characters as less worried and conflicted, and with less grandiosity and idealism than had been apparent at age 31. What had replaced that grandiose (but worried) exuberance at age 41?

As these men and women aged, they moved toward greater maturity, complexity, and integration and were more likely to write themes of positive, supportive relationships. The degree to which they wrote themes of achievement and idealizations lessened over time; themes associated with impact (*n* Pow) especially were lower in men at 41. On the other hand, Intimacy motivation did not change over these ten years.

The major question I have addressed has been whether thought contents change as people make the transition from early adulthood to middle age. The answer, based on results from TAT stories, is that there is both change and continuity. Despite the passage of time and the variety of individual life experiences over ten years, these adults were stable relative to each other in the strength of some of their motives and their level of maturity. At the same time, differences appeared in the content of their thoughts, changes in keeping with developmentally oriented personality theories. In general, these results support theoretical views of reduced self-concern and assertion and greater concern with communion and other people in middle age; of movement toward greater adaptation to the environment and of rising introspection (Erikson, 1963; Franz & White, 1985; Gutmann, 1975; Kegan, 1982; Rosen & Neugarten, 1964; Schaie, 1977–1978; Stewart, 1992; White, 1966). These changes can be highlighted by the stories of one adult written at two times to the same picture. At age 31 he wrote:

> It is mid-afternoon late Thursday and John has been pondering an extremely difficult problem encountered while building General Dynamics' latest supertanker. This vehicle will be far larger than any natural gas tanker used thus far. Safety conditions are being balanced against engineering and cost priorities. As John examines the theoretical/moral aspects of the new tanker his mind wanders elsewhere. The questions that perplex him call to mind the working conditions in the environment and the effects of his contributions to society on his family's welfare and that of mankind. Save the Whales!

At age 41, in response to the same cue, his story sounds like this:

> The man at the desk appears to be some kind of engineer who is working on a complex project. There are blueprints and other papers filling his desktop which he appears to be involved with. In the picture the man is looking at a picture of his wife and children. He is at the same time taking a break from his project and refreshing himself by thinking of his family.

Idealistic thinking, such as discovering a cure for an incurable disease, saving the whales, or single-handedly creating world peace at age 31 seems to benefit adult adjustment at age 41. In light of recent theorizing on the deficits of clinical narcissism (Kohut, 1977; Wink, 1992), it is interesting that this TAT-based measure of idealistic/grandiose thinking is associated with positive outcomes at midlife. These results support the sense that at least in this cohort, there are developmentally healthy aspects of grandiosity or the ability to dream (Gottschalk, 1990; Kohut, 1977; Levinson et al., 1978; Wink, 1992). Clearly, further research is needed to see if this thought process changes with age in other cohorts, over broader age ranges, and across different historical periods.

The empirically derived scoring system for age-related thoughts captured three characteristics of adults suggested by theorists: idealizations, realism, and warm, supportive relationships. The extent to which conflict, problems, and worry occurred in age-31 stories was not clearly reflected by theory. Although this uncertainty could be explained as evidence for the psychological costs of expansion or individuation (e.g., of fears of moving too far or too high), of difficulty in integrating the complexities of adult life (e.g., Levinson et al.'s (1978) age-30 transition), or simply as part of the questioning of one's identity in the context of intimacy (Erikson, 1963), the presence and prevalence of this thought-content category was unanticipated. Since the early forties can also be considered a transition period, conflicts and uncertainty would not seem to be unique to the thirties. To what extent, then, can this characteristic that is typical or normative for this group at age 30 also be found in other 30-year-olds?

The increase in caring for others—as captured by the category of non-role-related helping—though entirely absent in age-31 stories occurred so infrequently at age 41 that it was omitted from the scale. Since both Erikson (1963) and White (1966) emphasize the growth of caring as an aspect of mature adulthood, the absence of this imagery was as much of a surprise as the presence of so much uncertainty. There are three possible explanations: either this characteristic may not be evident yet (these subjects are only in early middle age); the picture cues may be oriented toward individuation and intimacy themes rather than caring; or the specification in the scoring system that the helping had to be beyond the typical role of a person (e.g., a teacher helping a student with schoolwork would not score) may have been too narrow. These results, then, qualify the broad (universalistic) generalizations of some life-span theorists.

I found only mixed support for Gutmann's role-related ideas concerning gender crossover at mid-life; in this sample, men and women changed in similar directions—both exhibiting lessened need for achievement and increased need for affiliation. The men, however, may appear less agentic than the women; both achievement and power decreased in the men, and men who were high in power at 31 were high in affiliation at 41. Although women decreased overall in the need for achievement, increased job status (which was most prevalent among the women) was associated with increased achievement strivings. In contrast, women in the Mills sample became more dominant at midlife (Helson & Moane, 1987); those women, however, were two years older, from a different historical period, and better educated than most of the women in this sample; and dominance was measured using a questionnaire. Women in the Mills sample also experienced a time of conflict in their 40s (Helson & Wink, 1992); the analyses of my sample suggest *decreased* conflict and worry from age 31 to age 41. Whether women in general increase in dominance as they continue into middle age (as did women studied by Helson & Moane, 1987) remains to be seen.

More changes are likely to occur as these adults experience the next two decades of middle age, including, for those who are parents, the postparental years. However, we should also consider the extent to which this cohort is different from that studied by Gutmann. These middle-class, educated men and women reaching adulthood in the 1970s and middle age in the late 1980s could expect lives less closely constrained by social roles than those of their parents or grandparents. What Gutmann viewed as biologically determined may have reflected the cultural constraints of the generation of midlife men and women he studied during the 1960s; what is normative for one cohort may not be for another.

The importance of the social context of this cohort cannot be overestimated; without additional cohorts it is impossible to discern the extent to which the changed thought contents were related to age, maturation, or social history. Born into the baby boom of the 1950s, these adults experienced adolescence in the overturn of cultural expectancies of the 1960s. Their early adulthood during the 1970s was one in which old rules no longer applied. The seventies were characterized by the emergence of new family structures, high divorce rates, feminism, more women in the workplace, the disillusionment of the war in Vietnam, Watergate, and the oil crisis of the early seventies. It is possible that the higher needs for power and achievement and the idealizations and uncertainty in the age-31 stories written in 1978 reflect the uncertainty, worry, and need for self-assertion necessary to establish a sense of self and a coherent life path during that confusing historical time. Similarly, the more contented, satiated, and relational stories at age 41 (in 1987) may reflect the relative economic prosperity of these well-educated middle-class adults before the economic difficulties of the late 1980s and early 1990s. Thus, the uncertainty present in this sample at age 31 may be cohort dependent, a reflection of sociohistorical conditions rather than a characteristic typical of 30-year-olds in general.

On the basis of these results, I am not yet ready to concur with Fiske and Chiriboga (1990) or McCrae and Costa (1990) that the *norm* in adulthood is continuity. It all depends on when and how people's lives and characteristics are examined. In this and other longitudinal studies, there is convincing evidence for both stability and change—especially normative change. It seems that we will make progress in life-span personality psychology when we develop models of personality that can help us discover what aspects of personality are more likely to be stable or change, what processes are involved, including factors such as sex, context, ethnicity, stress, and age, and when change is more or less likely to occur. That multiple models delineating nuances of stability and change are still needed and valuable (Gergen, 1978) is highlighted by the fact that no *single* theory I reviewed accounted for the changes I found in this sample. Without more sophisticated models and more informed longitudinal research, we are doomed—as Robert White (1966) suggested—to continue to create caricatures of human beings rather than portraits of lives in progress.

ACKNOWLEDGMENTS

I greatly appreciate the helpful comments on earlier versions of this chapter by Joel Weinberger, David McClelland, Jackie James, Abby Stewart, Todd Heatherton, Robert Bornstein, David Buss, and two anonymous reviewers. Part of this research uses follow-up data from the *Patterns of Child Rearing, 1951–1952* data set (Sears, Maccoby, & Levin, 1957). The original sample was started by R. Sears, E. Maccoby, and H. Levin; the data are archived at the Henry A. Murray Research

Center of Radcliffe College, Cambridge, Massachusetts. The 1978 follow-up by McClelland and the 1987 McClelland-Franz follow-up are also archived at the Murray Center.

NOTES

1. A score indicating the overall stance level of the person is determined using a weighted score: ((1 * the number of receptive images) + (2 * the number of autonomous images) + (3 * the number of assertive images) + (4 * the number of integrative images))/total number of images.

2. Systems are available, and can be created, based on what theorists say a priori *should* be found in adults (e.g., Stewart, Franz, & Layton, 1988). I was interested in what people said about themselves rather than how well they fit imposed theoretical schemas.

REFERENCES

Blatt, S., & Blass, R. (1990). Attachment and separateness: A dialectical model of the products and processes of development throughout the life cycle. *Psychoanalytic study of the child, 45,* 107–127.

Brim, O. G., & Ryff, C. D. (1980). On the properties of life events. In P. B. Baltes & O. G. Brim (Eds.), *Life-span development and behavior, Vol. 3* (pp. 368–387). San Diego, CA: Academic Press.

Buhler, C. (1968). The developmental structure of goal setting in group and individual studies. In C. Buhler & F. Massarik (Eds.), *The course of human life: A study of goals in the humanistic perspective* (pp. 27–54). New York: Springer.

Buhler, C., & Goldenberg, H. (1968). Structural aspects of an individual's history. In C. Buhler & F. Massarik (Eds.), *The course of human life: A study of goals in the humanistic perspective* (pp. 54–63). New York: Springer.

Caspi, A., & Bem, D. (1990). Personality continuity and change across the life course. In L. Pervin (Ed.), *Handbook of personality theory and research* (pp. 549–575). New York: Guilford Press.

DeCharms, R. (1992). Personal causation and the origin concept. In C. P. Smith, J. W. Atkinson, D. C. McClelland, & J. Veroff (Eds.), *Motivation and personality: Handbook of thematic analysis* (pp. 325–333). Cambridge, England: Cambridge University Press.

Elder, G. (1979). Historical change in life patterns and personality. In P. B. Baltes & O. G. Brim (Eds.), *Life-span development and behavior: Volume 2* (pp. 117–159). San Diego, CA: Academic Press.

Erikson, E. H. (1963). *Childhood and society* (2nd ed.). New York: Norton.

Fiske, M., & Chiriboga, D. A. (1990). *Change and continuity in adult life.* San Francisco: Jossey Bass.

Franz, C. E. (1992, September). *Do preoccupations change as people age?* Paper presented at a meeting of the MacArthur/Murray Center Network for Successful Midlife Development, Brewster, MA.

Franz, C. E., & McClelland, D. C. (1992). *Scoring manual for age related preoccupations.* Unpublished manuscript, Center for Health and Applied Social Science, Boston University.

Franz, C. E., & McClelland, D. C. (1994). The life course of women and men active in the social protests of the 1960s: A longitudinal study. *Journal of Personality and Social Psychology, 66,* 196–205.

Franz, C. E., McClelland, D. C., & Weinberger, J. (1991). Childhood antecedents of conventional social accomplishment in midlife adults: A 36-year prospective study. *Journal of Personality and Social Psychology, 60,* 586–595.

Franz, C. E., & Weinberger, J. W. (1993). Childhood antecedents of depression in midlife adults: A longitudinal study. Unpublished manuscript, Department of Psychology, University of Michigan.

Franz, C. E., & White, K. M. (1985). Individuation and attachment in personality development: Extending Erikson's theory. *Journal of Personality, 53,* 224–257.

Gergen, K. J. (1978). Toward generative theory. *Journal of Personality and Social Psychology, 36,* 1344–1360.

Gottschalk, L. A. (1990). Origins and evolution of narcissism through the life cycle. In R. A. Nemiroff & C. A. Colarusso (Eds.), *New dimensions in adult development* (pp. 73–90). New York: Basic Books.

Gould, R. L. (1980). Transformational tasks in adulthood. In S. I. Greenspan & G. H. Pollock (Eds.), *The course of life: Psychoanalytic contributions toward understanding personality development, vol. 3: Adulthood and the aging process* (pp. 117–127). Washington, DC: National Institute for Mental Health.

Gutmann, D. (1975). Parenthood: A key to the comparative study of the lifecycle. In N. Datan & L. Ginsberg (Eds.), *Life-span developmental psychology: Normative life crises* (pp. 167–184). San Diego, CA: Academic Press.

Helson, R. (1993). Comparing longitudinal studies of adult development: Towards a paradigm of tension between stability and change. *Studying lives through time: Personality and development* (pp. 93–119). Washington, DC: American Psychological Association.

Helson, R., & Moane, G. (1987). Personality change in women from college to midlife. *Journal of Personality and Social Psychology, 53,* 176–186.

Helson, R., & Wink, P. (1992). Personality change in women from the early 40s to the early 50s. *Psychology and Aging, 7,* 46–55.

Heyns, R. W., Veroff, J., & Atkinson, J. W. (1992). A scoring manual for the affiliative motive. In C. P. Smith, J. W. Atkinson, D. C. McClelland, & J. Veroff (Eds.), *Motivation and personality: Handbook of thematic analysis* (pp. 211–223). Cambridge, England: Cambridge University Press.

Jung, C. G. (1972). The transcendent function. In H. Read, M. Fordham, G. Adler, & W. McGuire (Eds.), *The structure and dynamics of the psyche, vol. 8 of*

The collected works of C. G. Jung (2nd ed., pp. 67–91). Princeton, NJ: Princeton University Press.

Kegan, R. (1982). *The evolving self: Problem and process in human development.* Cambridge, MA: Harvard University Press.

Koestner, R., Franz, C., & Weinberger, J. (1990). The family origins of empathic concern: A 26-year longitudinal study. *Journal of Personality and Social Psychology, 58,* 709–717.

Kohut, H. (1977). *The restoration of the self.* New York: International Universities Press.

Kohut, H. (1985). Thoughts on narcissism and narcissistic rage. In C. Strozier (Ed.), *Self psychology and the humanities: Reflection on a new psychoanalytic approach by Heinz Kohut* (pp. 124–160). New York: Norton.

Labouvie-Vief, G., Hakim-Larson, J., & Hobart, C. (1987). Age, ego-level, and the life-span development of coping and defense processes. *Psychology and Aging, 2,* 286–293.

Lachman, M. E. (1989). Personality and aging at the crossroads: Beyond stability versus change. In K. W. Schaie & C. Schooler (Eds.), *Social structure and aging: Psychological processes* (pp. 167–190). Hillsdale, NJ: Eribaum.

Levinson, D. J., Darrow, C. N., Klein, E. B., Levinson, M. H., & McKee, B. (1978). *The seasons of a man's life.* New York: Knopf.

Loevinger, J. (1976). *Ego development.* San Francisco: Jossey-Bass.

Lubin, M. I. (1964). Addendum to Chapter 4. In B. L. Neugarten (Ed.), *Personality in middle and late life: Empirical studies* (pp. 102–104). New York: Atherton Press.

Lundy, A. (1985). The reliability of the Thematic Apperception Test. *Journal of Personality Assessment, 49,* 141–145.

Lundy, A. (1988). Instruction set and Thematic Apperception Test validity. *Journal of Personality Assessment, 52,* 309–320.

McAdams, D. P. (1985). *Power, intimacy and the life story: Personological inquiries into identity.* Chicago: Dorsey Press.

McAdams, D. P. (1992). The intimacy motivation scoring system. In C. P. Smith, J. W. Atkinson, D. C. McClelland, & J. Veroff (Eds.), *Motivation and personality: Handbook of thematic analysis* (pp. 229–253). Cambridge, England: Cambridge University Press.

McCall, R. B. (1977). Challenges to a science of developmental psychology. *Child Development, 48,* 333–344.

McClelland, D. C., Atkinson, J. W., Clark, R., & Lowell, E. (1992). A scoring manual for the achievement motive. In C. P. Smith, J. W. Atkinson, D. C. McClelland, & J. Veroff (Eds.), *Motivation and personality: Handbook of thematic analysis* (pp. 153–178). Cambridge, England: Cambridge University Press.

McClelland, D. C., & Franz, C. E. (1992). Motivational and other sources of work accomplishments in mid-life. *Journal of Personality, 60,* 679–707.

McClelland, D. C., & Pilon, D. A. (1983). Sources of adult motives in patterns of parent behavior in early childhood. *Journal of Personality and Social Psychology, 44,* 564–574.

McCrae, R. R., & Costa, P. T., Jr. (1990). *Personality in adulthood.* New York: Guilford Press.

Mitchell, V., & Helson, R. (1990). Women's prime of life: Is it the 50s? *Psychology of Women Quarterly, 14,* 451–470.

Neugarten, B. L. (1970). Adaptation and the life cycle. *Journal of Geriatric Psychology, 4,* 71–87.

Picano, J. J. (1989). Development and validation of a life history index of adult adjustment for women. *Journal of Personality Assessment, 53,* 308–318.

Rix, S. E. (1988). *The American woman 1988–1989: A status report.* New York: Norton.

Rosen, J. L., & Neugarten, B. L. (1964). Ego functions in the middle and later years: A thematic apperception study. In B. L. Neugarten (Ed.), *Personality in middle and late life: Empirical studies* (pp. 90–101). New York: Atherton Press.

Schaie, K. W. (1977–1978). Toward a stage theory of adult cognitive development. *International Journal of Aging and Human Development, 8,* 129–138.

Sears, R. R., Maccoby, E. E., & Levin, H. (1957). *Patterns of child rearing.* Evanston, Ill.: Row Peterson.

Smith, C. P. (1992). Reliability issues. In C. P. Smith, J. W. Atkinson, D. C. McClelland, & J. Veroff (Eds.), *Motivation and personality: Handbook of thematic analysis* (pp. 126–142). New York: Cambridge University Press.

Stewart, A. J. (1982). The course of individual adaptation. *Journal of Personality and Social Psychology, 42,* 1100–1113.

Stewart, A. J. (1992). Scoring manual for psychological stances toward the environment. In C. P. Smith, J. W. Atkinson, D. C. McClelland, & J. Veroff (Eds.), *Motivation and personality: Handbook of thematic analysis* (pp. 451–480). Cambridge, England: Cambridge University Press.

Stewart, A. J., Franz, C. E., & Layton, L. (1988). The changing self: Using personal documents to study lives. *Journal of Personality, 56,* 41–74.

Stewart, A. J., & Healy, J. (1989). Linking individual development and social changes. *American Psychologist, 44,* 30–42.

Stewart, A. J., Lykes, B., & LaFrance, M. (1983). Educated women's career patterns: Separating social and developmental changes. *Journal of Social Issues, 38,* 97–117.

Vaillant, G. E. (1977). *Adaptation to Life.* Boston: Little, Brown.

Vaillant, G. E., & Milofsky, E. (1980). Natural history of male psychological health IX. Empirical evidence for Erikson's model of the life cycle. *American Journal of Psychiatry, 137,* 1348–1359.

Veroff, J. (1982). Assertive motivations: Achievement versus power. In A. J. Stewart (Ed.), *Motivation and society* (pp. 99–132). San Francisco: Jossey-Bass.

Veroff, J. (1986). Contextualism and human motives. In D. R. Brown and J. Veroff (Eds.), *Frontiers of motivational psychology: Essays in honor of John W. Atkinson* (pp. 132–145). Berlin: Springer-Verlag.

Veroff, J., Depner, C., Kulka, R., & Douvan, E. (1980). Comparison of American motives: 1957 versus 1976. *Journal of Personality and Social Psychology, 39,* 1249–1262.

Veroff, J., Reuman, D., & Feld, S. (1984). Motives in American men and women across the adult life span. *Developmental Psychology, 20,* 1142–1158.

White, R. W. (1966). *Lives in progress: A study of the natural growth of personality.* New York: Holt, Rinehart.

Wink, P. (1992). Three types of narcissism in women from college to mid-life. *Journal of Personality, 60,* 7–30.

Winter, D. G. (1992). A revised scoring manual for the power motive. C. P. Smith, J. W. Atkinson, D. C. McClelland, & J. Veroff (Eds.), *Motivation and personality: Handbook of thematic analysis* (pp. 311–324). Cambridge, England: Cambridge University Press.

Zung, W. K. (1965). A self-rating depression scale. *Archives of General Psychiatry, 12,* 63–70.

Do Aspects of Gender Identity Change from Early to Middle Adulthood? Disentangling Age, Cohort, and Period Effects

Rebecca A. Parker and Carolyn M. Aldwin

A hotly debated topic in developmental psychology is whether personality changes in adulthood (for reviews see Aldwin & Levenson, 1994; Caspi, Bern, & Elder, 1989; McCrae & Costa, 1990). Although several theories of adult development exist, much of the longitudinal research reported to date has been atheoretical; it simply examines stability and change using standardized personality inventories, with notable exceptions (e.g., Helson & Moane, 1987). One exception to this trend concerns the so-called crossover effect in studies of gender identity development, with gender identity encompassing both self-attributions and social role expectations (Deaux, 1985).

The crossover notion was derived from Jung's (1933) hypothesis about systematic changes in personality from early to middle adulthood. He believed that certain aspects of the personality that were suppressed during adolescence and early adulthood reemerged in midlife. In particular, Jung proposed that a woman suppresses her animus as a young wife and mother, but that the long-suppressed animus demands expression in midlife, resulting in increased interest in achievement and accomplishments, especially outside the home. In contrast, he thought that a man suppressed his anima in young adulthood in the service of the competitiveness and achievement orientation necessary for successful career development. In midlife, his anima demanded expression, resulting in an increased interest in familial and nurturant concerns.

This chapter is based partially on the first author's dissertation. The study was supported by the John D. and Catherine T. MacArthur Research Network on Successful Midlife Development, as well as Hatch Funds from the University of California at Davis Cooperative Extension Service. We would like to thank Paula Schnurr and Avron Spiro III for their recommendations on some of the analyses, Leanne Friedman for her help with data management and analyses, our colleagues in the MacArthur Foundation Network, Jacquelyn Boon James, Carol Franz, and Corinne Lewkowicz for suggestions on ways to improve the manuscript, and Rael Dornfest, Cory Fitzpatrick, and Tiffany Pfeffers for help with data collection and data entry.

The current conception of the crossover effect, however, implies a role reversal in midlife: women become more masculine than men, and vice versa. This emphasis on the absolute level of masculinity or femininity per se misrepresents Jung's focus on redressing the balance of anima and animus. Nonetheless, this simplified version of Jung's theory has received wide credence in the adult development literature (despite surprisingly little empirical support), and this has led to the neglect of other possible patterns of change in gender identity in adulthood. As we shall see, there is little agreement about the measurement of gender identity, what aspects of gender identity might change, whether this hypothesized change is continuous or discontinuous, and the age at which this process may begin.

Our purpose in this chapter is to organize what has been observed about gender identity development and then to build on that knowledge through analyses of two longitudinal data sets. We first analyze the psychological and sociological literatures to identify specific aspects of gender identity that have been shown to change (or not, as the case may be). We then present analyses that examine changes in two aspects of gender identity across age, cohorts, and period.

Gender Identity and Adult Development

There is a surprising amount of contradictory evidence concerning changes in gender identity in adulthood for both men and women, as can be seen from an examination of the studies reported in Tables 4.1–4.3. Research on men has variously reported increased femininity, increased masculinity, decreased masculinity, and increased androgyny. Similarly, studies of women have provided evidence of increased masculinity, increased femininity, decreased femininity, and decreased androgyny. At first glance, it would appear that few generalizations can be made about the development of gender identity in adulthood. However, we propose that there are two systematic sources of variation in these seemingly confusing results: (1) variation in types of measures used (i.e., personality- or value-based) and (2) a confound between age, period, and cohort effects.

In general, measures of gender identity are based on either personality traits or values. Since gender identity is unlikely to be a unidimensional construct, the various types of measures probably reflect its different aspects, and certainly yield differing results (cf. Deaux, 1985; Nash & Feldman, 1981; Spence, 1991). By personality measures of gender identity we mean those instruments that use self-attributions of traits thought to be differentially endorsed by men and women, while measures based on values assess goals, interests, achievement motivation, and gender role performance (Fultz & Herzog, 1991). Given that personality traits are thought to be fairly stable while values are more changeable (Conley, 1984), it may be that the disparity in findings regarding gender identity is due to the failure to distinguish between these two measurement approaches.

Additionally, contradictory findings in the literature may be due to confounds between age, cohort, and period effects (cf. Schaie, 1977). As mentioned earlier, it is unclear at what age changes in gender identity might occur. Studies vary considerably in the age groups that they examine, making comparison across studies difficult. Further, research in this area has been conducted for over four decades (Holahan, 1984). During this time, there has been massive social change concerning gender identity and gender-based expectations. The effect of these changes in social norms on gender-related behavior has not yet been disentangled from the effect of maturation.

To disentangle the various effects of measures and design, we separated the studies based on personality from those based on values measures (Tables 4.1 and 4.2, respectively) and further subdivided each table by design (i.e., cross-sectional vs. longitudinal). The cross-historical studies were presented separately in Table 4.3, because they had slightly different reporting requirements. We only include empirical studies which provide clear statistical analyses of age, cohort, or period effects on gender identity. The tables report information on sample size and composition, age range, and length of follow-up, as well as a summary of the results. We used symbols to indicate the direction of change reported in the results column. For example, under the subheading *Women,* a + in the F column indicates that women in the study increased in femininity within the age period indicated, while a + in the M column indicates an increase in masculinity. Similarly, − indicates a decrease and 0 indicates no change. Of course, for cross-sectional and cross-historical studies, these symbols refer to differences between age groups, cohorts, and/or periods.

Note that studies with multiple cohorts represent special reporting problems. For example, Spence & Helmreich (1979), presented in Table 4.1, compared differences between four age groups. The three rows in the results columns refer to contrasts between adjacent groups: the first row summarizes the differences between the first and the second age groups, the second row summarizes those between the second and third groups, and so forth. Thus, for studies with multiple cohorts, the number of results rows will usually be the number of cohorts minus 1. Note, however, that some studies used multiple assessments. If the results differed by measure, then a result row is provided for each measure. For example, Carlson & Videka-Sherman (1990), presented in Table 4.2, measured both work satisfaction and social network characteristics. The results column reflects the fact that these two measures varied differentially by age.

Personality-based studies. Table 4.1 summarizes eleven studies examining changes in gender identity using personality-based measures, grouped according to design. Longitudinal studies revealed a relatively clear pattern for women. Femininity evidenced a curvilinear trajectory, increasing from the early to the late 20s and then decreasing from the late 20s to the 40s (Helson & Moane, 1987). Helson and Wink (1992), following the same sample for an additional decade, reported a continued decrease in femininity from the 40s to the 50s. Consistent with this pattern, Kelly (1955) reported increased masculinity in women from the 20s to the 40s.

Cross-sectional studies provided partial support for this pattern. Three studies reported lower femininity scores for women in their mid-30s and older in comparison with younger women (Lowenthal, Thurnher, & Chiriboga, 1975; McDonald, Ebert, & Mason, 1987; Urberg, 1979). None reported the opposite pattern. In addition, Urberg (1979) reported that women in their 40s were more masculine than women in their late teens. Similarly, Fisher & Narus (1981) reported higher masculinity in mid-20s women than in early 20s women. And despite some drop in masculinity from the mid-20s to the mid-30s, middle-aged women remained significantly more masculine than women in their teens (Fischer & Narus, 1981). However, McDonald et al. (1987) reported a negative correlation between age and masculinity. The clearest trends, then, are for less femininity and greater masculinity in older women relative to those in their teens and twenties.

For men, neither of the articles reporting analyses of longitudinal data revealed a coherent pattern. Douglas and Arenberg (1978) reported that males' masculinity scores fluctuated between 20 and 70 years of age, with a generally downward trend, while Kelly (1955) reported that men increased in masculinity between their 20s and 40s.

In contrast, studies using a cross-sectional design yielded more consistent results. Spence and Helmreich (1979) reported higher masculinity for men in early adulthood (18–25) than for teenaged men. However, Urberg (1979) reported that men in their late 20s to their 40s were less masculine than men in their teens, while Douglas and Arenberg (1978) reported that older men were less masculine than younger men (between 17 and 98). Two studies reported greater femininity in men at midlife relative to men in their late teens or early 20s (Fischer & Narus, 1981; Urberg, 1979). In general, there appears to be a drop in masculinity across adulthood for men, following a short-term increase in early adulthood. Similarly, it appears that femininity increases over the same time period.

In summary, studies using personality-based measures appear to demonstrate a curvilinear relationship between age and gender identity, with each sex exhibiting an increase in the opposite gender identity (i.e., women increasing in masculinity) from very early adulthood to early midlife (late 20s to 30s), with a plateau or slight decrease thereafter. There is some support for an increase in same-gender identity as well, in both sexes, early in adulthood, although the general trend is for a decrease throughout adulthood.

Values-based studies. Table 4.2 presents eight studies examining gender identity development using values-based measures, rather broadly defined. These include both projective measures of achievement motivation (similar to the TAT) and a variety of nonstandardized questions about life goals and sources of life satisfaction. In general, feminine values orientations were assessed through measures of expressiveness, nurturance, or interest in social relationships. In contrast, masculine values orientations were assessed through measures of instrumentality, power, or strength of career orientations. In these studies, responses were content-analyzed and categorized as either instrumental (mastery, aggressive, or nonsocial imagery) or expressive (passive, nurturant, or social imagery). Table 4.2 uses the same symbol conventions as Table 4.1.

The values studies appear to provide a picture that is relatively consistent with that of the personality studies (see Table 4.2). Both longitudinal studies for women reported increased interest in masculine goals between early adulthood (27–30) and midlife through old age (43–70) (Helson & Moane, 1987; Holahan, 1984). Helson and Moane (1987) also reported an early increase in a feminine values orientation followed by a drop from the late 20s to the 40s.

The one cross-sequential study (Veroff, Reuman, & Feld, 1984)

TABLE 4.1 Studies Using Personality-Based Measures to Assess Changes in Gender Identity

Author	Sample	Ages	Method	Variable	Measure	Results Women F	Women M	Men F	Men M
Kelly, 1955	176 men 192 women	M = 26.7 M = 24.7	20 years longitudinal	Masculinity-femininity	Strong's MF Scale		+		+
Douglas & Arenberg, 1978	915 men	17–98	7 years longitudinal	Temperament	GZMS				−
Helson & Moane, 1987	104 women	21 27 43	Longitudinal	Femininity	CPI	+ −			
Helson & Wink, 1992	101 women	43 52	Longitudinal	Femininity	CPI	−			
Lowenthal, Thurnher, & Chiriboga, 1975	108 men 108 women	means 17 & 17 23 & 25 52 & 48 61 & 58	Cross-sectional	Masculinity-femininity	ARL	−	Younger groups vs. older groups 0	0	0

Study	N	Age	Design	Construct	Instrument			
Douglas & Arenberg, 1978	915 men	17–98	Cross-sectional	Temperament	GZMS			—
Urberg, 1979	men & women	12–14	Cross-sectional	Sex role concepts	ACL	0	0	0
		17–19				—	+	0
		25–40				0	0	0
		50–65				0	0	0
Spence & Helmreich, 1979	1909 men, 2047 women	15–18	Cross-sectional	Personality attributes	PAQ	0	0	+
		18–25				0	0	0
		29–44						
Fisher & Narus, 1981	127 men, 202 women	16–19	Cross-sectional	Sex role identity	BSRI	0	0	0
		20–21				0	+	0
		22–27				0	—	0
		28–39				0	0	+
Jobson & Watson, 1984	16 men, 16 women	<20	Cross-sectional	MF	Survey questions	0	0	0
		35+						
McDonald, Ebert, & Mason, 1987	87 men, 183 women	17–88	Cross-sectional	Gender role identity	PAQ	—	—	0

Note: ACL, Adjective Checklist; Block, 1961. ARL, Adjective Rating List; Lowenthal et al., 1975. BSRI, Bem Sex Role Inventory; Bem, 1974. GZMS, Guilford-Zimmerman Masculinity Scale; Guilford & Zimmerman, 1956. CPI, California Personality Inventory; Gough, 1987. Strong's Nonvocational Masculinity-Femininity Scale; Strong's Vocational Interest Inventory; Strong, 1943. + = increase; — = decrease; 0 = no change.

TABLE 4.2 Studies Using Values-Based Measures to Assess Changes in Gender Identity

| | | | | | | Women | | Men | |
Author	Sample	Age	Method	Variable	Measure	F	M	F	M
Levinson et al., 1978	40 men	40–44	4 years longitudinal	Life structure	Content analysis			+	−
Holahan, 1984	122 men, 141 women	30–70	40 years longitudinal	Marital role	Views on marriage		+		−
Helson & Moane, 1987	140 women	20–27, 27–43	23 years longitudinal	Role involvement	Content analysis	+, −	0, +		
Veroff, Reuman, & Feld, 1984	2571 men and women	24–34, 35–54, 55+	Cross-sectional	Motives	TAT	−, −	0, −	0, 0	0, 0
Neugarten & Gutmann, 1968	68 men, 64 women	40–54, 55–70	Cross-sectional	Role images	TAT	−	+	+	−
Gutmann, 1975	417 men	35–49, 50–59, 60+	Cross-sectional	Sex roles	TAT		+	+	−
Holahan, 1984	122 men, 141 women	26, 37	Cross-sectional	Marital role	Views on marriage	0	+	+	−
Carlson & Videka-Sherman, 1990	2374 men and women	24–39, 40–65	Cross-sectional	M/F	Work satisfaction, social network	−	0	+	0

Note: TAT, Thematic Apperception Test; Murray, 1938; + = increase; − = decrease; 0 = no change.

reported lower interest in masculine values in older women (55+) relative to midlife women. They also observed that older cohorts (55+) of women were lower in feminine concerns than were cohorts in their mid-20s to 30s.

Two of the three cross-sectional studies reporting data on women identified greater interest in masculine concerns from the mid-20s through the late 30s (Holahan, 1984) and from midlife (40–54) to late adulthood (55–70) (Neugarten & Gutmann, 1968). Similarly, two studies reported lower femininity from early adulthood (24–39) to midlife (40–65) (Carlson & Videka-Sherman, 1990) and from midlife to late life (55–70) (Neugarten & Gutmann, 1968).

The clearest pattern for women across these studies, then, is of an increasingly masculine values orientation from early to late adulthood. There is some support for an increase in feminine concerns early in the 20s, and more robust support for a decrease in those concerns from midlife into late adulthood.

For men, the longitudinal studies consistently reported a decrease in masculine concerns over the adult years: from the 30s to the 70s (Holahan, 1984) and from 40 to 44 (Levinson, 1978).

The cross-sectional studies, likewise, reported lower masculine concerns in older than in younger men (Gutmann, 1976; Holahan, 1984; Neugarten & Gutmann, 1968). Similarly, feminine concerns were higher in older than younger men (Holahan, 1984; Gutmann, 1975; Neugarten & Gutmann, 1968).

Overall, the preponderance of the values-based studies support a pattern of increased identification with the values and motives traditionally associated with the opposite sex (the crossover effect). This pattern was observed across studies using both longitudinal and cross-sectional designs. However, none of the studies adequately addressed the impact of cohort and period effects.

Cross-historical studies. From either cross-sectional studies or longitudinal ones with a single cohort, it is generally unclear whether observed changes are the effect of age, cohort, or period. Cohort effects represent the differential impact of social forces and life experiences on individuals as a function of their age when those experiences occurred (Veroff et al., 1984). For instance, Elder (1974) observed that the Great Depression had greater and more lasting effects on individuals entering adulthood than on children who were younger at the time.

Period effects represent the generalized impact of changing social conditions on all individuals alive at the time. For example, changing social norms with regard to women's employment represent changes in lifestyle options that would likely affect the personality development of people of many ages and cohorts (Rossi, 1980).

Table 4.3 presents literature that addresses changes in gender role beliefs using time-series or time-sequential analyses, that is, data were gathered at different times from different groups of individuals but in the same age group(s). While not directly addressing age effects on gender identity development, these studies provide insight into the possible patterns of change that could be attributed to cohort or period, while controlling for age of respondent. In three of the five cases, the studies used values-based measures. In the remaining two, a personality-based measure was used.

For women, the one personality-based study reported no change. One of the values-based studies reported that masculine concerns were lower among women in 1976 than among those women surveyed in 1957 (Veroff et al., 1984). The remaining two studies reported that respondents in recent periods (1979 and 1984) reported more masculine concerns than had those in an earlier period (1969 for both studies) (Fiorentine, 1988; Regan & Roland, 1985). It appears that there may have been a curvilinear pattern in women's identification with masculine-typed concerns, with a decrease from the 1950s into the mid-1970s and an increase from the late 1960s through the mid-1980s. Note the substantial cohort effects reported by Veroff et al. (1984). Finally, two studies reported decreased valuation of feminine goals between the late 1950s and the mid-1970s (Regan & Roland, 1985; Veroff et al., 1984).

Among men, the one personality-based study reported no change. Among values-based studies, however, Veroff et al. (1984) reported increased valuation of masculine values between 1957 and 1976, which is consistent with Fiorentine's (1988) report on the periods 1969 to 1984. In contrast, Regan and Roland (1985) reported decreased interest in masculine values between 1969 and 1979, which is similar to Douglas and Arenberg's (1978) report on the period between 1958 and 1974. In this instance, no singular pattern emerges. Rather, there is equally compelling evidence of both increased and decreased masculine values between the late 1950s and the mid-1980s. These differences could be attributed, at least in part, to the use of different measures. Finally, evidence for decreased valuation of feminine activities, particularly among younger cohorts in the 1970s and 1980s, was provided by Veroff et al. (1984) and Fiorentine (1988).

TABLE 4.3 Cross-Historical Studies Assessing Changes in Gender Identity

Author	Sample	Age	Birth Cohort	Period	Variable	Measure	Women F	Women M	Men F	Men M
Urberg, 1979	458 men and women	12–14	1962–1964	1976	Sex-role concepts	ACL	Comparing oldest two groups;			
		17–19	1957–1959	1978			0	0	0	0
		25–40	1936–1951							
		50–65	1911–1926							
Fiorentine, 1988	All U.S. college freshmen	18 (?)	1951–1966	1969 1984	Values, life plans	Survey items	0	+	—	+
Regan & Roland, 1985	1360 men 1426 women	college seniors	1946–1948 1956–1958	1969 1979	Values	Life satisfaction	—	+	0	—
Veroff, Reuman, & Feld, 1984	2571 men and women	21–60	1897 1898–1906 1907–1916 1917–1926 1927–1936	1957 1976	Motives	TAT	—	—	0/—	+
							Significant cohort effects, particularly among women			
Douglas & Arenberg, 1978	707 men	24–76	1892–1899 1900–1907 1908–1915 1916–1923 1924–1931 1932–1939	1958–1974 7 years after first test	Motives	TAT				—

Note: ACL, Adjective Checklist; Block, 1961.
+ = increase; — = decrease; 0 = no change.

Analyses of these five studies, then, provide a relatively steady picture of changes in social norms regarding gender-appropriate feelings, beliefs, and behaviors. Valuation of feminine concerns decreased between the late 1950s and the mid-1980s. No study reported the opposite pattern. The pattern for changes in regard to masculine concerns, however, is more complex. It appears that the general trend is for an increase from the mid-1950s into the 1980s, although there is also limited support for a decrease in those values from the 1950s to the mid-1970s. It is possible that the discrepancies observed across these studies reflect changes in social norms. Similarly, differences in measures or in age groupings could account for the differences.

Summary

Despite the initial appearance of considerable confusion, it is possible to discern patterns of gender identity development in adulthood if age, cohort, and period effects are examined and allowances are made for differences in measures. Studies using personality measures showed a curvilinear relation with age, with each sex increasing in the opposite gender identity and then plateauing or perhaps decreasing slightly. There was also evidence for increased identification with same-gender traits. Values-based studies provided support for the increase in opposite-gender values, but in a linear fashion, such that older respondents had the highest levels of opposite-gender scores (reminiscent of the crossover effect). Attributing these patterns to age, cohort, or period is still premature. However, the analysis of the cross-historical studies revealed that regard for feminine concerns has decreased for both men and women, and regard for masculine concerns has generally increased.

Nonetheless, there are still many problems with the studies that currently exist. Difficulties arise in trying to identify patterns because of the arbitrary age groupings in cross-sectional studies and the wide variance in time spans in longitudinal designs. All of the studies focused on either age, cohort, or period effects. None was structured to disentangle these effects. Finally, there are confusing discrepancies between the personality- and values-based literature that need clarification.

Present Study

We examined patterns of gender identity development during early and middle adulthood in two data archives, the Davis Longitudinal Study (DLS) and the Transition Study (TS). The databases were chosen

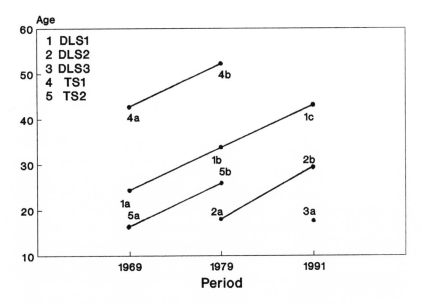

FIGURE 4.1. Design and Data Collection Points for the DLS and TS

because of the variety of comparisons they permitted. Both studies used personality- and values-based gender identity measures, and they overlapped considerably in terms of ages, cohorts, and periods. Figure 4.1 presents the data collection points from both archives used in the present study. As can be seen, both followed a cohort of 20-year-olds from 1969 to 1979, while the TS followed a cohort of 40-year-olds at the same time. The DLS, however, also followed 20- and 30-year-olds from 1979 to 1991. While the archives were roughly balanced by sex, they provided contrasts in education and socioeconomic status (the DLS comprised exclusively college graduates, while the TS sample was much more varied in educational attainment).

Combining the data sets permits us to examine age, cohort, and period effects in both personality and values. Specifically, we ask the following questions:

1. Does gender identity change from early to middle adulthood? If so, do changes in personality show the same pattern as those in values?

2. If age-related changes do exist, are the patterns of change consistent across cohorts and period?

On the basis of the literature we reviewed, we expect to observe differential patterns of change depending on the type of gender identity measure used. For the personality-based measure, we expect to see a nonlinear relation with age. When using the values-based measure, cohort and/or period effects will be significant, some of which will identify increased interests among women in masculine-typed values and among men in feminine-typed values.

Methods

Samples and Procedures

Two different archives were used in this study, the Davis Longitudinal Study (DLS) and the Transition Study (TS). The sample and procedures for these studies will be described separately.

Davis Longitudinal Study. The DLS sample consists of three cohorts of University of California at Davis alumni. Cohort 1 were surveyed as seniors (1968–1970; indicated as 1969) and as alumni in 1979 and 1991 (1*a*, 1*b*, 1*c* in Figure 4.1). Cohort 2 joined the study as seniors in 1979 and were also resurveyed in 1991 (2*a*, 2*b*). Finally, Cohort 3 graduated in 1989 and were surveyed in 1991 (3*a*). Details on the 1969 and 1979 surveys can be found in Yonge and Regan (1975) and Regan and Roland (1985).

Of the 2,695 surveys sent to current addresses in the summer of 1991, 1,093 were returned (41% overall response rate). The response rates varied by cohort, resulting in 581 (46%), 232 (40%), and 280 (33%) individuals from Cohorts 1, 2, and 3, respectively. While the age range was fairly narrow for Cohort 1, it became progressively wider for Cohorts 2 and 3, reflecting the increasing number of women (and men) returning to college in later adulthood. Thus, we selected only those respondents from each cohort who were within certain age ranges to assure consistency of age within cohort. Assuming it was unlikely that individuals had started college earlier than their 17th year, we established upper age limits for each cohort. For Cohort 1, only those who were 47 years old or younger in 1991 were included. For Cohort 2, the upper age limit was 37; and for Cohort 3, the upper age limit was 27. In addition, listwise deletion was used to create a sample that had complete data at all time points, eliminating the problem of trying to compare analyses based on varying subsamples. This resulted in 148 men and 187 women in Cohort 1, 53 men and 54 women in Cohort 2, and 87 men and 116 women in Cohort 3, for a total of 645 respondents.

The DLS sample is not representative of the general population. At the most recent survey time, 66% of the sample were working on or had completed postgraduate degree programs. Of those currently employed, 40% were employed at the upper-white-collar level, and 35% at the professional/executive level. The DLS sample varies considerably with regard to marital and parental status, with the majority of the first and second cohorts in marriage relationships and most of the third cohort still single.

The Transition Study. The TS (Lowenthal et al., 1975) recruited participants in the late 1960s. They were originally selected on the basis of impending transition events in their lives (high school graduation, marriage, empty nest, retirement) and were followed every two to three years during the ten years of the study. For this study, only data collected at the first and last interviews will be used (4a, 4b, and 5a, 5b, in Fig. 4.1). In contrast to the DLS sample, only 37% of the sample completed four years of college. Of those, 75% had started or completed a postgraduate program. At the last interview, 31% were employed in upper-white-collar positions and 9% were in professional occupations. Only data from the baseline and the final interviews are used in this study.

There were overlaps between the age ranges in some of the transition groups, so we reorganized the sample according to age. Individuals were selected for inclusion if they were between 20 and 29, or 40 and 49 years, at the first interview. In this way we created two cohorts, one that was entering adulthood at the beginning of the study, and one that was entering midlife at the beginning of the study. Unfortunately, we could not use listwise deletion with this sample, because of its already small size. Consequently, the sample size varies between the two analyses reported. The sample for cross-sequential analyses is 14 men and 20 women aged 20 to 29, and 9 men and 12 women aged 40 to 49. Time-sequential analyses have two samples: 19 men and 23 women aged 20 to 29; and 12 men and 15 women aged 40 to 49.

Measures

At each survey time, both studies used personality instruments and questions about sources of life satisfaction (i.e., values).

Personality measures. The DLS used the Masculinity-Femininity (MF) scale of the Omnibus Personality Inventory (OPI; Heist & Yonge, 1968), while the TS used the Adjective Rating List (ARL; Block, 1961). Thus, we administered the ARL and a short version of the OPI in 1991 to the DLS for comparison purposes. Note that the MF scales of both instruments were empirically, rather than theoretically, derived. That is, the scales consist of items on which there were gender differences in endorsement rates without regard to content. As such, these reflect sex differences in attitudes and self-attributions during the 1960s.

There are both benefits and drawbacks to using a "1960s ruler" to assess gender identity over the subsequent two decades. The benefit is that the only way to disentangle age, period, and effects is to consistently use the same instruments at each time point for all ages and cohorts. Then if the same pattern of age results is found in different periods, we know that we have shown a developmental pattern that holds regardless of period (to say nothing of the stability of gender stereotypes). However, if there are period effects, any changes seen relative to earlier studies may be simply reflections of changing social norms. Changing instruments in midstream would obviate the possibility of any such comparisons.

The drawback of using a 1960s ruler is that we are using an admittedly outmoded instrument. For example, current research on more modern instruments suggests that masculinity (M) and femininity (F) should be analyzed separately (Bem, 1974). However, when we analyzed the MF subscales separately, the results were simple mirror images of each other. Thus, we present only information on the single MF scale.

The OPI (DLS). The MF scale of the OPI (Heist & Yonge, 1968) consists of 56 true-false statements. High scorers on this scale, which ranges from 0 to 56, are more "masculine" in that they prefer physical sciences over poetry, are not easily excited, are usually calm, and do not enjoy social and cultural events. In the DLS sample, the range of means was 24.4 to 33.6; the range of standard deviations was 4.9 to 5.8.

In 1991, a brief version of the OPI, containing 24 items from the standard MF scale, was administered because of budgetary constraints. For longitudinal analyses which rely on correlational statistics a short form of a scale at one period is not problematic. However, the required use of MANOVAs to test our hypotheses necessitated the estimation of the full-scale scores from our subscale following procedures recommended by Spiro (1992, personal communication).[1]

ARL (DLS & TS). At every interview time, TS respondents were administered the ARL (Block, 1961), which rates a list of adjectives on a 3-point scale (1 = "unlike me," 2 = "both like and unlike me," and 3 = "like me"). Scale scores were constructed by summing the points for associated items. The masculinity scale was constructed by summing responses to 13 items, and the femininity scale by summing responses to 11 items. A MF balance score (representing a composite of responses to the masculine and feminine items) was created by subtracting the femininity scale score from the masculinity scale score and adding 100. The possible range of scores is 80 to 128; in the DLS and TS samples, the range of means was 99 to 108; the range of standard deviations was 4.3 to 5.7. Individuals scoring high on the MF balance scale described themselves as ambitious, assertive, competitive, hostile, and so forth. Those scoring low in this scale described themselves as charming, cooperative, easily embarrassed, friendly, sincere, and so forth.

Comparison of the OPI and ARL. To facilitate comparing the two data sets, the DLS was administered both the OPI and the ARL at the most recent survey. The initial correlation between the MF scales from the two instruments was modest ($r = .282$, $p < .01$). However, both scales had limited response ranges, so their reliabilities are rather low (alpha = .545, OPI; alpha = .439, ARL). Item-to-scale correlations demonstrated that this unreliability was not due to one or two discrepant items. Thus, we borrowed a technique used to correct for unreliability in longitudinal studies, and divided the correlation coefficient by the product of the square roots of the alphas of each instrument (Nunnally, 1978, pp. 237–239). This increased the magnitude of the correlation to a reasonable level ($r = .576$), suggesting that the two instruments are reasonably similar.

Values-Based Measures

Life value instrument (DLS). The Cornell Values Study (Goldsen, Rosenberg, Williams, & Suchman, 1960) was administered at each DLS study time. Respondents were asked to identify which items, from a list of seven, were primary, secondary, and tertiary sources of life satisfaction. Response options were: (1) literature, art, or music; (2) career or occupation; (3) family relationships; (4) leisure time, recreational activities; (5) religioius activities; (6) participation in community affairs; and (7) participation in activities directed toward national or international betterment. Dummy variables were created, one to distinguish those endorsing family as primary sources of life satisfaction (coded 1) from those who did not (coded 0), and the second to identify those endorsing work as primary (coded 1) from those who did not (coded 0).

Life values (TS). Respondents were asked, "What is the main purpose or task in life?" Content analysis identified the major categories:
personal achievement (social or occupational success), marriage and
family, humanitarian concerns, coping with the givens of life, happiness, religious life, and legacy (Lowenthal et al., 1975). As was done
with the DLS values data, dummy variables were coded to create family
and career variables, each coded 1 (if selected) or 0 (if not selected).

Data Analysis

A variety of longitudinal comparisons were conducted. The existence of multiple cohorts in the two longitudinal archives allowed the
differentiation of age, cohort, and period effects, using the cohort-
sequential, cross-sequential, and time-sequential models suggested by
Schaie (1977).[2] Unless otherwise noted, all analyses used repeated measures MANOVAs and were performed separately for personality and
values data. For all analyses, sex was entered as an independent variable.

As we indicated in the literature review, most longitudinal studies
simply follow one cohort over time. Thus, for comparison purposes,
we first examined simple longitudinal change using repeated measures
MANOVA for the three time periods in Cohort 1 (1*a*, 1*b*, and 1*c*, in
Fig. 4.1) to discover if there were any systematic age-related changes in
gender identity. However, this analysis confounded cohort and period
effects.

Cohort-sequential analysis compared changes between the same
ages (20–30 years) in two different birth cohorts over three periods
(that is, comparing 1*a*-1*b* to 2*a*-2*b* in Fig. 4.1). The cross-sequential
analysis examined cohort and period by comparing two different birth
cohorts over the same period (1*b*-1*c* to 2*a*-2*b*, in Fig. 4.1). The time-
sequential analysis examined age and period by comparing cross-
sectional differences in age groups at two different periods (2*a*-1*b* to
3*a*-2*b*, in Fig. 4.1). This analysis identified age as the within-subjects
factor and period as a main effect, but confounded cohort. Comparison
of results across analyses will allow us to disentangle age, cohort, and
period effects.

Results

The results section is divided into two overarching sections, personality, and values, that is, family and career orientations. We begin each
section with an analysis of DLS longitudinal data, and discuss subse-

quent analyses relative to the trends observed in the longitudinal analysis.

We use figures to illustrate the results of the longitudinal and sequential analyses. In addition, tables summarize the results of all analyses in each section. Each type of analysis is identified under the *Designs* column. The direction of change, or of difference (as in the case of sex or cohort), is described by a greater-than (>) or a lesser-than (<) symbol. We identify significant interactions effects by listing only the specific effects that are involved, for example, sex(*a*) by cohort(*c*) is identified as (*a*)(*c*). Not *every* effect was tested in each analysis. Consequently, to remind the reader which effects were tested in a given analysis, those that were tested but were not significant are indicated with an *ns*.

Personality

For this set of analyses we predicted that women and men would increase in masculinity between the early 20s and early 40s. We anticipated significant age effects but no cohort or period effects. For all analyses, men scored higher on masculinity measures than women. Thus, we do not mention this again in the text, but summarize it in the tables.

Does gender identity change between early and middle adulthood? As shown in the top left panel of Figure 4.2, both men and women increased in masculinity between their 20s and 30s, with a slight decrease for both groups from the 30s to the 40s; $F(2, 666) = 10.15$, $p < .001$ (see Table 4.4). There were no interaction effects between age and sex, supporting the expectation that men and women would change in similar ways.

Is the pattern of change consistent across cohorts? We conducted cohort-sequential analysis to determine whether the change in gender identity seen in the first cohort could be replicated in the second cohort. As shown in the lower left panel of Figure 4.2, men and women in both cohorts increased in masculinity between their 20s and their 30s in a remarkably similar pattern; $F(1, 438) = 23.01$, $p < .001$. Cohort was not a significant effect, and there were no interaction effects (see Table 4.4). This analysis could not rule out the possibility of period effects which might influence each cohort similarly, and thus it was necessary to analyze for cohort and period effects.

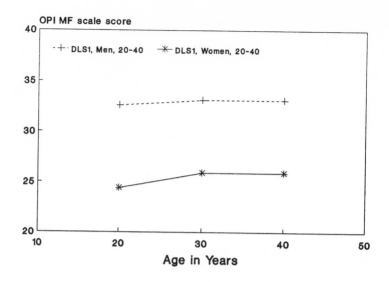

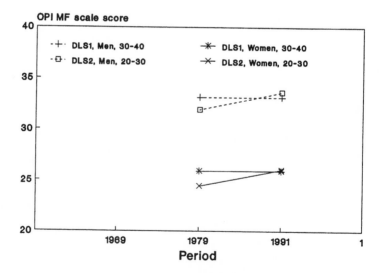

FIGURE 4.2. Analyses of the Personality Measures
a. Longitudinal analysis   c. Cross-sequential analysis (DLS)
b. Cohort-sequential analysis   d. Cross-sequential analysis (TS)

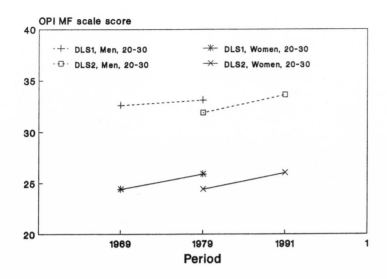

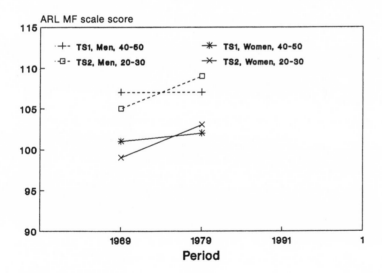

FIGURE 4.2. *continued*

TABLE 4.4 Longitudinal and Sequential Analyses
of the Personality-Based Measures

Designs	Sex (a)	Age (b)	Cohort (c)	Period (d)	Interaction
Longitudinal	M > F***	20 < 30 > 40***			
Cohort-sequential	M > F***	20 < 30***	ns		
Cross-sequential	M > F***		ns	79 < 91**	(c)(d)**
Time sequential	M > F***	20 < 30**		ns	

*p < .05; **p < .01; ***p < .001.

Is the pattern consistent across cohort and period?

OPI. We conducted a cross-sequential analysis on Cohorts 1 and 2 to evaluate the possibility that observed changes in gender identity were a function of period and cohort. There was a main effect of period, $F(1, 438) = 10.02$, $p < .01$, but not of cohort (see Table 4.4). There was a significant cohort-by-period interaction, however; $F(1, 438) = 10.49$, $p < .001$. As shown in the top right panel of Figure 4.2, masculinity increased for men and women only in the younger cohort. This finding supported the longitudinal results and demonstrated that masculinity increased only in early adulthood. At this point, however, period effects could not be eliminated until they were evaluated relative to age effects.

ARL. Once again, we performed a cross-sequential analysis, but this time with the TS sample and the ARL/MF scale data. This comparison enabled us to determine whether the pattern described above was consistent across an additional sample of young adults (20s to 30s, $d1$–$d2$) and an older cohort (40s to 50s, $e1$–$e2$).

As with the OPI/MF analysis, men and women in the younger cohort increased in masculinity, in contrast to the older cohort (cohort by period, $F(1, 51) = 7.54$, $p < .008$). The older cohort provided some evidence of the beginning of a crossover effect; women increased in masculinity and men decreased, although there was no significant sex-by-cohort effect (see Fig. 4.2, bottom right panel).

Is the pattern of change consistent across age and periods?

OPI. A time-sequential ANOVA enabled us to separate the effects of age from those of period and complete the set of needed comparisons. As shown in Table 4.4, the analysis revealed significant age effects, $F(1, 3) = 10.1$, $p < .002$, but no significant period effects or age-by-period interactions. These results demonstrated that the shift toward increased masculinity from 20 to 30, and the stable masculinity from 30 to 40 was a function of age, and not of cohort of period (see Fig. 4.3).

ARL/MF. A second time-sequential ANOVA, which combined the DLS and TS data sets, revealed significant period effects: $F(1, 3) = 30.33$, $p < .001$. This result runs counter to the pattern observed above. Perhaps there is, indeed, a period effect influencing gender identity, but one that occurs over a longer span of years than that examined above. An alternative explanation might be the possibility of a class or education effect, neither of which we could explicitly test.

Summary of results of the personality analyses. The analyses reported above provided strong evidence that personality change in early adulthood was a function of age, rather than cohort or period. The longitudinal analysis suggested an age effect, and the sequential analyses tested the alternative explanations (cohort or period effects). Table 4.4 shows that age was consistently a significant main effect and that, in no case, were there age-by-cohort or age-by-period interactions. In the one instance where period effects were significant, period was, in fact, a proxy for age (in that they both identify duration). The results were consistent in identifying the significance of age effects (i.e., development) on an increasingly masculine (relative to feminine) self-identification in the 20s to 30s, and stable masculine/feminine self-identifications in the next decade. These results were generally consistent with predictions based on the literature.

In the next section, we examine whether a similar or different pattern was seen for traditional female (family) and male (career) values.

Family and Career Orientations

All analyses utilized repeated measures MANOVAs, unless otherwise noted. Each value orientation was analyzed separately, with family values first. Again, figures are used to illustrate the longitudinal and sequential analyses; all analyses are summarized in Table 4.5. In most analyses, men were higher on career values and lower on family values than women, unless otherwise noted.

Do values change in early to middle adulthood? As shown in the upper left panel of Figure 4.4, men and women decreased in family orientation between their 20s and 30s, and increased between their 30s and

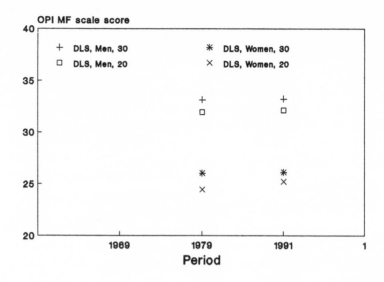

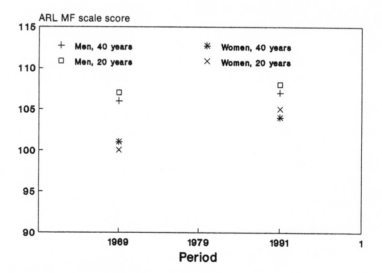

FIGURE 4.3. Time-Sequential Analyses of the Personality Measures
a. Time-sequential analysis (DLS)
b. Time-sequential analysis (DLS/TS)

TABLE 4.5 Longitudinal and Sequential Analyses of Values-Based Measures

Designs	Sex (a)	Age (b)	Cohort (c)	Period (d)	Interactions
Longitudinal					
Family	M < F***	20 > 30 < 40***			
Career	M > F	20 < 30 > 40**			
Cohort-Sequential					
Family	M < F***	ns	ns		(a)(c)* (b)(c)***
Career	M > F*	ns	ns		(a)(c)*
Cross-Sequential					
Family	M < F**		1969 < 1979*	1979 < 1991***	
Career	M > F*		ns	1979 > 1991*	
Time-Sequential					
Family	M < F***	ns		1979 < 1991**	(a)(c)*
Career	M > F**	ns		ns†	

†p < .10; *p < .05; **p < .01; ***p < .001.

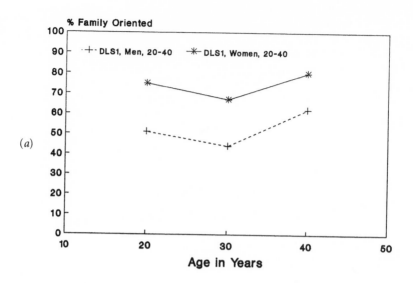

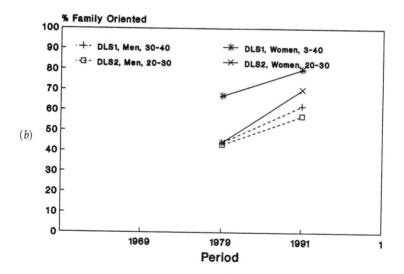

FIGURE 4.4. Analyses of the Family Values Measure
a. Longitudinal analysis   *c.* Cross-sequential analysis (DLS)
b. Cohort-sequential analysis   *d.* Cross-sequential analysis (TS)

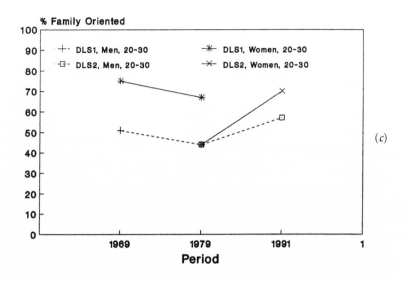

(c)

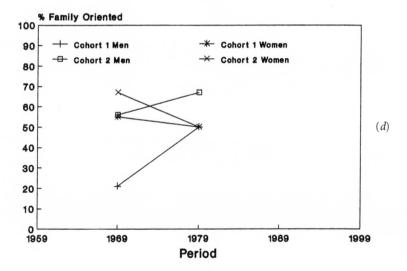

(d)

Figure 4.4. *continued*

40s; $F(1, 726) = 14.95$, $p < .001$ (Table 4.5). On average, more women (72%) than men (50%) selected family as their primary values orientation; $F(1, 363) = 39.08$, $p < .001$. There were no sex-by-age interactions. As shown in the upper left panel of Figure 4.5, the opposite pattern was observed for career values. For both men and women, career orientation increased between their 20s and 30s and decreased between their 30s and 40s; $F(1, 726) = 6.24$, $p < .01$. As with family orientations, there were no interaction effects.

Attributing this pattern to age, however, would be premature. Controlling, in turn, for age, cohort, and period will help identify the source of the differences.

Is the pattern of change consistent across cohorts? Comparing Cohorts 1 and 2 at the same ages revealed no main effects of age or cohort (Table 4.5). However, there were significant age-by-cohort, $F(1, 438) = 17.20$, $p < .001$, and sex-by-cohort, $F(1, 438) = 3.94$, $p < .05$, interactions. As shown in the lower left panel of Figure 4.4, this analysis revealed the significance of cohort on patterns of change in family orientation. In marked contrast to the decrease observed in the first cohort, respondents in the second cohort *increased* in family orientation between 20 and 30 (about 25%), women significantly more so (Fig. 4.4).

Similarly, cohort-sequential analysis of career values revealed no significant main effects of age or cohort (see Table 4.5). As with family values, however, changes in career orientation appeared to reflect the impact of cohort (see Fig. 4.5). Significant sex-by-cohort effects, $F(1, 438) = 6.14$, $p < .05$, revealed a general drop in career orientation between the first and second cohorts. This change was not attributable to age. Although sex had a significant effect, its substantive impact was minimal; this suggests that similar factors were affecting both men and women. It was possible that this putative cohort effect was actually an effect of period arising from the fact that the cohorts were assessed at different periods.

Is the pattern of change consistent across cohort and period? Although the older cohort was more family oriented than the younger, $F(1, 438) = 5.31$, $p < .05$, as shown in the upper right panel of Figure 4.4, the most important result of this analysis was that *all* groups increased in family orientation between 1979 and 1991, $F(1, 552) =$

32.69, $p < .001$ (Table 4.5). There were no significant age-by-cohort interactions.

A similar analysis on career orientation revealed significant effects of period, $F(1, 438) = 5.01$, $p < .05$. (see Table 4.5). In contrast to the pattern observed between 1969 and 1979, *all* groups either decreased or were stable in career orientation between 1979 and 1991 (see Fig. 4.5). There was a significant sex-by-cohort effect, $F(1, 438) = 5.40$, $p < .05$, indicating that men in Cohort 2 were stable in career orientations, in contrast to men in Cohort 1, who decreased.

Both analyses revealed significant period effects. Cohort also appeared to play a substantial role in value orientations.

TS. The TS data did not reveal any significant cohort or period effects in either family or career orientation (Table 4.5). Men increased in family orientation, while women decreased, creating a crossover effect for the older cohort that did not reach significance (Fig. 4.4). In general, all groups decreased in career orientation, young men being the exception (see Fig. 4.5). This pattern also did not reach significance, perhaps becasue of the small sample size.

Is the pattern of change consistent across age and periods? Again, significant effects of period, $F(1, 3) = 8.85$, $p < .01$, accounted for changes in family orientation between 1979 and 1991 (see Fig. 4.6). There was no effect of age (see Table 4.5). There were no significant interaction effects. As was found through the other sequential analyses, family orientation was more likely to be chosen, by both men and women, in 1991 than in 1979.

Analyzing changes in career values only identified a trend in period effects, $F(1, 3) = 3.51$, $p = .06$ (see Table 4.5). As shown in Figure 4.7, there was a pattern of decreased career salience for all groups in 1991 relative to 1979.

DLS and TS. The ANOVAs of the combined data revealed significant period effects, $F(1, 3) = 5.98$, $p < .05$, with all age groups more family oriented in 1991 than in 1969 (Fig. 4.6). Contrary to the findings discussed above, older cohorts were more family oriented than younger cohorts, $F(1, 3) = 6.25$, $p < .05$ (see Table 4.5).

For career values, however, the ANOVAs did reveal a significant age-by-cohort effect, $F(1, 3) = 8.69$, $p < .01$. Young women in the DLS sample were more career oriented than young women in the TS sample, a pattern that reversed for the older women (Fig. 4.7). This difference may be attributable to education.

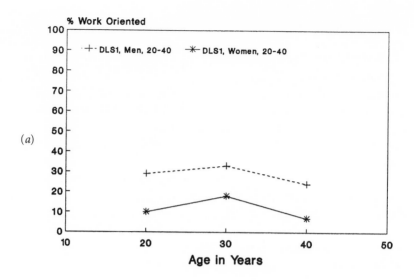

(a)

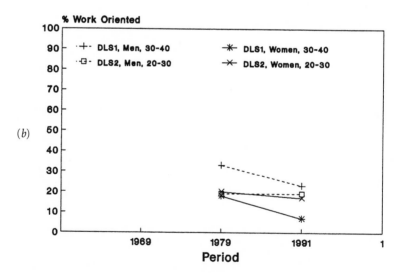

(b)

FIGURE 4.5. Analyses of Career Values Measure
a. Longitudinal analysis   c. Cross-sequential analysis (DLS)
b. Cohort-sequential analysis   d. Cross-sequential analysis (TS)

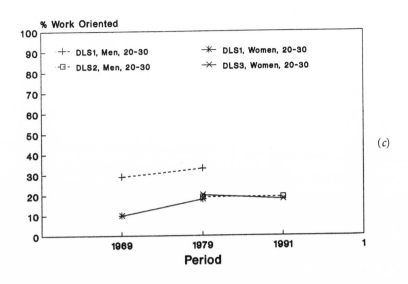

(*c*)

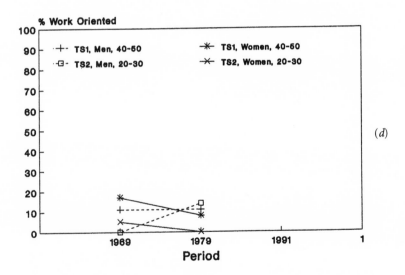

(*d*)

FIGURE 4.5. *continued*

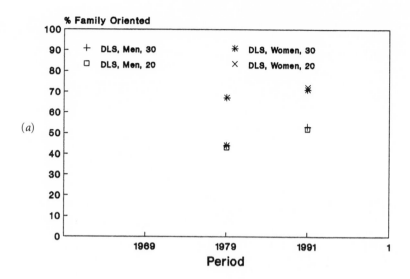

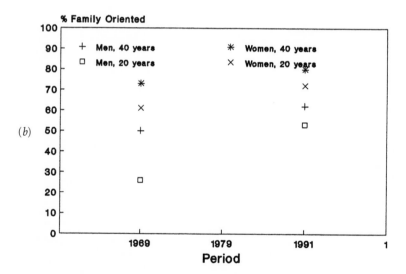

FIGURE 4.6. Time-Sequential Analyses of the Family Values Measure
a. Time-sequential analysis (DLS)
b. Time-sequential analysis (DLS/TS)

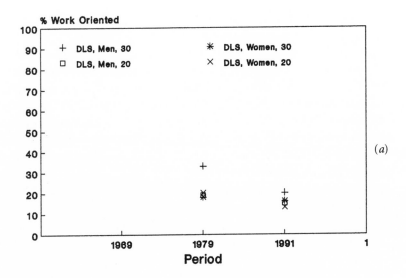

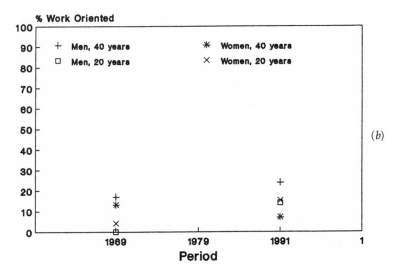

FIGURE 4.7. Time-Sequential Analyses of the Career Values Measure
a. Time-sequential analysis (DLS)
b. Time-sequential analysis (DLS/TS)

Summary of results of the values analyses. Analyses of changes in family and career values did not provide the relatively simple developmental picture found in analyses of the personality data. Rather, as can be seen in Tables 4.4 and 4.5, it appeared that cohort and period effects better accounted for changes in value orientations. The seemingly developmental pattern observed in the longitudinal analysis of values was not supported by the sequential analyses. The interaction terms (sex-by-cohort and age-by-cohort) indicated, instead, that social time had significant impact on value changes. Similarly, the significant cohort and period effects identified through the cross- and time-sequential analyses confirmed the importance of the sociohistorical context on the primacy of family and career in adults' lives. Overall, family roles decreased in salience between 1969 and 1979 but increased again between 1979 and 1991, while career values showed the opposite pattern.

DISCUSSION

In this project we had two major purposes. The first was to examine whether or not there were systematic changes in gender identity from young to middle adulthood. We used three different cohorts over two decades (1969–1991) and thus were able to examine both developmental (age) and social (cohort and period) influences on change in gender identity.

Our second purpose was to address the problem of distinguishing personality development from changes in value orientations vis-à-vis gender role identity in adulthood. In this study, since we could separate personality indices from values measures, we could describe the development of each trait independently, although with the same individuals followed at the same intervals.

Not surprisingly, men were always higher in masculinity than were women, regardless of age, cohort, or period. This supported the validity of the OPI as a measure of gender identity. At no point did the gender identity of the sexes cross over, supporting the similar observation of Lowenthal et al. (1975) with another personality measure, the ARL. Surprisingly, the differences between the sexes narrowed only slightly in subsequent cohorts (see Fig. 4.2), which does not argue for increasing androgyny in the population. Note, however, that Neugarten and Gutmann's (1968) argument for increasing androgyny was based on values, not personality, measures.

The primary influence on personality-related gender identity change was age. The longitudinal personality analysis suggested that men and women increased in masculinity between their 20s and 30s and then remained stable between their 30s and 40s. The cohort-sequential analysis eliminated cohort effects as an explanation for the pattern because respondents in the second cohort increased in masculinity at virtually the same rate as the first cohort. This pattern was seen regardless of cohort or period and thus constituted a true age-based (or maturational) change. Interestingly, the personality measure was most labile in the respondents' 20s, supporting McCrae and Costa's (1990) observations of greater probability of personality change in this decade.

With additional analyses, however, we determined that the effect we observed was the result of a relative shift between masculine and feminine self-identifications. Respondents decreased feminine self-identifications substantially over time, while masculine self-identifications were relatively stable. The result of this differential change was represented in our instruments as increased masculinity. We suspect this change actually represented a decrease in emotional lability.

Personality, then, did not appear to be affected by the social context, at least as measured in this study. This finding was consistent with Helson and Moane (1987). Despite their work associating life paths with antecedent and subsequent personality characteristics (Helson, Mitchell, & Moane, 1984), they have more recently stated that "changes in personality described as normative are not attributable to any particular sequence of role involvements" (Helson & Moane, 1987, p. 182). In other words, personality development followed a trajectory unrelated to attributes of the social environment.

We repeated this series of analyses with the values measures. As before, the longitudinal analyses revealed a nonlinear pattern of change in both family and career values. Using three points of longitudinal data from the first DLS cohort we showed that men and women decreased in family orientation and increased in career orientation between their 20s and 30s. They then increased in family orientation and decreased in career orientation between their 30s and 40s. When we analyzed for the effects of cohort, however, this pattern did not seem to be the result of developmental processes; the second cohort did not replicate the pattern of the first. Rather, respondents in both cohorts followed the same pattern between 1979 and 1991, increasing in family orientation and decreasing in career orientation. Time-sequential analyses confirmed the effect of period and substantiated the unimportance of age in accounting for changes in value orientations.

The majority of both men and women saw the family as the primary source of life satisfaction, regardless of cohort or period. While the 1979 cohort of women did value careers as much as family, the subsequent cohort returned to the pattern of the 1969 women. Further, by 1991, the second cohort was also highly family oriented.

Of particular interest was the persistence of family orientation among this college-educated, professionally employed sample. Contrary to oft-expressed concerns that the importance of the family is waning, the data suggested that the role of the family is increasingly important in the lives of successful, professional adults. This turn toward interpersonal connectedness was not the result of midlife crises (cf. Levinson, 1978). Rather it was individuals still in their early adulthood who were concurrently pursuing professional careers that turned toward interpersonal connectedness.

Also notable was the decreasing centrality of careers in these respondents' lives. In light of the rate of professional employment in this sample, it was surprising that the respondents did not depend on their careers to provide significant life satisfaction.

In sum, these analyses provided consistent support for differential impacts of age, cohort, and period on personality and values. Whereas personality change (in this case masculinity-femininity) is clearly an effect of developmental processes, changes in value orientation are clearly the result of changing sociohistorical norms and opportunities.

To interpret the persistent effects of cohort and period on value changes, we needed to examine the social environments the study respondents experienced. In the mid-1960s, the feminist movement was a major social issue. In the late 1970s, the economic recession seriously impacted the labor market. It can be argued, in fact, that the patterns of change presented here reflect an increasing complexity in social beliefs about the relationship between family and career role commitments. Whereas respondents in Cohort 1 were raised in the prefeminist era in which people believed that women should be primarily oriented around their families and men around their careers, respondents in Cohorts 2 and 3 were exposed to a significantly different value system during their childhood and adolescent years. The result of this is observed in women's heightened career focus and in men's decreased career focus (period effects seen in 1979). These role commitments, however, were still seen as relatively incompatible (cf. Machung, 1989). By the 1980s, however, Cohort 3 respondents were exposed to a wider variety of models for balancing career and family. Many of these models portrayed the roles as compatible, if, at times, overwhelming. We believe that the heightened focus on family in 1991, then, represents this young cohort's commitment to a dual-role lifestyle, which unfortunately we could not adequately represent with our values measure. Further support for this argument was presented by Parker and Aldwin (1994), who reported that Cohort 3 respondents aspired to professional careers while also being strongly committed to their families.

However, some caveats must be mentioned. Neither of the samples is representative. The DLS sample comprises well-educated, primarily White individuals who had the resources to continue their professional development. The Transition Study sample represents lower-middle-class Whites in a metropolitan area. Thus, the generalizability to a broader population of non-college-educated, lower socioeconomic status, and ethnic minority populations was uncertain. In addition to being nonrepresentative of the general population, the two samples were significantly different from each other.

However, the value of these databases is their longitudinal, multiple-cohort research designs and their use of multiple indicators of gender identity. With regard to the DLS, its large sample, containing nearly equal numbers of men and women representing multiple cohorts, all followed at regular intervals, provided an unusual opportunity to distinguish the effects of age, cohort, and period. Its homogeneity could have been a potential liability but was, in this case, a bonus. Results generated from this sample already represented a reasonable control of social class and education, making it easier to interpret effects of developmental and social forces.

The values measure required respondents to rank-order their role commitments. This strategy could be problematic because it tends to be unstable. However, few respondents indicated that any two role domains were equally important (e.g., that career and family were equal rather than rank-ordered). Consequently, there is little evidence that this measure misrepresents respondents' actual role hierarchies. In addition, the hierarchies were very similar to those in general use in the sociological literature.

This study clearly demonstrated the need to exercise caution when choosing an index of gender identity. Different measures resulted in completely different patterns. The need to develop clearer constructs and better measures has already been identified (Chaps. 1 & 5); our work substantiates this need. Further, any differences between the James and Lewkowicz study in Chapter 5 and ours can be attributed to differences in how gender identity was defined. In our study we used an older measure that relied on gender stereotypes and thus demonstrated differences between the sexes. Their study, however, purposefully sought to strip gender identity of these stereotypes, focusing on power and affiliation, and thus did not find the types of sex differences seen here.

In addition, our study confirmed the value of using complex longitudinal databases with multiple cohorts for assessing questions of personality and value change in adulthood. However, we did not assess the impact of the acquisition of social roles on changes in gender identity; this is a crucial next step toward understanding the impact of period and cohort. Life-span developmental psychologists have much to gain by incorporating measures of social life into their studies. This includes distinguishing the microcontext (social roles) from the macrocontext (cohort and period effects). It was also apparent that cross-disciplinary communication is both necessary and productive.

NOTES

1. The DLS archives included both the OPI scale scores and the items in 1979. Thus, we regressed the total MF score on each item and calculated a predicted score by weighting each item by the B value and adding the intercept. The predicted and actual means and standard deviations for the scale were nearly identical ($M_{observed}$ = 28.54, sd = 6.06; $M_{predicted}$ = 28.54, sd = 5.19). However, we did a repeated measures MANOVA to check the results and discovered a significant gender-by-time interaction, $F(1, 878) = 71.86, p < .001$. Thus, we computed separate regression equations by sex and recomputed the predicted scores ($M_{observed}$ = 28.82, sd = 6.11; $M_{predicted}$ = 28.80, sd = 5.46). This time, the repeated measures MANOVA demonstrated no significant differences between the two scores, $F(1, 456) = .01$, $p < .917$. Thus, we applied the B weights and intercepts from these analyses to the Time 3 data to calculate predicted scale scores.

2. We thank Paula Schnurr for suggesting this model for the study.

REFERENCES

Aldwin, C. M., & Levenson, M. R. (1994). Aging and personality assessment. In M. P. Lawton & J. A. Teresi (Eds.), *Annual Review of Gerontology and Geriatrics, Vol. 14* (pp. 182–209). New York: Springer.

Bem, S. L. (1974). Measurement of psychological androgyny. *Journal of Consulting and Clinical Psychology, 42,* 155–162.

Block, J. (1961). *The Q-sort method in personality assessment and psychiatric research.* Springfield, IL: Charles C. Thomas.

Carlson, B. E., & Videka-Sherman, L. (1990). An empirical test of androgyny in the middle years: Evidence from a national survey. *Sex Roles, 23,* 305–324.

Caspi, A., Bem, D. J., & Elder, G. H. (1989). Continuities and consequences of interactional styles across the life course. *Journal of Personality, 57,* 375–406.

Conley, J. J. (1984). The hierarchy of consistency: A review and model of longitudinal findings on adult individual differences on intelligence, personality, and self opinion. *Personality and Individual Differences, 5,* 11–26.

Deaux, K. (1985). Sex and gender. *Annual Review of Psychology, 36,* 49–81.

Douglas, K., & Arenberg, D. (1978). Age changes, cohort differences, and cultural change on the Guilford-Zimmerman Temperament Survey. *Journal of Gerontology, 33,* 737–747.

Elder, G. (1974). *Children of the Great Depression.* Chicago: University of Chicago Press.

Fiorentine, R. (1988). Increasing similarity in the values and life plans of male and female college students? Evidence and implications. *Sex Roles, 18,* 143–158.

Fisher, J. L., & Narus, L. R., Jr. (1981). Sex-role development in late adolescence and adulthood. *Sex Roles, 7,* 97–106.

Fultz, N. H., & Herzog, A. R. (1991). Gender differences in affiliation and instrumentality across adulthood. *Psychology and Aging, 6,* 579–586.

Goldsen, R. K., Rosenberg, M., Williams, R., Jr., & Suchman, E. (1960). *What college students think.* Princeton, N.J.: Van Nostrand Reinhold.

Gough, H. G. (1987). *Manual for the California Psychological Inventory.* Palo Alto, CA: Consulting Psychologists Press. (Original work published in 1957.)

Guilford, J. P., & Zimmerman, W. S. (1956). *The Guilford-Zimmerman Temperament Survey: Manual of instructions and interpretations.* Beverly Hills, CA: Sheridan Supply Company.

Gutmann, D. (1975). Parenthood: A key to the comparative study of the life cycle. In N. Datan & L. H. Ginsberg (Eds.), *Life-span developmental psychology: Normative life crises.* New York: Academic Press.

Heist, P., & Yonge, G. (1968). *Omnibus personality inventory, Form F, Manual.* New York: The Psychological Corporation.

Helson, R., Mitchell, V., & Moane, G. (1984). Personality and pattern of adherence and nonadherence to the social clock. *Journal of Personality and Social Psychology, 46*(5), 1079–1096.

Helson, R., & Moane, G. (1987). Personality change in women from college to midlife. *Journal of Personality and Social Personality, 53,* 176–186.

Helson, R., & Wink, P. (1992). Personality change in women from the early 40s to the early 50s. *Psychology and Aging, 7,* 46–55.

Holahan, C. K. (1984). Marital attitudes over 40 years: A longitudinal and cohort analysis. *Journal of Gerontology, 39,* 49–57.

Jackson, D. N. (1974). *Personality Research Form Manual.* Port Huron, MI: Research Psychologists Press.

Jackson, D. N. (1976). *Jackson Personality Inventory Manual.* Goshen, N.Y.: Research Psychologists Press.

James, J., Lewkowicz, C., Libhaber, J., & Lachman, M. E. (1995). Reconceptualizing the gender identity crossover. *Sex Roles, 32,* 185–2071.

Jobson, S., & Watson, J. S. (1984). Sex and age differences in choice behaviour: the object-person dimension. *Perception, 13,* 719–724.

Jung, C. G. (1933). The stages of life. In *Modern man in search of a soul.* Trans. W. S. Dell & C. F. Baynes. New York: Harcourt, Brace.

Kelly, E. L. (1955). Consistency of the adult personality. *American Psychologist, 10,* 659–681.

Kuhlen, R. G., & Johnson, G. H. (1952). Changes in goals with adult increasing age. *Journal of Consulting Psychology, 16,* 1–4.

Levinson, D. J., with Darrow, C. N., Klein, E. B., Levinson, M. H., & McKee, B. (1978). *The seasons of a man's life.* New York: Ballantine Books.

Lowenthal, M. F., Thurnher, M., & Chiriboga, D. (1975). *Four Stages of Life.* San Francisco: Jossey-Bass.

Machung, A. (1989). Talking career, thinking job: Gender differences in career and family expectations of Berkeley students. *Feminist Studies, 15,* 35–58.

McCrae, R. R., & Costa, P. T., Jr. (1990). *Personality in adulthood.* New York: Guilford Press.

McDonald, N. E., Ebert, P. D., & Mason, S. E. (1987). Marital status and age as related to masculine and feminine personality dimensions and self-esteem. *Journal of Social Psychology, 127,* 289–298.

Murray, H. (1938). *Explorations in psychology.* New York: Oxford University Press.

Nash, S. C., & Feldman, S. S. (1981). Sex role and sex-related attributes: Constancy and change across the family life cycle. In M. E. Lamb & A. L. Brown (Eds.), *Advances in Developmental Psychology* (pp. 1–35). Hillsdale, NJ: Lawrence Erlbaum Associates.

Neugarten, B. L., & Gutmann, D. L. (1968). Age-sex roles and personality in middle age: A Thematic Apperception study. In B. L. Neugarten (Ed.), *Middle age and aging* (pp. 58–74). Chicago: University of Chicago Press.

Nunnally, J. (1978). *Psychometric theory.* New York: McGraw-Hill.

Parker, R. A., & Aldwin, C. M. (1994). Desiring careers but loving families: Cohort, period, and gender effects in career and family orientations. In G. P. Keita & J. J. Hurrell, Jr. (Eds.), *Stress in the '90s: A changing workforce in a changing workplace* (pp. 23–38). Washington, DC: American Psychological Association.

Regan, M. C., & Roland, H. E. (1985). Rearranging family and career priorities: Professional women and men of the eighties. *Journal of Marriage and the Family, 47,* 985–992.

Rossi, A. S. (1980). Life-span theories and women's lives. *Signs, 6,* 4–32.

Schaie, K. W. (1977). Quasi-experimental research designs in the psychology of aging. In J. E. Birren & K. W. Schaie (Eds.), *Handbook of the psychology of aging* (1st ed., pp. 39–58). New York: Van Nostrand Reinhold.

Spence, J. T. (1991). Do the BSRI and PAW measure the same or different concepts? *Psychology of Women Quarterly, 15,* 141–165.

Spence, J. T., & Helmreich, R. L. (1979). Comparison of masculine and feminine personality attributes and sex-role attitudes across age groups. *Developmental Psychology, 15,* 583–584.

Strong, E. K., Jr. (1943). *Vocational interests of men and women.* Stanford: Stanford University Press.

Urberg, K. A. (1979). Sex role conceptualizations in adolescents and adults. *Developmental Psychology, 15,* 90–92.

Veroff, J., Reuman, D., & Feld, S. (1984). Motives in American men and women across the adult life span. *Developmental Psychology, 20,* 1142–1158.

Yonge, G. D., & Regan, M. C. (1975). A longitudinal study of personality and choice of major. *Journal of Vocational Behavior, 7,* 41–65.

FIVE

Themes of Power and Affiliation across Time

Jacquelyn Boone James and Corinne J. Lewkowicz

Themes of Power and Affiliation across Time

i have noticed
that men somewhere around forty
tend to come in from the field
with a sigh
and removing their coat in the hall
call into the kitchen
you were right
Grace
it ain't out there
just like you've always said
and she
with the children gone at last
breathless
putting her hat on her head
the hell it ain't!
coming and going
they pass in the doorway.

(Ric Masten, "Coming and Going")

The notion that at midlife women become more assertive and aggressive while men become more affiliative and expressive is deeply embedded in common lore. Derived in part from Jung's (1933) theoretical model of personality integration, this notion of *crossover* has received considerable acceptance within the field of psychology (Brown, 1992; Nemiroff & Colarusso, 1990; Rossi & Ohta, 1986; Rowles & Ohta, 1983). Yet findings within this body of research do not always converge (e.g., Abrahams, Feldman, & Nash, 1978; Spence & Helmreich, 1979; Urberg & Labouvie-Vief, 1976).

There are many inconsistencies among studies of personality crossover in midlife, inconsistencies that appear to be related to design issues and the crossover hypothesis (see James, Lewkowicz, Libhaber, &

109

Lachman, 1995). Adequate assessment of this hypothesis requires the longitudinal assessment of both men and women from a wide age range. Few studies meet these requirements (see Feldman, Biringen & Nash, 1981; Hyde, Kranjnik & Skuldt-Niederberger, 1991; Spence & Helmreich, 1979, for exceptions).

Measurement issues have proved to be more complicated and have necessitated a return to Jung's (1933) theoretical formulation for direction as to how best to study the question of whether a crossover in personality attributes can be demonstrated empirically. Many studies have used self-report instruments, assessing masculinity and femininity with a variety of instruments (over 150, according to Lenney, 1991), which have similar names but do not necessarily measure the same phenomena. In addition to definitional issues surrounding masculinity and femininity (see Epstein, 1988; Lott, 1990; Mednick, 1989; Morawski, 1985), these measures, because they consist of self-ratings, also have the disadvantage of being particularly vulnerable to a social desirability response set. Jung's theory, however, postulated that the midlife personality shift was an unconscious process; these processes do not readily lend themselves to empirical research and are even less accessible through self-report assessment techniques.

In fact, the strongest empirical support for the personality shift has come from projective data taken from the Thematic Apperception Test (TAT; Gutmann, 1964, 1975, 1985, 1987; Neugarten & Gutmann, 1968), which is believed to tap unconscious or intrapsychic processes. Even so, McGee and Wells (1982) have pointed out other methodological flaws in Gutmann's approach, including the use of small and nonrandom samples, the lack of information about the sociodemographic characteristics of his subjects, the lack of explanation of the precise nature of his coding categories and interrater reliabilities, and so on. McGee and Wells also assert that Gutmann's use of an interview to determine his subjects' images of an older and younger couple in a TAT picture reveal more about their stereotypes of old people than about their own inner strivings.

Thus, in a previous study (James, Lewkowicz, Libhaber, & Lachman, 1995) we set out to eliminate some of these biases and provide a new test of the midlife personality shift using cross-sectional data. We examined the crossover hypothesis using a personality attributes questionnaire recoded to assess *agency* and *communion* (our self-report measure) and *power* and *affiliation* (our projective measure) using reliable coding techniques from McClelland (1985). We found some support for a crossover for middle-aged men (but not for women) using projective assessment techniques. We speculated that the lack of evidence of a crossover for women in our study had to do with the extensive work histories of the women in our sample and thus the lack of specialization in traditional sex roles. Moreover, tests of these issues using self-report instruments are discussed more clearly in Chapter 4. Thus, we designed this study to examine similar questions with a more traditional cohort and with longitudinal data using assessment techniques that (1) take a systematic approach to the use of projective data, and (2) use constructs that are more relevant to Gutmann's model of the crossover hypothesis and contain fewer unwarranted assumptions about sex role appropriateness. We will now elaborate on why these are important directions to take.

Jung's Theoretical Model

According to Jung's derivation, normal personality development in middle and old age brings forward the unconscious anima (feminine archetype) in men and the animus (masculine archetype) in women. Thus, Jung (1933) described midlife men becoming more attentive to hearth, home, and relationships; and women, more worldly, work-oriented, and assertive. Jung regarded this shift as a process of integrating latent sides of the personality generated from within the self. He also considered this to be a developmental inevitability in adulthood, an ontogenetic phase transcending culture and time. This developmental phase has been widely interpreted as a time of incorporating assertiveness and agentic attributes for women and the interpersonal and communal attributes for men. It is, therefore, generally construed less as a full crossover or reversal of gender differences than as a time of integrating or balancing the personality.

Gutmann's Supporting Evidence

On the basis of studies from a number of preliterate agricultural societies, all of which appear to be extremely role differentiated, Gutmann (1987) uses ethnographic accounts to describe a similar "shift in the politics of the self" (p. 203). Using TAT cards to engage subjects in an interview about the picture, he identifies themes that reveal the subjects' perception that older men and women take on psychological attributes that were previously unavailable to them or that they had lived out vicariously through their partners.

In general Gutmann refers to a crossover, but he also mentions "sexual bimodality," transformations that "involve more than a drift away from [previous attributes], but an actual shift in gender distinctiveness, from univocal masculinity [or femininity] to sexual bimodality" (p. 94). Thus, it is not clear whether Gutmann truly embraces a crossover of attributes for men and women or whether he, too, observed more of a perception of integration, or a process of incorporating new attributes alongside the old ones. The latter interpretation is more consistent with Jung's theoretical model and has received more empirical support (Eichorn, 1981; Helson & Moane, 1987).

Gutmann, however, extends Jung's model by proposing a theory about why the crossover or personality integration occurs. Positing that it is a result of the end of the "parental emergency," he claims that the arrival of children requires an extensive period of "parental service" and therefore, strict polarities in sex-role-appropriate behaviors for the parents. Thus, for the good of society, mothers must become the nurturers and fathers, the providers. When this period of child rearing is over, men and women can expect the release of powers and potential previously unused (because previously unnecessary) for continued development during their later years.

This line of reasoning may be called into question when applied to current cohorts of working mothers (and fathers) who attempt to avoid this level of sex role specialization (Feree, 1990) and because of the lack of evidence that children fare any worse under these circumstances (see Betz & Fitzgerald, 1987, for a review). It also ignores the assertiveness and aggressiveness involved in the roles of homemaker and mother (see Malley & Stewart, 1988) and the relevance of interpersonal skills and capacities in the workplace. Most provocative is the suggestion that the mother role and the role of worker/provider are inherently incompatible (see Baruch, Barnett, & Rivers, 1983; Baruch, Biener & Barnett, 1987; and Crosby, 1987, for different views). Therefore, one important question for this research was whether the crossover occurs for women who have combined work and family roles.

Sex Role Identity

Even though Gutmann and his colleagues have amassed considerable support for the existence of the personality shift (Gutmann, 1964, 1975, 1990; Neugarten & Gutmann, 1968), the aforementioned methodological and conceptual flaws have led researchers to seek more systematic approaches to the question of whether such a gender role crossover could be observed in other ways. Quite logically, because Jung's notion of anima and animus has been translated as the feminine and the masculine within the personality, there has been a proliferation of studies of the gender role crossover using a variety of the available measures of sex role identity (Amstey & Whitbourne, 1981; Cunningham & Antill, 1984; Erdwins, Tyler, & Mellinger, 1983; Feldman et al., 1981; Fischer & Narus, 1981; Hyde et al., 1991). These studies have led to many inconsistencies and some criticism, mostly centering around the limitations of these instruments (see Constantinople, 1977, and Morawski, 1985, for discussions of limitations).

There are, however, more difficult issues involved in using these measures as assessment tools for the crossover hypothesis. First is the problem of using terms such as *masculinity* and *femininity* as bipolar opposites that link certain attributes to men and others to women. There have been repeated calls for these to be treated rather as separate dimensions, allowing for the possibility that men and women can carry both sets of characteristics (Epstein, 1988; Lott, 1990; Mednick, 1989). Some have advocated the replacement of these gender-linked labels with more descriptive terms, such as "affiliative," "expressive," "communal," instead of "femininity," and "instrumental," "assertive," "agentic," instead of "masculinity" (Bakan, 1966; Carlson, 1971; Rossi, 1980; Wiggins, 1991; and many others).

While we agree with this approach, it generates another set of problems when certain items within the particular measure of sex role identity are not relevant to either affiliation or assertiveness (or any of the other recommended substitutions for masculinity and femininity). Consider, for example, the items from three widely used measures of sex role identity. In the California Personality Inventory (Gough, 1956) we find items such as "I prefer a shower to a bathtub" from the masculinity scale, and "I would like to wear expensive clothes" from the femininity scale (Lenney, 1991, p. 628–629). In the Adjective Check List (Heilbrun, 1976), there are items such as *fickle, dependent,* and *frivolous* from the femininity scale and *handsome* from the masculinity scale. Likewise, the Bem Sex Role Inventory (Bem, 1981) femininity scale contains items such as *gullible, childlike,* and *flatterable,* and no uncomplimentary items on the masculinity scale. These kinds of items do not appear to be relevant to emotional expressivity or instrumentality; nor do the single items *masculine* and *feminine,* two items shared by all three of the above measures, which Feldman et al. (1981) suggest could be responsible for all the variance contributing to sex differences on these measures.

Since in our previous study we were interested in assessing clearer conceptions of Jung's model (and Gutmann's extension) using both self-report and projective data, we chose to assess attributes reflecting *agency* and *communion*. Because of the limitations of existing masculinity and femininity scales, we determined that a theoretically based scale derived from a personality trait inventory, the 50-Bipolar Personality Inventory (Goldberg, 1992) could be used as a self-report instrument. We accomplished this by selecting items from the measure that suggested communion (e.g., *warm, kind, cooperative, unselfish, good-natured, sociable*) and agency (e.g., *conscientious, bold, active, imaginative, self confident, hardworking, creative, forceful*), and conducting item analyses to test internal consistency. See Costos, 1986, for a similar recoding of the Bem Sex Role Inventory (BSRI).

Although we expected that these scales would represent the agentic and communal dimensions relevant to the hypothesized personality crossover more clearly than the traditional sex role identity scales, we found that self-report instruments are not the best measures for a valid test of Jung's hypothesis. Specifically, there is the aforementioned problem of the socially desirable response set inherent in these measures, and perhaps more importantly, the difficulty of expecting research participants to report unconscious processes through objective assessment techniques. Indeed, there were no age or sex differences on the basis of these scales (James et al., 1995). Thus, for this longitudinal research, we returned to Gutmann's (1987) assertion that the "special lenses" of projective tests were necessary to assess the personality shift. To overcome some of the methodological flaws in Gutmann's use of the TAT, we drew from Winter's (1991) use of interview materials to assess motives.

Motives as Unconscious Needs

A motive is defined as a "recurring concern around a goal state" (McClelland, 1980). Motives are also known as needs: the need for achievement, the need for power, the need for affiliation/intimacy.[1] According to McClelland (1980, 1981, 1985), these needs as assessed by the TAT reflect operant behaviors, "natural and spontaneous goal-directed strivings," while self-report instruments (such as sex role identity measures) reflect respondent behaviors, more likely to be a part of one's conscious beliefs or cognitions. Thus, the operant measures would appear to be a more "sensitive index of the relative strength of motive dispositions." "Such dispositions are conceived of as recurrent

and emotionally tinged goal-directed preferences for particular qualities of experience (such as 'doing better' for achievement or 'feeling
strong' for power)" (Emmons & McAdams, 1991, p. 648).

Thus, these motives or needs appear to be constructs that could be
useful as a test of Jung's theoretical model and a more systematic test
of Gutmann's extension of this model. Although Veroff, Reuman, and
Feld (1984) analyzed motives across the life span for a national survey
sample, no between-sex comparisons were possible because different
sets of pictures were administered to men and women (see also Baruch,
1967, and Jenkins, 1989, for motives analyzed over time for samples
of women). There appear to be parallels between Gutmann's constructs
of active and passive mastery (aspects of the personality shift) and two
of the social motives, the need for power (Npow) and the need for
affiliation (Naff). What follows is an outline of these parallels and a
brief discussion of motives that do not appear to be similar to Gutmann's constructs.

As Gutmann (1987) describes the midlife shift for women, he reveals their coming to terms with their own aggressiveness, involving
themselves in self-aggrandizing, expansive and vigorous activities. He
refers to this as "active mastery," but he describes it in terms of power.
The older woman, he says, becomes more of a power within the family;
she takes a more managerial role. She often uses her role to be a source
of authority and wisdom for those still vulnerable, but at the same
time, "an old woman may say things that no one else would dare to
say" (p. 164), things that can sound shameless and shocking. He describes the older woman as "feisty" and dominant over others. She
is forward moving and productive; she is authoritative, effective, and
increasingly less submissive.

Winter (1988) describes the power motive as "a concern for having
an impact on the world, arousing strong emotions in others or maintaining reputation and prestige" (p. 510). Thus, the older woman in
Gutmann's scenario can be seen as power motivated. She is the leader
in the family; she seeks validation and prestige in the world; and she
may even arouse strong emotions with her potential for shocking comments.

The need for affiliation, a concern with establishing and maintaining relationships, seems to characterize Gutmann's concept of passive mastery, which is a turn "toward the milder pleasure of hearth
and home," an interest in community and collaborative efforts. The
older man, according to Gutmann (1987), begins to claim his accom-

modative qualities: "sensuality, affiliation, and maternal tendencies" (p. 203). Both passive mastery and Naff are characterized by openness and receptivity, an orientation toward others and communality. Both also contain elements of inhibition and vulnerability to rejection.

The achievement motive, on the other hand, is the "disposition to perform activities in competition with some standard of excellence" (Veroff et al., 1984, p. 114), and has more to do with feeling challenged to improve performance than a desire for leadership and authority. Even though these motives are typically studied in relation to each other, our research questions centered around changes over time in power and affiliation/intimacy; therefore, we did not explore the need for achievement in the present investigation.

Reexamining the Crossover Hypothesis

Our purpose was to explore further the issue of whether there is a crossover in affiliative and power-related concerns. Thus, our first question was whether there is a shift in themes of dominance and power (agency) or themes of affiliation/intimacy (communion) for men and women in different age groups over a 10–12 year period. Were these themes consistent over time or did they change? Was there evidence of a crossover in affiliative and power-related concerns or was there more of a convergence over time? Additionally, since Gutmann emphasized the importance of the end of the "parental emergency" for the release of these midlife freedoms, we asked whether this shift is more a function of family stage than age.

METHODS

Subjects

The data for this research were drawn from Lowenthal, Thurnher, & Chiriboga's (1976) longitudinal study of *Transitions in Four Stages of Life* for the years 1968–1980 (currently housed at the Murray Research Center of Radcliffe College). This longitudinal study was of men and women who ranged in age from 18 years to over 50 and who were facing one of four transitions at the beginning of the study: (1) graduation from high school ($n = 25$ males, 27 females); (2) new marriage, less than one year and without children ($n = 25$ males, 25 females); (3) last child leaving home ($n = 27$ males, 27 females); and (4) retirement ($n = 30$ males, 30 females). Participants (total $n = 216$) were recruited from within a single school district. High school seniors identified as the youngest child in their families were selected as the group of high school graduates; their parents then constituted the empty nest group. The newlyweds and the preretirees were friends and relatives of the first two groups and also resided in the school district. Since the focus of our study was personality change in middle and later life, we eliminated the high school seniors from our analyses. Thus, the sample for our secondary analysis consisted of 164 (mostly White) men and women from the original study (see Lowenthal et al., 1976, for a detailed description of the sample).

According to Lowenthal et al. (1976), most participants in the study had some education beyond high school (few actually held a college degree) and in general had more education than their parents. The newlywed group had the most education, followed by the postparental group, followed by the preretirees. Nearly all the men in our sample worked full-time. The women differed by group: approximately three-fourths of the women in the newlywed group worked full-time; and about one-half of the empty-nest women and the preretirement women worked full-time. A small percentage of women worked part-time. Although the men worked more than the women and had more stable employment histories, half of the older working women had "work histories fully as stable as the men's, the majority having been on the same job for over ten years" (Lowenthal et al., 1976, p. 6). Both men and women of our sample were, however, quite family centered (as determined by the extent of time and activity oriented toward home when not working), and the women appeared to be working more to supplement the family income than for their own career development or self-satisfaction (Lowenthal et al., 1976).

In general, the sample appeared to represent the traditional values of the middle and lower-middle class. It is probably not inconsequential that at the time of this study (1969–1981), these values were being publicly called into question by the social unrest generated by the women's movement and other elements of counterculture. We would need similar longitudinal studies of other cohorts to test the actual impact of these events on the crossover phenomenon.

The sample is limited in that it was selected for convenience within one community and thus is not representative of the total population. It is also a small sample for these analyses, and the twelve-year period of the study is relatively short for an analysis of life-span changes. It is our view, however, that its strengths outweigh its weaknesses for these exploratory analyses of a new conception of the crossover hypothesis and for suggesting new lines of inquiry.

First, while the sample does not represent the population at large, it does appear to be an underrepresented group in psychological research, that of the middle, lower-middle and working class. Few studies have tested the crossover hypothesis in samples other than well-educated Americans (see Veroff et al., 1984, for an exception). Additionally, while 12 years is a short time across the adult life span, it is sufficiently long to observe the hypothesized changes in the middle years, especially when there is a very clear group of middle-aged adults (ages 36–50) and both younger and older comparison groups. Finally, and most importantly, these data provide an abundance of qualitative material for examining both the constructs of interest (power and affiliative themes) "at a distance" (Winter, 1991) and for closer contextual analysis of these constructs.

PROCEDURE

The procedure for the study involved the use of secondary analysis, which has many advantages (Colby, 1982; James & Paul, 1993; Stewart & Platt, 1982). The major advantage relevant to this study is the availability of in-depth interviews from a sample of adult men and women, followed over 10–12 years, and spanning a wide range of ages, which would be both difficult and expensive to obtain otherwise. The use of secondary analyses does have its limitations as well, which we will discuss below.

Age Grouping and Time Intervals

Age grouping. Because of the wide age range within, and age overlap between, some of the transition groups (e.g., 39–61 among the postparental group and 45–67 among the preretirees) and because of the age-related (and not family-stage-related) differences found in our cross-sectional study (James et al., 1995), we have chosen to organize the sample by age group for separate analyses of the effects of age. Thus, our reconfigured groups include young adults, ages 20–35, mean = 24 ($n = 19$ men, 21 women); young middle-aged adults, ages 36–50, mean = 46, $n = 15$ men, 21 women); and older middle-aged adults, ages 51+, mean = 58, ($n = 17$ men, 14 women).[2] The small size of the groups is due to this reorganization and the missing data from the final interview. All analyses were conducted with both the original transition groups and our reconfigured groups.

Time intervals. Participants were interviewed five times during the 10–12 year period of the study. For the purposes of our question of whether there is a personality crossover in midlife, we determined that the 2-year intervals were too short for such changes to be observed. Similarly, the change over the 12 years of the study (from time 1 to time 5) was too long to avoid missing changes that might occur during the middle years of the study. Consequently, three contact points were identified for analyses: wave 1, conducted in 1968–69; wave 3, 1974; and wave 5, 1979–80. These time points were used in combination with the age cohort groups as defined above and the transition groups used in the original study as independent variables.

Measures

Motives. Motives, defined as a "recurring concern around a goal state" (McClelland, 1980), and understood as individual differences in the extent of certain needs (achievement, power, affiliation/intimacy), are typically assessed by content coding of the TAT. McClelland (1980, 1981, 1985) views these motives as spontaneous strivings or "operant" behaviors. Each motive has its own coding system with acceptable interrater reliabilities, and each has impressive reported construct validity over many years of testing (see McClelland, 1980, for a summary of the psychometric properties).

Winter (1973, 1991) has ascertained, however, that motives can also be reliably assessed using interview material, using a method he refers to as "running text." Winter (1991) maintains that running text, based on a simplified revision of the original content coding scheme, can be "applied to any verbal material that is at least in part imaginative or 'aspirational,' rather than being purely factual; or that contains statements about goals, actions, or wishes: TAT stories, interviews, and press conference transcripts, speeches, dialogue" (p. 4).

Since each wave of the Lowenthal et al. (1976) data contained questions in the interview about present, past, and future goals, these sections were selected for the assessment of three motives: the need for achievement, the need for power, and the needs for affiliation/intimacy. Even though goal-oriented questions (what were your goals for the past? what are your goals for the present? what are your goals for the future?) were asked at each wave, the interviews differed in that

119

answers to the questions were longer and more in-depth for the first wave than for later waves. Several corrections for this lack of comparability were made. For wave 1, only the goal-oriented questions were coded; these were lengthy responses and clearly provided a valid assessment of the need for affiliation/intimacy and the need for power, according to Winter's (1991) scoring rules. For waves 3 and 5, however, all of the open-ended questions within the interview were coded; these were comparable in length to goal-oriented questions extracted from the wave 1 interview. Finally, motive scores were corrected for verbal fluency; the scores used for these analyses are based on proportions of the number of statements relevant to each motive to the number of words in the portion of the interview selected for coding.

Coding was conducted by two raters who were trained in the running text method by David Winter and who achieved interrater reliability with expert coding of .85 or better. Reliability with each other, and for coding of the current study, was also obtained at .85 or better. Coders were unaware of the hypotheses of the study.

RESULTS
Age Cohort Analyses

Analyses were conducted to assess whether the needs for power and affiliation/intimacy (ascertained from themes within interviews) change over time, and whether the course of these changes differs for people in different age cohorts and for men and women. A 3 (age cohort) by 2 (sex) by 3 (time) multivariate analysis of variance was conducted for each motive (power and affiliation), with time as a repeated measure. For confirmation of the hypothesis that there is a sex-related crossover in power-related and affiliative themes, we would expect a significant three-way interaction whereby middle-aged women (more than younger or older women) increased in their need for power, while middle-aged men (more than younger or older men) increased in their need for affiliation. For a true crossover, we would also expect to find that middle-aged women decreased in affiliative concerns while their male counterparts decreased in power-related concerns.

First, as can be seen in Tables 5.1 and 5.2, there were significant changes over time in both the need for power and the need for affiliation/intimacy for men and women and for all age cohorts. Thus, it is clear that these are not stable concerns, at least not for the men and women of this sample.

Table 5.1 Need for Power for Different Age Cohorts

Source of Variation	Sum of Squares	DF	Mean of Squares	F Ratio
Between subjects				
Sex	8623.57	1	8623.57	11.89***
Age cohort	6746.62	2	3373.31	4.56**
Sex by age cohort	8970.67	2	4485.33	6.18**
Error between	71809.94	99	725.35	
Within subjects				
Time	8948.27	2	4473.63	10.22***
Time by sex	795.43	2	397.72	.91
Time by age cohort	2851.16	4	712.79	1.63
Time by sex by age	3431.86	4	857.97	1.96t
Error within	86692.00	198	437.84	

$t = p < .10$. $* p < .05$. $** p < .01$. $*** p < .001$.

Table 5.2 Need for Affiliation for Different Age Cohorts

Source of Variation	Sum of Squares	DF	Mean of Squares	F Ratio
Between subjects				
Sex	29776.16	1	29773.16	16.72***
Age cohort	12518.82	2	6259.41	3.51*
Sex by age cohort	70.35	2	35.17	.02
Error between	176332.72	99	1781.14	
Within subjects				
Time	36025.87	2	18012.94	17.86***
Time by sex	721.52	2	360.76	.36
Time by age cohort	2993.64	4	748.41	.74
Time by sex by age	1575.41	4	393.85	.39
Error within	199641.90	198	1008.29	

$t = p < .10$. $* p < .05$. $** p < .01$. $*** p < .001$.

The Need for Power

As shown in Table 5.1, the expected sex-by-age-cohort-by-time interaction did not meet the conventional statistical significance requirement ($p < .05$) but did reveal a trend, $F (4,198) = 1.69$, $p < .10$ in that direction. Results did, however, indicate both between- and within-subject differences in the need for power. Follow-up analyses revealed that women in the middle-aged cohort were significantly higher in the need for power than all other groups, $F(5,107) = 5.55$, $p < .001$. Since this sex-by-age interaction was in the predicted direction and the sex-by-age-by-time interaction approached significance, we conducted follow-up analyses to assess differences over time among men and women in the three age cohorts.

These follow-up analyses revealed that women across all age cohorts were significantly higher in the need for power than the men at wave 1, $F(1) = 5.35$, $p < .05$; by wave 3, there was a significant age cohort–by–sex interaction whereby the middle-aged women were higher than men and higher than both younger and older women, $F(2) = 5.10$, $p < .01$; their need for power had increased still further by wave 5, $F(2) = 4.12$, $p < .05$. Thus, our hypothesis that middle-aged women increase in their need for power while men decrease was partially supported. As can be seen in Figure 5.1, the middle-aged women clearly exhibited change over time in the expected direction. Additionally, the middle aged men were significantly lower in their need for power than the middle-aged women, and they did decrease from wave 1 to wave 3 (not significantly); the pattern over time for these men, however, did not seem dissimilar to that of the younger or the older men.

The Need for Affiliation

There was no support for the crossover hypothesis on the basis of changes over time in the need for affiliation/intimacy. As can be seen in Table 5.2, the only within-subjects difference in the need for affiliation was with respect to time, $F(2,198) = 17.86$, $p < .001$; there were considerable changes from wave 1 to wave 5 in the need for affiliation. There were also significant sex differences and age-cohort differences. Follow-up analyses revealed that the young adults were significantly higher in their need for affiliation than older people. No other age groups differed significantly. Additionally, the women were higher in the affiliative motive (across all age cohorts) than the men. The expected age-group-by-sex interaction was not significant.

Thus, the answer to our question of whether men increase (while women decrease) in affiliative concerns as they move from middle age into old age is negative. As can be seen in Figure 5.2, across age groups the need for affiliation was at its highest level during young adulthood, and the pattern over time was similar for men and for women. Even though the need for affiliation was highest among the young adults (both men and women), it also increased over time in all three age groups. The fact that the men of our sample increased in their need

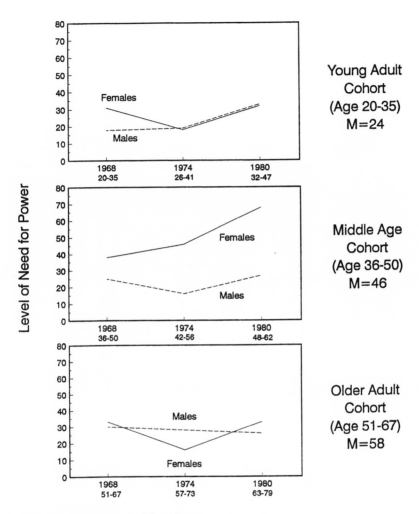

FIGURE 5.1. Motives over Time: Power

for affiliation over time provides some indication that this is the pattern for men. This increase, however, did not develop at midlife, nor did it ever approach the level of women's need for affiliation. Clearly, the women's scores for affiliative concerns were higher at all age groups and continued to increase across time, as did the men's; women did not decrease in affiliative concerns, as Gutmann's model suggests. The similarity in the patterns in the need for affiliation are suggestive of period effects; although we could not test this possibility, we will discuss it further below.

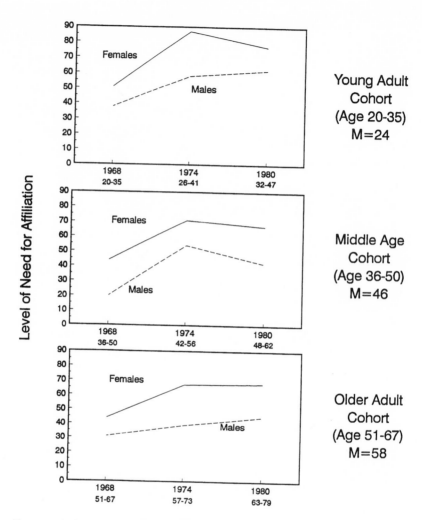

FIGURE 5.2. Motives over Time: Affiliation

Family Stage Analyses

In response to Gutmann's assertion that the release from the parental imperative directs the sex-role crossover in midlife, we also analyzed the needs for power and affiliation as a function of family stage (i.e., in terms of where in the parental cycle these individuals found themselves: those newly married and beginning the process of child rearing over the 12 years of the study, those facing the transition to the empty nest, and those about to retire). Therefore, we conducted the same multivar-

TABLE 5.3 Need for Power for Different Life Stages

Source of Variance	Sum of Squares	DF	Mean of Squares	F Ratio
Between subjects				
Sex	5051.30	1	5051.30	6.18*
Stage	4554.04	2	2277.02	2.79*t*
Sex by stage	2659.86	2	1329.93	1.63
Error between	80858.73	99	816.75	
Within subjects				
Time	8810.32	2	4405.16	9.63***
Time by sex	927.35	2	463.68	1.01
Time by sex by stage	340.01	4	85.00	0.19
Error within	90596.93	198	2457.56	

$t = p < .10.$ $* p < .05.$ $**p < .01.$ $***p < .001.$

iate analyses of variance (sex-by-family-by-time) on the needs for power and affiliation with time as a repeated measure. If the end of the parental emergency were the factor involved in women's increasing concern with power, these analyses should reveal a significant sex-by-stage-by-time interaction for both power and affiliation.

Once again, there were significant changes over time across the five waves of the study in the need for power. There was, however, no time-by-sex-by-stage interaction, nor any other within-subjects main effects (see Table 5.3). There were significant sex differences; women across all stages indicated higher need for power than did the men. The empty-nest women, however, did not show a different pattern than the younger or the older women.

With regard to the need for affiliation, there were significant main effects of sex, stage, and time, although none of the interactions was significant (see Table 5.4). As with the need for power, the women in this sample indicate a higher need for affiliation than did the men. Additionally, follow-up analyses indicate that those individuals who were newly married showed a higher need for affiliation than those about to retire. Neither the newlyweds nor the preretirees, however, differed significantly from the empty nesters.

Cohort Analyses among the Middle-aged

Because there were three different age cohorts across the twelve years of the study, there was enough overlap in age to allow for the

TABLE 5.4 Need for Affiliation for Different Life Stages

Source of Variance	Sum of Squares	DF	Mean of Squares	F Ratio
Between subjects				
Sex	33113.69	1	33113.69	18.79***
Stage	14089.70	2	7044.85	4.00*
Sex by stage	216.50	2	108.25	0.06
Error between	174509.13	99	1762.72	
Within subjects				
Time	34345.76	2	17172.88	16.93**
Time by sex	1721.61	2	860.81	0.85
Time by stage	1902.75	4	475.69	0.47
Time by sex by stage	1180.33	4	295.08	0.29
Error within	200873.95	198	1014.51	

$t = p < .10.$ * $p < .05.$ **$p < .01.$ ***$p < .001.$

assessment of newly constituted groups of people who were approximately the same age at different points in time for differences in their levels of concern with power and affiliation. Thus, there were those who were entering midlife (in their early 40s) composed of the young cohort at wave 5, 1980 (ages 32–47, $M = 36$) compared with the midlife cohort at wave 1, 1968 (ages 36–50, $M = 46$). A second group comprised those who were well established in middle age (mid-to-late 50s) and consisted of the midlife cohort at wave 5, 1980 (ages 48–62, $M = 58$) compared with the older cohort at wave 1, 1968 (ages 51–67, $M = 58$).

The Need for Power

ANOVAs revealed no differences between the two groups of early entrants to midlife in the need for power; there were also no differences between the men and the women. The early part of middle age appears to reflect similar levels of power-related themes both in 1968 and in 1980. As for differences between adults well established in midlife at different points in time, there were cohort differences. The midlife women (in their late 50s in 1980) were higher in the need for power than the older cohort of women (and men) who were in their late 50s in 1968. The older women, however, were higher in the need for power than the two groups of men (although this difference was nonsignificant). This analysis suggests a uniqueness among the midlife cohort of women surveyed here in their level of concern with power.

The Need for Affiliation

As can be seen in Figure 5.2, the pattern of change over time in the need for affiliation appears to be similar for all age cohorts. Across all age cohorts and across time, the women were higher in this concern. Comparison of two groups of early entrants to midlife revealed that the young cohort at age 32–47 was higher in the need for affiliation than was the midlife cohort at age 35–50. As for the well-established midlifers, the midlife cohort at age 48–62 was higher in need for affiliation than the older cohort at age 51–67. Thus, the concern with affiliation was least prevalent for the older cohort; it was greater for the midlife cohort and still greater for the young adult cohort. The similarity of the patterns suggests period effects which we cannot test, but which make sense in light of McClelland's (1987) finding that a collective concern with affiliation tends to increase in the aftermath of war, in this case the Vietnam War.

Discussion

This study extends previous research by providing a model for testing changes in personality with measures that are theoretically derived and more construct relevant and that contain fewer unwarranted assumptions about sex-role appropriateness. Our study also allows for the assessment of these characteristics over time, which is the only way to determine whether there is intraindividual change or personality shift.

Like many of the other approaches to examining the crossover hypothesis (Abrahams et al., 1978; Amstey & Whitbourne, 1981; Cunningham & Antill, 1984; Feldman et al., 1981; Fischer & Narus, 1981; Hyde et al., 1991; Livson, 1983; Veroff et al., 1984), these results provide partial support for Gutmann's model. The middle-aged women clearly demonstrated the expected increase in a concern with power, influence, and impact. They also appear to be different from the older cohort in this sample, although these analyses of cohort differences were comparisons of similar age groups at different points in time and thus are not longitudinal analyses.

The middle-aged and older male cohorts were less concerned with affiliation than were the young male cohort, yet over the 12 years of the study they increased in affiliative concerns. Clearly, the men and women did not cross over in their expression of these needs. It is also clear that these changes have more to do with age cohort than with the weakening of parental responsibilities. These data support the notion that this group of middle-aged women, while still preoccupied with affiliative concerns, also became increasingly more concerned with issues of power and influence. The pattern for men, however, is less clear. The men of this study did increase in the need for affiliation over time, but still remained significantly lower in this concern than the women. They did not show an overall decrease in the concern with power.

Similar to the findings from our cross-sectional study (James et al., 1995), the finding most consistent with the changes in direction that Gutmann predicted was again evident only with respect to one group, in this case the women. In our previous study there was evidence of the expected changes in the concern with power and affiliation only for the men, although this evidence was based on cross-sectional age differences, not intra-individual change.

On the basis of all the data that we have examined, including an intensive literature review, we can draw few robust conclusions except the obvious one—that the crossover phenomenon is more complicated than currently understood. Clearly, changes in concerns with power and affiliation do occur for some people some of the time. The factors contributing to these changes, however, remain less clear. Gutmann has suggested that these changes have to do with the end of active parenting. Our data do not support this hypothesis; age cohort was a better indicator of change than was family life stage (see also Cunningham & Antill, 1984; Erdwins et al., 1983; Friedman, Tzukerman, Wienberg, & Todd, 1992).

It appears that some of these changes depend on how traditional the participants are. Livson (1983) found that her "traditional" subjects changed very little over time in agentic and communal self-attributions (see also Amstey & Whitbourne, 1981; Cunningham & Antill, 1984; Erdwins et al., 1983). Similarly, Veroff et al. (1984) found that although women in general declined in the need for affiliation, this was not true for rather nontraditional women, that is, housewives without children, employed women with children, or women in high-prestige careers (regardless of parent status).

It has been suggested that the question of whether there is a personality shift in married men and women ignores the developmental changes of single and childless midlife adults (McGee & Wells, 1982). Even for couples, however, little attention has been given to the possibility that this role reversal (or balancing) is embedded in the partners' interactions over time and the way that they negotiate work and family commitments (as the poem quoted at the beginning of the chapter suggests). Only one study that we located considered attributes of husbands and wives in relation to each other. In a study of couples (married, divorced, cohabiting, dating) Cunningham and Antill (1984) (using the BSRI) showed that among couples where the wife was employed, there was a lessening of femininity for wives and of masculinity for husbands. They concluded that these changes represented a weakening of stereotypes rather than developmental changes.

Whatever its source, this change over time with respect to power and affiliation appears to be a rather subtle phenomenon that is hard to capture with unidimensional scales, whether projective or self-report. Indeed, the most compelling evidence of the crossover seems to come from longitudinal studies that use multiple measures that assess perceptions, behaviors, orientation to work and family (including the reasons for working), values, and attitudes. In fact, Fiske and Chiriboga (1990) report evidence of the personality shift from these data in terms of participants' values. "Men become more accepting of social and perhaps community and personal issues, while women become more instrumental and task-oriented" (p. 220). These conclusions were based on a picture that emerged from multiple indicators of values and attitudes (see also Chap. 4). Longitudinal data, when used in this way, consistently show changes in men and women that reflect reprioritizing to some degree (see Helson & Moane, 1987; and Maas, 1989, for a summary of these studies).

The shift in priorities (whether agentic or communal), then, does not appear to be necessarily related to family stage; it may be at least partially related to social context and social change with respect to family involvement and roles, and it appears to be more easily revealed in multiple assessments over time. Having drawn these rather tentative conclusions, we believe that the whole question of whether we can identify group differences in agentic and communal attributes or motives may be misguided. The assumption underlying all these conclusions is that the midlife shift is a rather homogeneous phenomenon, the same for all women (and men). Indeed, the patterns drawn in both Figure 5.1 and Figure 5.2 represent means at each wave and may not represent any one individual in the study (Mishler, 1993). A better analysis of change over time might involve classifying individual patterns and asking for whom crossover occurs and whether the crossover is the same for all who experience it.

Because our data included in-depth interviews, we selected a few of these to examine the patterns of change among the middle-aged women in our study who did exhibit the increase in concerns with power and the men who increased in their affiliative concerns.[3] In this exploratory way, we hoped to begin to suggest new lines of inquiry, that is, who changes over time in the expected way and what is the nature of those changes?

Of the 15 middle-aged women in our sample, 10 exhibited the increase that would be predicted by Gutmann's model.[4] Obviously, the fact that 5 women did not exhibit this pattern should be underscored, especially since the increase in the need for power among middle-aged women was statistically significant. For each of the 10 women, there were interesting patterns and themes that could be followed across all waves of the study.

Six of the 10 presented a pattern of increasing concern with the launching of children. Only 2 of these 6, however, referred to *freedom* from parenting. It was sad to note that neither of these two women used this perceived freedom to realize her dream; one wanted to pursue an art career, the other to own a small gift shop. Both remained very actively involved with their children and their children's "growing pains," their grandchildren, and leisure pursuits. While these are indeed worthy endeavors, these women seem to reflect the assumption prevalent among their cohort that if ones pursues self-interests (i.e., a career), then one has to abandon family interests. The other 4 women in this group never mentioned or indicated any perception of themselves as free of mothering.

To the contrary, the other 4 women manifested increasing efforts to hold on to some measure of parental control as their children approached adulthood and took on values not shared by their parents. Most of these conversations (and the increasing need for power scores) centered around issues presented by children of the 60s: worry over their social activism, long hair, sexual behavior, and style of dress, and deep concern over drugs. While these themes may be unique to parents of this cohort, the mothers of this group clearly did not exemplify increases in the need for power on the basis of the decreasing involvement in the parent role. Indeed Peterson and Stewart (1993) have suggested that women who are high in the power motive may express this need "in the more socially defined traditional manner through the care of offspring" (p. 195).

One of the women, whom we shall call "Laura,"[5] however, pre-

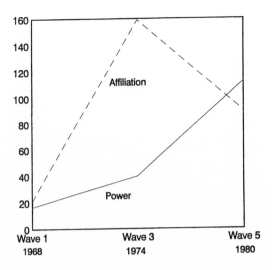

FIGURE 5.3. Laura: Power and Affiliation over Time

sented a dramatic and rather disturbing example of a concern with launching a particularly difficult child (see Fig. 5.3). In the first interview in 1969, we learn that her son "Michael" is not functioning well in school and has been referred for psychiatric help. Her efforts to deal with Michael in the first wave center around doing what is necessary to make things better, buying him books, taking note of his improvements, and having faith in his maturational process. Her power score is very low at this point. By 1975 (wave 3), Michael has been referred to the "probation department for possible incorrigibility." She expresses her worry about his future and begins to take a more active role in getting him on the right track. In the last wave (1980) we learn that Michael has been arrested for "possession [of marijuana] and contributing to the delinquency of a minor." Her emotional response was to hide, then try to figure out how to help him, then be furious, followed by trying to accept him with his limitations. She says her biggest worry is "trying to get [Michael] to become a self supporting citizen—get him to feel he is worthy." All these understandable efforts to provide help, to influence, to control and empower Michael are reflected in Laura's very high need for power at the time of the last wave of the study.

Since the crossover hypothesis would suggest that Laura might show a decreasing interest in affiliative concerns, it is interesting to note that Laura's need for affiliation increased as well (and was indeed higher

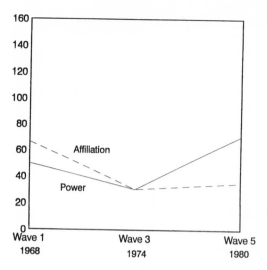

FIGURE 5.4. Sally: Power and Affiliation over Time

than her need for power until wave 5). She spoke of enjoying "activities involving interaction with people," "remain[ing] interested in people, both good and bad," "meeting new people," indicating that she "perhaps loves him [her son] more" now that she understands him, and is happy in her marriage, "realizing that her husband is a good friend." These themes in Laura's interviews were found alongside the themes of needing power and influence.

While all of the women among the ten who revealed the increase in the need for power were mothers, and all were still involved in becoming the parent of an adult, not all the interviews contained the launching of children as a central theme. Three of the women started out with low power scores that increased over time as they dealt with changing marital status; two experienced the illness and death of a spouse, and one went through the process of divorce.

"Sally," whose husband died, responded by becoming increasingly involved in political concerns (see Fig. 5.4). In 1969, at the time of the first interview, Sally speaks at length about preparation for her husband's retirement. She has thought about what it will be like (whether they will get on each other's nerves) and has observed other retired couples. At the same time we learn that her husband, Bill, has already had a heart attack, leaving them both fearful and vulnerable. We see that Sally has begun to prepare herself for life without Bill and has ideas about how she will conduct herself, even describing in some detail what kind of widow she would like to be, one that does not become a "pest to your kids."

Almost in the same breath, (and unlike the parents mentioned earlier), she expresses envy of the political activism among the youth (even though she says they have a list of complaints without offering any solutions). We learn in painful detail of the time in her youth when the "Germans invaded Czechoslovakia" and of the dismay she felt when her outrage about the newspaper headlines was met with lack of interest on the part of her friends. She expressed despair over the lack of social activism of her peers.

During the 1975 interview (wave 3), Sally makes no mention of her husband's heart condition; things seem to be fine, although the death of peers underscores confrontations with death. She also notes that her "birthday depresses her." She continues to identify herself as increasingly "politically oriented," insisting that her husband join her in watching Bill Moyers and maintaining a campaign of writing "letters to Senators and the President . . . [and] reading *The Best and the Brightest*." These themes are reflected in her increasing need for power scores. At the time of the last interview (1980), we learn that her husband had died (not of heart disease, but of cancer) some time during the last three years. Although not pursuing her previous political activities with the same energy as before Bill's death, her high power score is reflected in her rage over the insidiousness of the disease and her perception of ineptitude within the American Cancer Society. One is left with the distinct impression that she will actively pursue an activist role in supporting the search for a "cure for cancer."

Sally's need for affiliation score decreased over time as the crossover hypothesis would predict. Very high at time one of the study, her affiliative statements became fewer as her rage and disappointment with life increased in the face of deaths of her husband and a close friend. In her case, one mode (power and assertiveness) did seem to replace another (communality and affiliativeness).

Like Sally, the other two women whose husbands either were ill or died during the course of the study, worked actively to develop new lives. These were central themes in their increasing power scores. One became very involved in the care of her parents and her grown children (helping, providing, serving); the other became an outstanding travel agent who owned her own business and traveled extensively (winning awards, leading, directing).

The most compelling example of the building of a new life, however,

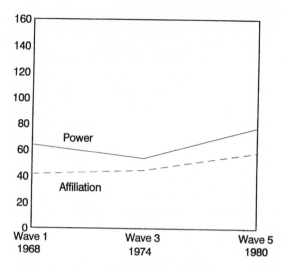

FIGURE 5.5. Marilyn: Power and Affiliation over Time

was the story of "Marilyn," who was divorced several years before her first interview in 1969 (see Fig. 5.5). We learn that after working as an assistant to the vice president of a retail jewelry company, she has been working weekends providing secretarial services for a criminal attorney. She says she gets a

> sense of self satisfaction when, under her [boss'] guidance and with her advice, someone's mind can be made a little easier over a problem that they consider overwhelming, which is really quite simple. And also, when I know that they are not going to be charged a fortune. It is sad for me to think that so many people are taken advantage of simply because of their lack of knowledge. It gives me a lot of satisfaction if I can save one of them from the clutches of a shyster. People just don't know their rights and they are taken advantage of and this is something that makes me mad.

It is not surprising then that we find that she has enrolled in law school herself in order to do things "helping other people and changing laws." "I have to make my mark," she tells the interviewer. Not interested in "fame or fortune per se," she indicates that she "would like to see people who can't afford legal advice to get it." Unlike our other examples, Marilyn already has a high need for power score at wave 1. By wave 3, she is applying to take the bar examination and looking forward to practicing law; delighted with her newfound attachment to work, she remembers an earlier time when she was contemplating suicide. By the last interview in 1980, she is a full partner in a firm and is dealing with the exigencies of power and politics within the organization. Less altruistic than when she began, she states her goal is making "a lot of money and keep[ing] it." Asked how she feels about it all, she responds, "Well, I think I have more self-confidence and inner security. I am more content with this life I am living." Her power score has increased dramatically, as her descriptions of delegating work, dealing with betrayals and "back stabbing" among partners, and handling a multitude of stressful situations permeated her last interview. This theme can also be seen in her willingness to acknowledge her aspirations for economic rewards, success, and social status. She has not given up her efforts to do good deeds on behalf of others, but she has accepted the relevance and importance of her own needs as well.

Like Laura's, Marilyn's need for affiliation increases at the same time as her need for power (even though the need for power was consistently higher than the need for affiliation). In the beginning of her new adventure, her friends express worry that she might "overdo it on the way." As she moves through her program she speaks of "closer relationships with people with whom I have a lot in common" and yearns for a "close relationship with a man." In the last wave, she refers to her pleasure in the company of the "husband of a friend," lets the interviewer know that she has a "big set of friends," and that she enjoys as one aspect of her work "the friendly encounter." Once again, themes of power and influence increase through and among affiliative themes in Marilyn's interviews.

Even though the middle-aged men of our sample did not reveal significant change over time in the predicted ways, we did find three men (among the eleven) who decreased in the need for power *and* increased in the need for affiliation. Two of these men faced rather dramatic midlife events: One became "disabled" and could no longer serve in the Navy, his lifetime career; the other lost so much money on a business endeavor that he had to drop it, regroup, and seek a new way of making a living.

The disabled seaman ("George") became an artist and described new joy in living and new pleasure in having time with and loving his wife (see Fig. 5.6). These themes dominated his interviews and increased over the 12-year-period. Similarly, the entrepreneur ("Harry")

135

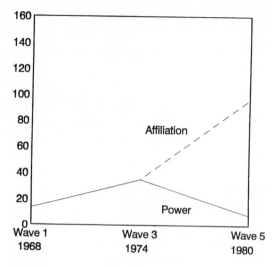

FIGURE 5.6. George: Power and Affiliation over Time

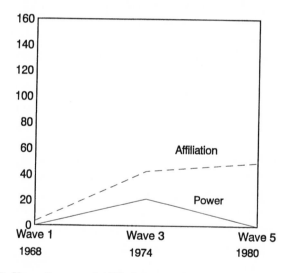

FIGURE 5.7. Harry: Power and Affiliation over Time

downscaled and found a less risky business, a "new definition of success," and new priorities that reflected better "family relations" (see Fig. 5.7). In the last interview, he speaks of "love and affection," "happy marriage," "having good friends," and "belonging to a group" as his most important goals. The third man ("Mark"), at wave 1, is looking forward to retirement at age 55 from years of service as a po-

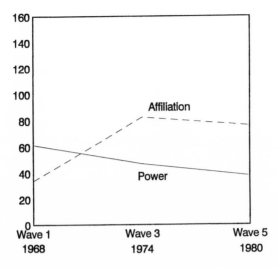

FIGURE 5.8. Mark: Power and Affiliation over Time

liceman (see Fig. 5.8). The main task, he says, is "to be a good person, spiritually, physically, mentally. To be willing to give of yourself to other people and to be open-minded—not to be jealous." By the last interview, his wife has died and he speaks of loneliness and troubled relations with relatives. He also tells the interviewer that he enjoys his family and wants to be close with them; he expresses a special concern over the maintenance of the close relationship with his father-in-law of 40 years.

Like the examples of the women's lives, the themes within the men's stories reveal change over time in the face of concrete and specific life events. There was no indication among these men that the changes occurred as a result of the lessening of the parent role.

Interwoven within all the interviews are some cohort-specific issues (the Vietnam War, the women's movement, Civil Rights activism, World War II and memories of the Great Depression), life events (divorce, illness, and death, job opportunities and losses, difficult children, even a mugging), and life stages (young adults starting lives of their own, empty nest, retirement). Disentangling these in any meaningful way appears to be a daunting task (at least with these data), but necessary nonetheless if we are to really understand the phenomenon of personality shifts at midlife.

We have suggested, with our case examples, that the personality shift is not the same experience for everyone. It is also not just a function of the end of parenting; moreover, these explorations through interview data suggest that the inconsistencies in the literature are a function of more than measurement and design (as we have suggested elsewhere; James et al., 1995). We have mentioned the lack of attention to interactive aspects of couple's lives; even less examined are the very real power and status differentials that exist between men and women. Our case studies suggest that within-sex differences are more telling than between-sex differences. They suggest that there are individual differences in the experience of the empty nest; these differences may have different effects on any changes in the nature of concerns with power and affiliation. Our cases suggest that it is more important to examine the qualities of the postparental years than the ages of children or the status of parenthood (e.g., Heidrich & Ryff, 1993). Likewise, our cases suggest that the meaning of work (more than the fact of work or the status of work) may be influential in changing concerns with power and affiliation. This has long been recognized as true of women's work (Grossman & Chester, 1990); it appears to be true for men as well. Finally, our cases suggest that the extent of political activism or level of social responsibility carried by individuals has relevance for changes in concerns with power and affiliation in middle age. This is a seldom examined but relevant source of individual differences. These are but a few new trails to travel with this question. Rather than continuing to proliferate studies of the crossover of personality characteristics, it may now be interesting to ask questions about what factors contribute to increases and decreases in the need for power and affiliation (or agentic and communal concerns), which do not, and why.

ACKNOWLEDGMENTS

Portions of this chapter are reprinted, with permission, from J. James, C. Lewkowicz, J. Libhaber, & M. Lachman (1995), Rethinking the gender identity crossover hypothesis: A test of a new model, *Sex Roles, 32*(3/4), 185–207. Ric Masten's poem "Coming and Going" is reprinted with permission. We gratefully acknowledge comments on earlier drafts by Margie Lachman, Erin Phelps, Anne Colby, Beth Paul, and two anonymous reviewers. We also appreciate support and assistance from Ana Abrantes, Rebecca Bureau, Sarah Igo, Joe Grolnic, Abigail Peck, Algernon Austin, Evelyn Liberatore, and Juliet McMains. Bill Peterson and Wendy Welsh were invaluable in producing reliable coding.

NOTES

1. Although the need for affiliation and the need for intimacy have separate coding schemes when applied to Thematic Apperception Tests (TAT), they are combined when using Winter's (1991) running text method. Thus, no distinctions between them will be made here.

2. These age groupings are identical to those used in our previous study (James et al., 1995).

3. Since nearly all the men increased in affiliation over time either at wave 1 or wave 5, we included for these case analyses only those men who both increased in affiliative concerns and decreased in the concern with power.

4. Women who increased in their concern with power from wave 1 to either wave 3 or wave 5 (or both) were selected as representatives of the changes over time found among the midlife cohort of our study; we examined changes in the need for affiliation as well. Few women actually decreased in their concern with affiliation.

5. All names and any other identifying information used to describe individual participants in the study are fictitious.

REFERENCES

Abrahams, B., Feldman, S. S., & Nash, S. C. (1978). Sex role self-concept and sex role attitudes: Enduring personality characteristics or adaptations to changing life situations? *Developmental Psychology, 14,* 393–400.

Amstey, F. H., & Whitbourne, S. K. (1981). Continuing education, identity, sex role, and psychological development in adult women. *Sex Roles, 7*(1), 49–58.

Bakan, D. (1966). *The duality of human existence.* Boston: Beacon Press.

Baruch, R. (1967). The achievement motive in women: Implications for career development. *Journal of Personality and Social Psychology, 5*(3), 260–267.

Baruch, G., Barnett, R., & Rivers, C. (1983). *Lifeprints: New patterns of love and work for today's women.* New York: Signet.

Baruch, G. K., Biener, L., & Barnett, R. C. (1987). Women and gender in research on work and family stress. *American Psychologist, 42*(2), 130–136.

Bem, S. L. (1981). *Bem Sex-Role Inventory professional manual.* Palo Alto, CA: Consulting Psychologists Press.

Betz, N. E., & Fitzgerald, L. E. (1987). *The career psychology of women.* Orlando: Academic Press.

Brown, J. K. (1992). Lives of middle-aged women. In V. Kerns & J. K. Brown (Eds.), *In her prime* (pp. 17–30). Urbana: University of Illinois Press.

Carlson, R. (1971). Where is the person in personality research? *Psychological Bulletin, 75,* 203–219.

Carlson, R. (1985). Masculine/feminine: A personological perspective. In A. J. Stewart & M. B. Lykes (Eds.), *Gender and personality* (pp. 296–311). Durham: Duke University Press.

Colby, A. (1982). The use of secondary analysis in the study of women and social change. *Journal of Social Issues, 38,* 119–123.

Constantinople, A. (1977). Masculinity-femininity: An exception to a famous dictum? *Psychological Bulletin, 80,* 389–407.

Costos, D. (1986). Sex role identity in young adults: Its parental antecedents and relation to ego development. *Journal of Personality and Social Psychology, 50*(3), 602–611.

Crosby, F. (1987). Multiple regressions and multiple roles: A note for the general reader. In F. J. Crosby (Ed.), *Spouse, parent, and worker* (pp. 39–43). New Haven: Yale University Press.

Cunningham, J. D., & Antill, J. K. (1984). Changes in masculinity and femininity across the family life cycle: A reexamination. *Developmental Psychology, 20*(6), 1135–1141.

Eichorn, D. H. (1981). *Present and past in midlife.* New York: Academic Press.

Emmons, R. A., & McAdams, D. P. (1991). Personal strivings and motive dispositions: Exploring the links. *Personality and Social Psychology Bulletin, 17*(6), 648–654.

Epstein, C. F. (1988). *Deceptive distinctions.* New Haven: Yale University Press.

Erdwins, C. J., Tyler, Z. E., & Mellinger, J. C. (1983). A comparison of sex role and related personality traits in young, middle-aged, and older women. *International Journal of Aging and Human Development, 17,* 141–152.

Feldman, S. S., Biringen, Z. C., & Nash, S. C. (1981). Fluctuations of sex-related self-attributions as a function of stage of family life cycle. *Developmental Psychology, 17*(1), 24–35.

Feree, M. M. (1990). Beyond separate spheres: Feminism and family research. *Journal of Marriage and the Family, 52,* 866–884.

Feree, M. M., & Hess, B. B. (1987). Introduction. In B. B. Hess & M. M. Feree (Eds.), *Analyzing gender: A handbook of social science research* (pp. 9–30). Newbury Park, CA: Sage Publications.

Fischer, J. L., & Narus, L. R., Jr. (1981). Sex-role development in late adolescence and adulthood. *Sex Roles, 7*(20), 97–106.

Fiske, M., & Chiriboga, D. A. (1990). *Change and continuity in adult life.* San Francisco: Jossey-Bass.

Fiske, M., Thurnher, M., & Chiriboga, D. (1968–1977). *Longitudinal Study of Transitions in Four Stages of Life, 1968–1977.* Machine-readable data files accessible at the Murray Research Center of Radcliffe College, Cambridge, MA.

Friedman, A., Tzukerman, Y., Wienberg, H., & Todd, J. (1992). The shift in power with age: Changes in perception of the power of women and men over the life cycle. *Psychology of Women Quarterly, 16,* 513–525.

Goldberg, L. R. (1992). Development of markers for the big-five factor structure. *Psychological Assessment, 4,* 26–42.

Gough, H. G. (1956). *California Psychological Inventory.* Palo Alto, CA: Consulting Psychologists Press.

Grossman, H. Y., & Chester, N. L. (Eds.) (1990). *The experience and meaning of work in women's lives.* Hillsdale, NJ: Lawrence Erlbaum Associates.

Gutmann, D. L. (1964). An exploration of ego configurations in middle and later life. In B. L. Neugarten and Associates (Eds.), *Personality in middle and later life* (pp. 114–148). New York: Atherton Press.

Gutmann, D. L. (1975). Parenthood: A key to the comparative study of the life cycle. In N. Datan & I. H. Ginsberg (Eds.), *Life span developmental psychology.* New York: Academic Press.

Gutmann, D. L. (1985). The parental imperative revisited: Towards a developmental psychology of adulthood and later life. *Contributions to Human Development, 14,* 31–60.

Gutmann, D. L. (1987). *Reclaimed powers: Toward a new psychology of men and women in later life.* New York: Basic Books.

Gutmann, D. L. (1990). Psychological development and pathology in later adulthood. In R. A. Nemiroff & C. A. Colarusso (Eds.), *New dimensions in adult development.* New York: Basic Books.

Heidrich, S. M., & Ryff, C. D. (1993). The role of social comparisons process in the psychological adaptation of elderly adults. *Journal of Gerontology, 48,* 127–136.

Heilbrun, A. B. (1976). Measurement of masculine and feminine sex role identities as independent dimensions. *Journal of Consulting and Clinical Psychology, 44,* 183–190.

Helson, R., & Moane, G. (1987). Personality change in women from college to midlife. *Journal of Personality and Social Psychology, 53*(1).

Hyde, S. J., Kranjnik, M., & Skuldt-Niederberger, K. (1991). Androgyny across the life span: A replication and longitudinal follow-up. *Developmental Psychology, 27*(3), 516–519.

James, J., & Paul, E. (1993). The value of archival data for new perspectives on personality. In D. Funder, R. Parke, C. Tomlinson-Keasey, & K. Widaman (Eds.), *Studying lives through time: Approaches to personality and development.* Washington DC: American Psychological Association.

James, J. B., Lewkowicz, C., Libhaber, J., & Lachman, M. (1995). Rethinking the gender identity crossover hypothesis: A test of a new model. *Sex Roles, 32,* 185–207.

Jenkins, S. R. (1989). Longitudinal prediction of women's careers: Psychological, behavioral, and social-structural influences. *Journal of Vocational Behavior, 34,* 204–235.

Jung, C. (1993). *Modern man in search of a soul.* New York: Harcourt Brace.

Lenney, E. (1991). Sex roles: The measurement of masculinity, femininity, and androgyny. In J. P. Robinson, P. R. Shaver, & L. S. Wrightsman (Eds.), *Measures of Personality and Social Psychological Attitudes.* New York: Academic Press.

Livson, F. B. (1983). Changing sex roles in the social environment of later life. In G. D. Rowles & R. J. Ohta (Eds.), *Aging and milieu* (pp. 131–151). New York: Academic Press.

Lott, B. (1990). Dual natures or learned behavior: The challenge to feminist psychology. In R. T. Hare-Mustin & J. Marecek (Eds.), *Making a difference: Psychology and the construction of gender*. New Haven: Yale University Press.

Lowenthal, M. F., Thurnher, M., & Chiriboga, D. (1976). *Four stages of life*. San Francisco: Jossey-Bass.

Maas, H. S. (1989). Social responsibility in middle age: Prospects and preconditions. In S. Hunter & M. Sundel (Eds.), *Midlife myths: Issues, findings, and practical Implications* (pp. 253–271). Newbury Park, CA: Sage Publications.

Malley, J. E., & Stewart, A. J. (1988). Women's work and family roles: Sources of stress and sources of strength. In S. Fisher & J. Reason (Eds.), *Handbook of life stress, cognition, and health* (pp. 175–190). New York: Wiley.

Masten, Ric. (1990). Coming and going. In *Ric Masten Speaking*. Watsonville, CA: Papier-Mache Press.

McClelland, D. C. (1965). Toward a theory of motive acquisition. *American Psychologist, 20,* 321–333.

McClelland, D. C. (1980). Motive dispositions: The merits of operant and respondent measures. *Review of Personality and Social Psychology, 1,* 10–41.

McClelland, D. C. (1981). Is personality consistent? In A. I. Rabin, J. Arnoff, & R. Zucker (Eds.), *Further explorations in personality* (pp. 86–113). New York: Wiley.

McClelland, D. C. (1985). *Human motivation*. New York: Free Press.

McClelland, D. C. (1987). Motivational trends in society. In D. C. McClelland, *Human Motivation* (pp. 415–472). Cambridge: Cambridge University Press.

McGee, J., & Wells, K. (1982). Gender typing and androgyny in later life: New directions for theory and research. *Human Development, 25,* 116–139.

Mednick, M. T. (1989). On the politics of psychological constructs: Stop the bandwagon, I want to get off. *American Psychologist, 44*(8), 1118–1123.

Mishler, E. G. (1993, June). *Missing persons: Recovering developmental stories/histories*. Paper presented at the Conference on Ethnographic Approaches to the Study of Human Development, Oakland, CA.

Morawski, J. G. (1985). The measurement of masculinity and femininity: Engendering categorical realities. In A. J. Stewart and M. Brinton Lykes (Eds.), *Gender and personality: Current perspectives on theory and research,* (pp. 108–135). Durham: Duke University Press.

Nemiroff, R. A., & Colarusso, C. A. (1990). *New dimensions in adult development*. New York: Basic Books.

Neugarten, B. L., & Gutmann, D. L. (1968). Age-sex roles and personality in middle age: A thematic apperception study. In B. L. Neugarten (Ed.), *Middle age and aging* (pp. 58–75). Chicago: University of Chicago Press.

Peterson, B. E., & Stewart, A. J. (1993). Generativity and social motives in young adults. *Journal of Personality and Social Psychology, 65*(1), 186–198.

Rossi, A. S. (1980). Life-span theories and women's lives. *Signs, 6*(1), 4–32.

Rossi, G. D., & Ohta, R. J. (1986). Sex and gender in an aging society. *Daedalus, 115*(1), 141–169.

Rowles, G. D., & Ohta, R. J. (1983). Emergent themes and new directions: Reflection on aging and milieu research. In G. D. Rowles & R. J. Ohta (Eds.), *Aging and milieu* (pp. 231–240). New York: Academic Press.

Spence, J. T., & Helmreich, R. L. (1979). Comparison of masculine and feminine personality attributes and sex-role attitudes across age groups. *Developmental Psychology, 15,* 583–584.

Stewart, A. J., & Platt, M. B. (1982). Studying women in a changing world: An introduction. *Journal of Social Issues, 38,* 1–16.

Urberg, K. A., & Labouvie-Vief, G. (1976). Conceptualizations of sex roles: A life-span developmental study. *Developmental Psychology, 12,* 15–23.

Veroff, J., Reuman, D., & Feld, S. (1984). Motives in American men and women across the adult life span. *Developmental Psychology, 20*(6), 1142–1158.

Wiggins, J. S. (1991). Agency and communion as conceptual coordinates for the understanding and measurement of interpersonal behavior. In D. Cicchetti & W. Grove (Eds.), *Thinking clearly about psychology: Essays in honor of Paul E. Francisco* (pp. 89–113). Minneapolis: University of Minnesota Press.

Winter, D. G. (1973). *The power motive.* New York: Free Press.

Winter, D. G. (1988). The power motive in women—and men. *Journal of Personality and Social Psychology, 54*(3), 510–519.

Winter, D. (1991). Measuring personality at a distance: Development of an integrated system for scoring motives in running text. In A. J. Stewart, J. Healey, & D. Ozer (Eds.), *Approaches to studying lives: Volume 3B* (pp. 59–90). In R. Hogan (Ed.), *Perspectives in personality.* London: Jessica Kingsley.

II Relations with Others

SIX

Concern with Others at Midlife: Care, Comfort, or Compromise?

Toni C. Antonucci and Hiroko Akiyama

While midlife has always been possible, the changing demographics of the industrialized world now make midlife an extended portion of the life span. To place this point in perspective, it is useful to note that the average life expectancy in the United States in 1775 was 35, whereas in 1995 it will be approximately 75 (Butler, Lewis, & Sunderland, 1991). Today we think of midlife as a period roughly between the ages of 35 and 60. Thus, midlife as we know it is a relatively new period of the life span. To be sure, one could argue that midlife existed in the 1700s as well. Then midlife might be ages 15 to 25. But the difference, both in terms of the duration of midlife and life expectancy, radically alters midlife's place in individual development. Demographic changes highlight the evolving nature of midlife. In Part 2 three chapters explore the concern with others that has been hypothesized to play a special role in the lives of midlife men and women. We consider the sociohisorical and life-span context of midlife and examine the function of social relations in successful midlife development.

Certainly, successful midlife development can be achieved through various paths. No one path will be successful for all men and women, all races, cultures, and ethnic groups. However, it is probably universally true that interpersonal relations, involvement with family, friends, and coworkers, are an important part of midlife development. Here we review what is known about relationships in midlife, with a special focus on how these relationships may vary and have different meanings for men and women. In addition to an overview of midlife as represented in the literature, we consider the changing nature of midlife, relationships, and roles.

To understand the changes in midlife development, it is necessary to consider both the macro- and microlevel context within which this development occurs. Thus, midlife development occurs within a sociohistorical as well as a life span context. In an effort to elaborate on what is already known in this area, we present findings from our work and that of others, and review these, along with the findings from chapters 7 and 8, for their contribution to the understanding of midlife development. In particular, we consider the possibility that interpersonal relations, especially concern with others, may function as a mechanism for the achievement of both midlife goals and personal development.

Sociohistorical Context

Socialization and the historical context within which that socialization occurs fundamentally influence individual development. Neugarten (1973) noted that people were influenced by their own concept of a social clock, that is, their sense of the prescribed time for specific roles and accomplishments. The social clock of young adults dictates that they should marry by a certain age and have children at a certain age. For the older adult it dictates when one should become a grandparent or retire. It is clear that socialization in midlife and to some degree the boundaries and prescriptions of the social clock at midlife have been changing over time. No cohort has experienced midlife with quite the same norms, expectations, and values to guide or interpret their experiences of midlife as the men and women of today. Nevertheless, the social clock clearly governs middle age even today. Instead of a time for certain roles, however, midlife may be better understood as the time when the social clock dictates what one should have accomplished. This appears to translate into accomplishing one's own goals but also assuring that family and friends achieve their goals. Midlife is the power period, the time when personal goals and accomplishments are being achieved. At the same time, this is also a period when these goals and accomplishments are reflected in our aspirations for others, especially our children. Of course, it is very likely that there are gender differences in what these goals are. Similarly, the way these goals should be accomplished may be viewed very differently by midlife men and women.

Differences between men and women about how they interpret similar situations have received increased attention of late. In 1972 Jessie Bernard suggested that women and men have different experiences in marriage and that marriage was a much less positive experience for women than for men. Veroff, Douvan, and Kulka (1981) provided evidence from their 1957 and 1976 cohort studies, *Americans View Their Mental Health*. They report that people seemed happier with their marriages in 1976, and that fewer people thought their marriages were average or not too happy in 1976 than in 1957. Since divorce is more common now, it might be hypothesized that many people unhappy with their marriage have already been divorced, thus increasing the percentage of middle-aged partners who report being happy in their marriage. It is also true that many more people reported having marital problems in 1976. It is especially interesting that although the latter finding is a general one across both sexes, men show this increased reporting of marital problems more than women. It may be the case that modern men are recognizing more of the internal workings of the marital relationships than they used to. A more recent longitudinal study of marriage (Johnson, Amoloza, & Booth, 1992) found that there was high stability in marital happiness. Moreover, while men were happier in their marriages than women in their early years of marriage, this sex difference disappeared in the later years of the study. Perhaps the experience of marriage is becoming more similar for men and women. Getting married is a source of satisfaction and happiness, but both men and women may now recognize that maintaining the same levels of satisfaction and happiness throughout marriage is a difficult and complicated task.

Clearly twenty or forty years ago a great deal of societal pressure came to bear on both men and women. Men were expected to have a family and to provide for family members financially. Women were expected to have a family and to provide care and nurturance to family members. Social norms and the pressure to achieve those norms were severe. Has this changed over the last generation or two? The answer seems to be yes, but not completely, and there are some important caveats that further define the situation.

Today it is clearly much more normative for women to work throughout their adult life, even after becoming a wife and mother. On the other hand, it is not less normative for men to occupy the three roles of worker, husband, and parent. It appears to be the case that men *must* work and *should* also be married and have children. Women *must* be married and have children and *should* (or is it *may*?) work. Data from different cohorts that we report below suggest that we are decidedly more tolerant of people occupying fewer roles and of their occupying any of these roles at a later age. But they are still considered major indicators of successful adult development. The biggest change appears to be that women more frequently occupy all three roles than previously, though it continues to be normative for men to occupy all three as well.

One can also gain understanding of the sociohistorical context for men and women by considering the literature that has developed over the last few decades concerning the effects of multiple roles and well-being (Baruch & Barnett, 1986; Baruch, Barnett, & Rivers, 1983; Crosby, 1987, 1993; Gore & Mangione, 1983). Historically this is perhaps best represented by the research exploring the effects of women's working on the development of their children. As middle-class women of recent years became increasingly likely to be employed, people feared that women were abandoning their children by having jobs and that a whole generation of children would be damaged because their mothers were not home to raise them. Nevertheless, some feminist researchers were radical enough to point out that poor women have been raising children for years, despite being employed. And researchers have discovered that even middle-class working women can raise their children adequately. What has always been downplayed but is nevertheless very important is that mothers' attitudes about their working situation and their guilt or pleasure at the prospect of having a job is very important for both the mother's and the child's well-being (Hoffman, 1974, 1989). Thus, as we review the literature that examines the effect of multiple roles on well-being, we must also consider both individuals' attitudes about those roles and the sociohistorical context within which they occupy them.

LIFE SPAN DEVELOPMENTAL PERSPECTIVE

As we examine the multiple paths people can take to achieve successful midlife, it becomes evident that the increasingly similar paths taken by men and women are just as important as the differences. We have learned from Kohlberg (1976) that men and women and boys and girls have different levels of moral development. We have been told that women are less likely to reach the advanced stages of moral development. But more recently we have learned from Gilligan (1982) what many had suspected all along, that different ways should be recognized as equally successful paths to development. Although not everyone agrees with Gilligan, we can at least point to this example as illustrative. Some things become more similar over time and some things more different, but under most circumstances we can benefit from recognizing that multiple ways can be useful and successful.

We seem to have learned a parallel lesson about sex role differentiation. Earlier researchers hypothesized that people were either highly feminine or highly masculine. But later research suggested that these are not two sides of one continuum but rather two separate continua. In fact, one individual can be high in both femininity and masculinity or low in both. The empirical evidence offered interesting and persuasive details about how different patterns of scoring (e.g., high femininity/low masculinity, high masculinity/low femininity) might operate. But the most interesting finding was that people who were high on both femininity and masculinity appeared to be among the best adjusted of all. This work was conducted in the 1970s (e.g., Bem, 1975). Broverman, Vogel, Broverman, Clarkson, & Rosenberg (1972) in related experimental work showed that most people, men and women, considered "masculine" traits, but not "feminine" ones, to be those of a healthy individual. More recent research conducted in the late 1980s and '90s indicates that in fact very few characteristics are now rated as masculine or feminine. With the exception of the specific words "masculine" and "feminine," all other adjectives were described as neither masculine or feminine but rather as neutral (Ballard-Reisch & Elton, 1992). Whereas Gilligan's work might be interpreted as demonstrating that different does not mean wrong or less, the work of Bem (1975), Broverman et al. (1972), and Ballard-Reisch & Elton (1992) suggests that not only can multiple paths be successful but the successful path can change and may be cohort specific. These points are critical to understanding development over the life span.

Midlife has been a neglected area of focus for developmental psychologists. But in many ways it is a prime arena for studying how individual life-span developmental experiences influence major life roles and at the same time how those roles influence human development. Child developmentalists and gerontologists may have recognized the importance of intra-individual development and a life-span perspective earlier, but their work is severely constrained by individual issues that dominate these periods of the life course. Children are enormously involved in rapid individual development; old people are coping with and struggling with functional limitations and declining health. It is only at midlife that we can really examine how intra-individual developmental experiences influence the now almost universal roles for midlife men and women of spouse, parent, child, and worker.

GENDER DIFFERENCES IN INTERPERSONAL RELATIONSHIPS

It is often assumed that we understand gender differences in interpersonal relationships (Huyck, 1990). However, closer examination suggests that things are more complicated than they look (Antonucci, 1994). Although the literature of adult development often claims that women have bigger and better social relationships than men, it is clear that bigger must be separated from better and that there are no life-span, gender, racial, or cultural universals to this claim. This point is important since it is often assumed that women evaluate their roles differently because they value different aspects of those roles. Thus, it has been argued that women like to work because they value their social contacts at work. Indeed, women themselves often said this. However, social relations became the most important aspect of work only if other aspects of work were not considered. Investigators assumed women were most interested in the social aspects of their jobs, so they asked only about those aspects of their jobs. In other studies, where women were asked about the relative importance of various aspects of work, women, like men, responded that money is an important—in fact, the most important—aspect of their work. Women do value interpersonal relationships, but they appear more similar to men than different in many aspects of role evaluation, especially when they are asked the same questions (Manis & Markus, 1978).

We still do not completely understand gender differences in interpersonal relationships. Although the common belief is that women have superior social relationships, we have now demonstrated empirically in a representative sample of community-dwelling Americans that quantitatively, girls and younger women appear to have fewer social relations than boys and younger men (Antonucci & Akiyama, 1993). This finding is not new. Maccoby and Jacklin noted in 1974 that boys have many social contacts. However, their review of the literature at the time noted that boys' contacts were of the general, even superficial type. Boys were more likely to be involved in sports than girls, and once involved in sports, were much more likely to be involved in team sports. Girls, on the other hand, were less likely to be involved in sports, and if they were, tended toward more individualized sports like gymnastics or tennis.

Similarly there were differences in the friendships patterns themselves (Maccoby & Jacklin, 1974). Girls had long talks with their friends, shared many important and intimate details of their lives, and often professed exclusivity in these relationships. Boys played games or sports with their friends, talked with them about the latest sports events, and tended to meet in groups and public playgrounds rather than in dyads or in visits to each other's homes. In the case of young girls and boys, then, it does not seem to be true that the social relationships of girls are quantitatively superior. Their qualitative superiority depends on whether we assume that it is valuable at this age (or any age) to have intimate, exclusive dyadic relationships.

Although we do not wish to discount the positive role that social relationships often play in the lives of women, we might entertain the paradox of these relationships. As girls move into adulthood, it may be that their social relationships handicap them for midlife. They have acquired numerous in-depth, close, personal, intimate relationships. It is often speculated that at midlife women have many significant relationships of this type. They are wives, mothers, daughters, and coworkers. And their roles, that is, the expectations of their behavior, in these relationships are relatively unique. In the traditional occupation of all these roles, but especially those of wife, daughter, and mother, these close and intimate relationships should be a source of pleasure and satisfaction. However, as problems develop for any of their significant others, such as husband, parents, and children, even coworkers and friends, women often report being more affected by these problems (Kessler, McLeod, & Wethington, 1985; Walker, Martin, & Jones, 1992). Women seem more likely to feel a personal responsibility to either solve the problem or share the burden of experiencing the problem than men are. The mental health repercussions of this assumption are evident in the higher rates of distress, depressive symptomatology, and other mental health problems reported for women (Eaton, Kramer, Anthony, Dryman, Shapiro, & Locke, 1989). The additional factor of more midlife women being employed outside the home may exacerbate the problem, although we explore an alternate possibility empirically in a later section of this chapter. In brief, it may be that multiple roles, especially employment outside the home, offer external benefits from which men have benefited for many years—the benefits of a more diverse multioptioned path. In fact, Stephens, Franks, and Townsend (1994) recently demonstrated that women can extract both stress and rewards from multiple roles.

As women occupy more roles, one cannot help but ask whether multiple roles will provide increased options or increased stress. With the changing times, will women's having more choices for major life roles mean that their satisfaction with marriage will increase to the level of men's? Or will men and women become more similar, because, as Johnson, Amoloza, & Booth (1992) reported, men believe they have more problems in their marriages. On the other hand, recent data indicate that multiple roles may offer additional resources, but only under specific circumstances. In social relations, interpersonal relations, social support, and marital interaction, much research indicates that women and men experience different worlds. Even couples married to each other report different experiences (Acitelli, 1992; Acitelli & Antonucci, 1994). In the following section we explore the specific relations of spouse, parent, adult child, and worker as experienced by men and women at midlife. As we examine these roles, a pattern of helping and caring for others, especially among women, becomes evident.

Convoys of Social Relations at Midlife

Some have argued that concern with others is a uniquely midlife development, since it would be impossible to invest in others without having achieved at least some level of development oneself. However, it is also clear that not all people reach the point where they are willing to be concerned with others. Also of interest, some have speculated that men and women reach and achieve this concern for others in decidedly different ways. We (Antonucci & Akiyama, 1987; Kahn and Antonucci, 1980) have suggested that people move through life surrounded by a convoy of social relations; convoy members protect and defend, aid, and socialize individuals as they move through life. Although not all relationships are long-term and significant, a sizable proportion of them are. These relationships fundamentally affect how the individual experiences the world. These relationships are assumed to be reciprocal and developmental. As the individual changes and develops through time, the nature of expectations and exchanges is also likely to change.

In previous years it has been necessary to speculate about the number and composition of men and women's close social ties throughout adulthood. Studies tended to focus on one age group or another and to vary considerably in the methodology used to assess social relations. From a study we recently completed, Social Relations and Mental Health over the Life Course, data are now available from a representative sample of people aged 8 to 93. We provide a brief overview of these not-yet-published data from midlife.

We asked people to describe their convoys of support. Consistent with the convoy concept that people structure their social relations in a hierarchical fashion, we asked respondents to report three levels of closeness. Using the hierarchical mapping technique described elsewhere (Antonucci, 1986), we first asked people to describe others who were so close and important to them that they could hardly imagine life without them. Their names were placed in the first (inner) of three concentric circles surrounding the individual. In the second (middle) circle, we asked respondents to place people that were not quite that close but were also very close and important to them. And finally in the third (outer) circle, we asked respondents to place people that were not as close as the other two groups but were important enough to be mentioned as part of their personal network.

Data are available for two groups of middle-aged men and women, those aged 35–49 and those aged 50–64. Compared with people of all other ages, these groups in general report the largest convoys. In addition there are interesting caveats concerning the size, distribution, and composition of their social relations. The younger middle-aged group, on the average, reported over eleven people in their convoys. This number includes two to three more people than are included in all other age groups. The older midlife group reports slightly fewer people in their networks, with an average of almost ten people. And as is true in other adult age groups, women report significantly more people in their convoys than men. Women aged 35–49 have a total of 11.52 people in their convoys, but men in this age group only report 10.23. Among those aged 50–64, the women have a total of 10.28 people and the men report only 9.06 people. The difference between the men and women in the 35–49 group is the largest for all adult categories from ages 20 through 94. These data support the hypothesis that there are many people with whom middle-aged men and women have close and intimate relationships and for whom they might logically feel concern. These figures also support Brody's (1981) notion that middle-aged women are "in the middle," being pulled by older and younger family members who look to them for emotional and tangible support.

Not only is the overall size of their convoys different but the placement of people in each circle (i.e., the levels of closeness they feel toward others) and the composition of their convoys is also different. Women aged 35 to 49 report an average of five people in their inner circle. This includes husband, daughter, son, mother, and sister. Men of this age report on average only four people in their inner circle. These include the same relations as those of the women (i.e., wife, son, daughter, and mother) but do not include a sister. The pattern is similar for people aged 50 to 64. Women report an average of slightly more than four people in their inner circles, while men again report about one less person. The composition of these circles changes very slightly;

mother is no longer included in the circles of men or women, and granddaughters are added to the inner circle of the women, replacing sister, who is no longer included.

If we examine middle circles at the younger group (35–49) we find very few gender differences in either the size or the composition of these circles. Younger middle-aged women and men include their brother, sister, friend, and other relatives as members of their middle circles, although the order of mention may be different. But the older age group both suggests a gender difference and reflects their older age. Older men no longer include their sister as a member of their middle-level convoy, but they now include both a son and a daughter. Brother remains, as does friend. For women, the changes are slightly different. Brother is no longer included, but son is added. Sister, friend, and other relative remain. And finally, both men and women at midlife include approximately two people in their outer circle, a friend and another relative. This is the case for both younger and older middle-aged people and is equally true for men and women. In sum, midlife men and women are surrounded by close family and friendship ties. There are slight age and gender differences in convoy membership. If we examine them closely we find that these differences are concentrated in the closest, inner-circle relationships.

We turn now to a consideration of the role relationships most often represented in these inner-circle memberships (i.e., the roles of spouse, parent, and child), and also consider one less-close relationship (that of coworker).

Midlife Roles: Spouse

Marriage is among the most central roles occupied by adult men and women. Marriage is often, though not always, entered into during young adulthood. By midlife the partners are assumed to have established the nature or rhythm of their relationship. Early research indicated that many people are less satisfied with their marriage in midlife when children are adolescents but that marital satisfaction increases again after the children leave home (Campbell, Converse, & Rodgers, 1976; Harris, Ellicott, & Holmes, 1986; Lowenthal, Thurnher, & Chiriboga, 1975). People have therefore often said that teenage children are the cause of decreased marital satisfaction.

Once again we find that data from several large national surveys indicate that men are happier with their marriage at midlife than women (Campbell et al., 1976; Veroff et al., 1981). Veroff et al. demonstrated that in both 1957 and 1976 (though to a lesser degree in 1976), it was very important to men and women to be married. But once married, women derived far less satisfaction from the marital state than did men. There was much speculation about this finding. What could account for the difference? No one had any trouble explaining why it was important to be married in 1957 and even in 1976. To a large degree, people are defined by their social roles, and being married or being a spouse was one of the most central roles for both men and women. How could the finding regarding satisfaction be explained? If women wanted so badly to be married, why did they not derive the same level of satisfaction from it that men did? Was it perhaps a cohort effect? A sign of the times? Did this finding hold only before women were liberated, that is, before they had freedom of choice? With few acceptable alternative adult roles, most women married and became parents. Did they feel a lack of choice? Is that why they derived so much less satisfaction from the role of spouse than men? Some argued that it was because they were required to derive their sense of achievement or accomplishment through others (i.e., indirectly rather than through their own direct achievements). Helson and Picano (1990) reported that traditional middle-aged women, those who married young, had children, and were full-time homemakers, were more likely to develop chronic health problems at middle age and showed greater declines in psychological well-being than women who were less traditional and worked. And Moen, Dempster-McClain, and Williams (1992), using unique panel data from 1956 and 1986, found that women who occupied multiple roles in 1956 had higher levels of health in 1986.

Our recent reanalyses of the data of Veroff et al. for two groups of young (21–39) and midlife (40–59) men and women suggest some interesting conclusions. Both men and women were more likely in 1976 than in 1957 to be tolerant of people who chose not to marry. But women were much more likely to report that marriage changed their life in negative ways, while both men and women reported that marriage restricted life in negative ways much more in 1976 than in 1957. On the other hand, both age groups of men and women were less likely ever to have felt inadequate as a spouse in 1976 than in 1957. Both men and women in the older age group were also happier in their marriages than those in the younger age group.

MIDLIFE ROLES: PARENT

At midlife most adults are the parents of adolescents or young adults. If the adults have divorced and remarried, the additional complication of blended or stepfamilies may also be present. Generally, this is a time of preparing children for adulthood and launching them into adulthood (Erikson, 1968). Parenting of adolescents has been considered a time of storm and strife, for the parents. Adolescents are struggling to become young adults. Much has been made of the potential for conflict around values, sexuality, discipline, and life goals (Alpert & Richardson, 1980). While adolescents are reaching for adulthood, their parents are trying to maintain their position of power and to influence their children's development. The generation gap is hypothesized to be strong at this time (Kidwell, Fischer, Dunham, & Baranowski, 1983; Smetana, 1988). Adolescents strive to be different from their parents, while their parents are invested in the relationship and the similarity between the two generations (Bengtson, Cutler, Mangen, & Marshall, 1985; Bengtson, Rosenthal, & Burton, 1990). On the other hand, several researchers have noted that there is, in fact, less conflict during this period than we have been led to believe (Bengtson & Troll, 1978).

Launching children into adulthood leaves the home empty. Earlier writers discussed the devastating effect of the empty nest on the psychological well-being of the parents, especially the mother (Bart, 1971), while later research suggests that the evidence is inconclusive and contradictory at best (Raup & Myers, 1989). Transitions offer special challenges to both parents and their children, but most seem successfully accomplished (Harris, Ellicott, & Holmes, 1986). Empirical evidence suggests that most parents, including women, experience their children's launching into adulthood as a successful and happy time. Parents are more likely to feel freed of the demands of parenting while at the same time enjoying their children's accomplishments (Krystal & Chiriboga, 1979; Lowenthal & Chiriboga, 1972; Troll & Bengtson, 1982). However, another cohort difference seems to be emerging. An increased number of adult children are continuing to or returning to live with their parents (Glick & Lin, 1986). Reports of the success of this arrangement, sometimes called the boomerang phenomenon, have been variable at best.

In an attempt to explore possible explanations for the contradictory evidence accumulated in the literature, we (Adelmann, Antonucci, Crohan, & Coleman, 1989) examined the data of Veroff et al. in a

unique manner, identifying empty-nest families in two different cohorts. We found little evidence for the empty-nest syndrome in 1957
and even less in 1976. However, if we look at the two cohorts, it is
quite clear that women who experienced their early adulthood during
the time of the feminine mystique were much more likely to report
lower levels of psychological well-being when their children left the
home than women who were young adults during World War II, when
young women were encouraged to enter the labor force. Our more
recent analyses of their data examining middle-aged people's view of
parenting also offers some interesting insights. Both men and women
were more likely in 1976 than in 1957 to report that their lives changed
in a negative way after they had children; women reported this to a
significantly higher degree than men in both years. Similarly, while in
1957, both men and women were not very likely to feel that their life
was restricted because they had children (scoring between 1 and 2 on
a five-point scale), both men and women, but younger women significantly more so, believed that their life was much more restricted if they
had children in 1976 (scoring consistently over 2 on the five-point
scale). Both younger (21–39) and middle-aged (40–59) adults reported
feeling the strain of parenting more. Both men and women were more
likely in 1976 than in 1957 to feel inadequate as a parent, with men
more likely to report this than women.

It appears that raising teenagers and launching them into adulthood
is an especially critical aspect of midlife in our society. While much
has been made of this as a negative time, midlife men and women
seem to take pleasure and pride in launching their children. And while
many have emphasized the conflicts of this period, others have shown
that there is much less conflict than we had previously been led to
assume. Once children are launched, parents in late midlife seem to
enjoy their children's successes and their own new freedom from the
day-to-day tasks of parenting. The tasks of parenting seemed to be
marked by concern, care, and perhaps celebration at this period of life.

MIDLIFE ROLES: ADULT CHILD

Among the roles that seem to have changed considerably for recent
cohorts is that of adult child at midlife. While their children are going
through the struggles of adolescence and early adulthood, their parents
are confronting the challenges of aging. Although from time to time
Americans have been labeled uncaring or unfeeling with respect to
older family members, in fact, most research shows that middle-aged

adults are deeply involved with and do care for their aging parents. Most old people live close to and are in frequent contact with their children (Brubaker, 1983; Shanas, 1962). Cicirelli (1983) reported that approximately 90% of all adult children have close or very close relationships with their parents. Similarly, Richards, Bengtson, and Miller (1989) reported what they called optimistic reconstruction of intergenerational relationships in their longitudinal study of families. As the younger generation moved from young adulthood to middle age, they became more positive about their relationship with their parents.

This relationship is usually not stagnant. Older people in their sixties and seventies are relatively healthy, often with some chronic but not major illnesses and very few functional limitations. Most Americans of this age live independently, relying on their children for help only in times of stress or crises (Brubaker, 1983). As their health begins to deteriorate, they often turn to their adult children for help (Moss & Moss, 1992; Suitor & Pillemer, 1988). As noted earlier, Brody (1985) referred to these midlife adult children as the women in the middle or the sandwich generation. Most data indicate that when elder relatives fail, people turn to their daughters or daughters-in-law, rather than their sons or sons-in-law, for help. Thus, a significant portion of the midlife experience of these adult children is caring for and comforting their parents through the difficult challenges of old age.

It would be inaccurate, however, to leave the impression that this support provision is unidirectional, that is, that middle-aged children are only the sources of support for their parents. There is also evidence that parents provide aid, comfort, and care for their children in midlife. This help can be instrumental when parents give financial or other tangible aid or emotional support as a middle-aged adult child copes with the problems of having a teenage child, of a divorce, or of coping with a significant health crisis (Akiyama, Antonucci, & Campbell, 1990; Giordano & Beckman, 1985; Troll, 1982).

Midlife Roles: Worker

And finally, although we have emphasized the family roles that most midlife men and women occupy, that is, the roles of spouse, parent, and adult child, the worker role is also an important aspect of the midlife experience. In the past, work was considered a primary role for men, and relatively few women were fully employed throughout their adulthood. This has certainly changed in recent years. Not only

160

are both men and women more likely to be employed at midlife but women are more and more likely to be employed throughout their adulthood, that is, are less likely to have interrupted their career for child rearing.

Researchers have explored the role of work in the life and well-being of men and women at all ages. It has always been known that work is an important source of gratification and self-actualization for men (Tamir, 1982). More recently it has been recognized that employment outside the home may be an important source of psychological well-being for women as well (Crosby, 1987, 1993). Our own analyses (Coleman, Antonucci, & Adelmann, 1987) indicate quite clearly that the employment role seems to provide women with an additional source of successful midlife experience.

As women and men move through midlife and cope with the challenges of being sandwiched in the middle, how does the work role accommodate? Although very little research has focused on this specific question, what is available indicates that women can be stressed by having to maintain this additional role. However, they often report that their worker or employment role is the one role that offers independence and a sense of competence away from the demands of the family (Crosby, 1993). As the crush of opposing demands becomes greater, some women cope by dropping the employment role and others cope by hiring people to help with the caregiving roles. Women often chose their option on the basis of finances. Women who are making enough money through their employment to hire caregiving help often do so. In other cases, women who wish to maintain the work role but cannot afford to hire help may share the caregiving with other family members or relatives. Still other women quit their job to fulfill their caregiving responsibilities (Brody, Kleban, Johnson, Hoffman, & Schoonover, 1987). Men almost never quit their jobs because of caregiving responsibilities, although some men have been known to take early retirement in order to provide care for their wives if that option was available. In sum, research suggests that the worker role is often a source of accomplishment for both men and women. However, it is interesting that even in this role, as MacDermid, Heilbrun, and Dettaan suggest in Chapter 8, women often derive satisfaction from their jobs through their concern for others when they mentor junior coworkers. We now turn to a consideration of the two empirical investigations reported in the two remaining chapters in Part 2.

Concern for Others: Two Empirical Investigations

Chapters 7 and 8 explore the role of relationships in the lives of midlife men and women. They suggest that the relationships of midlife adults centrally involve concern for others and are multifaceted in nature. Paul (Chap. 7) extends the findings presented above of the study of Social Relations and Mental Health over the Life Course. Using the data of Lowenthal et al. (1975), she finds that men and women are involved with multiple relationships at midlife. These relationships— mother, spouse, children, siblings, and extended family—directly parallel those mentioned in the Social Relations study. Her analysis further extends the implication of the Social Relations data by indicating that the general psychological well-being of women is affected by these relationships much more than that of men. Others have also shown that men and women respond to and evaluate support exchanges differently (Spreecher, 1992). These findings suggest that the concern for others that has been hypothesized to be especially present at midlife may be a predominantly female concern. Paul (Chap. 7) reminds us and demonstrates that these close and important relationships can have both positive and negative effects on mental health for both men and women. Her findings support Lepore's (1992) conclusion that multiple sources of support provide the individual with resources to buffer the effect of negative social interactions. To the extent that men and women with multiple roles have additional sources to turn to to buffer negative social interactions, these resources offer multiple paths to successful adaptation. These longitudinal studies also document the changing nature and importance of both the sources and functions of significant relationships throughout midlife. Furthermore, while recognizing similarities between men and women, they also provide solid support for the different experiences of men and women in midlife.

MacDermid, Heilbrun, and DeHaan (Chap. 8) specifically investigate the generativity of employed women in multiple roles. Their data spans fifteen years and different cohorts. Their investigations clearly support the hypothesis raised in the literature and in this chapter that having multiple roles provides greater resources. They found generativity to be role specific and to be related to satisfaction in a role much more than competence. Hence, it seems clear that women differentiate between roles and are not motivated by their own perceived ability in

162

a task or role. It is especially interesting that role specificity was greater for the 1991 sample than the 1978–1979 sample. They speculate, and we would agree, that role-specific approaches are increasingly necessary to study how women function in different roles. We interpret this as an improvement. Women separate and separately evaluate the different roles they are now increasingly likely to occupy. The distinction of these multiple roles provides multiple paths for generativity as well as for sources of satisfaction and well-being. It will be interesting to compare the parallel investigation with men. When such analyses become available, it will be possible to explore the similarities and differences in patterns of generativity among men and women at midlife.

FUTURE DIRECTIONS

As we have examined the midlife experience of men and women, we have considered existing theory and empirical evidence that this is a time marked by a concern for others. Our overview of this literature is suggestive. Studies considering the experience of being a working mother and wife in the fifties compared with occupying the same role in the seventies and nineties clearly indicates that these roles are experienced differently by the women of the two cohorts. Reflection on divorce in the fifties, seventies, and nineties yields the same conclusion. Societal changes affect the experience of these roles. Hence it is critically important to maintain a sociohistorical perspective on the experience of midlife. Similarly, we can understand the nature and experience of midlife better within a life-span developmental framework. To be a working mother who is herself the child of a working mother is a very different life-span experience than that of the midlife adult who is the first in her family to return to work to earn a little extra money after the children have left for college. The role of working mother and wife as a critical and long-term contributor to the family finances is a much more recent phenomenon. The essential importance of having two incomes to maintain a middle-class standard of living is increasingly recognized and seems to fundamentally affect how these roles are experienced by both the midlife women and their families.

As these and other changes become common, it will be interesting to examine how these multiple roles differentially affect the relationships midlife women have with their husbands, children, parents, and friends. While there is some evidence to suggest that more roles mean more stress, other data suggest that more roles provide more resources.

The empirical questions remain: Under which conditions do multiple roles affect relationships positively and under which conditions negatively?

Other more fundamental questions should also be the focus of future research. We need to clarify the ways in which women affect and are affected by social relations differently from men. With women more likely to occupy the same spouse, parent, child, and worker roles as men, it will be interesting to examine whether men's and women's social relationships become more similar over time. We have noted that at midlife, people, especially women, seem to become more concerned with others. As men and women become more similar in their roles, will women become more caring and concerned in more roles? Or will these characteristics of women's midlife social relationships be compromised? An alternative possibility, of course, is that women's relationships will come to look more like those of men. On the other hand, it is possible that certain characteristics of both role and the role occupant combine to produce caring, concerned role occupants at midlife. If this is the case, then those characteristics need to be further identified. For example, as more and more families have mothers and fathers who are employed outside the home, and as fathers play a more active parenting and adult child role, it is possible that the very nature of men's relationships with their children and parents will change. They, too, may exhibit increased signs of care and concern. Of course, the alternative possibility must also be considered: that women will have less time to care for or be concerned about others and will consequently compromise their intimate close relationships. Fortunately, the following chapters do not support this pessimistic view.

One clear limitation of our current work is that we have not considered the role of friends at midlife. We and others (Adams & Bliezsner, 1989; Crohan & Antonucci, 1989) have written of the unique role friends play in adulthood. Certainly they are likely to be a source of satisfaction and support and at midlife are less likely to be a cause for concern. Friends are likely to be a source of comfort as midlife men and women struggle with and care for their spouses, children, and parents.

As we look to the future, we must recognize that thus far our methods have been relatively limited, as have our data. Ideally future research would consistently offer longitudinal data related to these questions and would be more diverse with respect to subject populations. Little attention has been paid to race, ethnic, or cultural differences, although even the limited comparative research available suggests that there are race differences in the effects of multiple roles on the midlife experiences of men and women. Additional research must be more sensitive to this diversity.

Recognizing the limits of the data we have thus far examined, we can draw the following conclusions. It appears to be the case that men and women continue to grow and develop at midlife and that social relations are critically influential to this development. Although the evidence suggests that there are many ways in which men and women have very similar social convoys or networks, for example, they are similar in size, we need to achieve a much better understanding of how the composition and content of these relationships differs for men and women.

We need to understand these differences at a more fundamental and psychological level. We have suggested that women may have a different level of concern for others. Women seem to spend much of their midlife caring for and being concerned with others. We do not know how much this care comforts women or compromises their well-being, but it may represent a central component explaining the multiple paths that men and women take in midlife and how these paths differentially influence their optimal development.

REFERENCES

Acitelli, L. (1992). Gender differences in relationship awareness and marital satisfaction among young married couples. *Personality and Social Psychology Bulletin, 18,* 102–110.

Acitelli, L., & Antonucci, T. C. (1994). Gender differences in marital support and satisfaction in older couples. *Journal of Personality and Social Psychology.*

Adams, R. G., & Blieszner, R. (1989). *Older adult friendship: Structure and process.* Newbury Park: Sage Publications.

Adelmann, P. K., Antonucci, T. C., Crohan, S. E., & Coleman, L. M. (1989). Empty-nest, cohort, and employment in the well-being of midlife women. *Sex Roles, 20*(3/4), 173–189.

Akiyama, H., Antonucci, T. C., & Campbell, R. (1990). Exchange and reciprocity among two generations of Japanese and American women. In J. Sokolovski (Ed.), *Cultural context of aging: Worldwide perspectives* (pp. 127–138). Westport, CT: Greenwood Press.

Alpert, J., & Richardson, M. (1980). Parenting. In L. Poon (Ed.), *Aging in the 1980s: Psychological issues* (pp. 441–454). Washington, DC: American Psychological Association.

Antonucci, T. C. (1986). Social support networks: A hierarchical mapping technique. *Generations, 10*(4), 10–12.

Antonucci, T. C. (1994). A life-span view of women's social relations. In B. F. Turner & L. E. Troll (Eds.), *Women growing older* (pp. 239–269). Thousand Oaks, CA: Sage Publications.

Antonucci, T. C., & Akiyama, H. (1987). Social networks in adult life and a preliminary examination of the convoy model. *Journal of Gerontology, 42*(5), 519–527.

Antonucci, T. C., & Akiyama, H. (1993). Convoys through the life course. *Encyclopedia of Adult Development.* Phoenix: Oryx Press.

Ballard-Reisch, D., & Elton, M. (1992). Gender orientation and the Bem Sex Role Inventory: A psychological construct revisited. *Sex Roles, 27*(5/6), 291–306.

Bart, P. B. (1971). Depression in middle-aged women. In V. Gornick & B. K. Moran (Eds.), *Women in sexist society.* New York: New American Library.

Baruch, G., & Barnett, R. (1986). Role quality, multiple role involvement, and psychological well-being in midlife women. *Journal of Personality and Social Psychology, 51,* 578–585.

Baruch, G., Barnett, R., & Rivers, C. (1983). *Life-prints: New patterns of love and work for today's woman.* New York: McGraw-Hill.

Bem, S. (1975). Sex role adaptability: One consequence of psychological androgyny. *Journal of Personality and Social Psychology, 31,* 634–643.

Bengston, V., Cutler, N., Mangen, D., & Marshall, V. (1985). Generations, cohorts, and relations between age groups. In R. Binstock & E. Shanas (Eds.), *Handbook of aging and the social sciences* (2nd ed.). New York: Van Nostrand-Reinhold.

Bengtson, V., Rosenthal, C., & Burton, L. (1990). Intergenerational relations. In R. H. Binstock & L. K. George (Eds.), *Handbook of aging and the social sciences.* New York: Academic Press.

Bengtson, V., & Troll, L. (1978). Youth and their parents: Feedback and intergenerational influence in socialization. In R. Lerner & G. Spanier (Eds.), *Child influences on marital and family interaction: A life-span perspective* (pp. 215–240). New York: Academic Press.

Bernard, J. (1972). *The Future of Marriage.* New York: Bantam Books.

Brody, E. (1981). Women in the middle and family help to older people. *The Gerontologist, 21,* 471–480.

Brody, E. (1985). Parent care as a normative family stress. *The Gerontologist, 25*(1), 19–29.

Brody, E., Kleban, M., Johnson, P., Hoffman, C., & Schoonover, C. (1987). Work status and parent care: A comparison of four groups of women. *Gerontologist, 27,* 201–208.

Broverman, I., Vogel, S., Broverman, D., Clarkson, F., & Rosenberg, P. (1972). Sex role stereotypes: A current appraisal. *Journal of Social Issues, 28,* 59–78.

Brubaker, T. (1983). *The family in later life.* Beverly Hills, CA: Sage.

Butler, R. N., Lewis, M., & Sunderland, T. (1991). *Aging and mental health: Positive Psychosocial and biomedical approaches.* (4th ed.). New York: Merrill.

Campbell, A., Converse, P., & Rodgers, W. (1976). *The quality of American life.* New York: Russell Sage Foundation.

Cicirelli, V. (1983). Adult children and their elderly parents. In T. H. Brubaker (Ed.), *Family relationships in later life* (pp. 31–46). Beverly Hills, CA: Sage.

Coleman, L. M., Antonucci, T. C., & Adelmann, P. K. (1987). Role involvement, gender, and well-being. In F. Crosby (Ed.), *Spouse, parent, worker: On gender and multiple roles* (pp. 138–153). New Haven, CT: Yale University Press.

Crohan, S. E., & Antonucci, T. C. (1989). Friends as a source of social support in old age. In R. G. Adams & R. Blieszner (Eds.), *Older adult friendship: Structure and process.* Newbury Park: Sage Publications.

Crosby, F. (1987). *Spouse, parent, worker on gender and multiple roles.* New Haven, CT: Yale University Press.

Crosby, F. (1993). *Juggling: The unexpected advantages of balancing families.* New York: Free Press.

Eaton, W. W., Kramer, M., Anthony, J. C., Dryman, A., Shapiro, S., & Locke, B. Z. (1989). The incidence of specific DIS/DSM-III mental disorders: Data from the NIMH Epidemiologic Catchment Area Program. *Acta Psychiatrica Scandinavica, 79,* 163–178.

Erikson, E. H. (1968). *Identity, youth, and crisis.* New York: Norton.

Gilligan, C. (1982). *In a different voice.* Cambridge: Harvard University Press.

Giordano, J., & Beckman, K. (1985). The aged within a family context: Relationships, roles, and events. In L. L'Abate (Ed.), *Handbook of family psychology and therapy.* (Vol. 1, pp. 284–320). Homewood, IL: Dorsey.

Glick, P., & Lin, S. (1986). More adult children living with their parents: Who are they? *Journal of marriage and the family, 48,* 107–112.

Gore, S., & Mangione, T. (1983). Social roles, sex roles, and psychological distress: Additive and interactive models of sex differences. *Journal of Health and Social Behavior, 24,* 300–312.

Harris, R. L., Ellicott, A. M., & Holmes, D. S. (1986). The timing of psychosocial transitions and changes in womens' lives: An examination of women aged 45–60. *Journal of Personality and Social Psychology, 51*(2), 409–416.

Helson, R., & Picano, J. (1990). Is the traditional role bad for women? *Journal of Personality and Social Psychology, 59,* 311–320.

Hoffman, L. W. (1974). Effects on child. In L. W. Hoffman & F. I. Nye (Eds.), *Working mothers* (pp. 126–166). San Francisco: Jossey-Bass.

Hoffman, L. W. (1989). Effects of maternal employment in the two parent family. *American Psychologist, 44,* 283–292.

Huyck, M. H. (1990). Gender differences in aging. In J. E. Birren & K. Warner Schaie (Eds.), *Handbook of the Psychology of Aging* (3rd ed. pp. 124–132). San Diego: Academic Press.

Johnson, D. R., Amoloza, T. O., & Booth, A. (1992). Stability and developmental change in marital quality. *Journal of Marriage and the Family, 54*(3), 582–594.

Kahn, R. L., & Antonucci, T. C. (1980). Convoys of social support: A life-course approach. In P. B. Baltes & O. Brim (Eds.), *Life-span development and behaviors* (Vol. 3, pp. 383–405). New York: Academic Press.

Kessler, R. C., McLeod, J. D., & Wethington, E. (1985). The costs of caring: A perspective on the relationship between sex and psychological distress. In I. G. Sarason & B. R. Sarason (Eds.), *Social support: Theory, research and applications* (pp. 49–55). The Hague: Nihoff.

Kidwell, J., Fischer, J., Dunham, R., & Baranowski, M. (1983). Parents and adolescents: Push and pull of change. In H. McCubbin & C. Figley (Eds.), *Stress and the family* (Vol. 1). New York: Brunner/Mazel.

Kohlberg, L. (1976). Moral stages and moralization: The cognitive-developmental approach. In T. Lickona (Ed.), *Moral development and behavior: Theory, research, and social issues* (pp. 31–53). New York: Holt, Rinehart, & Winston.

Krystal, S., & Chiriboga, D. (1979). The empty nest process in midlife men and women. *Maturitas, 1,* 215–222.

Lepore, S. J. (1992). Social conflict, social support, and psychological distress: Evidence of cross-domain buffering effects. *Journal of Personality and Social Psychology 63*(5), 857–867.

Lowenthal, M. F., & Chiriboga, D. A. (1972). Transition to the empty nest: Crisis, challenge, or relief? *Archives of General Psychiatry, 26,* 8–14.

Lowenthal, M. F., Thurnher, M., & Chiriboga, D. (1975). *Four stages of life.* San Francisco: Jossey-Bass.

Maccoby, E. E., & Jacklin, C. N. (1974). *The psychology of sex differences.* Stanford, CA: Stanford University Press.

Manis, J. D., & Markus, H. (1978). *Career and career attitudes: age, education, and timing effects.* Paper presented at the meeting of the American Psychological Association, Toronto, Canada.

Moen, P., Dempster-McClain, D., & Williams, R. M., Jr. (1992). Successful aging: A life-course perspective on women's multiple roles and health. *American Journal of Sociology, 97*(6), 1612–1638.

Moss, M. S., & Moss, S. Z. (1992). Themes in parent-child relationships when elderly parents move nearby. *Journal of Aging Studies, 6*(3), 259–271.

Neugarten, B. L. (1973). Personality change in late life: A developmental perspective. In C. Eisdorfer & M. P. Lawton (Eds.), *The psychology of adult development and aging.* Washington, DC: American Psychological Association.

Raup, J. L., & Myers, J. E. (1989). The empty nest syndrome: Myth or reality? *Journal of Counseling and Development, 68*(2), 180–183.

Richards, L., Bengtson, V., & Miller, R. (1989). The "generation in the middle": Perceptions of changes in adults' intergenerational relationships. In K. Kreppner & R. M. Lerner (Eds.), *Family systems and life-span development.* Hillsdale, NJ: Lawrence Erlbaum Associates.

Shanas, E. (1962). *The health of older people: A social survey.* Cambridge: Cambridge University Press.

Smetana, J. G. (1988). Adolescents' and parents' conceptions of parental authority. *Child Development, 59,* 321–35.

Spreecher, S. (1992). How men and women expect to feel and behave in response to inequity in close relationships. *Social Psychology Quarterly, 55*(1), 57–69.

Stephens, M. A. P., Franks, M. M., & Townsend, A. L. (1994). Stress and rewards in women's multiple roles: The case of women in the middle. *Psychology and Aging, 9*(1), 45–52.

Suitor, J. J., & Pillemer, K. (1988). Explaining intergenerational conflict when adult children and elderly parents live together. *Journal of Marriage and the Family, 50,* 1037–1047.

Tamir, L. (1982). *Men in their forties.* New York: Springer.

Troll, L. E. (1982). *Continuations: Adult development and aging.* Monterey, CA: Brooks/Cole.

Troll, L. E., & Bengtson, V. (1982). Intergenerational relations throughout the lifespan. In J. Wolman (Ed.), *Handbook of developmental psychology.* Englewood Cliffs, NJ: Prentice-Hall.

Veroff, J., Douvan, E., & Kulka, R. (1981). *The inner American.* New York: Basic Books.

Walker, A. J., Martin, S. S. K., & Jones, L. L. (1992). The benefits and costs of caregiving and care receiving for daughters and mothers. *Journal of Gerontology, 47,* S130–139.

A Longitudinal Analysis of Midlife Interpersonal Relationships and Well-being
Elizabeth L. Paul

In the past two decades, we have witnessed intensified research on the contributions of relationships to individual development and physical and psychological well-being. This is particularly apparent in studies of infants and children (e.g., Arend, Gove, & Sroufe, 1979), and more recently in studies of older adults (e.g., Blieszner & Adams, 1992; Lee, 1985). However, the role of relationships at other points in adulthood, such as middle adulthood, has received relatively little attention (with the exception perhaps of the marital relationship). My purpose here is to explore midlife adults' multifaceted social networks and the associations between adults' experiences of relationships and individual well-being over time. Furthermore, do associations between relationships and well-being during midlife differ from the associations in late adolescence and early adulthood? Do relational correlates of midlife well-being vary over time?

The scant research on relationships in adulthood primarily concentrates on the marital relationship. Marriages have predominantly been studied from three vantage points: the communications perspective, the behavioral interactionist perspective, and the family life cycle perspective. The communications and behavioral interactionist perspectives begin with the assumption that marriage and well-being are intricately linked and aim to determine communication and interaction patterns that predict marital resiliency.

From a family life cycle perspective, marriages are most often studied in relation to the transition to parenthood and the postparental or empty nest phase of the family life cycle in which adult children are no longer living in the parental home. An often-asked research question regarding both family transitions is, what impact does the transition have on adults' relationship with their spouse? (e.g., Bozett, 1985; Bumagin & Hirn, 1982; Cassidy, 1985; Harris, Ellicott & Holmes, 1986; Krystal & Chiriboga, 1979; Mancini & Bird, 1985). The assumption has been that the parenthood and empty-nest phases of the family life cycle are typically experienced as difficult or, in the case of the postparental transition, even traumatic; however, empirical support for this hypothesis is mixed (Raup & Myers, 1989). Just as many studies have documented resultant improvement in the marital relationship after children leave home as have pointed to deterioration. Rather than determining whether the marital relationship improves or deteriorates, we should examine the importance of the marital relationship for individual well-being and the change in this salience over time. Do the associations between the experience of the marital relationship and well-being vary during adulthood? Perhaps the importance of the marital relationship waxes and wanes in terms of what it contributes to each partner's well-being. Other relationships may sometimes act as the primary contributor to well-being during adulthood.

This emphasis in adult research on a *focal* relationship (i.e., the marital relationship) has precluded attention to other salient relationships in adulthood. As a result, the simultaneous importance of other relationships (e.g., friends, children, and nuclear and extended family members) is virtually unknown; rarely are these relationships viewed as contributing to adaptation (i.e., well-being) in adulthood. This is especially surprising in light of the multiplicity of relational demands experienced by many adults (Brody, 1981; Cherlin, 1981; Hagestad, 1984; Richards, Bengtson, & Miller, 1989). Recently the gerontological literature has pointed to the importance of a variety of relationships in later adulthood, such as those with friends (Blieszner & Adams, 1992; Fiebert & Wright, 1989), siblings (Bedford, 1989; Matthews, Delaney, & Adamek, 1989), children (Clemens & Axelson, 1985; Schnaiberg & Goldenberg, 1989; Shehan, Berardo, & Berardo, 1984), and grandchildren (Bozett, 1985). For the most part, these relationships in adulthood and their associations with adult outcomes have yet to be explored.

Another common vantage point on relationships in adulthood and other phases of adulthood is their service as supports during times of transition. The supporting role of relationships has been studied in such life transitions as marriage (Milardo, 1982; Surra, 1988) parenthood (Belsky & Rovine, 1984; McCannell, 1988; Miller & Sollie, 1980; Stueve & Gerson, 1977), divorce or separation (Huston & Levinger, 1978; Rands, 1988), retirement (Blumstein & Schwartz, 1983), taking care of elderly parents (Shanas, 1979) and posthospitalization of elderly adults (Johnson, 1988). These studies typically use cross-sectional designs and rely on retrospective data, or they use short-term longitudinal designs (usually with only two waves—pre-and post-transition). As in studies of the transition to parenthood or the postparental transition, many studies of other transitions focus on changes in the marital relationship. If the role of more than one relationship is considered (e.g., familial and extrafamilial), often a structural social network approach is applied whereby the network composition (e.g., size, density) is studied, disallowing differentiation among relationships or indicators of relational affect or valence (e.g., Gottlieb, 1980). The assumption is that support is always good; thus, the larger the social network, the better. When individual relationships are assessed, the indicator most often used in the structural social network approach is degree of contact or proximity; again the assumption is the more contact or the closer the proximity, the better.

Antonucci (1989) draws attention to the importance of relational affect or valence in studying relationships as she points to a serious shortcoming in the social support literature: bias toward the positive effects of social support. She states: "social relationships are neither always positive nor always negative—it is important to approach the study of these relationships without directional bias. Whereas social relationships can have a positive effect on health and well-being, . . . the reverse is also true" (p. 309). Similarly, Hirsch (1981) argues that supportive relationships can be either limiting or expanding. Antonucci (1989) notes: "The expanding or limiting effects of social relationships are thus far understood in a very restricted sense. It remains for future research to explore the influences of individual life cycle and family stage on the expanding vs. limiting effects of social relationships" (p. 311). For this reason, in addition to structural network indicators, relational affect or other subjective indicators—differentiating between positive and negative (i.e., conflict) dimensions—are vital in the study of relationships in adulthood. As yet, the associations between structural and affective relationship indicators are not clear; however, current research on older adults' intergenerational family relationships suggests a weak (or nonexistent) association (Mangen, Bengtson, & Landry, 1988). Does this association hold for other types of relationships? For other phases of adulthood? Furthermore, associations between structural and affective relationship indicators and well-being have yet to be studied. Additionally, questions remain about the association between positive and negative affective relationship indicators. Are these separate dimensions of affective relationship quality that show different associations with midlife well-being?

Another criticism we may make of the literature on the role of social support networks during various phases of the individual and family life cycle is that we do not know how the experience of one transition compares to that of other qualitatively different transitions (Fiske & Chiriboga, 1990; Lowenthal (Fiske), Thurnher, & Chiriboga, 1975). Without such comparisons, how are we to understand variations across the life course? Fiske and her colleagues aimed to redress this issue in their longitudinal study of four life cycle transitions, yet very few longitudinal analyses were conducted, much less analyses of the role of relationships during these transitional periods.

Thus, in moving beyond these limitations in studying the associations between relationships and midlife adult well-being, five steps must be taken:

1. The role of *multiple* relationships (including with nuclear and extended family members and friends) must be explored
2. Positive and negative affective dimensions of relational experiences must be used
3. Experiences of multiple relationships must be considered in relation to adult outcomes such as well-being
4. The associations between relationships and well-being must be compared across qualitatively different periods so that we can gain a more complete picture of the experience and role of relationships in various phases of adulthood (e.g., midlife)
5. Changes over time in associations between relationships and well-being must be studied so that variation across the transition process is assessed

Secondary analysis of the Fiske, Thurnher, and Chiriboga Longitudinal Study of Transitions in Four Stages of Life (1968) allows a unique opportunity to apply these steps, particularly with regard to the experiences of relationships during various periods of life. This data set is valuable for exploring the associations between relationships and well-being over time because of the longitudinal design (five waves of data collected over a 10-year time period); the wealth of qualitative and quantitative data on relationships, individual development, and well-being; and the inclusion of individuals spanning several stages of life, ranging from late adolescence to middle adulthood.

We asked the following exploratory questions: What is the relationship between affective relational qualities and the more structural characteristic of the degree of contact in specific relationships?

The assumption is that the relationships that involve a higher frequency of contact are stronger than the relationships in which partners spend little time with each other. For instance, are sibling relationships in which siblings rarely see each other less close than relationships characterized by a higher frequency of contact? More recent work casts doubt on this strong positive association. Low to zero-order correlations between affective relational qualities and degree of contact are expected.

The emphasis in social support and personal relationships research has been on positive elements of relating. Less attention has been paid to negative experiences of relationships and their implications for individual well-being. What is the association between positive and negative affective experiences of specific relationships? It is expected that the positive relationship qualities of satisfaction and closeness will be moderately negatively associated with conflict, indicating that satisfaction/closeness and conflict reflect two different dimensions of affective relationship quality.

What are the associations between indices of individual well-being and affective relational qualities and the degree of contact? Do these associations in midlife differ from the associations in late adolescence and early adulthood? Do these associations vary across time (across different points in the transitional process)?

Most individuals are involved in a variety of familial and extrafamilial relationships at any given time. Do all interpersonal involvements contribute to well-being? Or do different subsets of relationships correlate with well-being at different phases of the life cycle? It is expected that different constellations of relationships will be significantly associated with various dimensions of well-being for each of the three phases studied. Furthermore, as Hirsch (1981) has suggested, some relationships may be negatively associated with well-being. Moreover, it is expected that these patterns of associations will vary at different points in the transition process.

Method

Participants

Data were drawn from Fiske, Thurnher, and Chiriboga's Longitudinal Study of Transitions in Four Stages of Life (1968), archived at the Henry A. Murray Research Center of Radcliffe College. Participants in this study were 107 men and 109 women, selected from an urban area and representative of middle- and lower-class socioeconomic backgrounds. Participants were contacted five times over a ten-year period (overall attrition rate was 26%). Individuals who were confronting one of four normative transitions were selected. For this secondary analysis, individuals in the first three transition groups were selected, resulting in a group of 155 men and women ranging in age from 16 to 61. This subsample was partitioned into three age groups: late adolescence (age 16 to 21), early adulthood (age 22 to 39), and middle adulthood (41 to 61). Table 7.1 lists the three age groups represented in the subsample and information on the age range at each of the three waves of data used in the present secondary analysis, cohort, and the sex composition of each age group. Individuals focused on in this study, the middle adulthood group, were approaching the empty-nest phase of the life cycle at the start of the study.

The majority of participants were White (91%). The sample also included Black, Filipino American, Chinese American, Japanese American, and Mexican American individuals (particularly in the younger age group). Participants were of low- to lower-middle socioeconomic

TABLE 7.1 Age Range, Cohort, and Sex Composition
of Each Age Grouping

	Age Range	Cohort	Males (N)	Females (N)
Late adolescence (1968)	16–21	1950–1955	25	37
Follow-up 2 (1973)	22–27		17	30
Follow-up 4 (1978–80)	28–33		23	32
Early adulthood (1968)	22–39	1929–1950	24	16
Follow-up 2 (1973)	27–44		22	14
Follow-up 4 (1978–80)	33–50		21	15
Midlife (1968)	41–61	1907–1927	27	26
Follow-up 2 (1973)	46–66		20	21
Follow-up 4 (1978–80)	52–72		14	21

status. The sexual preference of 9% of the late adolescents was homo-sexual. All other participants were heterosexual.

Measures
Affective relationship qualities

To glean information about specific relationship qualities, I developed a coding system that would be global enough to be applicable to all waves of data collection (richness of relationship data varied somewhat across waves), yet detailed enough to retain the richness of the data. Most waves of data collection included a section of open-ended interview/questionnaire questions on "Family, Social Networks, and Social Perceptions." Sometimes the same questions were repeated in successive waves; more often than not, however, questions varied somewhat from wave to wave. The most complete set of information on interpersonal relationships was gathered in wave 1. Waves 3 and 5 also contained assays of relationship involvement that were fairly consistent with those of wave 1. Because of the scanty data in waves 2 and 4, these waves were not included in this secondary analysis.

A global content analytic coding system was developed containing five qualities on which each relationship discussed could be scored (see Appendix for code definitions):

Contact: frequency of personal contact and time spent together
Satisfaction: degree of pleasure from or comfort in the relationship
Closeness: degree of emotional involvement or connectedness
Conflict: problematic differences of opinion or other interpersonal problems
Importance: significance of the relationship in one's life

To enhance the codability of the data, two coding rules were used: (1) a narrow rating scale was used (4 points, ranging from low to high for all codes except conflict, which ranged from high to low), and (2) the unit of analysis was kept broad (however, in no instance were specific statements scored for more than one category). Thus, coders used all available information from the social network section of the interview/questionnaire, and if sufficient data were not available on specific relationships mentioned, they looked through other sections of the protocol (e.g., values and goals, life evaluation, activities, etc.) for supplemental information.

Coders were instructed to first list all relationships included by respondents in their social network and then to score each relationship mentioned for as many of the five coding categories as possible. Coders were generally successful at coding all five relationship qualities for most relationships in the social network. Interrater reliability was assessed between two scorers trained on 15 protocols from a different subsample of the larger Lowenthal, Thurnher, and Chiriboga study. Percentage agreement of individuals listed as part of the social network was 99%. Pearson product moment correlations between all possible pairs of raters (6 raters in toto) on the five relationship scores for each social network member ranged from .89 to .97. This was sufficiently high reliability to enable coders to rate the remaining protocols independently.

Since any relationship mentioned by participants was coded, a broad network of possible relationships resulted. Up to four sisters, four brothers, five friends, ten children, and five extended family members were included. Few individuals, however, have social networks this large. Thus, to maximize the sample sizes across relationship types, scores for some relationships were aggregated. For instance, if more than one sibling relationship was mentioned, relationship qualities were averaged. Multiple friends, extended family members, and children were also averaged. Seven relationship categories resulted: mother, father, siblings, extended-family members, friends, spouse/ partner, and children. Thus, for each participant, 35 scores per wave resulted: five relationship quality codes for seven relationship categories. In general, midlife men and women were involved in interpersonal ties spanning the seven relationship categories. However, many of the participants experienced the death of one or both parents over the course of the study. This approach sacrificed the variance across different relationships within any aggregated relationship category. For instance, in many cases, not all sibling relationships were experienced similarly. A challenge for future research is to include this variance in analyses.

Well-being. Five indicators of well-being included by Fiske et al. in the Transitions study were used:

1. Negative Self-Concept. A 70-item adjective checklist (ACL; representing items suggested by Block, 1971) was administered at each wave of data collection. Participants were asked to rate each adjective as (1) like themselves, (2) unclear or in between, or (3) unlike themselves. The Negative Adjective Checklist Index represents the sum of the ACL

self-ratings for items drawn from a principal components analysis (items loading .30 or higher) as reflecting negative self-concept. Items include absentminded, affected, cruel, defensive, dissatisfied, dull, easily embarrassed, easily hurt, hostile, impulsive, jealous, lazy, rebellious, resentful, restless, sarcastic, self-pitying, stubborn, suspicious, touchy, tactless, undecided, unhappy, uninterested, unworthy, withdrawn, worried.

2. Affect Balance. Affect Balance is based on Bradburn Affect-Balance Scale (1969) items. The Bradburn items were coded 1 for "not experienced" to 4 for "experienced often during the past week." The positive subtotal is the sum of the codes for "on top of the world," "excited or interested," "pleased about accomplishment," and "proud." The negative subtotal is the sum of the codes for "very lonely or remote," "depressed," "bored," and "restless." To compute the affect-balance score, the negative subtotal is subtracted from the positive subtotal and a constant of 13 is added to eliminate negative numbers.

3. Symptomatology. Symptomatology was assessed via the total count of positive (yes) responses to the 42-item California Symptoms Checklist (CSC) (Lowenthal, Thurnher, Chiriboga, & Associates, 1975) designed to assess psychological symptomatology (including associated somatic symptoms). The CSC includes such items as "Do you usually get up tired and exhausted in the morning?" "Are you constantly keyed up and jittery?" and "Do you worry a lot about your health?"

4. Loneliness. Participants were asked how many times during the past week they had felt lonely. Responses were grouped into low (rarely felt lonely), moderate (sometimes felt lonely), and high (often felt lonely) groups. This index of well-being differs from the other indices in its time specificity.

5. General Morale Index (GMI). The GMI is based on the sum of responses to "dissatisfied" and "unhappy" on the ACL, the Bradburn overall happiness rating, and the rating for the present year on the life evaluation chart.

The five well-being indices were standardized and placed on a common scale so that all scores ranged from low to high well-being. The five indices of well-being were significantly intercorrelated in most cases for the three waves of data. However, correlation coefficients rarely exceeded .50 (average correlations: wave 1: .33; wave 3: .46; wave 5: .45), indicating that each index maintains some unique meaning. Thus, all five indices were used individually in all analyses.

RESULTS

Associations between Affective Relationship Qualities and Degree of Contact

The five relationship qualities (four affective qualities and degree of contact) were intercorrelated for each relationship type in waves 1, 3, and 5. (See Table 7.2 for a summary of these results.) Satisfaction and closeness were significantly positively correlated (at a high magnitude) in all cases. Conflict was significantly negatively correlated with satisfaction and closeness in most cases. In many cases, importance was significantly positively correlated with satisfaction and closeness and negatively correlated with conflict; the magnitude of correlations with importance was lower than the magnitude of those between conflict, closeness, and satisfaction. In many correlation matrices contact was *not* significantly correlated with the other relationship qualities; when significant, correlation coefficients were of a lesser magnitude than those between satisfaction, closeness, and conflict.

Associations between Well-being and Relationship Indicators

On the basis of the pattern of intercorrelations among relationship qualities, three summary relationship indicators were derived for each relationship in an effort to streamline further analyses. Two aggregated affective relationship quality scores were generated for each relationship: positive (satisfaction/closeness) and negative (conflict) affective relationship quality. Because of the relatively weak associations be-

TABLE 7.2 Intercorrelations of Affective Relationship Qualities and Degree of Contact across Waves 1, 3, and 5

	Mean r	Range		Significance
Closeness/satisfaction	.72	.44 to	.85	all $p < .001$
Closeness/importance	.65	.45 to	.81	all $p < .001$
Satisfaction/importance	.60	.40 to	.75	all $p < .001$
Conflict/satisfaction	−.48	−.70 to	−.35	all $p < .01$
Conflict/importance	−.32	−.60 to	−.19	9 out of 21 $p < .01$
Conflict/closeness	−.40	−.69 to	−.27	all $p < .01$
Contact/satisfaction	.24	−.13 to	.64	6 out of 21 $p < .05$
Contact/closeness	.23	−.14 to	.58	6 out of 21 $p < .05$
Contact/conflict	−.04	−.39 to	.27	1 out of 21 $p < .05$
Contact/importance	.28	.04 to	.48	7 out of 21 $p < .05$

tween importance and the other affective relationship qualities, importance was treated as related to but nonredundant with satisfaction, closeness, and conflict. Hence the positive and negative affective relationship quality indicators were weighted by importance (e.g., the more important a relationship, the more magnified the experience of conflict). This approach is in keeping with Schuster, Kessler, and Aseltine's (1990) finding that close social ties have a stronger emotional impact than more distant social ties. Thus, positive affective relationship quality was determined using the following formula: (*Satisfaction* + *Closeness*) × *Importance;* negative affective relationship quality was measured as *Conflict* × *Importance.* Given the common lack of significant associations between contact and the affective relationship qualities, contact was treated as a separate relationship indicator in the following analyses.

Table 7.3 displays descriptive statistics for standardized positive and negative affective relationship quality and contact scores for each of the seven categories of relationships.

As indicated in Table 7.3, midlife males and females generally expressed moderate to high positive affect and low negative affect regarding their various relationships across all three waves (although variances indicate a great deal of variability among participants in their relationship experiences). Midlife males had less positive relationships with children in wave 1, with their mothers in waves 3 and 5, and with their spouse/partner in wave 5. Moderate conflict was experienced by midlife men in their spouse/partner relationship in wave 1, with siblings and children in waves 3 and 5, and with friends in wave 5. In contrast, midlife women expressed less positive affect regarding their spouse/partner relationship in wave 1 and with siblings in wave 3. Midlife women expressed moderate negative affect regarding their relationships with children in all three waves.

The degree of contact midlife adults had (in aggregate) with their various network members was more varied. Midlife males were in frequent contact with their fathers and spouses/partners in wave 1; with their mothers, friends, spouses/partners, and children in wave 3; and with their mothers and children in wave 5. Midlife women were in frequent contact with friends and spouse/partner in all three waves; additionally, midlife women frequently interacted with children in wave 3.

Table 7.4 displays descriptive statistics on standardized scores for the five indices of well-being. As indicated in Table 7.4, midlife adults

TABLE 7.3 Descriptive Statistics for Midlife Adults' Positive and Negative Affective Relationship Quality and Degree of Contact

	MO	FA	SIB	EXT	FR	SP	CH
Wave 1							
Males							
Positive	.08(.98)	.63(1.0)	.37(1.2)	.27(1.06)	.16(.97)	.30(.93)	−.11(.8)
Negative	−.34(1.03)	−.19(.52)	−.13(1.19)	−.56(.59)	−.02(1.4)	.07(1.25)	−.12(.83)
Contact	−.17(1.18)	.18(1.2)	−.27(1.01)	−.06(1.21)	−.05(1.1)	.20(.49)	−.05(1.1)
Females							
Positive	.32(1.06)	.26(1.39)	.12(.77)	.37(1.0)	.51(1.09)	−.13(1.02)	.10(1.19)
Negative	−.50(.50)	−.64(.83)	−.07(.75)	−.61(.35)	−.21(.63)	−.11(.81)	.10(1.15)
Contact	−.41(1.10)	−.51(.81)	−.83(.74)	−.26(.92)	.13(.93)	.26(.38)	.02(.91)
Wave 3							
Males							
Positive	−.30(.80)	<5	.48(1.01)	<5	.31(.91)	.46(.71)	.08(.68)
Negative	−.24(1.36)	<5	.14(1.25)	<5	−.15(.65)	−.12(.96)	.17(.74)
Contact	.12(1.23)	<5	−.20(.95)	<5	.25(1.06)	.29(.80)	.46(.91)

Females							
Positive	.32(.80)	<5	−.19(1.05)	<5	.55(.99)	.23(.81)	.39(1.37)
Negative	−.22(.60)	<5	.01(.94)	<5	−.25(.58)	−.43(.86)	.35(1.17)
Contact	−.12(1.13)	<5	−.75(.81)	<5	.10(.98)	.53(.01)	.34(.84)
Wave 5							
Males							
Positive	−.13(.95)	<5	.62(.89)	<5	.39(1.16)	−.20(.93)	.10(.56)
Negative	−.68(1.06)	<5	.06(1.26)	<5	.28(1.59)	−.44(.91)	.06(.66)
Contact	.64(1.23)	<5	−.07(1.03)	<5	−.11(1.21)	−.02(1.03)	.33(.85)
Females							
Positive	.58(1.18)	<5	−.02(1.05)	.63(.68)	.36(.93)	.21(1.14)	.32(1.41)
Negative	−.14(.81)	<5	.01(1.06)	−.33(.58)	−.16(.71)	−.58(.71)	.20(1.34)
Contact	.04(1.15)	<5	−.54(1.04)	−.05(1.21)	.14(1.04)	.36(.41)	−.07(.96)

Note: Means for each relationship indicator are followed by standard deviations in parentheses.

MO = Mother.
FA = Father.
SIB = Siblings.
EXT = Extended family.
FR = Friends.
SP = Spouse/partner.
CH = Children.

TABLE 7.4 Indices of Midlife Well-Being by Sex and Wave

	Negative Self-Concept	Affect Balance	Loneliness	Symptoms	Morale
Wave 1					
Males	.40(1.28)	.02(.85)	.54(.58)	.43(.82)	.11(1.02)
Females	.14(.77)	.12(1.15)	.25(.87)	−.21(1.20)	−.20(.95)
Wave 3					
Males	.37(1.03)	−.09(.96)	.40(.54)	.41(.75)	−.02(1.15)
Females	.22(.82)	.06(.88)	.24(.93)	−.21(1.05)	.07(.96)
Wave 5					
Males	.34(.99)	−.29(.91)	.32(.83)	.38(.65)	.36(.88)
Females	.13(.79)	.05(.92)	.52(.52)	−.27(1.08)	−.17(1.07)

Note: Means for each relationship indicator are followed by standard deviations in parentheses.

generally showed a favorable self-concept and few feelings of loneliness. Midlife females showed favorable affect balance (especially in wave 1), whereas midlife males had a more troubled affect balance (especially in wave 5). Midlife males generally had high morale (especially in waves 1 and 5), whereas midlife females had low morale in waves 1 and 5. Finally, midlife women experienced high degrees of symptomatology across all waves; midlife men consistently reported low degrees of symptomatology.

Given the significance of sex of participant in previous analyses of the Fiske et al. data, we broke down the following analyses by sex in addition to age groupings. This six-cell breakdown resulted in adequate cell sizes for most relationship categories, with the occasional exception of extended family members and children. The low frequencies of extended family members in waves 3 and 5 was likely an artifact of cross-wave interview discrepancies. However, the insufficient cell frequencies for children in the late-adolescent and early-adulthood wave 1 and 3 data were due to family life cycle differences among the age groups. In the cells in which the frequency of respondents fell below five, the variable was dropped from the analyses.

Though the cell sizes were satisfactory for some statistical procedures, the use of other statistical approaches was limited. For instance, while conceptually appropriate, hierarchical linear modeling necessitates far larger cell sizes than are present in this data set. Even multiple regression approaches are of limited use, because it is necessary to eliminate missing variables casewise rather than listwise. This is antithetical to my position that individuals' social networks naturally differ in structure. For instance, just because a respondent has no siblings does not mean that overall this case lacks meaning.

Because of these statistical limitations, we relied primarily on Pearson product-moment correlations in assessing associations between relationship qualities and well-being. Relationship quality and contact for the seven relationship categories were correlated with the five indices of well-being within the six age-by-sex groups in waves 1, 3, and 5. Fisher's z transformation was used to compare correlation coefficients: (1) Associations of midlife men were compared with the same associations for midlife women; (2) correlations for midlife men and women were compared with comparable correlations of men and women in the two other age groups; (3) correlations for the midlife group were compared across the three waves of data collection. Statistically significant correlations and differences between correlations at the .05 probability level and below are reported; trends ($p < .10$) will not be reported.

Table 7.5 displays statistically significant correlations between relationship qualities and well-being by wave for midlife men and women, indicating the ways in which midlife men and women differed from each other, the ways in which these correlations differed from parallel associations in the two younger groups, and cross-time differences. We will describe significant findings for the midlife adults here, with special attention to ways in which they differ from the other age groups.

Midlife men. In wave 1, the positive affective quality of relationships with mother and extended family members was positively related to well-being. More specifically, midlife males' general morale was linked to their positive relationship experiences with mother and extended family members (more than for late adolescents); positive relations with the mother were also associated with midlife males' loneliness in the past week. Likewise, negative affective relationship quality with the mother was negatively associated with affect balance. Contact with siblings was linked with less symptomatology (significantly more than for midlife females and late adolescents).

In wave 3 (5–6 years later), the only relational correlates of well-being for midlife men concerned their sibling relationships. Midlife males' positive affect regarding siblings was linked with fewer feelings of loneliness and with higher general morale. The association with gen-

TABLE 7.5 Relationship Qualities and Well-being at Midlife

	Negative Self-Concept	Affect Balance	Loneliness	Symptoms	Morale
Wave 1					
Males			MO(+).43*	SIB(CT)-64***a	EXT(+).66***a MO(+).42*
Females	SIB(+)67*5 MO(−)−.60*a	MO(−)−.51* SP(+).44*	FR(−).−48**	SIB(−)−.68*	
Wave 3					
Males			SIB(+).55*5	MO(−)−.72*a	SIB(+).62*ae
Females	CH(−)−.45*			FR(+).51*	FR(+).45* SP(+).78***a

Wave 5

Males

MO(+).94**ae1
FR(−).−79***a1,3

SIB(+)−.75*1,3

FR(+).66*1

Females

SIB(−)−.69*a

EXT(+).90***e1
EXT(CT).80*1

MO(CT).97*a1,3

SIB(−).−76**a
SIB(CT)−.51*a

SP(+).68**
SP(CT).51*

EXT(+).82*

SP(+).72***a

Note: MO = mother; FA = father; SIB = Siblings; EXT = Extended family; FR = Friend; SP = Significant other; CH = Children.
Relationship indicator in parentheses following relationship category notation: (+) = Positive affective relationship quality; (−) = Negative affective relationship quality; (CT) = Contact.
Italics indicate a statistically significant sex difference (i.e., between midlife men and women).
Lower case letters following correlation coefficients indicate significant differences between the correlation coefficient and comparable correlation coefficients for the other age groups (comparisons were matched on sex, i.e., midlife men were compared with late adolescent and early adult men).
Roman text letters indicate significant differences at the p < .05 level or better. a = Late adolescence; e = Early adulthood. Numbers following correlation coefficients indicate significant differences between the correlation coefficient and comparable correlation coefficients for midlife adults at other waves of data collection: 1 = Wave 1; 3 = Wave 3; 5 = Wave 5; *p < .05; **p < .01; ***p < .001

eral morale was significantly different from that in the two other age groups. The linkage between positive affect in sibling relationships and less frequent feelings of loneliness was significantly different from the comparable linkage in wave 5.

In wave 5 (5–6 years after wave 3), a striking contrast with wave 3 findings emerged. Midlife males' positive affect regarding siblings was highly related to loneliness (thus, the more positive the affect, the more frequent were feelings of loneliness in the past week). This association differed significantly from the comparable association in waves 1 and 3. The positive affective quality of relations with mother and friends were significantly positively associated with well-being in wave 5. More specifically, positive affect regarding the mother was associated with a more positive self-concept. This linkage was in contrast with the comparable linkage for the other two age groups and for midlife men in wave 1. Midlife males' positive affect toward friends was linked with less symptomatology (significantly more than for wave 5 midlife females and for midlife males in wave 1). In addition, negative affect regarding friends was negatively linked with self-concept, more than for wave 5 midlife females and for the midlife males in the other two waves.

Midlife women. A more complex pattern of correlates emerged for midlife women, especially in wave 5. In wave 1, a variety of relational correlates of well-being emerged. Positive affective quality of midlife women's relationships with siblings was associated with a favorable self-concept (more than for midlife men at this time and for midlife women in wave 5). Additionally, positive affect regarding their spouse/partner was associated with a healthier affect balance for midlife women. Less conflict (low negative affect) in sibling relationships, friendships, and relations with the mother was associated with less symptomatology, fewer feelings of loneliness, and a more positive self-concept. The linkage between friendship and well-being for midlife women significantly differed from the association for midlife men. In addition, the association between midlife women's relation with the mother and self-concept significantly differed from the comparable correlation for late adolescent women.

In wave 3, relations with mother, friends, and spouse/partner again emerged as correlates of well-being. In addition, relationships with children also showed a significant linkage with well-being. More specifically, positive affect toward friends was associated with fewer symptoms and higher general morale. Positive affect regarding midlife women's spouse/partner was also linked with a more positive general morale, more than for midlife men and late adolescent women. As negative affect regarding the mother decreased, midlife women's symptomatology decreased (more than for late adolescent females). Similarly, the less negative affect toward their children, the more positive was midlife women's self-concept.

The most complex pattern of relational correlates of well-being for midlife women was found in wave 5. A wide array of relationships showed linkages with well-being. Greater negative affect regarding siblings was linked (more than for late adolescent women) with a more negative self-concept and with more symptomatology. The linkage with symptomatology also significantly differed from the comparable linkage for midlife men. Contact with siblings at midlife (more than for late adolescents) was also associated with symptomatology (the more contact, the less symptomatology reported).

Positive affect toward extended family members (most often grandchildren for the seven midlife women who discussed extended family members) was significantly positively linked with affect balance (more than for early adults and for wave 1 midlife women) and general morale. Additionally, contact with extended family members was also linked with affect balance (more than for wave 1 midlife women).

Contact with the mother was strongly *negatively* associated with loneliness for midlife women. Thus, the more frequent their contact with the mother, the lonelier they felt. Finally, midlife women's positive affect toward their spouse/partner was associated with a more favorable general morale (more than for late adolescents) and with a healthier affect balance. Contact with spouse/partner was also linked with a healthier affect balance.

DISCUSSION

My aim was to explore the interpersonal worlds of midlife adults and the implications of these connections for individual well-being. More specifically, I used a multiple relationships approach, wherein I explored the well-being correlates of the *variety* of relationships comprising midlife adults' social networks. I assessed as indicators of relationship experiences, positive and negative affective quality as well as the degree of contact within seven different categories of familial and extrafamilial relationships. While caution needs to be exercised so as not to overinterpret the specific findings of this secondary analysis given the less than desirable cell sizes, evidence exists to support further efforts in the directions I have advocated.

The first set of exploratory questions I posed were aimed at clarifying the distinctions between various dimensions of relationship experiences. The findings support recent assertions about the distinction between the quality and the interaction patterns (e.g., contact) of interpersonal relationships (Beckman, 1981; Conner, Powers, & Bultena, 1979; Mancini, 1980; Mancini & Blieszner, 1989; Mangen, Bengtson, and Landry, 1988; Tracy & Whittaker, 1990) and argues for their retention as distinct contributors to the understanding of the experience of interpersonal relationships.

I made a further distinction between positive and negative affective relationship indicators, consistent with findings of Schuster, Kessler, and Aseltine (1990) and Abbey, Abramis, and Caplan (1985), who found moderate inverse correlations between positivity and negativity in specific relationships. Because less than half of the variance of positivity is explained by negativity (in most cases), such findings support recent assertions of the importance of treating positive and negative affective relationship quality as separate indicators in the study of personal relationships (Cramer, Riley, & Kiger, 1991; Grisset & Norvell, 1992).

The distinctions supported in this chapter between affective and structural indicators of relationships and between positive and negative affective relationship quality reflect a trend in the personal relationships and social support literatures of developing more multiplex conceptualizations and operationalizations of interpersonal processes (Clark & Reis, 1988). My efforts to move in this direction in this secondary analysis were restricted by limited availability of data; however, even global distinctions between positive and negative affective quality and contact resulted in a more detailed understanding of interpersonal relationship experiences at midlife.

The second set of exploratory questions focused on linkages between the three different dimensions of relationship experiences (positive and negative affective relationship quality and contact) in different relational contexts and midlife well-being. My analyses revealed complex patterns of relational correlates of midlife well-being. I tried to diversify conceptions of midlife adults' relational worlds (by considering various dimensions and contexts of their multiple relationship experiences) as well as their well-being. Midlife well-being was operationalized in a variety of ways so as to reflect the multifariousness of such a construct. Thus, the five well-being indices used represent various dimensions of well-being, including cognitive (negative self-concept), emotional (affect balance, general morale), social (loneliness), and psychological health (symptomatology) dimensions. The use of multiple indices of well-being follows the suggestion of Baruch (1984) to attend to the complexity of well-being, especially for adults. Indeed, as I will discuss below, each well-being index showed a different pattern of relational correlates.

The resultant patterns of correlations support not only the use of diverse indicators of well-being but also the assessment of midlife adults' *multiple* relationships that comprise their complex social networks. I will discuss these results in three parts, each relating to the suggestions for furthering our knowledge of associations between interpersonal relationships and midlife well-being.

First we consider affective dimensions and structural properties of *multiple* relationships in relation to midlife well-being. The predominant focus in the literature on midlife adults is the marital relationship. The marital relationship is presumed to be the focal point of midlife adults' relational worlds and is often considered alone as the relational predictor of well-being. The salience of other interpersonal relationships for midlife well-being has not been as closely considered.

If I had viewed the connections between the relational dimension of midlife experience and psychological well-being solely through studying the marital relationship, I would have found a slim pattern of associations. Midlife adults' relational lives (as represented by the marital relationship) would be seen to be most important for their affective well-being (as reflected by affect balance and general morale), but only for women. More specifically, the positive affective quality of midlife women's relationship with their husband/partner showed a fairly stable association with affect balance and general morale over time. Additionally, ten years after they launched their last child, more frequent interaction of a woman with her husband was associated with a healthier affect balance. *No* marital relational correlates of well-being were found for midlife males throughout the ten-year period.

We might conclude from this focal analysis of a single relationship predictor that relational correlates of midlife well-being were meaningful only for women's healthy affect balance and their general level of morale. Such a finding is generally consistent with some research on relational correlates of postparental well-being (White & Edwards, 1990) and contentions that women are more "relational" than men and that their psychological health is more strongly affected by their interpersonal connections (Henderson, Byrne, Duncan-Jones, Scott, & Adcock, 1980; Schuster et al., 1990).

We gain a different picture, however, when we consider the *multiple* relationships that make up midlife adults' relational worlds. In this study, I assessed seven categories of relationships in which midlife adults are involved, including relationships with mother, father, siblings, extended family, spouse/partner, friends, and children. Most individuals were involved concurrently in relationships fitting five or more of these categories. I assert not only that individuals' multiple relationships are complex and varied in the ways in which they are experienced but also that such relationship experiences have differing implications for well-being and other adult outcomes. Some relationships might bode well for psychological health, whereas others might diminish well-being (e.g., Antonucci, 1989; Hirsch, 1981). It is important to consider the pattern of positive and negative correlations in better understanding associations between relational involvement and well-being.

Each of the five dimensions of well-being had significant relational correlates, albeit each was associated with different relationship experiences. This is most evident in midlife women 10 years into the launching phase (wave 5). Four different relationship categories emerged as important for their well-being (siblings, mother, spouse/partner, and extended family). Some relationships seemed to provide two different psychological resources. There was also some overlap in relationships that provided psychological resources. For example, positive extended family (in this case grandchildren) *and* spouse/partner relations were linked with midlife women's affect balance as well as their general morale. The importance of grandchildren to midlife adults' well-being is just beginning to be addressed (Thomas, 1990).

However, siblings and mother played unique roles for midlife women. Conflict with siblings was associated with a more negative self-concept and with more symptomatology. More frequent contact with siblings, however, was linked with less symptomatology. Perhaps some of the conflict experienced in sibling relationships at midlife centers on mismatched needs for sibling companionship, such that less relational stress for the more invested partner is incurred when contact is more frequent. In contrast, more frequent contact with the mother was associated with more frequent recent feelings of loneliness for midlife women. Of course, the causal direction of such a finding is in question—perhaps midlife women who experience loneliness seek the company of their mothers to fill this void.

This pattern of correlates of well-being suggests that multiple relationships may be necessary for meeting our various psychological needs. Some interpersonal relationships may be quite specialized in the psychological needs they meet, as Weiss has suggested (1969, 1974, 1976), whereas others may be interchangeable in the psychological resources they provide (Simons, 1984; Weiss, 1974, 1986).

These findings also show the significance of both positive and negative relationship experiences. In many instances, negative affect (conflict) appears to be diminishing some element of well-being, while positive affect seems to be concurrently bolstering some aspect of well-being. Sometimes negative and positive affect in the same relationship show this juxtaposition. At other times, negative affect in one relationship is coincident with positive affect in another relationship. Some studies have suggested that negative relationship experiences may have an impact on well-being that outbalances positive experiences (Fiore, Becker, & Coppel, 1983; Henderson, Byrne, Duncan-Jones, Scott, & Adcock, 1980; Pagel, Erdly, & Becker, 1987; Rook, 1984; Ruehlman & Wolchik, 1988; Schuster, Kessler, & Aseltine, 1990; Stephens, Kinney, Ritchie, & Norris, 1987). Another possibility is that cross-domain buffering occurs (Lepore, 1992) whereby positive experiences in one interpersonal domain reduce psychological distress in another domain. For example, midlife males' self-concept in wave 5 seemed to be bolstered by positive affective relations with the mother but diminished by negative affective relations with friends. It is possible that the more positive relations with the mother were buffering the negative effects of conflict experienced in their friendships.

After reviewing the literature on the cross-domain buffering effect, Lepore (1992) concluded that the studies "suggest that individuals who have diverse social support resources might be more resilient in the face of negative social interactions than individuals who must rely on few social support resources" (p. 859). My study adds suggestive evidence to this assertion, though further analyses are necessary at the network level to lend greater support.

If we take a multiple relationships approach to gaining understanding of the relational correlates of midlife well-being, we also see that the psychological health of men as well as women is associated with their relationship experiences. Across the three waves, various dimensions of midlife men's well-being were associated with the qualities of relationships with siblings, extended family, mother, and friends. In terms of the sheer number of significant relational correlates of well-being, men appear to have fewer relationship/well-being connections than midlife women (especially five to six years into the launching phase). But it is noteworthy that while different patterns of relational correlates of well-being emerged for midlife men and women, the magnitude of most of the relational correlates did not differ between men and women.

The few relational correlates of well-being that did differ between men and women suggest that men and women sometimes draw different psychological benefits (and sometimes decrements) from various relationships. For example, in wave 1, midlife males' contact with their siblings was associated with less reported symptomatology than for midlife females. On the other hand, if midlife females had positive affective sibling relationships, this was associated with a more positive self-concept than was the case for midlife males. Thus, while sibling relationships appear to be important for both men's and women's well-being, their specific psychological resources appear to differ for men and women. This finding supports recent research calling attention to the significance of sibling relationships in adulthood (Bedford, 1989; Carstensen, 1992; Cicirelli, 1989; Depner & Ingersoll-Dayton, 1988; Simons, 1984) and suggests that researchers consider the specific resources served by siblings for midlife men and women.

Other interesting sex differences occurred for spouse/partner, mother, and friendship correlates of well-being. For instance, ten years into the launching phase, midlife women's contact with the mother was more strongly associated with less loneliness as compared with that of men. This might reflect the higher likelihood that midlife women will become the caretakers of their aging parents (Brody, 1981). Although the caretaking role often creates a great deal of stress (Stephens, Norris, Kinney, & Ritchie, 1988), Moss and Moss (1992) as well as Walker and Thompson (1983) assert that parent-adult child relations often remain close and vital, especially for women.

We may differentiate relational worlds at midlife from those of earlier periods of adulthood. Adulthood spans a lengthy period of time and encompasses numerous life transitions. It is important to differentiate among various phases of adulthood so as to gain a richer understanding of individuals' changing life experiences. Comparisons of midlife adults' associations between their relationship experiences and their well-being and the experiences of the two groups of younger adults yielded some interesting contrasts.

Few distinctions emerged between midlife and earlier adulthood. In most relational contexts of well-being, there was continuity between earlier and middle adulthood. Exceptions were the positive impact of males' relationships with siblings and the mother and females' relationships with extended family members. Midlife males' positive affect toward siblings was more strongly associated with positive general morale five to six years into the launching phase than that of early adults. Midlife men's positive affective relationship with the mother in wave 5 was more strongly associated with positive self-concept than that of early adult men. This may in part be due to the experience of the death of their fathers some of the midlife men had between waves 1 and 5. Perhaps this drew them closer to their mothers, which in turn helped them to maintain a positive self-concept (e.g., Douglas, 1990–91). Midlife women's positive affect toward extended family relations was more strongly associated with a healthy affect balance in wave 5 as compared with that of early adult women. This probably reflects these midlife women's transition to grandparenthood, an experience making midlife extended family relations different from early adults' extended family ties (Thomas, 1990).

Not surprisingly, more contrasts were found between late adolescent and midlife relational correlates of well-being. The connections of the well-being of midlife males and females with their relationships with mother, siblings, and partner/spouse were frequently different from those of late adolescents. The age-group differences for family of origin relationships provide support for the continuance of these relationships as important interpersonal ties in the lives of adults and may reflect the developmental shift from the emphasis on separation often characteristic of late adolescents' family relationships to the more individuated connected relationships often characteristic of adults' family relationships (White, Speisman, & Costos, 1987). This is not to say, of course, that family relationships are devoid of conflict at this age; in fact, the combination of both positive and negative correlates of relationships with well-being found in this study suggest that family relationships might both contribute to and detract from midlife adults' well-being differently from those of late adolescents. Further research is necessary on adults' relationships with their family of origin to better understand the unique psychological resources these families provide.

We may explore changes in associations between relationships and well-being over the transition process. Few studies of the launching phase and the empty-nest transition have explored the impact of this change on people's multiple relational involvements. Moreover, few studies have followed individuals into the extended launching phase to determine longer-term outcomes. This is especially important in light of recent attention to young adults *returning* to the nest, thus prolonging the launching phase and making it more complex.

The differing associations between relationship experiences and well-being found over time in this study point to the fluidity of relationships over time. The way certain relationships provided specific psychological functions varied over time. Midlife adults seem to be flexible in drawing necessary psychological supports and benefits from their various relationships. This finding is in agreement with others' assertions that some relationships are interchangeable in the psychological needs they fulfill (Simons, 1984; Weiss, 1974, 1986), especially when viewed over time. More idiographic level analyses in future research would help us to better understand the waxing and waning over time of the functions served by midlife adults' close relationships.

Although different patterns of well-being correlates emerged for midlife men and women in all three waves, wave 5 seemed to be the most distinct period, especially for midlife men. While midlife women's friends were important for their well-being (loneliness, symptomatology, general morale) during the first five to six years of the launching phase, midlife men's friends became important for their well-being ten years into the launching phase. In wave 5, males' negative affective friendship quality was associated with a more negative self-concept than for comparable associations in the previous two waves. In addition, males' positive affective friendship quality was associated with more positive general morale than that for comparable associations in wave 1. These findings document the significance of friendships in the lives of midlife men ten years into the launching phase (Reisman, 1988).

Positive affect toward the mother and siblings was also significantly more strongly associated with midlife males' well-being in wave 1. More specifically, positivity toward the mother was associated with midlife males' more positive self-concept. However, positivity toward siblings was associated with more frequent feelings of loneliness. Perhaps this reflects a longing to have more frequent interactions with siblings to whom they feel close.

These four relational correlates of well-being, mostly unique to this period for midlife men, all reflect a shift in orientation from family of procreation to family of origin and extrafamilial contexts ten years into the launching phase. Paralleling these associations, midlife women's well-being at this time was associated with family of origin (with siblings and mother) *and* family of procreation (including their spouse/ partner and their grandchildren). Also in contrast with midlife males' experience ten years into the launching phase, the significance of friendships for midlife women's well-being seems to diminish from wave 3 to wave 5 (although there was not a statistically significant difference between the magnitude of the correlations across waves). These cross-time shifts in the importance of various relationships for midlife men's and women's well-being pose interesting questions regarding shifting interpersonal involvements and changing sources of psychological resources as adulthood progresses. For example, is the experience of grandparenthood similar for midlife men and women? Do women become more involved with grandchildren than men and therefore receive more psychological resources from their interactions with grandchildren? If so, is this related to the men's shift toward friendships?

We must be cautious, however, in interpreting these findings as due solely to the transitional changes in familiy structure. Cohort and sociohistorical time effects must also be considered. For instance, the emergence of friendship as a positive correlate of well-being for men may result more from the increased acceptance of friendships as an important close relationship for men in their late seventies and eighties.

Conclusion

Using a multivariate multiple relationships approach, I have shown that the complex interpersonal worlds of midlife adults are intricately tied to the psychological well-being of midlife men and women. Moreover, it appears that midlife adults gather psychological resources from a collection of relational sources. The longitudinal design revealed that the relational sources of well-being also show variation over time— sometimes siblings are important, at other times friends are central. In some instances, these sources offset each other; some tax the individual and others feed the midlife adult in diverse ways.

I provide evidence for the usefulness of a multivariate multiple relationships approach for gaining a richer understanding of connections between interpersonal relationships and well-being. I suggest new directions for the study of relational predictors of midlife adults' well-being, including seriously considering men's active relational lives, attending to understudied relational contexts (e.g., extrafamilial relationships), and exploring the juxtaposition of positive and negative experiences within relationships. By analyzing some of the study's limitations, I can offer some challenges for future research using a multiple relationships approach.

First and foremost is the complexity of this design. Such multivariate designs make it necessary to collect a rich data set with a large sample size, enabling the use of more robust statistical techniques such as hierarchical linear modeling. Additionally, such complex nomothetic-level quantitative designs can be complemented by intensive idiographic-level qualitative studies (see, e.g., Paul, 1994). Qualitative studies would enable us to analyze intensely how specific interpersonal relationships contribute to and detract from well-being, and to develop new research questions and hypotheses.

A limitation of the multiple relationships approach taken here was that we needed to aggregate individual relationships into relationship categories because of limited sample sizes. Thus, the aggregated relationship qualities score may not always reflect all individual relationship experiences it represents. For example, some individuals had several siblings and had varying relationships with them—some relationships with siblings were relatively smooth and enjoyable whereas others were full of conflict and dissatisfaction.

This limitation is related to a larger issue endemic to personal relationships research: the ambiguity of *relationship category* as a unit of analysis. When studying a specific type of relationship such as relationships with siblings, sometimes one sibling is chosen to represent the category, or all sibling relationships are aggregated to yield an average of sibling relationships. Both approaches, though methodologically or statistically more manageable, have limited validity for fully understanding the many unique experiences that make up the larger category. Within-category variance needs to be studied. Alternatively, other ways (other than role categories) to group different relationships together should be explored. A multiple relationships approach allows for attention to the broader social context of individual functioning, which need not be limited to particular relationship contexts or categories.

The contrasting associations of affective relationship quality and contact with well-being suggest that it is important to differentiate various dimensions of the relationship experience and assess the contribution of each aspect to individual well-being. In this secondary analysis, content analysis enabled me to develop a complex depiction of midlife adults' relational worlds. However, limitations in the existing data made it difficult for me to assess relationship experiences. In future research, we could use richer assessments of various relationship dimensions—structural, affective, and functional—to further understand the complexities of midlife relationships. Rook (1990), for example, has differentiated among various types of negative social encounters, and Cutrona and Russell (1990) have attempted to determine the most effective components of support. Furthermore, it is necessary not only to make further distinctions among various relationship properties but also to retain differentiation among different dimensions of well-being in midlife for this area of research. Moreover, as Ryff (1989) recommends, future research should also consider adults' own definitions of well-being in addition to more conventional indicators of well-being.

In sum, the challenge in future research will be to further delve into the complex interconnections between interpersonal relationships and psychological well-being in midlife and to explore the transactional mechanisms by which the relational and individual worlds are connected.

ACKNOWLEDGMENTS

This research used the *Longitudinal Study of Transitions in Four Stages of Life, 1968–1980* data set (made accessible in 1979 and 1981; raw and machine-readable data files). These data were collected by M. Fiske, M. Thurnher, and D. Chiriboga and are available through the archive of the Henry A. Murray Research Center of Radcliffe College, Cambridge, Massachusetts (Producer and Distributor). Funding for this research was received from the Midlife Research Program. I am grateful to Junko Kaji, Kim Santagate, Amy Baumgartel, Nga Pham, and Niku Thomas for their assistance in data coding. Thanks also to Jacquelyn James for her many insights regarding this project and to Joanne Gold and two anonymous reviewers for their helpful suggestions.

APPENDIX: INTERPERSONAL RELATIONSHIP QUALITIES CODING CATEGORIES—BRIEF DESCRIPTIONS OF CATEGORIES AND ASSOCIATED RATING SCALES

Contact (frequency of personal contact or time spent together)

1. *No contact* (see each other no more than once a year)
2. *Little contact* (see each other approximately every other month or no more than six times a year)
3. *Moderate contact* (see each other once or twice a month)
4. *Much contact* (see each once or more weekly)

Satisfaction (degree of pleasure from or comfort in the relationship)

1. *Very dissatisfied* (bitter, angry, intense unhappiness in the relationship; respondent can say nothing good about the relationship)
2. *Somewhat dissatisfied* (respondent reports problems in the relationship that make it uncomfortable but acknowledges that the relationship is not *all* bad)
3. *Somewhat satisfied* (relationship is generally enjoyable but there are some aspects that detract from the satisfaction)
4. *Very satisfied* (reports feelings of happiness, joy, or comfort in the relationship; acknowledged conflicts do not detract from the satisfaction)

Closeness (degree of emotional involvement or connectedness)

1. *Very distant* (relationship is emotionally detached; including relationships with very little, if any, emotional involvement or sharing of personal issues or information, or bitter disconnected relationships as a result of a severed tie)
2. *Somewhat distant* (personal disclosure or sharing of feelings is very uncharacteristic of the relationship, yet some connection exists)
3. *Somewhat close* (individuals feel connected to one another and disclose personal and emotinal information, yet such sharing is sometimes approached cautiously)
4. *Very close* (individuals are closely allied with one another and comfortable with open sharing of personal feelings and issues)

Conflict (problematic differences of opinion or other interpersonal problems)

1. *Much conflict* (individuals are in conflict more often than not; general inability to handle conflicts)

2. *Moderate conflict* (conflicts often arise and are met by inconsistent attempts at resolution)
3. *Little conflict* (relationship is generally smooth, but sometimes conflicts arise that are not handled constructively)
4. *No conflict* (relationship is virtually conflict free or conflicts are handled constructively or resolved)

Importance (significance of the relationship in one's life)
1. *Unimportant* (relationship is of no significance or importance and is not characterized as committed; if the relationship ended tomorrow, no one would think about it)
2. *Somewhat unimportant* (little value is attached to the relationship; there is only minimal commitment to the furtherance of the relationship)
3. *Somewhat important* (individual is committed to the relationship and thinks of the connection as significant yet *not* as one of the individual's most important bonds)
4. *Very important* (individual is strongly committed to the relationship and considers it to be one of the individual's most valuable connections)

REFERENCES

Abbey, A., Abramis, D. J., Caplan, R. D. (1985). Effects of different sources of social support and social conflict on emotional well-being. *Basic and Applied Social Psychology, 6*(2), 111–129.

Antonucci, T. C. (1989). Understanding adult social relationships. In K. Kreppner & R. M. Lerner (Eds.), *Family Systems and life-span development.* Hillsdale, NJ: Lawrence Erlbaum Associates.

Arend, K., Gove, F. I., & Sroufe, L. A. (1979). Continuity of individual adaptation from infancy to kindergarten: A predictive study of ego-resiliency and curiosity in preschoolers. *Child Development, 58,* 958–959.

Baruch, G. K. (1984). The psychological well-being of women in the middle years. In G. K. Baruch & J. Brooks-Gunn (Eds.), *Women in midlife.* New York: Plenum Press.

Beckman, L. J. (1981). Effects of social interaction and children's relative inputs on older women's psychological well-being. *Journal of Personality and Social Psychology, 41,* 1075–1086.

Bedford, V. H. (1989). A comparison of thematic apperceptions of sibling affiliation, conflict, and separation at two periods of adulthood. *International Journal of Aging and Human Development, 28*(1), 53–66.

Belsky, J., & Rovine, M. (1984). Social network contact, family support, and the transition to parenthood. *Journal of Marriage and the Family, 46,* 455–462.

Blieszner, R., & Adams, R. G. (1992). *Adult Friendship.* Newbury Park, CA: Sage Publications.

Block, J. (1971). *The Q-sort method in personality assessment and psychiatric research.* Springfield, IL: Thomas.

Blumstein, P., & Schwartz, P. (1983). *American Couples.* New York: Morrow.

Bozett, F. W. (1985). Male development and fathering throughout the life cycle. *American Behavioral Scientist, 29*(1), 41–54.

Bradburn, N. M., & Caplovitz, D. (1969). *Reports on happiness: A pilot study of behavior related to mental health.* Chicago: Aldine.

Brody, E. M. (1981). "Women in the middle" and family help to older people. *Gerontologist, 21*(5), 471–480.

Bumagin, V. E., & Hirn, K. F. (1982). Observations on changing relationships for older married women. *American Journal of Psychoanalysis, 42*(2), 133–142.

Carstensen, L. L. (1992). Social and emotional patterns in adulthood: Support for socioemotional selectivity theory. *Psychology and Aging, 7*(3), 331–338.

Cassidy, M. L. (1985). Role conflict in the postparental period: The effects of employment status on the marital satisfaction of women. *Research on Aging, 7*(3), 433–454.

Cherlin, A. (1981). A sense of history: Recent research on aging and the family. In B. Hess & K. Bond (Eds.), *Leading Edges.* Washington, DC: National Institute of Health.

Cicirelli, V. G. (1989). Feelings of attachment to siblings and well-being in later life. *Psychology and Aging, 4*(2), 211–216.

Clark, M. S., & Reis, H. T. (1988). Interpersonal processes in close relationships. *Annual Review of Psychology, 39,* 609–672.

Clemens, A. W., & Axelson, L. J. (1985). The not-so-empty nest: The return of the fledgling adult. *Family Relations, 34*(2), 259–264.

Conner, K. A., Powers, E. A., & Bultena, G. L. (1979). Social interaction and life satisfaction: An empirical assessment of late life patterns. *Journal of Gerontology, 34,* 116–121.

Cramer, L. A., Riley, P. J., & Kiger, G. (1991). Support and antagonism in social networks: Effects of community and gender. *Journal of Social Behavior and Personality, 6*(4), 991–1005.

Cutrona, C. E., & Russell, D. W. (1990). Type of social support and specific stress: Toward a theory of optimal matching. In B. R. Sarason, I. G. Sarason, & G. R. Pierce (Eds.), *Social Support: An interactional view* (pp. 319–366). New York: Wiley.

Depner, C. E., & Ingersoll-Dayton, B. (1988). Supportive relationships in later life. *Psychology and Aging, 3*(4), 348–357.

Douglas, J. D. (1990–91). Patterns of change following parent death in midlife adults. *Omega Journal of Death and Dying, 22*(2), 123–137.

Fiebert, M. S., & Wright, K. S. (1989). Midlife friendships in an American faculty sample. *Psychological Reports, 64*(3, Pt. 2), 1127–1130.

Fiore, J., Becker, J., & Coppel, D. B. (1983). Social network interactions: A buffer or a stress? *American Journal of Community Psychology, 11,* 423–439.

Fiske, M., & Chiriboga, D. (1990). *Change and continuity in adult life.* San Francisco, CA: Jossey-Bass.

Gottlieb, B. H. (Ed.). (1980). *Social networks and social support.* Beverly Hills, CA: Sage Publications.

Grisset, N. I., & Norvell, N. K. (1992). Perceived social support, social skills, and quality of relationships in bulemic women. *Journal of Consulting and Clinical Psychology, 60*(2), 293–299.

Hagestad, G. O. (1984). The continuous bond: A dynamic multigenerational perspective on parent-child relations between adults. In M. Perlmutter (Ed.), *Minnesota Symposium on Child Psychology* (Vol. 17). Mahwah, NJ: Lawrence Erlbaum Associates.

Harris, R. L., Ellicott, A. M., Holmes, D. S. (1986). The timing of psychosocial transitions and changes in women's lives: An examination of women aged 45 to 60. *Journal of Personality and Social Psychology, 51*(2), 409–416.

Henderson, S., Byrne, D., Duncan-Jones, P., Scott, R., & Adcock, S. (1980). Social relationships, adversity, and neurosis: A study of associations in a general population sample. *British Journal of Psychiatry, 136,* 574–583.

Hirsch, B. J. (1981). Social networks and the coping process: Creating personal communities. In B. H. Gottlieb (Ed.), *Social networks and social support.* Beverly Hills, CA: Sage Publications.

Huston, T., & Levinger, G. (1978). Interpersonal attraction and relationships. *Annual Review of Psychology, 29,* 115–156.

Johnson, C. L. (1988). Relationships among family members and friends in later life. In R. M. Milardo (Ed.), *Families and Social Networks.* Beverly Hills, CA: Sage Publications.

Krystal, S., & Chiriboga, D. (1979). The empty nest process in midlife men and women. *Maturitas, 1,* 215–222.

Lee, G. R. (1985). Kinship and social support of the elderly: The case of the United States. *Aging and Society, 5*(1), 19–38.

Lepore, S. J. (1992). Social conflict, social support, and psychological distress: Evidence of cross-domain buffering effects. *Journal of Personality and Social Psychology, 63*(5), 857–867.

Lowenthal (Fiske), M., Thurnher, M., Chiriboga, D., & Associates (1975). *Four stages of life: A comparative study of women and men facing transitions.* San Francisco, CA: Jossey-Bass.

Lurie, E. E. (1974). Sex and stage differences in perceptions of marital and family relationships. *Journal of Marriage and the Family, 36*(2), 260–269.

Mancini, J. A. (1980). Friend interaction, competence, and morale in old age. *Research on Aging, 2,* 416–431.

Mancini, J. A., & Bird, G. W. (1985). Six steps toward a happy midlife marriage. *Medical aspects of human sexuality, 19*(10), 163–177.

Mancini, J. A., & Blieszner, R. (1989). Aging parents and adult children: Research themes in intergenerational relations. *Journal of Marriage and the Family, 51*(2), 275–90.

Mancini, J. A., & Blieszner, R. (1992). Social provisions in adulthood: Concept and measurement in close relationships. *Journals of Gerontology, 47*(1), P14–P20.

Mangen, D., Bengtson, V., & Landry, P. (Eds.). (1988). *Measurement of intergenerational relations.* Newbury Park, CA: Sage Publications.

Matthews, S. H., Delaney, P. J., & Ademek, M. E. (1989). Male kinship ties: Bonds between adult brothers. *American Behavioral Scientist, 33*(1), 58–69.

McCannell, K. (1988). Social networks and the transition to motherhood. In R. M. Milardo (Ed.), *Families and Social Networks.* Beverly Hills, CA: Sage Publications.

Milardo, R. M. (1982). Friendship networks in developing relationships: Converging and diverging social environments. *Social Psychology Quarterly, 45,* 162–172.

Miller, B., & Sollie, D. (1980). Normal stresses during the transition to parenthood. *Family Relations, 29,* 459–465.

Moss, M. S., & Moss, S. Z. (1992). Themes in parent-child relationships when elderly parents move nearby. *Journal of Aging Studies, 6*(3), 259–271.

Pagel, M. D., Erdly, W. W., & Becker, J. (1987). Social networks: We get by with (and in spite of) a little help from our friends. *Journal of Personality and Social Psychology, 53,* 793–804.

Paul, E. L. (1994). The complexities of a young adult woman's relational world: Challenges, demands, and benefits. In C. Franz & A. Stewart (Eds.), *Women Creating Lives.* Boulder, CO: Westview Press.

Pierce, G. R., Sarason, B. R., & Sarason, I. G. (1992). General and specific support expectations and stress as predictors of perceived supportiveness: An experimental study. *Journal of Personality and Social Psychology, 63*(2), 297–307.

Rands, M. (1988). Changes in social networks following marital separation and divorce. In R. M. Milardo (Ed.), *Families and Social Networks.* Beverly Hills, CA: Sage Publications.

Raup, J. L., & Myers, J. E. (1989). The empty nest syndrome: Myth or reality? *Journal of Counseling and Development, 68*(2), 180–183.

Reisman, J. M. (1988). An indirect measure of the value of friendship for aging men. *Journals of Gerontology, 43*(4), P109–P110.

Richards, L., Bengtson, V., & Miller, R. (1989). The "generation in the middle": Perceptions of changes in adults' intergenerational relationships. In K. Kreppner & R. M. Lerner (Eds.), *Family systems and life-span development.* Hillsdale, NJ: Lawrence Erlbaum Associates.

Rook, K. S. (1984). The negative side of social interaction: Impact on psychological well-being. *Journal of Personality and Social Psychology, 46,* 1097–1108.

Rook, K. S. (1990). Parallels in the study of social support and social strain. *Journal of Social and Clinical Psychology, 9,* 118–132.

Ruehlman, L. S., & Wolchik, S. A. (1988). Personal goals and interpersonal support and hindrance as factors in psychological distress and well-being. *Journal of Personality and Social Psychology, 55,* 293–301.

Ryff, C. D. (1989). In the eye of the beholder: Views of psychological well-being among middle-aged and older adults. *Psychology and Aging, 4*(2), 195–210.

Schnaiberg, A., & Goldenberg, S. (1989). From empty nest to crowded nest: The dynamics of incompletely-launched young adults. *Social Problems, 36*(3), 251–269.

Schuster, T. L., Kessler, R. C., & Aseltine, R. H. (1990). Supportive interactions, negative interactions, and depressed mood. *American Journal of Community Psychology, 18,* 423–438.

Shanas, E. (1979). The family as a social support in old age. *Gerontologist, 19,* 169–175.

Shehan, C. L., Berardo, D. H., & Berardo, F. M. (1984). The empty nest is filling again: Implications for parent-child relationships. *Parenting Studies, 1*(2), 67–73.

Simons, R. (1984). Specificity and substitution in the social networks of the elderly. *Intergenerational Journal of Aging and Human Development, 18,* 121–139.

Stephens, M. P., Kinney, J. M., Ritchie, S. W., & Norris, V. K. (1987). Social networks as assets and liabilities in recovery from stroke by geriatric patients. *Psychology and Aging, 2,* 125–129.

Stephens, M. P., Norris, V. K., Kinney, J. M., & Ritchie, S. W. (1988). Stressful situations in caregiving: Relations between caregiver coping and well-being. *Psychology and Aging, 3*(2), 208–209.

Stueve, C. A., & Gerson, K. (1977). Personal relations across the life cycle. In C. Fischer (Ed.), *Networks and places: Social relations in the urban setting.* New York: Free Press.

Surra, C. A. (1988). The influence of the interactive network on developing relationships. In R. M. Milardo (Ed.), *Families and Social Networks.* Beverly Hills, CA: Sage Publications.

Thomas, J. L. (1990). Grandparenthood and mental health: Implications for the practitioner. *Journal of Applied Gerontology, 9*(4), 464–479.

Thurnher, M. (1976). Midlife marriage: Sex differences in evaluations and perspectives. *International Journal of Aging and Human Development, 7*(2), 129–135.

Tracy, E. M., & Whittaker, J. K. (1990). The social network map: Assessing social support in clinical practice. *Families in Society, 71*(8), 461–470.

Walker, A. J., & Thompson, L. (1983). Intimacy and intergenerational aid and contact among mothers and daughters. *Journal of Marriage and the Family, 45,* 841–849.

Weiss, R. S. (1969). The fund of sociability. *Transaction, 9,* 36–43.

Weiss, R. S. (1974). The provisions of social relationships. In Z. Rubin (Ed.), *Doing unto others* (pp. 17–26). Englewood Cliffs, NJ: Prentice-Hall.

Weiss, R. S. (1976). *Loneliness.* Cambridge, MA: MIT Press.

Weiss, R. S. (1986). Continuities and transformations in social relationships from childhood to adulthood. In W. Hartup & Z. Rubin (Eds.), *Relationships and Development*, (pp. 95–110). Hillsdale, NJ: Erlbaum.

White, K. M., Speisman, J. C., & Costos, D. (1983). Young adults and their parents: Individuation to mutuality. In H. D. Grotevant & C. R. Cooper (Eds.), *Adolescent development in the family: Vol. 22. New Directions for Child Development*, pp. 61–76. San Francisco, CA: Jossey-Bass.

White, L., & Edwards, J. N. (1990). Emptying the nest and parental well-being: An analysis of national panel data. *American Sociological Review, 55*(2), 235–242.

EIGHT

The Generativity of Employed Mothers in Multiple Roles: 1979 and 1991

Shelley M. MacDermid, Gabriela Heilbrun,

and Laura Gillespie DeHaan

Although women's roles have received increasing attention in recent years, partly because of steadily rising participation by women in the paid labor force, women's development during middle adulthood still is not well understood. Our research focuses on generativity (Erikson, 1950) in the context of multiple roles as a major component of employed mothers' midlife experiences.

We attempt to measure generativity separately in three major roles and then to link role-specific generativity to women's evaluations of their role involvements and their well-being. We examine generativity in two samples of women who all are mothers, workers, and wives. Data were collected from the first sample in 1978–79 (Baruch, Barnett, & Rivers, 1983), and from the second sample in 1991 (MacDermid & Gillespie, 1992). During the intervening years, both the context and the level of women's participation in multiple roles changed considerably: employment became the statistical norm for women, fertility rates fell, and divorce rates stabilized. In this chapter, we examine differences between these two samples in the interrelationships of generativity, role performance, and well-being.

PARTICIPATION IN MULTIPLE ROLES: THE CONTEXTS OF GENERATIVITY

Generativity, the seventh and longest of Erikson's eight stages of psychosocial development, was originally defined as "the concern in establishing and guiding the next generation . . . the concept of generativity is meant to include such more popular synonyms as productivity and creativity, which, however, cannot replace it" (Erikson, 1950, p. 267). Erikson associated with each stage a basic strength or virtue. In the case of generativity, this was "care," whereby "the vitality of an order of care [is assured] to those wide areas of adult involvements which, according to a Hindu expression, guarantee the 'maintenance of the world'" (Erikson, Erikson, & Kivnick, 1986). Finally, Erikson viewed individual development as occurring in the context of role involvements: "matured adulthood, then, means a set of vital involvements in life's generative activities . . . participation in areas of involvement in which one can learn to take care of what one truly cares for" (Erikson, Erikson, & Kivnick, 1986, p. 50).

Interest in adult development during midlife surged during the 1980s after a lull during the previous decade. New evidence showed that among adults approaching midlife, generativity was positively related to age (Darling-Fisher & Leidy, 1988; Ochse & Plug, 1986; Ryff & Heincke, 1983). And it is related to successful functioning in public and private life (Vaillant & Milofsky, 1980). Extending Erikson's theory, McAdams, Ruetzel, and Foley (1986, p. 802) demonstrated that "adults whose biographical scripts for the future emphasize generativity . . . [scored] high on both power and intimacy motivation combined" (though results were stronger for men than for women). The nature of postmidlife relationships between generativity and age is less clear (McAdams, St. Aubin, & Logan, 1993).

Although frequently acknowledged as important, links between generativity and role involvements have seldom been studied empirically, although Sherman (1987), for example, suggests that "problems of identity in midlife are frequently those arising from a mismatch between the person's sense of self and his or her role(s) in life" (p. 102). Conceptualizing generativity as a global personality trait, some researchers have implicitly assumed that (1) individuals who perceive themselves as generative are more likely to behave in generative ways, and (2) generative individuals will be consistently generative across role domains. Possibly as a result of these assumptions, assessments of generativity have focused on *either* thoughts *or* role involvements more often than on both. In some cases, respondents have been judged by researchers to be more or less generative on the basis of their general perceptions of themselves (Ryff & Heincke, 1983) or on expert observers' ratings of generative themes in their plans or goals for the future (McAdams, Ruetzel, & Foley, 1986), regardless of the degree to which they were involved in roles where generative behavior might occur. In other cases, respondents have been classified as generative or not generative *primarily* on the basis of their participation in particular roles (Vaillant & Milofsky, 1980): "the overriding factor governing the clinical decision to put a man in this stage was his assumption of responsibility for other adults" (p. 1355).

An important contribution of recent studies by McAdams and his colleagues is the measurement of both perceptual and behavioral aspects of generativity. For example, Van de Water and McAdams (1989) examined respondents' paper-and-pencil self-reports of generativity and coders' ratings of generative themes in respondents' descriptions of their four most important current commitments to reveal a correlation of $r = .32$. They concluded that "general cognitive attitudes about generativity, . . . are modestly related to generative behavior in the area of adults' main life commitments (p. 447). In a study of 23 males and 56 females, McAdams and St. Aubin (1992) found that scores on the Loyola Generativity Scale (LGS) correlated .59 with a 49-item behavior checklist. More recently, McAdams, St. Aubin, and Logan (1993) observed a correlation of .53 between respondents' reports of generative concern (via the LGS) and generative action (via a 40-item behavioral checklist) and concluded that "there are meaningful conceptual and empirical differences among generative concern, generative commitment, generative action, and generative narration" (p. 227).

We found these investigations intriguing. Since they demonstrate that measures of self-perceived *global* generative concern and generative action may be at least somewhat distinct, we became interested in trying to pull apart generativity to examine it separately in specific roles.

The notion of studying development in the context of roles is not new. Researchers of adolescence have been especially active in pointing out that different identity domains (e.g., occupational, civic, interpersonal) may develop at different rates and thus should be attended to separately (Archer, 1992; Waterman, 1985). Indeed, Grotevant (1987) argues that the management of investments in roles and the forces competing with those investments constitute the process through which individuals form their identities. Regarding adults, Hornstein (1986) calls for a "dynamic model of identity that incorporates this notion of multiple role commitments" (p. 552), and Juhasz (1989) proposes a triple-helix model of development embedded in the roles of family, work, and self. Empirical supporting evidence comes from Kroger and Haslett (1991), who found significant variability within individuals across five identity domains (vocation, religion, politics, general role values, and relationships) in adults' recollections from adolescence to adulthood. Thus, "developments across identity components are not parallel, even for people choosing the same life-style" (p. 323).

Women's generativity has so long been associated with mothering that it can be difficult to conceive of generativity in other contexts such as employment and marriage. Erikson's inclusion of productivity and care (among others) as generative expressions encourages us, however, to broaden our conception. As adult role systems become more complex and diverse, and as parenthood becomes less predominant, a broad view of the loci and expressions of generativity increases in importance. But what does generativity in workplaces or in marriage look like? In workplaces, individuals who choose to take less experienced workers under their wing or to serve as mentors are demonstrating procreative generative behavior intended to maintain the world of the workplace and to invest in a younger generation. In marriage, such investments might focus on supporting spouses in their efforts to become better parents. Productivity, another key Eriksonian generative endeavor, might take the form of traditional workplace accomplishments like career advancement or the construction of a good marriage.

Interrelationships among Women's Roles

It may be particularly important to understand women's generativity in the context of multiple roles. Women's life courses are especially likely to include discontinuities (Long & Porter, 1984) such as moving in and out of the roles of worker, student, and caregiver many times. The role patterns displayed by women vary considerably, both across individuals and over time (Barnett & Baruch, 1978; Giele, 1982). In the past, some theorists focused primarily on men's development, proposing incremental and orderly developmental sequences that raised questions about the applicability of their work to women's lives (Barnett & Baruch, 1978; Hornstein, 1986). In the future, however, both women's and men's role patterns are likely to become increasingly fluid (Juhasz, 1989). Men's careers have become less orderly as the likelihood of having only one employer has fallen and as the need for periodic retraining has risen. As women have become increasingly involved in the labor force, pressure for men to become more involved in domestic work has risen. Longevity has risen and fertility has fallen, increasing the likelihood of caring for both dependent children and elders. Consequently, both role demands and the complexity of interdependence among roles may increase (Barnett & Baruch, 1987), increasing the utility of role-specific approaches.

Women may be particularly likely to experience conflicting demands from their various roles (Long & Porter, 1984). Since women occupy lower status jobs, on average, than men do, they have less power to modify their conditions of work (Barnett & Baruch, 1987); and since wives tend to have less power at home than husbands do, they also have less power to modify their conditions of domestic work. Thus, while men often may be able to substitute workplace labor for unappealing family tasks, particularly when the workplace labor is lucrative, women less frequently have this option (Barnett, 1991; Barnett & Baruch, 1978). While Barnett and Baruch (1987) characterize the traditional husband-father role as "low-strain" because it includes both low demand (i.e., minimal involvement in domestic work) and high control (i.e., marital power) relative to their wives, "being a mother is rarely associated with psychological well-being and is often associated with psychological distress" (Barnett, 1991, p. 11).

Studies of the interconnectedness of women's roles also show, however, that role demands do not always conflict. In some instances, positive experiences in one role may compensate for negative ones in another: stress in the parental role may be moderated by positive experiences in the worker role, for example (Barnett, 1991; Baruch & Barnett, 1986); it does not appear, however, that dissatisfaction in the marital role can be compensated for (Barnett & Baruch, 1987). Such data support the role enhancement perspective which proposes that multiple roles generate energy for one another, as opposed to the conflict and tension predicted by the role scarcity perspective.

Although it might be tempting to expect, on the basis of the interdependence of women's roles, that women would display generativity consistently across roles, the negotiation and juggling carried out by many women in order to participate in multiple roles may invalidate such an expectation. The role patterns displayed by women are extremely diverse, and the nature of the interconnections among roles varies as a function of both the roles and the individuals involved. Further, variations in meaning and importance among roles may result in individual differences in the consequences of involvement in the same number of roles across individuals (Barnett & Baruch, 1985).

The implication for the present research is that misleading observations could result from assuming that global and role-specific generativity are fully redundant. We expected women to be generative in many different domains of their lives and the degree to which they were generative to vary across domains. Given the possibility of considerable variation even among individuals displaying the same role patterns, it seemed useful to control role pattern variation by studying a sample of people who are all involved in the same roles.

Limited existing evidence of links between generativity and specific roles focuses primarily on the role of parent. In a longitudinal examination of the Radcliffe class of 1964 at ages 37, 44, and 48, Peterson and Stewart (1992) found that women whose scores on the California Q-Sort most closely conformed to those of a generative prototype defined by expert judges were also more likely to have had children ($r = .42$ on average over time). These women were also "less tense, depressed, angry and fatigued" (p. 8), and had higher well-being scores on the California Psychological Inventory. McAdams and St. Aubin (1992) observed in a study of 66 male and 83 female respondents that "among men especially, having been a parent was positively associated with scores on the LGS (Loyola Generativity Scale)" (p. 1012). In a study of adult men, Vaillant and Milofsky (1980, p. 1358) reported that generativity was correlated with experiences in the roles of parent (i.e., closeness to adolescent children), worker (i.e., assumption of managerial responsibilities), spouse (i.e., enjoyment of first marriage), and citizen (i.e., voluntary public service). Although these studies focus on *inter*individual rather than *intra*individual variations, they do suggest that particular kinds of role involvements may be more strongly related than others to generativity and in turn to well-being.

Looking beyond Role Occupancy

Rather than simply considering whether or not an individual occupies a particular role, existing research suggests that it may be important to consider respondents' *evaluations* of their experiences in particular roles. Barnett and Baruch (1985) found significant relationships among the quality of experience in the work and parental roles and role overload, anxiety, and role conflict. Later research with the same sample (Baruch & Barnett, 1986) showed that the quality of experience in particular roles was differentially related to aspects of well-being. Giele (1982) argued that a theme in recent studies of depression and well-being was the importance of "a sense of competence" (p. 21).

In this study we were more interested in respondents' assessments of their experiences than in whether or not they occupied particular roles. Only women who occupied all three roles of parent, worker, and wife were selected for analysis. Extending the premises of the role-quality research to generativity, we presumed that women who evaluated their involvement in a particular role positively would be more likely to report perceiving generativity in that role. We thus focused on respondents' evaluations of their involvements, specifically on how competent and satisfied they felt in each role, expecting perceptions of generativity to be a partial function of feelings of competence and satisfaction.

MULTIPLE EXPRESSIONS OF GENERATIVITY

In addition to broadening the range of roles within which generativity is examined, it may also be useful to consider a diverse array of generative expressions, or ways in which individuals might be generative. In the past, the study of generativity has been plagued by subtle gender biases. Despite the breadth of Erikson's *conception,* it has often been *operationalized* to emphasize expression by means of traditionally masculine qualities like dominance rather than the equally important quality of caring (see Hulsizer, Murphy, Noam, Taylor, Erikson, & Erikson, 1981), even in studies of women (e.g., Ryff & Migdal, 1984). Several scholars have argued that considerations of adult development have devalued or ignored the importance of nurturance and relationships, thus systematically excluding individuals (most often women) who are socialized to concentrate on those domains (Stewart & Gold-Steinberg, 1990). For example, Gergen (1990) points out that the "studies of Vaillant . . . and Gould . . . emphasize a male-oriented, individualistic, rationalistic, and egocentric orientation to life," suggesting that "to judge from the major studies on lifespan development at midlife, one would think only men survived the third decade of life" (p. 475). Stewart and Gold-Steinberg (1990) argue that "much of the theory and research about midlife adults has been "universal" in principle, but limited to men in terms of examples . . . , populations, samples . . . , and theorists (Becker, Erikson, Gould, Guttman, Kotre, Levinson, McAdams, Vaillant; see Neugarten, 1968, and Fiske, 1980, for female exceptions)" (p. 544). A concrete example is evident in Ryff and Migdal's (1984) selection of measures focusing on dominance, breadth of interest, and innovation to operationalize generativity.

At the other extreme, motherhood and nurturance sometimes have been assumed to be women's only possible generative outlets, excluding the possibility of leadership (Barnett, 1991; Long & Porter, 1984).

Gergen (1990) argues that "women's adult development is staged around the core notion of woman as reproducer" (p. 474), even though "women are very responsible for the maintenance of all life forms within the culture, at least from the standpoint of their moral responsibility, their contributions to social cohesion, their support of the lives of the competitively unsuccessful (e.g., the aged, ill, and young), and their position as spiritual leaders, educators and as a yet-unfathomed political force. Women might be viewed as those who create most of the art, control much of the money, support most of the cultural institutions, lead most of the volunteer groups, and influence most of the decision-making processes in some manner" (p. 483). (See also Franz & White, 1985; Giele, 1982; Gilligan, 1982; Stewart & Gold-Steinberg, 1990).

In recent years, however, a wider array of generative expressions has been acknowledged. For example, Kotre (1984) proposed the existence of four types of generativity (i.e., biological, parental, technical, and cultural) and argued that historical changes powerfully influence the contexts within which generative behavior occurs and the type of generative behavior that might occur. Perhaps because his conceptualization merged generative activity with the context or role within which it might occur (e.g., biological generativity was narrowly defined as begetting, bearing, and nursing children and thus would occur only in the parental role), and because his detailed case studies focused exclusively on eight subjects (four of them women in their midthirties or older), however, Kotre was able to observe only parental and cultural generativity.

Additional discussions of diversity in generative themes focus on the notions of agency and communion. Kotre (1984) argues that generativity may be Agentic or Communal, with agency springing from the "self-asserting, self-protecting, self-expanding existence of the individual" (p. 16), and communion "representing the participation of the individual in a mutual, interpersonal reality or in some larger organism" (p. 16). McAdams (1988) suggests that generativity involves *both* agency and communion, "challeng[ing] us as adults to be both powerful and intimate, expanding the self and surrendering to others in the same generative act" (p. 274), and cites significant correlations between generativity and the sum of power and intimacy motivations as evidence supporting his view (McAdams, 1988; McAdams, Ruetzel, & Foley, 1986). Echoing these findings, in recent analyses of California Q-Sort items forming a generative prototype, Peterson and Stewart (1992) observed a factor pattern suggesting what the researchers called Nurturant (corresponding to communal) and Prosocial (corresponding to agentic) generativity.

Several researchers have used the fiction, letters, and diaries of British feminist, pacifist, and author Vera Brittain to identify diverse generative themes and to understand them in the role contexts within which they occur (e.g., Peterson & Stewart, 1990; Stewart, Franz, & Layton, 1988; Stewart, Franz, Paul, & Peterson, 1991). Generative themes identified by this psychobiographical research include productivity, parenting, caring for others, and a need to be needed. Peterson and Stewart (1990) observed the ebbing and flowing of generative themes as Brittain's context and commitments were altered by World War II. For example, while "caring generativity" rose sharply with the onset of the war and the departure of her children for safety, Brittain's "productive generativity" reached its highest level in a decade when her children returned in 1943.

In this research, we focus on the two generative themes mentioned by Erikson that seem to us to be most closely related to existing studies: productivity and procreativity. According to Erikson, "the productive [aspect of generativity] . . . integrates work life with family life within the political and technical framework" (Hulsizer et al., 1981, p. 269). He acknowledges that productivity may occur in "business" (p. 255), but leaves open the possibility of productivity in other settings. Thus, "products" could include children of whom one is proud, a good marriage, or a successful career.

Procreativity is "primarily a concern in establishing and guiding the next generation" (but not necessarily one's own offspring; see Erikson, 1950, p. 267). The "procreative [aspect of generativity] . . . gives birth and responds to the needs of the next generation" (Hulsizer et al., 1981, p. 269). Mentoring colleagues or otherwise "bringing others along" thus may be procreative activities.

McAdams and St. Aubin (1992) contend that "generativity cannot be understood from a single personal or social standpoint, but that it must instead be viewed as a psychosocial patterning of demand, desire, concern, belief, commitment, action, and narration . . . situated in a particular social and historical context" (p. 1013). Although we cannot examine here all of the psychosocial components of McAdams's theoretical vision, we do attempt to understand patterns of women's generativity across roles, as related to role perceptions and well-being, in social and historical context.

Research Questions

We explored answers to the following questions: (1) Does generativity vary across roles? (2) How does generativity expressed in particular roles relate to women's assessments of their competence and satisfaction in those roles and to their well-being? (3) How do relationships among role-specific generativity, role performance, and well-being differ as a partial function of sociohistorical time (i.e., data collected in 1978–1979 vs. 1991)?

Procedures

Sample

1978–1979 subsample. Procedures used to collect data from the 1978–1979 subsample are described fully in Baruch, Barnett, and Rivers (1983). Data were collected in a northeastern city near Boston whose inhabitants worked in jobs with a wide variety of occupational prestige levels. Community voting lists were used to identify all women aged 35–55; the 6,000 women identified were then contacted in random order to determine if their family and employment circumstances qualified them for the study (e.g., women were considered to be employed only if they had worked for pay at least 17.5 hours per week for the three months prior to data collection). Certain groups of women (i.e., those in high-prestige jobs) were oversampled to ensure their representation in sufficiently large numbers for analysis. Over 76% ($n = 238$) of the women invited to participate completed structured face-to-face interviews. Analyses in the present study focus on the 45 women who were mothers, workers, *and* wives.

1991 subsample. Procedures used to gather data from the 1991 subsample are described fully in MacDermid and Gillespie (1992). All respondents were employed at a medium-sized bank in a midwestern community of 50,000 near a large urban center. Because bank employees are predominantly women who work at a wide variety of occupational prestige levels, they were considered a suitable comparison group for the 1978–1979 sample. All employees ($n = 367$) were invited to participate in a study of families and jobs in their workplace during work time. Screening questionnaires administered to the 257 employees (70%) who volunteered for the study identified women who had worked at the bank for at least six months, who lived with a spouse or partner, and who had children no younger than six. Of the 68 women that satisfied these conditions, 90% completed longer questionnaires, in the presence of research staff, tapping well-being, generativity, and aspects of role involvement. The 45 mothers aged 35–55 constitute the sample of interest for this study.

Measures

Unless otherwise indicated, measures were identical in the 1978–1979 and the 1991 data sets.

Role performance variables
Competence. Respondents' perceived competence in each of three roles (parent, worker, spouse) was assessed using a single item: "In general, how good or competent would you say you are [as a parent, at work, as a spouse]?" with four answer options, ranging from "Excellent" to "Not very good." In spite of the limited number of answer options, distributions of the competence variables were well shaped with minimal skewness ($-.1$ on average across roles) and kurtosis ($-.3$ on average). The average intercorrelation of competence scores across roles was .31.

Satisfaction. Respondents' satisfaction with each role was assessed using a single item: "All things considered, how satisfied or dissatisfied have you been with your [parenting, work, relationship with spouse] over the last two months?" The seven answer options ranged from "Completely satisfied" to "Completely dissatisfied." Although the distribution was somewhat skewed (-1 on average across roles; .6 kurtosis on average), this single-item measure correlated well in each role ($r = .58$ on average) with eight-item semantic differential measures of satisfaction in each role (available only in the 1991 data). The average intercorrelation of satisfaction scores across roles was .32.

The competence and satisfaction items were widely dispersed throughout the data collection instruments. Means, standard deviations, and ranges for competence and satisfaction in the roles of parent, worker, and spouse are presented in Table 8.1.

To examine the validity of our measures, we first examined intercorrelations between competence and satisfaction, expecting stronger correlations *within* than *across* roles. The average correlation between competence and satisfaction within roles was more than twice as large ($r = .25$) than the correlation across roles ($r = .12$). We also examined intercorrelations with indicators of well-being, focusing specifically on life satisfaction and self-esteem, because we expected these aspects of

TABLE 8.1 Characteristics of Measures

	Number of Items	Mean	Standard Deviation	Possible Range	Obtained Range
Parent role					
Generativity	4	13.4	1.9	0–16	7–16
Competence	1	2.9	.63	1–4	1–4
Satisfaction	1	5.6	1.2	1–4	2–7
Worker role					
Generativity	4	12.2	1.9	0–16	7–16
Competence	1	3.3	.59	1–4	2–4
Satisfaction	1	5.2	1.4	1–7	1–7
Spouse role					
Generativity	4	12.9	2.9	0–16	4–16
Competence	1	2.8	.64	1–4	1–4
Satisfaction	1	5.5	1.4	1–7	2–7

well-being to relate differently to satisfaction and competence. Consistent with our predictions, life satisfaction was more strongly related to role satisfaction ($r = .28$) than to competence ($r = .19$), while self-esteem was more strongly related to competence ($r = .52$) than to role satisfaction ($r = .25$).

Role-specific generativity. Measures of generativity in the parent, worker, and spouse roles comprised items developed by Baruch, Barnett, and Rivers (1983) to indicate respondents' perceived rewards and concerns in each role. Respondents were asked to indicate the extent to which they perceived certain features of their involvement in a particular role as rewarding or of concern (e.g., "too many conflicts with children" was a potential concern associated with the parental role). On the basis of descriptions gleaned from the generativity literature (Erikson, 1950; Erikson, Erikson, & Kivnick, 1986; Hulsizer, Murphy, Noam, Taylor, Erikson, & Erikson, 1981; McAdams, Ruetzel, & Foley, 1986; Ryff & Heincke, 1983), one reward item and one concern item were chosen to represent the best (i.e., most consistent with Erikson's views on generativity) example of each of five possible ways of being generative within each role (productivity, procreativity, creativity, care, and mastery). Productivity, procreativity and creativity are explicitly mentioned in Erikson's earliest definitions of generativity (e.g., Erikson, 1950). Care also is mentioned explicitly as a strength or virtue associated with generativity (Erikson, Erikson, & Kivnick, 1986). Finally, mastery is implicated in the work of generative individuals "to develop and maintain those societal institutions and natural resources without which successive generations will not be able to survive" (Erikson, Erikson, & Kivnick, 1986, pp. 73–74).

A total of 30 items was chosen, 5 reward items and 5 concern items for each of the roles of parent, worker, and spouse. Three expert judges then replicated the item selection process. When the judges converged on an item that was theoretically sensible but diverged from our a priori choice, we altered our choice. Final percentage agreements between our choices and those of the judges ranged from 76% to 92%, with a mean of 84%; final Kappa coefficients were adequate, ranging from .32 to .77, with a mean of .59 (Bakeman & Gottman, 1986; Cohen, 1960).

It is important to note that different items were chosen to represent each generative theme in each role. The pool of items used to construct the generativity measures in both samples did not permit the use of the same items for every role. However, even if we had been able to do so, we were not convinced that the apparent comparability of such measures would necessarily ensure construct validity. As a result, we relied upon theory and agreement by expert judges to determine our final measures. Although the merit of our strategy for dealing with this thorny problem certainly can be debated, we feel that our results at least justify further study.

Establishing measurement equivalence. In order to establish the comparability of our generativity measures across the 1978–1979 and 1991 samples, we used LISREL VII software (Joreskog & Sorbom, 1988) and a maximum likelihood nested hypothesis testing procedure that compares the relative fit to the existing data of factor loadings set equal across samples with unique loadings for each sample (Joreskog, 1979). In this procedure, measures are usually considered equivalent if the difference between chi-square tests of the fit of equivalent and unique loadings (called a "change in chi-square" test) is not significant. Once equivalence is established, the quality of the fit of the factor structure to the data can be assessed using several criteria: a chi-square/degrees of freedom ratio of less than 2.0 (Joreskog, 1979; Tanaka & Huba, 1984); a goodness of fit index of .85 or better (Barnett, Marshall, & Sayer, 1991); root mean square residuals less than .10 (Rupp & Segal, 1989); and t tests of the significance of each individual factor loading.

TABLE 8.2 Measurement Equivalence Testing

		1991 Sample		1978–1979 Sample		
χ^2/df	χ^2_{diff}	Goodness of Fit	RMSR	Goodness of Fit	RMSR	Change in χ^2
		Parent Role				
1.71	64.89 (38)**	.85	.08	.86	.08	
1.62	71.34 (44)**	.82	.07	.84	.09	6.45 (6)
		Worker Role				
1.05	39.80 (38)	.94	.02	.89	.08	
1.23	54.15 (44)	.90	.04	.87	.13	14.35 (6)*
		Spouse Role				
1.66	26.59 (16)*	.94	.05	.88	.06	
1.58	31.59 (20)*	.93	.07	.87	.08	5.00 (4)

*$p < .05$. **$p < .01$.

The 1991 data were used to identify the number of factors and their related items; findings then were cross-validated on the 1978–1979 data. There were two correlated factors for each role, a reward factor and a concern factor, with each reward or concern item loading on only one factor. Since sample size did not permit simultaneous estimation of the applicability of the equivalent model to both samples for all three roles, each role was analyzed separately.

As Table 8.2 shows, the change in chi-square was nonsignificant in the parent and spouse roles, indicating measurement equivalence across samples. Although the change in chi-square was significant in the work role, the chi-square test of the equivalent model was nonsignificant (indicating good fit), and the other criteria indicated good fit. For these reasons and on theoretical grounds, we did not reject the equivalent model. One item in the work role did not have a loading significantly greater than zero but was retained for the purposes of estimating the model. The fit of the equivalent model to the data for each sample also was adequate in the parent and spouse roles.

Scale scores and validity. Although we established measurement equivalence using all 23 items common to both the 1978–1979 and 1991 data sets (only 8, 9, and 6 items were available in the 1978–1979 data for the parent, worker, and spouse roles, respectively), we selected only the productivity and procreativity items for further analysis because these items were present in both samples for all roles. These items are listed in Table 8.3. Items associated with productivity, for example, focus on opportunities for advancement (as a worker), good communication (as a wife), and feeling proud of how children are turning out (as a mother). We created total generativity scores in each role by summing the raw reward and concern scores (with concern items reversed). Raw scores were used instead of weighted scores because raw scores are easier to interpret, because raw and weighted scores were correlated .96 on average, and because weighting is "seldom worthwhile" (Gorsuch, 1983, p. 269). We summed rewards and concerns because the factors were correlated. Final generativity scores in the parent, worker, and spouse roles were moderately intercorrelated (average $r = .31$). Table 8.1 describes the final measures.

Validity of the role-specific generativity measures was supported by their anticipated moderate correlations with the 10-item Darling-Fisher and Leidy (1988) generativity subscale, which measures generativity as a global personality trait (available only in the 1991 data): $r = .26$, .36, and .35 ($p < .05$), respectively, for parent, worker, and spouse generativity.

TABLE 8.3 Role-specific Generativity Items

Reward Items	Concern Items
Worker Role	
Procreativity	
Helping others develop	Job doesn't fit my skills or interests
Productivity	
Opportunity for advancement	Job conflicts with other responsibilities
Spouse or Partner Role	
Procreativity	
Spouse being a good parent	Conflicts about children
Productivity	
Good communication	Poor communication
Parent Role	
Procreativity	
Helping them (children) develop	Worry about the teenage years
Productivity	
Feeling proud of how they are turning out	Disappointment in what they are like

Outcome measures

Locus of control. Perceptions of the degree to which circumstances in life are under one's personal control were measured with a seven-item scale developed by Pearlin and Schooler (1978). Respondents were asked to strongly agree, agree, disagree, or strongly disagree with descriptive statements like, "I have little control over the things that happen to me." Scores ranged from 14 to 28, with a mean of 22.2 (*SD* = 3.7). Cronbach's alpha was .77.[1]

2. *Depression.* Defined as "signs of withdrawal of life interest, lack of motivation, and loss of vital energy . . . feelings of hopelessness and futility . . ." (Derogatis, Lipman, Rickels, Uhlenhuth, & Covi, 1974, p. 4), depression was measured with 10 items from the Hopkins Symptom Checklist (Derogatis et al., 1974). Respondents were asked "How much has each of the following symptoms bothered or distressed you during the past week including today?" using four answer options ranging from "not at all" to "quite a bit." Sample items included "feeling lonely" and "feeling trapped or caught." Cronbach's alpha was .86 in a large validation sample (Derogatis et al., 1974), quite comparable to the .87 value obtained in this study.[2] Scores ranged from 10 to 24 (out of a possible 40; higher scores indicate more depression), with a mean of 14.4 (*SD* = 3.6).

Self-esteem. The Rosenberg Self-Esteem scale (Rosenberg, 1979) is a 10-item scale that asks respondents to strongly agree, agree, disagree, or strongly disagree with a set of statements that describe themselves. Example of items in the scale include "On the whole I am satisfied with myself" and "At times I think I am no good at all." Scores ranged from 20 to 40 (higher scores indicating higher self-esteem), with a mean of 35.4 (*SD* = 4.5). Cronbach's alpha was .86.[3]

Life satisfaction. We used the Campbell, Converse, and Rodgers (1976) Overall Life Satisfaction item to measure life satisfaction. This item is a 7-point semantic differential; scores ranged from 2 to 7 (higher scores indicating greater satisfaction), with a mean of 5.3 (*SD* = 1.2). This single-item measure correlated well (*r* = .81, *p* < .001) with an eight-item semantic differential measure of satisfaction (available only in the 1991 data).

Because depression, locus of control, self-esteem, and life satisfaction were strongly intercorrelated (.59 on average), a well-being factor was created to reduce the number of variables for analysis. A scree test indicated the existence of a single factor, and the chi-square test of the sufficiency of a single factor indicated adequate fit (5.1 (2) *p* = .08).

222

Factor loadings ranged from .66 to .83 ($M = .76$; higher scores indicate greater well-being).

ANALYSES AND RESULTS

Demographic Comparison of the 1978–1979 and 1991 Samples

Table 8.4 indicates that the predominantly European American samples did not differ significantly in age, duration of marriage, or number of children. The samples, of course, came from different birth cohorts: the 1978–1979 sample was born between 1924 and 1944, while the 1991 sample was born between 1936 and 1956. All members of the 1991 sample had at least one child over 6 living at home, while 9 members of the 1978–1979 sample had children under 7, and 4 members had children who had all left home[4] (chi-square $(2) = 15.2, p < .001$). Not surprisingly, given historical trends, the 1991 sample reported longer work weeks than the 1978–1979 sample: while the 1978–1979 sample was almost evenly split between part-time and full-time employees (46.7% and 53.3%), the 1991 sample almost exclusively worked full-time (13.3% and 86.7%; chi-square $(2) = 11.9, p < .001$). Husbands of respondents in the 1991 sample also more strongly preferred that their wives be employed. While no husband in 1978–1979 expressed a preference for his wife to be employed, 72% of the husbands of the 1991 respondents preferred that their wives be employed[5] (chi-square $(3) = 45.7, p < .001$).

There was a clear social-class difference between the samples, indicated by differences in education, occupation, and income. Members of the 1978–1979 sample were more educated than the 1991 sample, perhaps a partial function of their geographic proximity to a large number of universities. While 23 of the 1978–1979 respondents reported completing advanced graduate degrees, none of the 1991 respondents had advanced beyond an undergraduate degree. While 24 of the 1978–1979 respondents' husbands had professional degrees, only 2 of the 1991 respondents' husbands had such degrees. These differences were concentrated in the upper two occupational prestige levels; there were no educational differences between the samples in the lowest occupational prestige group.

Whereas the 1978–1979 sample was almost evenly divided among women in high, medium, and low prestige jobs, the 1991 sample was concentrated in medium prestige jobs (chi-square $(2) = 10.1, p < .01$). *Family* income was significantly higher in the 1978–1979 sample than in the 1991 sample, but there were no significant differences in respon-

TABLE 8.4 Demographic Characteristics of Samples

	1978–1979 Sample			1991 Sample			
	M	SD	Observed Range	M	SD	Observed Range	Significance[a]
Age	44.4	6.5	35–55	42.9[b]	5.7	35–55	1.1 (87)
Length of marriage	21.2[b]	8.5	3–33	19.6	7.1	3–35	1.0 (87)
Number of children	2.6	1.0	1–6	2.9	1.6	1–7	1.1 (88)
Occupational prestige[c]	56.4	5.6	16–81	47.8	7.9	26–72	3.3 (65)**
High (%)		31.1	($n = 14$)		13.5	($n = 6$)	
Medium (%)		35.6	($n = 16$)		68.9	($n = 31$)	
Low (%)		33.3	($n = 15$)		17.8	($n = 8$)	
Work hours/week	32.6	9.8	17–50	40.3	7.2	16–55	4.1 (75.1)***
Annual income[d]	21.6[e]	14.8	2.6–45.5	16.7[f]	7.9	3.0–40.0	1.9 (62.6)+
Family income[d]	70.8[g]	28.7	25.8–103.1	45.8[h]	15.8	11.0–80.0	4.7 (62.5)***
Education[i]	4.9[b]	1.9	2–7	2.7	0.9	2–5	7.1 (60.3)***
Spouse's education[j]	4.0	1.2	2–5	2.8	1.0	1–5	5.4 (86.1)***

[a]Comparisons were conducted using t tests; noninteger degrees of freedom are reported when comparisons were based on harmonic means.
[b]Based on an n of 44 because 1 case has missing data.
[c]Classified as high, medium, or low prestige using 1970 National Opinion Research Center codes. High-prestige jobs: bank officers and systems analysts; medium-prestige jobs: technicians and tellers; low-prestige jobs: clerks and proofreaders.
[d]In thousands. Incomes by the 1978–1979 sample were adjusted for inflation and geographic variations in cost of living using tables for Annual Percentage Change in Earnings and Compensation (Bureau of the Census, 1980, 1987, and 1991) and the Consumer Price Index for Selected Areas (Bureau of Labor Statistics, 1979, 1990).
[e]Based on an n of 41 due to 2 cases missing data and the exclusion of 2 outliers who reported $60,000 (unadjusted) annual income.
[f]Based on an n of 36 due to 9 refusals to report income.
[g]Based on an n of 40 due to 3 cases missing data and exclusion of 2 outliers.
[h]Based on an n of 34 due to 11 refusals to report income.
[i]1 = some high school or less; 2 = high school diploma; 3 = some college or trade school without degree; 4 = associate or trade school degree; 5 = B.A.; 6 = M.A.; 7 = postgraduate work beyond M.A.
[j]1 = some high school or less; 2 = high school diploma; 3 = some college or trade school without degree; 4 = associate or trade school degree; 5 = professional.
+ $p < .10.$ * $p < .05.$ ** $p < .01.$ *** $p < .001.$

dents' *individual* income across samples *within* occupational prestige levels (footnotes for Table 8.4 explain how incomes reported in 1978–79 were adjusted for inflation and geographic disparities in cost of living).

Because the demographic characteristics were strongly intercorrelated (average $r = .57$), a socioeconomic status factor was created to use as a control variable in subsequent analyses. This factor comprised respondent's education, occupational prestige (continuous score), and income, respondent's husband's education, and family income; a scree plot supported the existence of a single factor. Factor loadings ranged from .69 to .82, with a mean loading of .76.

Do Levels of Generativity Vary across Roles?

To answer our first research question, we used a repeated-measures analysis of variance in which the three role-specific generativity scores were treated as a repeated measure (we called this within-subjects factor Role). A significant effect for Role ($F [2, 178] = 8.5$, $p < .001$) confirmed that there was significant variation across roles; we then conducted t tests of the differences between each pair of roles. Results showed that average levels of generativity reported in the parent role were higher than those in either the worker or the spouse roles (parent-work: $t = 4.8$, $p < .001$; parent-spouse: $t = 2.0$, $p < .05$). Somewhat higher generativity was reported in the role of spouse than in the role of worker ($t = 1.9$, $p < .07$).

Since the variation we observed in generativity across roles could simply be an artifact of measurement noise, we performed median splits on each generativity score (creating high and low groups) and examined the likelihood of falling into the high group in multiple roles. Presumably if generativity is displayed consistently across roles (i.e., does not vary), a person who is above the median in one role should be above the median in the others. This was not borne out by our chi-square tests (average chi-square (1) = 1.7, $p =$ n.s.).

How Is Role-Specific Generativity Related to Role Performance and Well-Being?

We next used path analysis to examine the links among respondents' perceptions of competence and satisfaction in each role, their generativity in each role, and their well-being. Intercorrelations among all analysis variables are shown in Table 8.5. Four hierarchical stepwise regressions were conducted: each of the measures of role-specific gen-

TABLE 8.5 Pearson Correlations among Variables Used in Path Analyses

	SES	PC	PS	WC	WS	SC	SS	P	W	S
Socioeconomic status (SES)										
Role performance										
Parent competence (PC)	28**									
Parent satisfaction (PS)	18+	29**								
Work competence (WC)	41***	24*	12							
Work satisfaction (WS)	23*	07	23*	16						
Spouse competence (SC)	18+	46**	23*	22*	09					
Spouse satisfaction (SS)	24*	02	35***	17	37***	31**				
Generativity										
Parent (P)	17	32**	51***	16	17	17+	15			
Worker (W)	22*	24*	27**	13	35***	10	14	27**		
Spouse (S)	23*	18+	52***	15	24*	28**	61***	44***	21*	
Well-being (WB)	27**	29**	38**	29**	28**	36**	47**	32**	30**	56**

+ $p < .10$. * $p < .05$. ** $p < .01$. *** $p < .001$.

erativity was first regressed on competence and satisfaction in all three roles; the well-being factor was then regressed on the three role-specific generativity scores. Socioeconomic status was entered first as a control variable into each regression.

As Figure 8.1 shows, the path model accounted for an average of 42% of the variance in the dependent variables (ranging from 22% for worker generativity to 50% for spouse generativity). Generativity in each role was related to satisfaction but not to perceived competence in that role. In addition, generativity in the spouse role was related to both spousal and parental satisfaction. Well-being was significantly related to generativity in the worker and spouse roles; it was not significantly related to generativity in the parental role.

We next conducted analyses to compare the relative explanatory power of our path model (which included only indirect relationships between competence, satisfaction, and well-being) with (1) path analyses including only the competence and satisfaction variables (thus omitting the generativity variables) as predictors of well-being; and (2) analyses including all competence, satisfaction, and generativity variables as direct predictors. The generativity variables explained significantly more variability in well-being than the satisfaction and competence variables (difference in R^2 = .04, F [1, 89] = 5.0, p < .05), and if we included the six satisfaction and competence variables as direct predictors, did not significantly increase the explained variability beyond what was accounted for by generativity (difference in R^2 = .03, F [1, 89] = 3.0, p > .05). Thus, our original model, which included only indirect relationships between well-being and competence and satisfaction, provided a better fit to our data than any of the alternatives we tested.

Do Relationships among Role Performance, Generativity, and Well-Being Differ by the Timing of Data Collection?

We first conducted an analysis of variance to compare means across the two samples. There were two significant differences: 1978–1979 respondents perceived themselves as more competent at their jobs (3.5 vs. 3.0, F = 18.48, p < .001) and as more generative in the spousal role (13.6 vs. 12.1, F = 6.4, p < .01) than did 1991 respondents. Consistent with our earlier demographic comparisons, 1978–1979 respondents also reported significantly higher socioeconomic status than did 1991 respondents (.52 vs. −.51 on the SES factor, F = 38.1, p < .001); this variable was controlled in subsequent path analyses but was never significant.

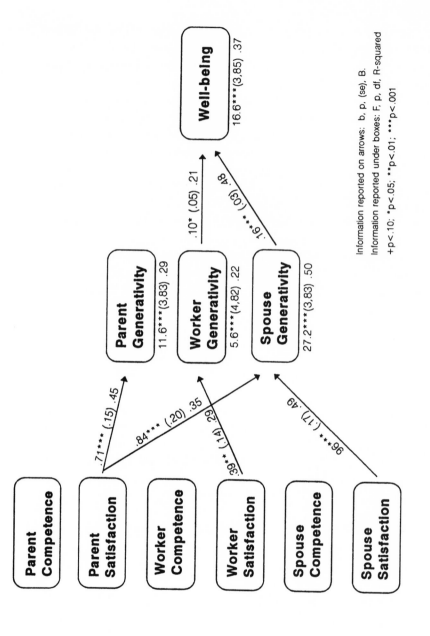

Information reported on arrows: b, p, (se), B.
Information reported under boxes: F, p, df, R-squared
+p<.10; *p<.05; **p<.01; ***p<.001

FIGURE 8.1. Path Analysis of Full Sample

Next, we replicated the path analyses separately within the 1978–1979 and 1991 subsamples. Results for the 1978–1979 subsample are shown in Figure 8.2. The explained variance ranged from 26% for well-being to 61% for spouse generativity, with a mean of 41%. As in the analyses of the full sample, generativity in each role was related to satisfaction, but not to competence, the one exception being a positive relationship between competence and generativity in the worker role. Generativity in the spousal role was related to both spousal and parental satisfaction. In contrast to the analyses of the full sample, well-being was related exclusively to generativity in the parental role, which explained 26% of its variation.

Figure 8.3 shows that the variance explained by the path analysis of the 1991 subsample ranged from 16% for worker generativity to 54% for well-being, with a mean of 33%. Generativity in both the parent and the worker roles was related to satisfaction in the parental role. Generativity in the spousal role was related to satisfaction in that role. Well-being was significantly related only to generativity in the spousal role, which accounted for 56% of its variation.

As a final exploration of the utility of the role-specific approach, we replicated our regressions of well-being using global indicators of generativity so that we could compare the proportions of explained variance. In each subsample, we averaged generativity scores across roles to represent global generativity and then regressed well-being on the new measure. We also regressed well-being in the 1991 sample on the Darling-Fisher and Leidy (1988) global generativity scale (available only in the 1991 data). In the 1978–1979 data, the global approach accounted for virtually the same percentage of variance as the role-specific approach (25% and 26%, respectively). In the 1991 data, however, the role-specific approach accounted for significantly more variance (54%) than either of the global approaches (47% and 37%, respectively, for generativity averaged across roles and the Darling-Fisher and Leidy scale).

DISCUSSION

We found support for the value of examining generativity as it is perceived in specific roles. We first proposed that observation of variation across roles would support the usefulness of considering generativity in the context of role involvements, rather than as a global personality trait. Respondents did report significantly different levels of generativity across roles, though one of the differences was only at

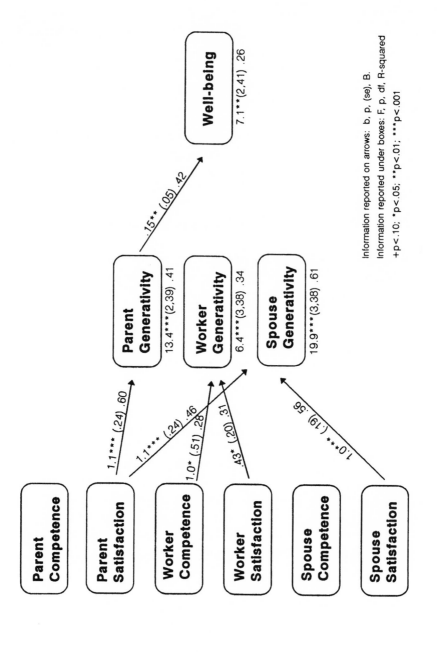

Information reported on arrows: b, p, (se), B.
Information reported under boxes: F, p, df, R-squared
+p<.10; *p<.05; **p<.01; ***p<.001

FIGURE 8.2. Path Analysis of 1978–1979 Subsample

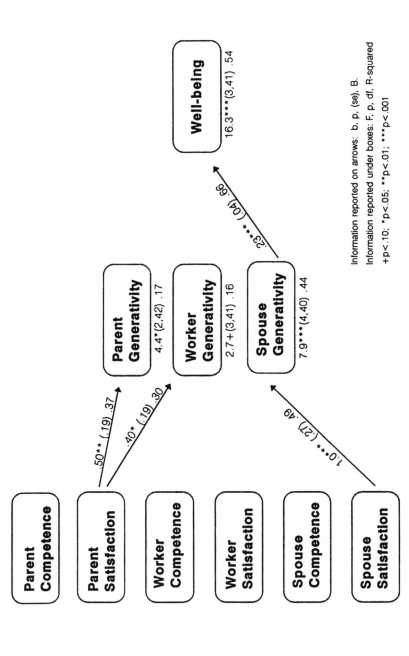

Information reported on arrows: b, p, (se), B.
Information reported under boxes: F, p, df, R-squared
+p<.10; *p<.05; **p<.01; ***p<.001

FIGURE 8.3. Path Analysis of 1991 Subsample

the level of a trend. In addition, women who reported high generativity in one role were no more likely than other women to report high generativity in other roles. We interpret these findings as providing modest evidence that there is significant variation across roles.

We next explored connections between role-specific generativity, women's feelings of competence and satisfaction in each role, and their well-being. We proposed significant interconnections that would vary from role to role. We showed that generativity in particular roles was generally related to satisfaction but not to competence, and that satisfaction in the parental role was also related to generativity in the worker or spouse roles, depending on which subsample was being examined.

The relationships between satisfaction in the parental role and generativity in other roles are not surprising given the prominence of the parenting role in social expectations of women, the amount of time women devote to the role, and the degree to which women adjust other role involvements to accommodate parenting demands.

Generativity in particular roles was differentially related to women's well-being. Specifically, in the sample as a whole, generativity in the spouse and worker roles, but not the parent role, was significantly related to well-being. The magnitude of the standardized regression coefficient for the spouse role was more than twice as large as that for the worker role (see Fig. 8.1), a further indication that the strength of the relationships between generativity and well-being varies across roles.

Finally, we were interested in how the relationships among role-specific generativity, role performance, and well-being might differ as a partial function of sociohistorical factors. We found that while worker generativity was related to both competence and satisfaction in the 1978–1979 sample, it was related to neither in the 1991 sample. Well-being was linked to parental generativity in the 1978–1979 sample but to spouse generativity in the 1991 sample. Caution is necessary, however, in interpreting these findings because of the large differences between our samples, although it is worth noting that the control variable for socioeconomic status was not significant in any analysis.

Thus, our findings provide some evidence in favor of all three of our propositions, supporting the value of considering generativity in the context of multiple roles. We do not, however, suggest that global approaches have no utility, since our role-specific measures were correlated with a global measure of generativity, and a global approach accounted for as much variance as the role-specific approach in one subsample.

Clearly, the parental role was important in the lives of the women in this research regardless of when data were collected. Respondents reported higher generativity (on average) in the parental role than in the roles of either worker or spouse. Parental satisfaction was related to generativity in more roles than satisfaction or competence in any other role. Among 1978–1979 respondents, parental satisfaction was related to both parental and spousal generativity, while among 1991 respondents, parental satisfaction was related to parental and worker generativity. These patterns are consistent with some earlier views that women's major generative expression is the nurturing and caring they provide in the family context. Our path analyses showed, however, that while the well-being of the 1978–1979 subsample was tied primarily to parental generativity, well-being in the 1991 subsample was most strongly related to generativity in the *spouse* role. While the parental role is clearly important, it is not the only significant role context for generativity.

Although we expected generativity to be related to perceptions of both competence and satisfaction, in general only satisfaction proved to be related to generativity. While the merit of the competence measures can be debated, it also may be the case that women choose to be more or less generative independent of how competent they feel in a particular role. For example, one might choose to invest time and energy in socializing a less experienced colleague regardless of how competent one feels in one's own position.

Differences between the 1978–1979 and 1991 subsamples raise questions about the power of the social context. The 1978–1979 respondents had higher-level, more lucrative positions than did the 1991 respondents. On average, they represented a group of unusually powerful and well-off women in their social context, in which only about 1 in 20 employed women was an executive (Bureau of Labor Statistics, 1991). Among these women, both competence and satisfaction in the worker role predicted worker generativity, but only generativity in the parental role was related to well-being. By 1990, the historical context had changed considerably: the percentage of lawyers who were women had quintupled from 4% to 20.6%; the percentage of computer programmers who were women had almost doubled, from 19.9% to 36%; and the percentage of physicians who were women had jumped from 10.1% to 19.3% (Bureau of Labor Statistics, 1991). More than 1 in 10 employed women was an executive. Among the 1991 respondents, generativity in the worker role was independent of worker competence and satisfaction, and well-being was related to generativity in the spousal role and marginally related to generativity in the worker role.

Given their generally distinguished work roles, it was somewhat surprising that the well-being of the 1978–1979 respondents was exclusively a function of generativity in the parental role. Conversely, it was surprising that the worker generativity of women in the 1991 subsample, who spent more time working than women in the earlier sample, was unrelated to competence and satisfaction.

One possible explanation is that links between generativity and well-being conform to social expectations. Thus, even though the 1978–1979 women worked in higher-level positions, on average, than the 1991 women, they lived in a social and historical context within which parenthood was expected to be their primary source of identity. Consistent with these expectations, the well-being of women in the 1978–1979 sample was related only to generativity in the parental role. At the same time, the powerful work positions occupied by these women may have afforded them more opportunities to be generative; hence the positive relationships we observed between work competence, satisfaction, and generativity. Since 1979, social expectations regarding the prominence of the parental role for women may have loosened with patterns of reduced fertility and delayed marriage, leading to the greater importance of generativity in the role of spouse for well-being among the 1991 respondents. Given that employment for women had become the modal pattern, the women in the 1991 sample were much less unusual than their earlier counterparts; they also occupied lower-level positions, which may have limited their opportunities to be generative; hence the lack of connection between worker competence, satisfaction, and generativity. Of course, differences between findings for the two samples might simply be an artifact of differences between the samples independent of any changes in the sociohistorical context. It is also important to note that well-being was related to generativity in the worker role when the two subsamples were analyzed together.

It is interesting to consider the findings of this study in light of recent research concerning the role of spouse. Recall findings by Barnett and Baruch (1987) reported earlier that women's negative evaluations of the spousal role do not appear to be compensated for by positive experiences in other roles. They also suggest (1987, p. 139) that the rising prevalence of dual-earner families is affecting the role of husband by increasing its demands, with increased marital strain as one consequence. McKinlay, Triant, McKinlay, Brambilla, and Ferdock

(1990) reinforce this suggestion: "Perhaps the most important finding regarding the impact of nurturing roles is the persistent effect of stress from a spouse" (p. 133). Thus, the greater importance of generativity in the spouse role for well-being in the more recently collected data is consistent with observations from other research about possible shifts in the implications of particular roles.

Finally, the differences in the relative utility of global and role-specific approaches at different times of measurement are intriguing. Among data collected in 1978–1979, the global and role-specific approaches accounted for virtually equal proportions of variance in well-being, while in the 1991 data, role-specific approaches accounted for significantly greater variability than global approaches. Again, although these results could stem from important preexisting differences between the samples, they are also consistent with increasing discontinuity in women's role patterns and support our earlier suggestion that role-specific approaches may become increasingly useful.

There are important limitations that must be taken into account when considering our findings. First, the research was cross-sectional, precluding any conjecture about the direction of the links between perceived generativity in specific roles and well-being. It is quite possible that individuals with positive well-being simply report perceiving themselves as more generative because they have a generally positive outlook (Kotre, 1984). Presumably, however, such individuals also would be more likely to report higher competence and satisfaction. The discrepant patterns for satisfaction and competence in this study seem to argue against a contagion perspective, although only longitudinal research will sort out this relationship.

Another concern is that the items we used to indicate generativity were originally developed as indicators of role quality (Baruch, Barnett, & Rivers, 1983). In our view, the ability to be generative in a given role may be a very legitimate, though distinct, component of role quality. On the basis of the work of our judges, we are confident that the items we selected represent role-specific generativity. Stronger comparability of generativity measures across roles would be gained, however, if the items could be more similar in both content and meaning.

Our sample is small and certainly not representative, given that all the 1991 respondents worked in one bank. We believe that we have provided sufficient evidence to justify larger and more rigorous studies of both men and women.

Finally, there are many other domains of generative activity we should have asked about. The most serious omission probably was that of generativity expressed in the role of friend. In the future, more freedom needs to be allowed for respondents to tell us how they construct generativity. More sophisticated ways of thinking about and measuring the breadth of generative expressions also need to be developed. Finally, because of our desire for comparability between the 1978–1979 and 1991 data, only two (i.e., productivity and procreativity) of the five types of generative expression that were of interest could be explored.

Important research tasks lie ahead. First, we need to understand the relationships between role-specific generativity and the factors that shape participation in a given role. For example, what impedes generative perceptions and behaviors? What facilitates generativity? What is the process through which individuals choose to be (or not be) generative, and how is the mode of expression chosen? In short, which individuals will *feel* generative and which individuals will *be* generative, and in which domains under which conditions? The generativity of men and women must be studied longitudinally, in a wider array of domains. It also would be very helpful to understand differences between birth cohorts, since our findings hinted at possible shifts in patterns of generativity across time. Finally, we need to understand the consequences of generativity (and stagnation) for other domains of life, making clear distinctions among generativity, well-being, and personality.

We have contributed to a way of thinking about generativity that acknowledges expression in multiple roles. Our aim was to explore an approach that allows us to better understand individual differences across time and context. In so doing, we hope to come closer to doing justice to the full complexity of the lives of both women and men.

Acknowledgments

In addition to funding from the MacArthur Network for Research on Successful Midlife Development, support for this research was received from the Purdue Agricultural Experiment Station and a Purdue University Biomedical Research Support Grant (5111187-0700). We gratefully acknowledge support and assistance from Rosalind Barnett, Phame Camarena, Ann C. Crouter, Cynthia Darling-Fisher, Tim Dwyer, Joanne Gold, Joan Jurich, Eric McCollum, Elizabeth Paul, Carol Ryff, Dena Targ, the staff of the Murray Center, and the respondents whose efforts made this research possible. We also appreciate helpful suggestions from three anonymous reviewers.

NOTES

1. Because individual item scores were not available in the Baruch and Barnett data archive, Cronbach's alphas are calculated using only the 1991 data set.

2. See note 1 above.

3. See note 1 above.

4. All path analyses were run with and without the women who had children under seven or who had left home; findings were virtually identical.

5. There was one difference in the answer options offered spouses in 1978–1979 and 1991: in 1978–1979 spouses were given the option of responding "uncertain"; in 1991 spouses were not given this option. The 16 respondents who responded "uncertain" in 1978–1979 were excluded from the comparison of responses on this item. Path analyses were done separately for full-time and part-time workers in each subsample. In the 1978–1979 subsample, findings were virtually identical for full-time and part-time workers. Although there were not enough part-time workers in the 1991 subsample for reliable path analyses, the patterns for the full-time workers were similar to those in the overall sample.

REFERENCES

Archer, Sally L. (1992). A feminist's approach to identity research. In G. R. Adams, T. P. Gullotta, & R. Montemayor (Eds.), *Adolescent identity formation.* Newbury Park, CA: Sage.

Bakeman, Roger, & Gottman, John M. (1986). *Observing interaction: An introduction to sequential analysis.* Cambridge: Cambridge University Press.

Barnett, Rosalind C. (1991). *Multiple roles, gender, and psychological distress.* Wellesley College Working Paper no. 233. Wellesley, MA: Wellesley College Center for Research on Women.

Barnett, Rosalind C., & Baruch, Grace K. (1978). Women in the middle years: A critique of research and theory. *Psychology of Women Quarterly, 3*(2), 187–197.

Barnett, Rosalind C., & Baruch, Grace K. (1985). Women's involvement in multiple roles and psychological distress. *Journal of Personality and Social Psychology, 49,* 135–145.

Barnett, Rosalind C., & Baruch, Grace K. (1987). Social roles, gender, and psychological distress. In R. C. Barnett, L. Biener, & G. K. Baruch (Eds.), *Gender and Stress.* New York: Free Press.

Barnett, Rosalind C., Marshall, Nancy L., & Sayer, Aline. (1991). *Positive spillover effects from job to home: A closer look.* Wellesley College Working Paper no. 222. Wellesley, MA: Wellesley College Center for Research on Women.

Baruch, Grace K., & Barnett, Rosalind. (1986). Role quality, multiple role involvement, and psychological well-being in midlife women. *Journal of Personality and Social Psychology, 51*(3), 578–585.

Baruch, Grace K., Barnett, Rosalind C., & Rivers, Caryl. (1983). *Lifeprints.* New York: Plume Books.

Bureau of the Census. (1980). *Statistical Abstract of the United States, 101st Edition.* U.S. Department of Commerce.

Bureau of the Census. (1987). *Statistical Abstract of the United States, 107th Edition.* U.S. Department of Commerce.

Bureau of the Census. (1991). *Statistical Abstract of the United States, 111th Edition.* Economics and Statistics Administration.

Bureau of Labor Statistics. (1979, January). *CPI Detailed Report.* U.S. Department of Labor.

Bureau of Labor Statistics. (1990, December). *CPI Detailed Report.* U.S. Department of Labor.

Bureau of Labor Statistics. (1991, August). *Working women: A chartbook.* U.S. Department of Labor.

Campbell, A., Converse, P., & Rogers, W. L. (1976). *The quality of American life.* New York: Russell Sage Foundation.

Cohen, Jacob. (1960). A coefficient of agreement for nominal scales. *Educational and Psychological Measurement, 20,* 37–46.

Darling-Fisher, C., & Leidy, D. Kline. (1988). Measuring Eriksonian development in the adult: The modified Erikson psychosocial stage inventory, *Psychological Reports, 62,* 747–754.

Derogatis, L. R., Lipman, R. S., Rickels, K., Uhlenhuth, R. H., & Covi, L. (1974). The Hopkins Symptom Checklist: A self-report symptom inventory. *Behavioral Science, 19,* 1–14.

Erikson, Erik H. (1950). *Childhood and Society.* New York: Norton.

Erikson, Erik H., Erikson, Joan M., & Kivnick, Helen Q. (1986). *Vital involvement in old age.* New York: W. W. Norton.

Fiske, Marjorie. (1980). Changing hierarchies of commitment in adulthood. In Neil J. Smelser & Erik H. Erikson (Eds.), *Themes of work and love in adulthood* (pp. 238–264). Cambridge, MA: Harvard University Press.

Franz, Carol E., & White, Kathleen M. (1985). Individuation and attachment in personality development: Extending Erikson's theory. *Journal of Personality, 53,* 224–255.

Gergen, Mary M. (1990). Finished at 40: Women's development within the patriarchy. *Psychology of Women Quarterly, 14,* 471–493.

Giele, Janet Zollinger. (1982). Women in adulthood: Unanswered questions. In Janet Zollinger Giele (Ed.), *Women in the middle years* (pp. 1–35). New York: John Wiley and Sons.

Gilligan, C. (1982). Adult development and women's development: Arrangements for a marriage. In Janet Zollinger Giele (Ed.), *Women in the middle years* (pp. 89–114). New York: John Wiley and Sons.

Gorsuch, Richard L. (1983). *Factor Analysis.* Hillsdale, NJ: Lawrence Erlbaum.

Grotevant, H. D. (1987). Toward a process model of identity formation. *Journal of Adolescent Research, 2*(3), 203–222.

Hornstein, Gail A. (1986). The structuring of identity among midlife women as a function of their degree of involvement in employment. *Journal of Personality,* *54,* 551–575.

Hulsizer, D., Murphy, M., Noam, G., Taylor, C., Erikson, E., & Erikson, J. (1981). On generativity and identity: From a conversation with Erik and Joan Erikson. *Harvard Educational Review, 51,* 249–269.

Joreskog, Karl G. (1979). A general approach to confirmatory maximum likelihood factor analysis with addendum. In Karl G. Joreskog & Dag Sorbom, *Advances in factor analysis and structural equation models* (pp. 21–44). Cambridge, MA: Abt Books.

Joreskog, Karl G., & Sorbom, Dag. (1988). *LISREL 7-A Guide to the Program and Applications.* Chicago: SPSS.

Juhasz, Anne McCreary. (1989). A role-based approach to adult development: The triple-helix model. *International Journal of Aging and Human Development,* *29*(4), 301–315.

Kotre, John. (1984). *Outliving the self: Generativity and the interpretation of lives.* Baltimore, MD: Johns Hopkins University Press.

Kroger, Jane, & Haslett, Stephen J. (1991). A comparison of ego identity status transition pathways and change rates across five identity domains. *International Journal of Aging and Human Development, 32*(4), 303–330.

Long, Judy, & Porter, Karen L. (1984). Multiple roles of midlife women: A case for new directions in theory, research, and policy. In G. Baruch & J. Brooks-Gunn (Eds.), *Women in midlife.* New York: Plenum.

MacDermid, Shelley M., & Gillespie, Laura K. (1992, May). *Generativity in multiple roles.* Paper presented during symposium *Emerging perspectives in adult personality development: Research concerning generativity,* chaired by E. de St. Aubin at the annual meeting of the Midwestern Psychological Association, Chicago.

McAdams, Dan P. (1988). *Power, intimacy and the life story.* New York: Guilford.

McAdams, Dan P., Ruetzel, Karin, & Foley, Jeanne M. (1986). Complexity and generativity at midlife: Relations among social motives, ego development, and adults' plans for the future. *Journal of Personality and Social Psychology, 50*(4), 800–807.

McAdams, Dan P., & St. Aubin, Ed de. (1992). A theory of generativity and its assessment through self-report, behavioral acts, and narrative themes in autobiography. *Journal of Personality and Social Psychology, 62*(6), 1003–1015.

McAdams, Dan P., St. Aubin, Ed de, & Logan, R. L. (1993). Generativity among young, midlife, and older adults. *Psychology and Aging, 8*(2), 221–230.

McKinlay, Sonja M., Triant, Randi S., McKinlay, John B., Brambilla, Donald J., & Ferdock, Matthew. (1990). Multiple roles for middle-aged women and their impact on health. In M. Ory & H. Warner (Eds.), *Gender, health and longevity.* New York: Springer.

Neugarten, Bernice L. (1968). The awareness of middle age. In B. L. Neugarten (Ed.), Middle age and aging (pp. 93–98). Chicago: University of Chicago Press.

Ochse, R., & Plug, C. (1986). Cross-cultural investigation of the validity of Erikson's theory of personality development. *Journal of Personality and Social Psychology, 50*, 1240–1252.

Pearlin, L. K., & Schooler, C. (1978). The structure of coping. *Journal of Health and Social Behavior, 19*, 2–21.

Peterson, Bill E., & Stewart, Abigail J. (1990). Using personal and fictional documents to assess psychosocial development: A case study of Vera Brittain's Generativity. *Psychology and Aging, 5*, 400–411.

Peterson, Bill E., & Stewart, Abigail J. (1992, May). The assessment of generativity using the California Q-Sort. Paper presented during the symposium *Emerging perspectives in adult personality development: Research concerning generativity*, chaired by E. de St. Aubin at the annual meeting of the Midwestern Psychological Association, Chicago.

Rosenberg, M. (1979). *Conceiving the self.* New York: Basic Books.

Rupp, Michael T., & Segal, Richard. (1989). Confirmatory factor analysis of a professionalism scale in pharmacy. *Journal of Social and Administrative Pharmacy, 6*(1), 31–38.

Ryff, Carol D., & Heincke, S. G. (1983). Subjective organization of personality in adulthood and aging. *Journal of Personality and Social Psychology, 44*, 807–816.

Ryff, Carol D., & Migdal, Susan. (1984). Intimacy and generativity: Self-perceived transitions. *Signs, 9*(3), 470–481.

Sherman, Edmund. (1987). *Meaning in mid-life transitions.* Albany: State University of New York Press.

Stewart, Abigail J., Franz, Carol E., & Layton, L. (1988). The changing self: Using personal documents to study lives. *Journal of Personality, 56*, 41–74.

Stewart, Abigail J., Franz, Carol E., Paul, Elizabeth, L., & Peterson, B. E. (1991). *Revised coding manual for three aspects of development of the adult self: Identity, intimacy, and generativity.* Unpublished coding manual. Ann Arbor: University of Michigan.

Stewart, Abigail J., & Gold-Steinberg, Sharon. (1990). Midlife women's political consciousness: Case studies of psychosocial development and political commitment. *Psychology of Women Quarterly, 14*, 543–566.

Tanaka, J. S. & Huba, G. J. (1984). Confirmatory hierarchical factor analyses of psychological distress measures. *Journal of Personality and Social Psychology, 46*, 621–635.

Vaillant, George E., & Milofsky, Eva. (1980). Natural history of male psychological health IX: Empirical evidence for Erikson's model of the life cycle. *American Journal of Psychiatry, 137*(11), 1348–1359.

Van de Water, Donna A., & McAdams, Dan P. (1989). Generativity and Erikson's "Belief in the Species." *Journal of Research in Personality, 23*, 435–449.

Waterman, A. S. (1985). Identity in the context of adolescent psychology. In Alan S. Waterman (Ed.), *Identity in adolescence: Processes and context.* San Francisco: Jossey-Bass.

III Health and Stress

NINE

Promoting Health and Minimizing Stress in Midlife
Ilene C. Siegler

Part 3 shifts our focus to health and the role that health plays in midlife. I would like to argue that health is very much a part of the definition of what it means to be middle-aged. This is apparent only when we consider when the cognitive transition of thinking of ourselves as no longer middle-aged comes about. It may not be extreme to say that a preoccupation of the middle-aged person is to find a way to deny aging and therefore stay middle-aged forever. It may be that old age is achieved when we are no longer doing or wishing to do or able to do the developmental tasks of adulthood. It is the changes in health status, the accumulation of illnesses, and the extent to which those health problems impact on our ability to remain in control of our lives that give health its prominence in the study of middle age. Rarely are the changes in health normative in this phase of the life cycle. However, fears of declining future health are a part of midlife.

The study of adult development, including middle age, has reached a developmental milestone of sorts with the publication of an *Encyclopedia of Adult Development* (Kastenbaum, 1993b). This publication is important because it shows convincingly that people have been studying adult development (including middle age) for a long time. The midlife crisis hit the popular imagination with the writings of Sheehy (1976), followed by the academic writings of Gould (1978) and Levinson (1978). Jung (1933), however, had laid the theoretical foundation for a transition at midlife, as discussed cogently by Kastenbaum (1993a) and by Schlossberg (Schlossberg, 1993; Schlossberg & Robinson, 1996).

In this chapter I will first comment on stress and then on health, including some examples from my current work, and finally, I will make a few remarks about Chapters 10 and 11.

Rather than a review of the literature (that is the function of handbooks, Goldberger & Breznitz, 1982; or edited collections, Eisdorfer & Elliot, 1982; Wykle, Kahana, & Cowal, 1992). I would like to pose a set of questions about the current status of stress and health that have implications for understanding midlife at the end of the 20th century and set the stage for the chapters in Part 3: (1) What is the optimal level of stress? Does it change with age? What about work stress? Does it cause illness? What are the roles of income and social class in defining middle age and setting its parameters? (2) What is the expected level of health and stress at midlife? Are these issues gender related?

THE STATUS OF STRESS AT MIDLIFE

Asking about stress in terms of its level assumes a particular definition. Defining stress is not easy. Kasl (1992), as usual, gets to the point: "The reader must be in a position to translate stress, when the word is used, into the actual operationalizations that were used and the actual data that were collected" (p. 6). Thomas (Chap. 10) defines stress as a set of symptoms indicative of psychological distress. Chiriboga (Chap. 11) uses small, medium, and large stressors as a framework for discussion of the content of the life course. I define stress in the interactional model, linking the environmental demands and a person's capacity to meet those demands (Kasl, 1992, p. 7).

My reading of the literature suggests to me that some level of stress is normative in adulthood, and that the variations in stress generally are *not* age related. When a life crisis perspective is taken, there is little evidence for the influence of age on reactions to life events, even though the occurrence of those events is related to age and life stage (Lieberman & Peskin, 1992, p. 124). An example of work on stress, health, and middle age that I find the most useful is the one that looks at stress in the workplace. There is very interesting discussion of the health effects of stress in the workplace in the work of Frankenhaeuser (1991) and Karasek and his colleagues (Karasek & Theorell, 1990).

Frankenhaeuser's research program at the Karolinska Institute in Sweden focuses on psychophysiological correlates of work for both men and women, with a particular emphasis on the role of catecholamines and cortisol in response to stress, and linkages to cardiovascular risk. It suggests that stress on the job is an important risk. Karasek and Theorell (1990) review findings from their long-standing research program on job strain and its components—decision latitude and psychological demands. They discuss the evidence that relates psychosocial job environment to coronary heart disease and to other health outcomes, including suicide, alcohol-related injuries, traffic accidents, and psychiatric and gastrointestinal diseases. They give a comprehensive review of the methods, issues, and findings, and the issues concerning occupational stress and its associations with health during the working years. Both of these research programs suggest interventions to make the workplace less stressful and to teach individuals to manage the stress in order to reduce the potential health effects. Given the importance of work in the lives of most middle-aged men and women, these research programs provide important models for future research. Most of the literature has been on industrial jobs, where there is both high demand and low control. However, the workplace is more varied. Stress and health are also related to voluntary and involuntary job changes. As our economy changes, it will be important to study the potential health effects of economic change on different individuals.

What role do income and social class play in defining middle age and setting its parameters? Anderson and Armstead (1995) have shown the tremendous difference that race and class make in health. Adler et al. (1994) have shown that the social class and health gradient has impact all along the scale. House et al. (1992) have shown that for advantaged persons, the average number of chronic diseases at age 70 is characteristic of the most impoverished at age 40. In most current studies of stress and health and midlife, far too little attention has been given to the role of social class and socioeconomic status within the United States. Cross-cultural studies also present interesting and relatively unexplored perspectives. For example, Markson and Gognalons-Nicolet (1991) contrast the United States with France, where economic and population pressures are encouraging early retirement at age 50.

Gender contrasts are important to the extent that men and women live different lives. We know that the men and women in the Second Duke Longitudinal Study had the traditional sex differences in terms of personality (Siegler, George, & Okun, 1979). Thus it is not surprising that they reported different events as stressful (Siegler & George, 1983), and that what the events demanded determined people's effectiveness in coping. Because the events that men reported tended to be their own events, they used active coping strategies that worked. Women tended to report events that happened to family members, where only palliative strategies were possible. Also, women's events, such as heart attacks, may happen to them later in life (Eaker et al., 1993), which may help to explain our findings.

THE STATUS OF HEALTH AT MIDLIFE

Most individuals seem to expect good health at midlife. What are the national figures? The U.S. Department of Health and Human Services (HHS) defines the adult population as persons aged 25–64. In 1977 the death rate for this population was 532.9 per 100,000. The 1990 goal was to reduce mortality to 400 per 100,000. This was achieved by 1989 and represented a 30% decline in mortality (U.S. Department of Health and Human Services [HHS], 1992, p. 18). This is because death rates from coronary heart disease in this age group have declined (41% decline for ages 55–64), while the death rates for cancers in this age group have increased only slightly. Although in later life increases in survival often imply increased rates of disability, this does not appear to be true during the middle years (Siegler & O'Keefe, 1992) or for the expert survivors who get to be centenarians (Poon, 1992).

In 1989 the five leading causes of death at ages 25–44 were unintentional injuries (35.4 per 100,000, of which motor vehicle crashes accounted for 20.6 deaths per 100,000), cancer (26.2 per 100,000), HIV (20.3), heart disease (19.0), and suicide (14.8). For persons aged 45–64, the five leading causes of death in 1989 were cancer (290.9 per 100,000), heart disease (241.5), stroke (32.5), unintentional injuries (32.4), and chronic obstructive pulmonary disease (28.0). The goal for *Healthy People 2000* (a long-range plan for the health of the nation) is to reduce the death rate from the 1990 rate of 400 per 100,000 to 340 per 100,000. Thus, the illnesses of middle age that are most likely to be responsible for premature mortality are cancer, heart disease, and AIDS. All of these have strong behavioral components. In general, levels of physical health tend to be stable during midlife. Around 40–50, the incidence of many diseases starts to increase. My view of health and aging was summed up in what I called developmental health psychology (Siegler, 1989). I attempted to understand how aging and health interact and to consider whether health status rather than age per se may be controlling the important variation that we normally attribute to age.

This makes studying health at midlife difficult. Normal populations have relatively few persons with disease, and middle-aged persons with disease are often nonrepresentative of midlife. A possible solution might be to study the same problems in populations selected for health status. Another solution might be using longitudinal data archives of large samples that started in midlife and following the groups into later life when differential health outcomes could be observed. However, it is hard to find studies whether ongoing or archival that have good psychosocial predictor data and good health outcome data on the same persons.

The index chosen to measure health during the middle years is critical. Reports of symptoms and self-rated health are two popular choices that are problematic. Symptom reports indicate neither health nor stress. Rather they are contaminated with neuroticism (Costa & McCrae, 1985, 1987; Watson & Pennebaker, 1989). These two indices of health (self-related health and symptom reports) tend to have spuriously high associations with psychosocial constructs because they *are* psychosocial constructs.

Watson and Pennebaker (1989) state in their thoughtful review:

> Thus NA (negative affectivity or neuroticism) can be expected to act as a general nuisance factor in health research, one that taps psychologically important but organically spurious variance in physical symptom measures. We must remain skeptical of any study that uses a health complaint scale as its criterion for health and that includes a psychological predictor, a measure with a subjective distress component. The danger always exists that such a predictor is assessing—either partly or completely—variance that is uninteresting from an objective health standpoint (however interesting it may be psychologically). (pp. 248–249)

SELF-RATED HEALTH

Self-rated health is not a proxy of objective health (Mossey & Shapiro, 1982). Mitchell and Helson (1990), in describing the prime of life for women in their early 50s, point to the importance of self-related health as a correlate of quality of life at age 52. Our analysis from the Augmented Second Duke Longitudinal Study essentially replicates this finding; self-rated health is a predictor of life satisfaction (Hooker & Siegler, 1992). Self-rated health also figures prominently in the work of Ware and associates (1993) who have developed the SF (Short Form)-36 as a measure of Quality of Life in health-related situations. It features perception of health as a component of the General Health Scale. Thinking of self-perceptions of health as a part of health-related quality of life is not a bad place to start, on the basis on current work (Dimsdale & Baum, 1995; Shumaker & Czajkowski, 1993). Spiro and Bosse (1993) have shown that health-related quality of life is associated with psychological well-being. It will be interesting to see if their findings can be replicated with younger samples.

TABLE 9.1 Self-rated Health (SRH) and the Five Personality Factors

Measures	Neuroticism	Extraversion	Openness	Agreeableness	Conscientiousness
SRH	−0.26	0.19	—	0.10	0.22

Source: I. C. Siegler, B. H. Kaplan, D. D. Von Dras, and D. B. Mark, "Cardiovascular Health, in S. L. Willis and J. R. Reid (Eds.), *Life in the Middle,* in press, Orlando, FL: Academic Press.

TABLE 9.2 Levels of Self-Rated Health by Age in UNC Alumni Heart Study Respondents

Response Option	At age 40 in 1986–1987	At age 42 in 1988–1989	Age 44 in 1990
Health is excellent	2,000 (57.3%)	1,914 (54.9%)	1,855 (53.2%)
Health is good	1,391 (39.3%)	1,479 (42.4%)	1,513 (43.4%)
Health is fair	90 (2.6%)	92 (2.6%)	115 (3.3%)
Health is poor	7 (0.2%)	3 (0.1%)	5 (0.1%)

Note: From UNC Alumni Heart Study Laboratory, 23 June 1995.

Self-rated health has been measured in the University of North Carolina Alumni Heart Study (UNCAHS) (Siegler, Peterson, Barefoot, Harvin, et al., 1992; Siegler, Peterson, Barefoot, & Williams, 1992). Personality was measured using the NEO Personality Inventory (Costa & McCrae, 1992). The correlations of self-rated health with the Big 5 personality factors are given in Table 9.1. Individuals higher in neuroticism are less likely to report that their health is excellent than their less neurotic peers. Similarly, extraverts, agreeable people, and those who are conscientious are more likely to report excellent health.

How excellent do the participants in the UNCAHS think their health is, and how stable is self-rated health? We can look at the responses of the group of 3,488 UNCAHS participants who were members of the study at the first three waves of data collection from age 40 to age 44. As can be seen in Table 9.2, there is a slight tendency for more to be in good health rather than excellent health. We have reports of illness that are being verified, so it is premature to speak about the associations of self-rated health with actual health status. However, in the future we expect to be able to do so. We are also collecting data on psychological well-being and should be able to evaluate self-rated health in that context. Distributions of self-rated health in a middle-aged population measured longitudinally are shown in Table 9.2.

We present these data is to illustrate that in a population unselected for a disease or for health problems, health is generally seen as excellent to good in the middle years, and this is stable during the middle years.

Another view of health at midlife comes from our work on the Mediators of Social Support, or MOSS study (Mark, 1994). This is a study of persons who are being evaluated for a diagnosis of coronary heart disease. The study is designed to replicate and explain an earlier finding that social support and economic status predict mortality in this population when disease severity is controlled (Williams et al., 1992).

Siegler (1995), as part of a symposium on social support and health, compared middle-aged and older respondents (cutting at age 65) who participated in the intensive interview portion of the study. There are data on 659 persons aged 31–94. The mean age of the sample is 63.88, and 65% of the sample are male. This is not surprising for a study based on coronary patients. We can look at the impact of age, gender, and disease severity on a variety of health, quality-of-life, and psychosocial factors measured while the participants were in the hospital for evaluation and again one month later when they were interviewed at home. The data from the one-month follow-up are important, because they will allow us to assess the impact of answering questions while in the hospital rather than at home. And this is a very important lesson for studying health issues—both the population and the site of the research are important variables that need to be considered.

Table 9.3 suggests that when we study consecutive admissions for evaluation for coronary heart disease (CHD) there is a wide range of ages and disease severity. The medhazard score involves all of the prognostic information about one-year survival. It combines all of the various indices of medical history and cardiovascular anatomy and physiology (Williams et al., 1992). Thus those in the low-risk group have a 94% chance of surviving for a year, while those in the high-risk group have an average 62% chance of surviving a year. People were classified into these groups as part of the design of the MOSS study to see if social support operated in the same way across levels of disease severity. So the term high versus low risk is descriptive. The Center for Epidemiologic Studies Depression Scale (CES_D) was measured in the hospital and one month later at a home visit. This scale is related to age and to disease severity at both times, but there is no interaction. Two measures of functional health were part of the data collection: one is a health interference item where 1 means "not at all" and 4 means "completely." The other is the General health perceptions from the Short

TABLE 9.3 The Role of Age versus Disease Severity in Coronary Patients from the MOSS Study

Variables	Middle-aged	Older	Low-Risk	High-Risk	Significant Difference
Age	53.85 (7.45)	73.23 (5.08)	60.19 (10.98)	68.31 (11.10)	AG/DxSev[a]
MEDHAZARD[b]	0.86	0.73	0.94	0.62	AG/DX/AG*D[c]
					x
CES_D[d]	20.32	18.28	19.04	20.79	Ag/DxSev
CES_D home[e]	17.64	16.21	16.69	17.29	Ag/Dx[f]
Health Interference	2.41	2.70	2.31	2.87	Dx Severity[g]
General health	36.71	33.39	38.50	30.49	DxSeverity

[a] Age Group and Disease Severity Group means are significantly different from each other.
[b] Hazard score is the percentage of the group predicted to survive.
[c] Age, severity, and their interaction are all statistically significant.
[d] Center for Epidemiologic Studies Depression scale, baseline in hospital.
[e] Center for Epidemiologic Studies Depression scale measured one month later at home.
[f] Age and disease severity are statistically significant.
[g] Disease Severity means all differ.

Form (SF) 36 item questionnaire; this is normalized such that a score of 100% is "uniformly excellent health," "being as healthy as anybody I know", "not expecting your health to get worse," and "not getting sick easier than others." Both of these scales are related only to disease severity. The means in Table 9.3 indicate that the groups being studied are reporting considerable symptoms of depression and a reduced quality of life, in contrast to the UNC Alumni Heart Study population. Middle-aged people and those with less severe disease report lower depression and higher quality of life and functional health; but these factors do not interact in this population. These brief illustrations from ongoing work with middle-aged people indicate that the population selected for study makes a critical difference when we try to understand health at midlife.

WHAT WE LEARN FROM PART 3

Chapters 10 and 11 are each based on an excellent parent study that was well conceptualized and designed to answer important questions about midlife. Neither was designed to measure health and thus the possibility of doing so is limited. Thomas (Chap. 10) defines stress as subjective emotional experience as indexed by symptoms of anxiety and depression on the Symptom Check List (SCL-90). She defines health as subjective, including health worries, health-limiting activities, and self-rated health. As she reports in Table 10.1, the strongest correlation is between these two constructs ($-.40$). It is not at all surprising that those who are more neurotic report lower health-related quality of life. I do not see what is gained by redefining symptoms of anxiety and depression as stress and defining health-related quality of life as health. Understanding the role of anxiety and depression in middle-aged women for their health-related quality of life—or perceived general health—is an important topic worthy of study, as Chapter 10 illustrates.

In Chapter 11, Chiriboga takes a very different view. He presents a catalog of stressors (high, medium, and low) and defines health only as a potential problem area that emerges from his data as a major area of concern for his middle-aged respondents (17.6% of respondents with health concerns overall compared to 19.2% in the work area), with the peak of over 40% of the empty nesters reporting health problems. Also, it is interesting that the correlations of psychological with physical health symptoms remain significant over time for both high- and low-stress persons, as defined by Chiriboga (see Chap. 11).

Final Thoughts

Is longevity changing the way we think about life stages? The whole concept of middle age seems to me to divide the life span psychologically into thirds—a beginning, a middle, and an end. Perhaps we are entering a new phase. If it should become common for people to become centenarians (Poon, 1992), then maybe we will be taking about quarters: first, second, third, and fourth. Thus, instead of middle age we will be talking about the second quarter.

My assigned title for this chapter was "promoting health and minimizing stress." Maybe it is promoting health that is becoming stressful. A front-page *New York Times* article in 1994 stated that "Eat, drink and be merry" may be the next trend. The article suggested a popular backlash on dieting and moderation. Seligman's (1994) new book counsels us to work on what works and to give up on what does not work. The promote-your-health-if-it-kills-you ethic may be starting to fade as a popular preoccupation. Perhaps as the crest of the baby boom approaches full middle age—the 1946 cohort is now 50—the reality of dealing with health-related issues in midlife in a nonstressful way will start to predominate as this cohort seeks the wisdom of its own aging.

Acknowledgments

My work on this chapter has been supported by Grants HL36587 HL45702 and HL55356 from the National Heart, Lung, and Blood Institute, AG09276 and AG12458 from the National Institute on Aging, and grants from the AARP Foundation. I would like to thank Nancy K. Schlossberg and Avron Spiro for sharing prepublication copies of their work.

References

Adler, N. E., Boyce, T., Chesney, M. A., Cohen, S., Folkman, S., Kahn, R. L., & Syme, S. L. (1994). Socioeconomic status and health: The Challenge of the gradient. *American Psychologist, 49,* 15–24.

Anderson, N. B., & Armstead, C. A. (1995). Toward understanding the association of socioeconomic status and health: A new challenge for the biopsychosocial approach. *Psychosomatic Medicine, 57,* 213–225.

Costa, P. T., Jr., & McCrae, R. R. (1985). Hypochondriasis, neuroticism, and aging: When are somatic complaints unfounded? *American Psychologist, 40,* 19–28.

Costa, P. T., Jr., & McCrae, R. R. (1987). Neuroticism, somatic complaints, and disease: Is the bark worse than the bite? *Journal of Personality, 55,* 299–316.

Costa, P. T., Jr., & McCrae, R. R. (1992). *The NEO Personality Inventory manual.* Odessa FL: PAR (Psychological Assessment Resources).

Dimsdale, J. E., & Baum, A. (1995), *Quality of life in behavioral medicine research.* Hillsdale NJ: Lawrence Erlbaum Associates.

Eaker, E. D., Chesebro, J. H., Sacks, F. M., Wenger, N. K., Whisnant, J. P., & Winston, M. (1993). Cardiovascular disease in women. *Circulation, 88,* 1999–2009.

Eisdorfer, C., & Elliot, G. R. (Eds.). (1982). *Stress and Human Health.* Washington DC: National Academy Press.

Frankenhaeuser, M. (1991). The psychophysiology of work load, stress, and health: Comparison between the sexes. *Annals of Behavioral Medicine, 13*(4):197–204.

Goldberger, L., & Breznitz, S. (Eds.). (1982). *Handbook of Stress.* New York: Free Press.

Gould, R. L. (1978). *Transformations: Growth and change in adult life.* New York: Simon and Schuster.

Hooker, K., & Siegler, I. C. (1992). Separating apples from oranges in health ratings: Perceived health includes psychological well-being. *Behavior, Health, and Aging, 2*(2), 81–92.

House, J. S., Kessler, R. C., Herzog, A. R., Mero, R. P., Kinney, A. M., & Breslow, M. J. (1992). Social stratification, age, and health. In K. W. Schaie, D. Blazer, & J. S. House (Eds.), *Aging, health behaviors, and health outcomes* (pp. 1–32). Hillsdale NJ: Lawrence Erlbaum Associates.

Jung, C. G. (1933). *Modern man in search of a soul.* New York: Harvest.

Karasek, R., & Theorell, T. (1990). *Health work stress, productivity, and the reconstruction of working life.* New York: Basic Books.

Kasl, S. V. (1992). Stress and health among the elderly: Overview of issues (pp. 5–34). In M. L. Wykle, E. Kahana, & J. Cowal (Eds.), *Stress and health among the elderly.* New York: Springer.

Kastenbaum, R. 1993. Mid-life crisis. In R. Kastenbaum (Ed.), *Encyclopedia of Adult Development* (pp. 346–351). Phoenix, AZ: Oryx Press.

Kastenbaum, R. (Ed.) (1993b). *Encyclopedia of Adult Development.* Phoenix, AZ: Oryx Press.

Levinson, D. J. (1978). *The seasons of a man's life.* New York: A. E. Knopf.

Lieberman, M. A., & Peskin, H. (1992). Adult life crises. In J. E. Birren, R. B. Sloane, & G. D. Cohen (Eds.), *Handbook of mental health and aging* (pp. 119–143). San Diego: Academic Press.

Mark, D. B. (1994, April). *Psychosocial factors and prognosis in established CAD.* Symposium at the Society of Behavioral Medicine, Boston, MA.

Markson, E. B., & Gognalons-Nicolet, M. (1991). Mid-life: Crisis or nodal point? Some cross-cultural views. In B. B. Hess and E. W. Markson (Eds.), *Growing old in America* (pp. 55–65). New Brunswick, NJ: Transaction Publishers.

Mitchell, V. & Helson, R. (1990). Women's prime of life: Is it in the 50s? *Psychology of Women Quarterly, 14,* 451–470.

Mossey, J. M., & Shapiro, E. (1982). Self-rated health: A predictor of mortality among the elderly. *American Journal of Public Health, 72*(8), 800–808.

Poon, L. W. (1992). The Georgia Centenarian Study: Special Issue. *International Journal of Aging and Human Development, 34*(1).

Schlossberg, N. K. (1993, June). Facing the ups and downs of mid-life. Lecture given as part of the series *The Transitional Years: A Psychological Look at Mid-Life in the 90's. APA Lectures the Smithsonian.* Washington, DC.

Schlossberg, N. K., & Robinson, S. P. (1996). *Going to Plan B.* New York: Simon and Schuster.

Seligman, M. E. P. (1994). *What you can change and what you can't.* New York: Knopf.

Sheehy, G. (1976). *Passages: Predictable crises of adult life.* New York: Dalton.

Shumaker, S. A., & Czajkowski, S. M. (1993). A review of health-related quality of life and psychosocial factors in women with cardiovascular disease. *Annals of Behavioral Medicine, 15*(2/3), 149–155.

Siegler, I. C. (1989). Developmental health psychology. In M. Storandt & G. R. Van den Bos (Eds.), *The adult years: Continuity and change* (pp. 119–142). Washington DC: American Psychological Association.

Siegler, I. C. (1995, March). *Social support in established coronary heart disease: Report of ongoing findings from the MOSS Study.* Presented in a symposium at the meetings of the Society of Behavioral Medicine, San Diego, CA.

Siegler, I. C., & George, L. K. (1983). Sex differences in coping and perceptions of life events. *Journal of Geriatric Psychiatry, 16*(2), 197–209.

Siegler, I. C., George, L. K., & Okun, M. A. (1979). A cross-sequential analysis of adult personality. *Developmental Psychology, 15*(3), 350–351.

Siegler, I. C., Kaplan, B. H., Von Dras, D. D., & Mark, D. B. (in press). Cardiovascular health: A challenge for mid-life. In S. L. Willis & J. R. Reid (Eds.), *Life in the Middle.* Orlando, FL: Academic Press.

Siegler, I. C., & O'Keefe, J. E. (1992). Aging and health. Invited address at the American Psychological Association, Washington DC.

Siegler, I. C., Peterson, B. L., Barefoot, J. C., Harvin, S. H., Dahlstrom, W. G., Kaplan, B. H., Costa, P. T., Jr., & Williams, R. B. (1992). Using college alumni populations in epidemiologic research: The UNC Alumni Heart Study. *Journal of Clinical Epidemiology, 45*(11), 1243–1250.

Siegler, I. C., Peterson, B. L., Barefoot, J. C., & Williams, R. B. (1992). Hostility during late adolescence predicts coronary risk factors at mid-life. *American Journal of Epidemiology, 138* (2), 146–154.

Spiro, A., & Bosse, R. (1993). *Relations between health related quality of life and well-being.* Paper presented at the meetings of the Gerontology Society of America.

U.S. Department of Health and Human Services. (1992). *Health United States 1991 and Prevention Profile.* Hyattsville, MD: PHS, CDC, NCHS, DHHS Pub No. 92-1232.

Ware, J. E., & Associates. (1993). SF-36 Health Survey: Manual and interpretation guide. Boston, MA: Health Institute, New England Medical Center.

Watson, D., & Pennebaker, J. W. (1989). Health complaints, stress, and distress: Exploring the central role of negative affectivity. *Psychological Review, 96,* 234–254.

Williams, R. B., Barefoot, J. C., Califf, R. M., Haney, T. L., Saunders, W. B., Pryor, D. B., Hlatky, M. A., Siegler, I. C., & Mark, D. B. (1992). Prognostic importance of social and economic resources among medically treated patients with angiographically documented coronary artery disease. *Journal of the American Medical Association, 267,* 520–524.

Wykle, M. L., Kahana, E., & Cowal, J. (Eds.). (1992). *Stress & health among the elderly.* New York: Springer.

TEN

Psychosocial Correlates of Women's Self-Rated Physical Health in Middle Adulthood

Sandra P. Thomas

Health is undeniably a key element in a woman's experience of middle adulthood as a time of productivity and personal fulfillment, yet research on psychosocial factors related to midlife health is sparse. The literature is notably deficient in studies of women's health during this period, except for narrowly focused investigations of the experience of menopause and its discomforts. Psychosocial variables are not only highly salient to health but also potentially modifiable by women themselves—if they receive accurate information or counseling from their health care providers.

I used a multivariate, multitheoretical approach to the study of health to examine a variety of psychosocial variables in a secondary analysis of data collected by Baruch and Barnett (1986) on 238 women. I build on some of my previous investigations of midlife health, including a longitudinal study that began at the 1982 World's Fair in Knoxville, Tennessee (Thomas, 1983). Among the predictors of women's health that I (Thomas, 1990) examined previously were locus of control, optimism, stress, and social network ties. The Baruch and Barnett data set included all of these variables and offered the opportunity to examine two additional variables (psychological well-being and quality of experience in social roles) hypothesized to impact women's health. One of the chief contributions of Baruch and Barnett's work was their emphasis on investigating women's *subjective* experience in their primary roles, in contrast to other projects in which the focus was merely on *occupancy* of roles. For example, their measurement tool made it possible to evaluate whether the rewards of being a mother outweighed a woman's concerns about her parenting competence and her worries and disappointments about her children's behavior. Insufficient attention has been given to the health consequences of women's experience in their daily roles in the home and workplace. Individuals internalize the roles they play and the statuses they occupy in the groups with which they are identified (Meltzer, Petras, & Reynolds, 1975). There fore, the benefits and costs of a woman's role commitments may be critically important to her health.

WOMEN'S HEALTH: THE KNOWLEDGE GAP

Rodin and Ickovics (1990), noting the "large gap in our knowledge base concerning women's health" (p. 1018), proposed an explicit research agenda with special attention to the health of aging women. Although women live longer than men, they spend their later years with more disabling conditions (in many cases, three or more chronic illnesses) (Verbrugge, 1985a). Virtually all studies show that women, regardless of age, report more health problems than men do. Women are more dependent on medical services, reporting more acute conditions and having higher prevalence of chronic diseases (Lempert, 1986). Compared to men, women of all ages report more physician contact through both office visits and telephone calls (Adams & Benson, 1990). Women restrict their activities for health problems about 25 percent more days each year than men do, and they spend about 40 percent more days in bed per year on the average (Verbrugge, 1985b).

Statistics specific to middle adulthood are consistent with those cited for women in general. Midlife women visit physicians, on the average, 5.9 times per year, compared to 4.7 visits for men (Givens, 1979). Restriction due to illness is 46 percent greater for midlife women than for midlife men; incidence of acute conditions is 24 percent greater for women (Givens, 1979). Women's traditional mortality advantage over men has begun to decline in recent years, particularly for persons aged 45 and older (Rodin & Ickovics, 1990). Despite the obvious need for research, female subjects have been woefully underrepresented in studies funded by the National Institute of Health, as documented by the U.S. General Accounting Office (1990).

Research specific to middle adulthood is particularly scanty. De-Lorey (1984) noted that "Until recently, little information has been available concerning the health or health care of mid-life women" (p. 277). DeLorey found that medical literature focused on menopause as the major health issue for midlife women; among 30 textbooks, few even mentioned other aspects of health (DeLorey, 1981). Although the discomforts of menopause should not be minimized, research shows that for most women it is not the negative, distressing experience portrayed in medical literature (MacPherson, 1981). In a longitudinal study of 541 initially premenopausal women, natural menopause did not adversely affect anxiety, anger, depression, perceived stress, or other psychological characteristics, and the researchers concluded that menopause was a benign event (Matthews et al., 1990). Further, menopause is not the predominant health issue of this period of a woman's life (McKinlay, McKinlay, & Brambilla, 1987).

In an extensive review of nursing research on women's health from 1980 to 1985, Woods (1988) found that only 15 percent of papers dealt with women in the middle years. Existing studies of midlife women's health or health-promoting behaviors (Duffy, 1988; Engel, 1987) have failed to explain much of the variance, and the use of homogeneous samples of midlife women limited generalizability. A model I developed accounted for 59 percent of the variance in perceived health status of a more diverse sample of midlife women (Thomas, 1990); however, the sample size was small and several variables that could be salient to health were not included.

The significance of this study lies in its potential for improving prediction of health status for midlife women. By the year 2000, the number of midlife women between the ages of 35 and 64 will have increased to slightly more than 50 million, approximately 42 percent of the entire female population (U.S. Bureau of the Census, 1978). Women in middle adulthood have half of their adult years remaining; with good health, these women have abundant potential for personal achievement and continued contributions to the health and welfare of their husbands, children, extended kin networks, friends, communities, and social institutions.

Conceptual Framework

The framework guiding the study is depicted in Figure 10.1. Health is conceptualized within a holistic philosophical perspective that differs from the disease-oriented medical model. Although some laypersons and health care providers continue to view health narrowly as absence of disease or ability to perform social roles, newer models have been introduced (e.g., Newman's [1986] conceptualization of health as expanding consciousness; Seeman's [1989] systems model of positive health), and there is greater acceptance of broader concepts of health emphasizing vitality and actualization (Smith, 1983). Investigators have begun to realize that we cannot study health by focusing on disease; health is most appropriately examined in relatively healthy people. Further, we cannot operationalize health with tools that list physi-

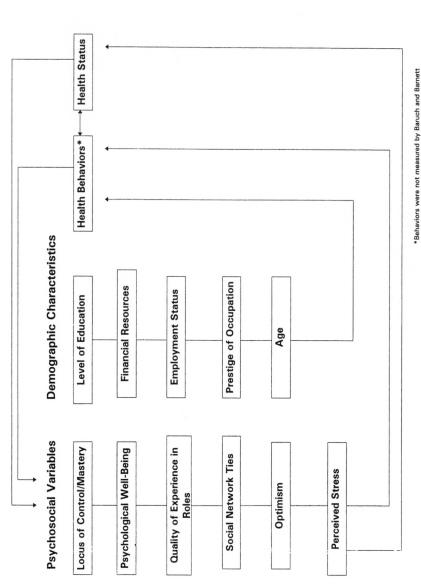

FIGURE 10.1. Conceptual Framework of Factors Related to Health of Midlife Women

*Behaviors were not measured by Baruch and Barnett

cal symptoms such as back pain and stomach discomfort. Health is in fact a rather subjective phenomenon; attempts to assess it by objective ratings have not been entirely satisfactory.

Health involves a dynamic interplay of physical, psychological, and social factors, not all of which can be examined here, because Baruch and Barnett (1986) did not assess physical health indicators (e.g., mobility, energy, physiologic symptoms) or self-care behaviors (e.g., getting proper rest). Therefore, the study focus is psychosocial, examining women's beliefs, emotions, and relationships. However, there is a great need for investigation of psychosocial variables that may influence propensity to engage in health-promoting behaviors or ability to cope successfully with health problems. Most Americans are aware that exercise, adequate sleep, proper weight, moderate drinking, and abstinence from smoking are correlated with better health (Wiley & Camacho, 1980), but they do not behave according to their knowledge.

We now examine the various concepts hypothesized to be salient to the health of midlife women. Although most of these variables have been studied individually in relation to health indicators, they have not been examined in combination for this particular age group.

Locus of Control/Mastery

Locus of control (LOC) is a construct from Rotter's (1954) social learning theory. According to Rotter, individuals develop beliefs about their ability to control desired outcomes or rewards through the reinforcement patterns to which they are exposed. Eventually most people have a stable general expectancy that reinforcements (rewards) are contingent upon their own behavior (internal locus of control) or an expectancy that rewards are received on a purely random basis or dispensed by powerful others (external locus of control). This stable general expectancy has been given a variety of names. For example, Pearlin and Schooler (1978) used the term *mastery* to describe "the extent to which one regards one's life-chances as being under one's own control in contrast to being fatalistically ruled" (p. 5). The personal control construct is also found in attribution theory (Heider, 1958), which explains future behavior according to the perceived causes of past events. Locus of control is subsumed in Kobasa's (1979) multidimensional *hardiness* construct and Antonovksy's (1984) *sense of coherence,* both of which have been associated with favorable health outcomes in a number of studies during the past decade.

What does locus of control have to do with health status? Logically, individuals that have an internal locus of control are more likely to engage in positive health behaviors; they believe that the reinforcement (good health) is directly related to their own actions, not controlled by powerful others (doctors) or by fate. Although there have been some discrepant findings, a large body of literature supports this association of internality with indicators of physical and mental health; researchers using the LOC construct have examined weight reduction, smoking cessation, health information seeking, and preventive health practices such as exercise (Strickland, 1989). In a yearlong prospective study, Seeman and Seeman (1983) found that subjects who scored high on a locus of control measure at pretest had better self-rated health and fewer sick days than individuals with a lower sense of personal control. My investigation (Thomas, 1983) of predictors of current health for midlife men and women revealed that internal locus of control was the strongest predictor. In a later study (Thomas, 1990) of middle-aged females participating in the third phase of my longitudinal study, internal locus of control was one of seven variables in a regression model predicting 59 percent of the variance in health status. Verbrugge (1990) found low mastery to be one of the most important risk factors for poor health status in a Detroit study of White adults; women were at greater risk than men. As Strickland (1988) has noted, women have less control over their lives than men do.

Psychological Well-being

The association between psychological well-being and health has been examined by a number of researchers. In a meta-analysis based on studies of U.S. adults, health and subjective well-being were found to be positively and significantly related (Okun, Stock, Haring, & Witter, 1984), with an average correlation of .32. Using different methods of research review, George and Landerman (1984) and Zautra and Hempel (1984) reached the same conclusion. George and Landerman conducted a secondary analysis of seven large data sets, finding a median correlation between health and well-being of .24; Zautra and Hempel used the traditional narrative literature review approach. Despite the convergence of evidence, the mechanism linking the two constructs remains unclear. Zautra and Hempel (1984) proposed that reduced well-being could play a causal role in physical health problems, either directly or indirectly through life-style changes.

What is meant by the term *well-being?* In their review of 81 studies, Zautra and Hempel (1984) reported lack of consensus on a definition of this multidimensional construct. Consequently, well-being has been operationalized quite differently by various researchers (e.g., life satisfaction, happiness). In recent literature, well-being is construed as more than happiness or "feeling good." Virtually all of the conceptualizations of well-being include self-acceptance or *self-esteem*. It stands to reason that persons who feel better about themselves would be more inclined to enact self-care behaviors that promote good health. According to Ryff (1989), another important component of well-being is a sense of meaning and *purpose in life*. Purpose in life includes having goals and a sense of directedness. It logically follows that persons having clear goals may devote more effort to health maintenance, as most goals cannot be achieved without good health. Ryff (1989) also emphasizes *personal growth* (realizing one's unique potential) in her discussion of the dimensions of well-being. In Ryff's view, a high scorer on this dimension would be developing, expanding, and becoming more effective, in contrast to a low scorer characterized by personal stagnation or boredom. This aspect of well-being appears particularly crucial for persons in middle adulthood, a period characterized by existential questioning (Gould, 1972), changes in life-style or role responsibilities (Levinson, 1978), and significant contributions to society (Erikson, 1968).

Quality of Experience in Roles

The next construct in the model is from interactionist role theory. Roles are contextually situated patterns of behaviors and attitudes (Turner, 1990); they evolve from societal expectations and are enacted in daily interactions with others in a variety of arenas. Rodin and Ickovics (1990) proposed that changes in social structure and roles in the past few decades have contributed to the decline in women's mortality advantage respective to men. By 1988, 65% of women were in the labor force (U.S. Department of Labor, 1990). Not surprisingly, the effects of the paid worker role, superimposed on the traditional roles of wife and mother, have commanded considerable attention from researchers. In early studies it had been hypothesized that the addition of employment to family roles would produce role overload and psychological distress, possibly compromising women's health. Research has not supported this proposition, however. Barnett and Baruch (1985) examined midlife women's psychological distress in relation to (1) number of roles; (2) occupancy of roles of paid worker, wife, and mother; and (3) quality of experience in these roles. The researchers found that the role of parent rather than paid worker was the major source of stress for women in the middle years, and that the *quality* of experience in social roles was more salient than the *number* of roles a woman occupied. In a subsequent analysis using the same data set, Baruch and Barnett (1986) examined role quality in relation to psychological well-being. The three role-quality variables were significant predictors of well-being, except that quality of experience in the parental role did not predict pleasure. Although subjects were questioned about their health, neither the 1985 nor the 1986 paper reported correlations between role quality and health status.

Helson, Elliott, and Leigh (1990), building on Baruch and Barnett's work, tested whether number and quality of roles were associated with health in 100 privileged midlife women. Number of roles was not related to physical health. The authors did not include the correlation of role quality and physical health in their report. A research team headed by Barnett recently examined quality of experience in roles in relation to physical symptoms, using a sample of women employed in helping professions. Rewarding aspects of the work role, such as helping others, were associated with lower levels of physical symptoms, even when the women felt overloaded by having too much to do. Conversely, under conditions of low reward from helping others and high overload, reports of physical symptoms were high (Barnett, Davidson, & Marshall, 1991).

Role *dissatisfaction* (respondents' feelings about their main role: job or housework) proved to be an important risk factor for poor health status in Verbrugge's (1990) Detroit study; risk was greater for women than for men. Unfortunately, it is not possible to ascertain *which* role the subjects were evaluating. Women were less likely than men to be employed, suggesting that for many women the role they evaluated was that of housewife. Women occupying the role of housewife were more likely to experience "role disenchantment" and depression than were employed women in a large longitudinal study by Pearlin, Lieberman, Menaghan, and Mullan (1981).

Loss of roles has been a focus of some research. During the 1960s and 1970s, the empty-nest syndrome attracted considerable attention; relinquishing the parental role was assumed to be traumatic for midlife women. However, later studies (Black & Hill, 1984) have negated this assumption. Midlife women frequently report that departure of children from the home creates opportunities for self-development through pursuit of further education, career moves, or community activities. For contemporary women, the "refilled-nest syndrome," in which adult children return home due to economic or personal crises, has become a greater stressor (Witkin, 1991).

Some studies (Waldron & Jacobs, 1989) have shown that the more roles a woman occupies, the healthier she is likely to be. It has been suggested that married women who juggle paid work and family responsibilities may use each role as a resource or buffer for coping with the stresses of the other (Stewart & Salt, 1981). In a sample of professional women, Amatea and Fong (1991) found that those occupying a greater number of roles reported lower levels of strain symptoms.

Stress

Research on stress has at various times focused on (1) the body's physiologic adaptation to environmental stimuli (Selye, 1956); (2) major life events such as bereavement, divorce, financial setbacks (Holmes & Rahe, 1967); (3) minor daily hassles which in themselves are not devastating but *cumulatively* tax one's frustration tolerance (Kanner, Coyne, Schaefer, & Lazarus, 1981); and (4) the interaction of person and environment (Lazarus, 1991). The Lazarus transactional view, which dominates contemporary literature, emphasizes the individuals' subjective appraisal that environmental circumstances or demands are too much for them to handle; thus, stress is now considered a perceptual construct rather than a particular external event or accumulation of events. An event appraised as threatening by one woman could be construed as challenging by another.

Although there is a voluminous literature on stress and its health consequences, including experimental, clinical, and epidemiological research (Steptoe, 1991), women have been neglected until recently (Barnett, Biener, & Baruch, 1987). There is evidence that a woman's level of stress is profoundly affected by misfortunes occurring to others in her social network (Kessler & McLeod, 1984), a phenomenon that has been termed "vicarious stress." In their study of over 500 women, Thomas and Donnellan (1993) found that vicarious stresses (e.g., son's divorce, grandson's illness, friend in jail, nephew's car accident) comprised the largest category of responses to the question: "What is your greatest stress right now?" The added burden of vicarious stress may account for the consistency of research reports showing that women are more stressed than men (Turner & Avison, 1989; Verbrugge, 1990), a gender difference evident as early as adolescence (Groër, Thomas, & Shoffner, 1992; Thomas, Shoffner, & Groër, 1988). In a study of stress factors of wives in dual-career marriages, husbands greatly underestimated the amount of stress their wives were experiencing; primary stresses were family related rather than job related (White, Mascalo, Thomas, & Shoun, 1986).

Midlife women appear to be particularly vulnerable to stress due to the simultaneous demands of caring for children as well as aging parents; the term *sandwich generation* has been applied to middle-aged Americans caught between the younger and older generations' dependency on them (Zal, 1992). Further, women are dealing with their own intrapsychic issues during this life stage. In my (Thomas, 1990) study of midlife women, the majority (66%) reported severe daily stress; primary concerns of highly stressed women were "health of a family member" (a vicarious stressor) and "troubling thoughts about one's future" (an intrapsychic stressor). High responsibility for family health care was an important risk factor for poor health status in the Detroit study by Verbrugge (1990); the risk was greater for females than for males. When middle-aged Cleveland women (ages 35–65) were asked to rank their top 5 health concerns from a list of 20, stress was the number 1 response (Kennedy & Comko, 1991).

Social Network Ties

Connectedness to others is a central element in women's health and well-being throughout the life span. There is considerable empirical evidence that solid, stable, connections to a social group produce improved resistance to disease (Ornstein & Sobel, 1987), although debate continues about whether social networks exert a direct effect or buffer the effects of stress. Caplan (1981) asserts that individuals are more likely to achieve mastery over stress if they receive adequate social support. Benefits of support from one's relatives and friends include concrete material help with problems (e.g., money), provision of information, affirmation of self-worth, and encouragement to maintain hope of a satisfactory outcome. A support network could also provide encouragement regarding health-promoting behaviors or compliance with treatment regimens prescribed for medical conditions. Connell and D'Augelli (1990) examined the direct effects of social support on physical health using LISREL; significant paths for their model indicated that individuals who perceive themselves as affiliative and nurturant have larger networks, receive more support from others, and rate their physical health more positively.

The connection between social support and mortality has been examined by several researchers. Berkman and Syme's (1979) longitudinal study revealed that subjects with few ties to other people had higher mortality rates than those with greater social connectedness. However, in replications of Berkman and Syme's work, gender differences were noted; the relationship between social ties and mortality rates was statistically significant *only for men* (Minkler, 1986). In the Tecumseh Community Health Study, indices of social relationships and activities were inversely associated with mortality, but associations were stronger for males than for females. The researchers concluded that men may benefit more from social relationships than women (House, Landis, & Umberson, 1988). Shumaker and Hill (1991) pointed out anomalies in three longitudinal studies of social support–mortality linkages with respect to women in certain age groups; in all three instances, women with high levels of support had *higher* mortality rates. The cost of caring for some women in large social networks may exceed the benefits.

Optimism

Scheier and Carver (1985) assert that optimism is a stable personality characteristic with important implications for the manner in which people regulate their actions, particularly actions relevant to their health. The construct of optimism, as used in psychological literature, includes global tendencies to (1) expect the best, (2) look on the bright side, and (3) anticipate good things in the future (Scheier & Carver, 1985). The construct does not overlap with internal locus of control; expectations of favorable outcomes may be derived from perceptions of being lucky or blessed by God as well as from convictions of personal control. Scheier and Carver (1992), in a study of adaptation to college life, found effects of optimism to be independent of locus of control. A number of studies have examined the influence of optimism on health variables. In a longitudinal study, Scheier and Carver (1985) found that highly optimistic students were less likely to report physical symptoms during a stressful period, even when statistical correction for initial symptom levels was done. Reker and Wong (1983) investigated optimism in relation to physical symptoms and overall physical and mental well-being in older adults. Two years after measurement of optimism, persons assessed at time 1 as optimists reported fewer symptoms and greater well-being than did those subjects initially categorized as pessimists. Higher levels of optimism have been associated with the likelihood of completing an alcohol treatment program (Strack, Carver, & Blaney, 1987) and with faster recovery of coronary artery bypass surgical patients (Scheier & Carver, 1992).

What accounts for these findings on linkages between optimism and health? Several mechanisms have been proposed, although none has adequate empirical support. The physiological mechanisms include immunological functioning (presumed to be superior in optimists) and cardiovascular reactivity to stress (presumed to be greater in pessimists). Behavioral mechanisms that may explain optimism's link to health include coping strategies and health habits. Researchers have found that optimists and pessimists differ in the kinds of coping techniques they used to manage stress; optimists focus on solving the problem and finding positive aspects of the situation, whereas pessimists deny, distance, and disengage (Scheier, Weintraub, & Carver, 1986). Optimistic persons are believed to be more persistent and to work harder at attaining their goals. Thus, if health goals (e.g., fitness, weight loss) are valued, optimists may behave as necessary to achieve them.

Demographic Variables

Although the primary emphasis was on psychosocial variables, selected demographic characteristics were included in the study framework. Matthews (1989) pointed out that health researchers neglect demographic variables, because they believe that such characteristics as education are not readily modifiable. Thus, we do not know much about the role of these variables in disease processes. But we obviously need to learn more. For example, among survivors of heart attack, mortality is associated with less education (Ruberman, Weinblatt, Goldberg, & Chaudhary, 1984). Health-damaging behaviors such as smoking are more prevalent in women with less education than in women with more education (Woods, Lentz, & Mitchell, 1993). Individuals with better education are more likely to read and comprehend written information about health-promoting activities and may be less intimidated about articulating their health concerns to care providers. Education may also covary with psychological processes yet to be identified (Matthews, 1989). Regardless of the mechanisms involved, when education is included as a predictor of health outcomes, strong positive relationships are usually found (Franks & Boisseau, 1980).

The employment-health link has been the subject of much speculation but little research involving large samples of women followed over time. One five-year study of over 2,000 Massachusetts midlife women showed that employment had a positive impact on perceived health; employed women had fewer restricted activity days and fewer new chronic conditions. The researchers concluded that employment may play a protective role for women, actually alleviating the stress of nurturing roles and preventing morbidity (McKinlay, Triant, McKinlay, Brambilla, & Ferdock, 1990). Several cross-sectional studies have provided additional support for the positive relationship between employment and health. Coleman and Antonucci (1983) found that women who were employed in middle adulthood had better physical health than homemakers. I found that employment outside the home was positively correlated with health (Thomas, 1990), while lower participation in paid employment was one of five factors placing women at greater risk of health problems in Verbrugge's (1990) study. Hornstein (1986) suggested that employment may have special meanings to midlife women, serving to minimize the stress of the midlife transition (i.e., a stabilizing element). However, the prestige of the occupation is an important factor to be considered when evaluating the influence of women's employment on their health. Women in highly prestigious fields such as medicine and law have much greater autonomy and control than women in lower prestige fields such as clerical and service work.

A final demographic factor is financial status. Consistent with commonsense prediction, higher income has been correlated with good health in numerous studies. Both physical and mental illnesses tend to be more prevalent among those of lower socioeconomic status. Individuals with lower incomes are more concerned about the possibility of contracting debilitating diseases and view themselves as more susceptible to illness in general (Johnston & Ware, 1976). Additionally, inadequate financial resources prevent them from obtaining required nutrients, preventive measures such as influenza immunizations, and proper medical care when ill. Midlife women with higher incomes reported fewer physical health problems in the study by Coleman and Antonucci (1983).

METHOD

I participated in the Midlife Research Program of the Henry A. Murray Research Center at Radcliffe College, a part of the Research Network on Successful Midlife Development funded by the John D. and Catherine T. MacArthur Foundation. I did a secondary analysis of the Baruch and Barnett data set, which is housed at the Murray

Center archive. Although health had been assessed at the time of data collection, the original study was conducted for a different purpose, and the health data had not been used in any of Baruch and Barnett's published reports.

Sample

Because role patterns were a primary concern in the original study, the sample was selected to ensure inclusion of (1) groups of theoretical relevance and (2) relatively rare groups (such as women in high-prestige occupations) rather than to comprise a representative sample of midlife women. To obtain the sample, Baruch and Barnett had first scrutinized census data in the Boston area to locate a community with adequate numbers of employed women and a wide range of occupational prestige levels; Brookline met their criteria. Brookline women in the 35 to 55 age group were contacted in order of the random numbers assigned to the community's list of registered voters; 6,000 women were screened by telephone. Home interviews were conducted with the final sample of 238 women; the response rate of women who met the inclusion criteria was reported by the researchers as 76 percent (Baruch & Barnett, 1986). The sample included women from four family statuses: never married ($N = 50$), married without children ($N = 54$), married with children ($N = 88$), and divorced with children ($N = 46$). These family statuses were crossed by employment status: half the married women were employed, as were all of the never-married and divorced women. The employed women were equally distributed by occupational prestige into high, medium, and low groupings according to Siegel's (1971) system of categorization. Unemployed women were classified according to the prestige of their husbands' occupations. All subjects were White; mean age was 43.6 years ($SD = 6.5$); mean number of years of marriage was 18 ($SD = 8.4$); and mean number of children was 2.6 ($SD = 1.2$). Of the 134 women who were mothers, 23 percent had younger children (7 years or less), while 66 percent had at least one child at home but none under age 8, and 11 percent had an empty nest. The majority (60%) of the women had baccalaureate or higher degrees; 76 percent were employed outside the home.

As noted by the researchers (Baruch, Barnett, & Rivers, 1983) in the preface to their 1983 book, the average woman in the sample was born in 1935 to parents living through the depression years; she had experienced the World War II years as a child and moved into adolescence in the postwar years. Despite a cultural climate that had promulgated the homemaker role as the ideal feminine choice, by 1979–1980 when the data were collected, she was living in a world radically altered by the women's movement. Thus, the unique aspects of this cohort of women must be kept in mind by researchers conducting secondary analyses over a decade later.

Instruments

Although some scales from the original test battery were retained intact, I created several new scales for this study. According to psychometric theory, scores based on scales with multiple items are more reliable than scores for single-item scales (Cronbach, 1951). Therefore, in several instances I combined compatible items rather than relying on the single-item measures that were used in the original study. In some cases, revisions were deemed necessary to reflect contemporary theorizing (e.g., psychological well-being). I used Cronbach's alpha to ascertain internal consistency reliability of the new scales.

Self-rated Health Index

In keeping with the conceptualization of health as a subjective phenomenon, three items were aggregated into a general index of self-rated health:

1. How would you describe your present health? (excellent, good, fair, or poor)
2. How often does your health get in the way of things you want to do? (5-point response format, anchored by "never" and "all the time")
3. To what extent, if any, are health worries a concern? (4-point response format, anchored by "not at all" and "extremely")

Cronbach's alpha for the scale was .75, and the average interitem correlation was .50. Good variability was achieved, with no problematic skewness, although there were more women in the sample scoring higher, indicating good health. Items in the health index are virtually identical to items included in Ware's (1976) Health Perceptions Questionnaire, which is the most widely used measure of self-rated health status. Presumption of validity for the scale relies on previous research in which similar subjective ratings of health have been found to correspond well with objective assessments by health care providers (Hunt et al., 1980; Martini & McDowell, 1976). In some cases self-assessment has even proved to be superior. Mossey and Shapiro (1982) tracked a sample of elderly individuals for eight years following subjective and physician ratings of their health; the subjective ratings were more highly correlated with mortality than were the physician ratings.

Locus of Control/Mastery

Baruch and Barnett had used Pearlin and Schooler's (1978) seven mastery items to assess women's sense of personal control over events and problems in their lives. The mastery scale was part of a battery used in a large study in Chicago by Pearlin and Schooler (1978); factor analysis was used in validation of the test battery. Internal consistency of the scale was reported at .75 by the test developers. No alterations of this measure were attempted for the present study.

Psychological Well-being

In keeping with current thinking about the construct of well-being (Ryff, 1989), my operationalization for this study departed from Baruch and Barnett's (1986) measure in some respects. Although the self-esteem component (measured by Rosenberg's 10-item [1965] scale) was retained, the pleasure and depression components were not. Instead, I gleaned items from the data set that more accurately reflected current conceptualizations of well-being. Illustrative items include "having pride in your accomplishments," "knowing your own strengths and limitations," and "feeling a need to justify your way of life to yourself and others" (the latter item reverse-scored). One item assessed general satisfaction with "life as a whole." The 10-item well-being scale achieved good variability of scores and acceptable internal consistency reliability (Cronbach's alpha = .72), with an average inter-item correlation of .32.

Role Quality Measures

On the basis of responses of the women interviewed in their pilot study, Baruch and Barnett had constructed scales assessing *rewards* and *concerns* (distressing or negative aspects) of each role. For example, a reward in the role of paid worker was salary; a concern was lack of challenge. A Likert-type response format was used. For all items, the possible range of responses was 1–4. After mean reward and concern scores were computed, a *balance* score (reward minus concern) constituted the index of the woman's subjective *quality of experience* in each role. For this study I used the scores for rewards, concerns, and balance as derived by Baruch and Barnett. I examined quality of experience in the roles of wife, mother, paid worker, homemaker, childless wife, never-married woman, and divorcée.

Perceived Stress

Consistent with current conceptualizations of stress as a subjective emotional experience, I selected subjects' mean scores on the anxiety and depression items of the Hopkins Symptom Checklist to operationalize the construct. The larger instrument (now known as the SCL-90) is a self-report inventory of psychological symptoms. It has been widely used in clinical and research studies, and there is extensive evidence of its reliability and validity; in the *Handbook of Stress* it is described as "a standard in the multidimensional measurement of psychological distress" (Derogatis & Coons, 1993, p. 209). Coefficient alpha was .89 for anxiety and .88 for depression in a study of women by Barnett, Marshall, and Singer (1992). I found precedent for combining the anxiety and depression items into a single distress score in the work of Folkman, Lazarus, Gruen, and DeLongis (1986) and Barnett, Marshall, and Singer (1992). The two scales were found to be highly correlated ($r = .80$) and there was high internal consistency reliability for the combined scale (Cronbach's alpha = .90) in the sample of Barnett et al. (1992).

Social Network Ties

Four items were aggregated into a new social ties index. Three items assessed the extent to which good close friends, social activities and groups, and volunteer or service activities were a rewarding part of the women's lives, and the final item asked to what extent not enough social life was a concern (reverse-scored). The full range of possible scores was observed on the scale, and there was no problematic skewness. Although Cronbach's alpha was less than desirable at .52, no other items were located in the data set that elevated the coefficient.

Optimism

Optimism was assessed by the single question "When you think about the future, how do you usually feel: extremely hopeful, somewhat hopeful, or not at all hopeful?" This item directly captures the construct of optimism as defined by Scheier and Carver: "expectations for the future" (1992, p. 221). A search of the data set revealed no other suitable items to combine into a scale.

Demographic Variables

Demographic variables (age, education, employment, occupational prestige) were used in their original form or recoded as dummy variables, with the exception of financial status. Because income figures had become obsolete, I created a 2-item financial resources index. Questions were: "How threatened do you feel financially from inflation?" and "To what extent is not having enough money a concern?" The full range of scores was observed, with no problematic skewness and an interitem correlation of .59.

Analysis

I considered various analytic strategies. Because path analysis does not accommodate reciprocal relationships (Billings & Wroten, 1978), it was inappropriate for this study. One-way causal paths cannot be specified for linkages between variables such as stress and health. Although LISREL accommodates reciprocal relationships, sample size was not adequate for this procedure. To examine relationships of psychosocial variables with perceived physical health, I used correlational and regression analyses. Because one of the strengths of the Baruch and Barnett data set was its purposeful inclusion of women pursuing different life paths, separate regressions were done for subgroups of the sample, which preserved the uniqueness of the different combinations of role responsibilities. To examine differences between various subgroups, I performed *t* tests and ANCOVA.

RESULTS
Relationships of Psychosocial Variables to Health

In bivariate analyses (see Table 10.1), stress was the strongest correlate of health (inversely related), with locus of control and optimism next in order of magnitude of the *r* values (positively related). A modest positive correlation was also found between psychological well-being and health. The role quality variables most salient to health pertained to the women's experiences in their marriages and in parenting children; quality of experience in the work role, although statistically significant, was a weak predictor. Likewise, social network ties and demographic variables were only weakly related to health. Although quality of experience in the single role was significantly related to health for the 50 women in this status, the remaining role quality variables (i.e., divorcée, homemaker, childless wife) were unrelated to the health of women enacting those roles.

TABLE 10.1 Psychosocial Correlates of Women's Physical Health
in Middle Adulthood ($N = 238$)

Variable	r	p
Stress	−.40	.0001
Locus of control	.29	.0001
Optimism	.29	.0001
Quality of wife role experience ($N = 141$)	.28	.0008
Quality of mother role experience ($N = 133$)	.27	.0020
Psychological well-being	.22	.0007
Social network ties	.16	.0132
Financial resources	.16	.0133
Occupational prestige	.16	.0145
Employment (coded 1 = yes, 0 = no)	.15	.0178
Age	−.15	.0255
Quality of work role experience ($N = 179$)	.15	.0400
Education	.13	.0450

Note: Quality of experience in the single role was significant ($r = .34$, $p = .02$), for the 50 women in this status; quality of experience in roles of divorcée, homemaker, or childless wife was unrelated to health.

The next step of the data analysis involved multiple regression procedures for subjects grouped according to role occupancy. The backward elimination type of stagewise variable selection procedure was used because it allows all variables to interact together; variables with the smallest partial F values are dropped in successive steps until a final model comprising predictors significant at .10 is derived. Before regression procedures, I examined the intercorrelation matrix to ascertain whether there was multicollinearity among the psychosocial variables. All correlations were below .65, indicating that the variables were not redundant (Tabachnick & Fidell, 1983). For each regression, self-rated physical health was the dependent variable and the psychosocial and demographic variables were predictors.

The first of these procedures involved all women who were *mothers*, whether married or divorced. Twenty-seven percent of the variance in health was accounted for by 5 predictors: stress ($\beta = -.29$), optimism ($\beta = .17$), employment outside the home ($\beta = .14$), occupational prestige ($\beta = .18$), and quality of experience in the maternal role ($\beta = .14$). In the second procedure, all women who were *employed*, regardless of marital or parental status, were included. Again, health was regressed on the psychosocial and demographic predictors; the resultant model included only stress ($\beta = -.27$) and locus of control ($\beta = .14$); occupational prestige and quality of experience in the work role were not useful predictors. Eleven percent of the variance in health was explained. The next model was developed using all women who were *married*, regardless of employment status or parental status. In this model the significant predictors of health were stress (negatively related) ($\beta = -.36$), quality of experience in the wife role ($\beta = .12$), employment ($\beta = .15$), and occupational prestige ($\beta = .14$); 22 percent of the variance was explained.

For the final regression analyses, a mean role quality score was created so that the entire sample of 238 women could be used. Using only the demographic variables as predictors of health in the first model, 9% of the variance was explained. Adding the psychosocial variables boosted the R^2 in the second model to 26%; significant predictors of health were stress (inversely related) ($\beta = -.28$), well-being ($\beta = .22$), role quality ($\beta = .21$), employment outside the home ($\beta = .16$), and optimism ($\beta = .15$). In summary, regression results consistently demonstrated the negative impact of stress. The strong impact of stress on health has been noted in previous studies of midlife women, as well as individuals in other life stages. Quality of experience in roles contributed to prediction of health, particularly quality in the roles of wife and mother. It is puzzling that *occupying* the work role showed up as beneficial to health in several of the models, but *quality of experience* as a worker did not. Perhaps the rewards of employment are not as important to women as the rewards derived from their marriage and family roles. This explanation is plausible given the role socialization of this particular cohort of midlife women during a time when employment was not a primary role for women.

Comparisons of Most Healthy and Least Healthy Midlife Women

In what ways are the most healthy and least healthy midlife women different? Using subjects who scored in the upper and lower 25 percent of the sample on the Health Index, I made comparisons on demographic variables (see Table 10.2). Fewer of the women in the healthiest group (55.5%) were married, as compared to 66.2 percent in the least-healthy group. A greater percentage of the healthiest group fell into the high-prestige occupational category, while the percentage of homemakers married to men in medium- or low-prestige occupations was greater in the least-healthy group. Another notable difference pertained

TABLE 10.2 Demographic Comparisons of Healthiest and
Least-Healthy Midlife Women (upper and lower 25% of sample)

	Healthiest (%)	Least Healthy (%)
Family status		
Never married	23.3	17.6
Married, no children	22.2	24.3
Married, children	33.3	41.9
Divorced, children	21.1	16.2
Work status		
Employed, high-prestige occupation	27.8	16.2
Employed, medium-prestige occupation	28.9	28.4
Employed, low-prestige occupation	25.6	24.3
At home, husband in high-prestige occupation	7.8	6.8
At home, husband in medium-prestige occupation	4.4	9.5
At home, husband in low-prestige occupation	5.6	14.9
Stage of family life cycle		
No children	45.6	41.9
Youngest child age 7 or less	13.3	12.2
No children under 8, at least 1 at home	36.7	39.2
All children out of home	4.4	6.8
Education		
Less than college degree[a]	33.3	51.4
Baccalaureate or advanced degree	66.7	48.6

[a]High school, trade school, or some college without degree

to educational level: the healthier group had a higher percentage of women with baccalaureate or advanced degrees. Marriages were of longer duration, on the average, in the unhealthiest group (mean = 19.2 years, $SD = 8.5$), than in the healthiest group (mean = 16.9 years, $SD = 7.8$); and there was a slight age difference (mean age 44.9 years, $SD = 6.8$ for unhealthiest; 43.1 years, $SD = 6.3$ for healthiest). The two groups also differed in mean scores on financial resources (mean = 4.4, $SD = 1.5$ in the unhealthiest group; mean = 4.9, $SD = 1.4$ in the healthiest). Number of children averaged two for both groups.

In the next set of procedures I controlled demographic variables, so that the psychosocial variables could be examined without their influence. Using tertiles, the sample was categorized by Health Index scores as "healthiest," "moderately healthy," and "least healthy." ANCOVA (with financial resources, education, and employment as co-variates) was used to compare the three groups on each of the psycho-social variables. The healthiest women (upper tertile) scored higher on locus of control than the other two groups ($F = 6.34$, $p = .0001$), whereas the moderately healthy and least healthy did not differ from each other. Findings with regard to well-being were similar, in that the healthiest women displayed greater psychological well-being than the other groups ($F = 4.43$, $p = .0007$), but the two lower-scoring groups did not differ from each other. On optimism ($F = 7.80$, $p = .0001$) this pattern was repeated, but on stress all three groups differed significantly from each other ($F = 10.75$, $p = .0001$). Mean scores on stress were incrementally ordered, such that the healthiest women had lowest stress, the moderately healthy somewhat greater stress, and the least healthy the highest stress. Groups also differed on quality of experience in the wife role, with the healthiest women scoring higher but with no difference between the other two groups ($F = 5.45$, $p = .0001$). On quality of experience in the role of mother (with age controlled), the two upper tertiles had higher scores (not differing from each other), whereas the lowest tertile had the lowest scores, differing from both of the other groups ($F = 3.95$, $p = .0012$). Groups did not differ on quality of experience in the work role or in social network ties.

Given the converging evidence that midlife women's roles appear to be of considerable salience to their self-rated physical health, the next step in the analysis was to examine mean scores on the two elements of role quality more closely (i.e., the *rewards* and *concerns* scales for each role). Again, the healthiest and least healthy women were compared. Women in better health in middle adulthood had fewer *concerns* regarding their work ($t = -2.03$, $p = .04$), marital ($t = -4.57$, $p = .0001$), and child-rearing ($t = -3.89$, $p = .0002$) roles, as compared to their counterparts who were less healthy. Further, single women reporting better health had fewer *concerns* pertaining to their unmarried status ($t = -2.88$, $p = .007$) than did single women who did not rate their health as highly. In most comparisons of the two groups on the *rewards* of the various life roles, there were no significant differences—with one notable exception. The healthiest women scored higher on rewarding aspects of their marriages ($t = 2.12$, $p = .04$) than the less-healthy group. Consistent with other analyses, neither rewards nor concerns of the homemaking role proved to be salient to health;

perhaps that role is not one in which this sample of well-educated women was deeply invested.

Item Analyses of Marital Rewards and Child-Rearing Concerns Scales

To ascertain what *distressing* or negative aspects of women's roles were more prominent in differentiating healthy and less healthy women, I compared responses to individual items of the marital and child-rearing concerns scales. Because of the large number of item comparisons, I did not use statistical tests to ascertain the significance of differences between means; the purpose of these comparisons was exploratory. Mean scores on marital concerns were higher for the least healthy group on virtually every item (see Table 10.3). Differences between the two groups were particularly notable on items regarding con-

TABLE 10.3 Mean Scores on Marital Concerns for Healthiest and Least-Healthy Midlife Women (upper and lower 25% of sample)

Concerns	Healthiest		Least Healthy	
	Mean	SD	Mean	SD
Husband unavailable or not home enough	1.48	0.73	1.69	1.04
Poor communication	1.38	0.57	1.80	0.99
Husband's physical health	1.78	1.05	2.18	1.20
Not getting enough appreciation or attention	1.28	0.49	1.65	0.80
If children, conflicts about children	1.50	0.84	2.06	1.13
Husband's job/career problems	1.28	0.61	1.65	0.97
Problems in sexual relationship	1.08	0.27	1.46	0.74
Lack of companionship	1.40	0.78	1.57	0.96
Husband's job instability	1.33	0.72	1.59	0.84
Problems caused by demands of husband's job	1.18	0.44	1.67	0.92
Husband has emotional problems	1.18	0.39	1.63	0.75
Not getting along, personality clashes	1.28	0.64	1.22	0.47
Conflict over who does housework	1.12	0.33	1.56	0.77
Not getting enough emotional support	1.23	0.50	1.41	0.68
If children, conflicts over sharing child care	3.12	1.11	3.15	1.01

Note: Possible range is 1–4 for all items (4 indicating the highest level of concern); the full range was observed for the least-healthy group on all items except no. 7 (sexual problems), no. 12 (personality clashes), and no. 14 (lack of support), for which the maximum score was 3. For the healthiest group, there was a more restricted range of scores; there were no scores of 4 on 7 of the 15 items, and for items 7, 11, and 13 there were no scores higher than 2.

TABLE 10.4 Mean Scores on Child-Rearing Concerns for Healthiest and Least-Healthy Midlife Women (upper and lower 25% of sample)

Concerns	Healthiest		Least Healthy	
	Mean	SD	Mean	SD
The financial strain	2.06	0.94	2.23	0.99
Feeling trapped or bored	1.37	0.63	1.64	0.85
Worrying about children's well-being	1.92	0.95	2.81	1.05
Children fighting or not getting along	1.78	0.85	2.21	1.12
The heavy demands and responsibilities	2.08	0.93	2.30	1.01
Worrying about the teenage years	2.19	1.02	2.69	1.06
Not being sure if you're doing the right thing	1.90	0.91	2.31	0.97
Children not showing appreciation or love	1.41	0.67	1.77	0.89
Problems with their schooling	1.84	0.87	2.24	1.14
Feeling disappointed in what they're like	1.16	0.37	1.51	0.74
Not having enough control over them	1.43	0.74	1.77	0.78
Children needing you less as they get older	1.18	0.44	1.50	0.75
Having too many arguments and conflicts with them	1.33	0.62	1.79	0.81
Children's interference in relationship with husband	1.25	0.59	1.44	0.61

Note: The full range of scores was observed on most items for both groups, with the exception of 2 items for each group. For the healthiest group, restricted range was observed on no. 10 (disappointed in what the children are like), with no scores higher than 2, and no. 12 (children needing mother less as they age), with no scores higher than 3; for the unhealthiest group, restricted range was observed on no. 11 (not having enough control) and no. 14 (interference in marital relationship), with no scores higher than 3.

flicts about children, problems due to husband's job demands, husband's emotional problems, and conflict over who does the housework. The women in the unhealthiest group were more likely to select the 4 response (highest level of concern). It is of interest that conflict over sharing child care was of greatest concern to women in *both* groups; groups did not differ appreciably on this item.

Scores on child-rearing concerns (see Table 10.4) indicate that the least healthy group scored higher on *every* item than did the women who were healthiest. The discrepancy was greatest for scores on an item pertaining to worry about children's well-being; groups also differed in amount of worry about the teenage years, having arguments and conflicts with children, children fighting, and "not being sure if you're doing the right thing."

Item Analyses of Marital Rewards and Child-Rearing Rewards Scales

In the final analyses I examined mean scores of healthy and less-healthy women on individual items in the Marital Rewards and Child-Rearing Rewards Scales. As shown in Table 10.5, on 11 of 15 marital reward items, the healthiest group of women scored higher than their counterparts who were less healthy. The largest discrepancy between groups was observed on item 6, "being able to go to husband with problems"; healthier women were more likely to find a listening ear. Physical affection and sexual intimacy were also more rewarding to the healthier group, along with husband being a good provider. Fewer differences were seen between the two groups on child-rearing rewards (see Table 10.6); on 8 of 14 items there was virtually no difference. The healthiest women scored higher on 3 items, including no. 14 ("the way children change you for the better"), whereas the unhealthiest women scored higher on several items pertaining to the importance

TABLE 10.5 Mean Scores on Marital Rewards for Healthiest and Least-Healthy Midlife Women

	Healthiest		Least Healthy	
	Mean	SD	Mean	SD
The companionship	3.60	0.70	3.35	0.91
Having someone to take care of you	2.75	1.02	2.89	1.02
Having a husband who is easy to get along with	3.42	0.76	3.10	1.07
The physical affection	3.50	0.74	3.08	1.02
Husband is a good father	3.30	0.91	3.10	1.12
Being able to go to husband with problems	3.36	0.90	2.82	1.07
The sexual relationship	3.70	0.54	3.27	1.04
Husband's backing you up in what you want to do	3.44	0.67	3.14	0.89
Enjoyment of doing things for husband	3.64	0.66	3.29	0.91
Husband's seeing you as special, appreciating you	3.35	0.89	3.13	0.91
Having a husband who is a good provider	3.27	0.81	2.84	1.01
Having a husband whose personality fits yours	2.74	1.10	2.78	1.10
Husband's willingness to share in housework	3.38	0.75	3.08	1.08
Good communication	3.27	0.83	3.31	1.04
Husband's willingness to share in child care	1.48	0.74	1.69	1.04

Note: Possible range is 1–4 for all items (4 indicating extremely rewarding); the full range of scores (1–4) was observed on all items for the least healthy group. For the healthiest group there were no scores of 1 (i.e., not at all rewarding) on items 1, 3, 7, 8, 9, and 13.

TABLE 10.6 Mean Scores on Child-Rearing Rewards for Healthiest and Least-Healthy Midlife Women

	Healthiest		Least Healthy	
	Mean	SD	Mean	SD
Being needed by them	2.90	0.80	3.07	0.86
The pleasure you get from their accomplishments	3.61	0.57	3.60	0.62
Helping them develop	3.53	0.77	3.60	0.66
The love they show	3.73	0.53	3.72	0.50
Feeling proud of how they are turning out	3.69	0.55	3.48	0.83
Liking the kind of people they are	3.67	0.59	3.62	0.66
Being able to go to them with problems	2.63	1.01	2.33	1.10
Enjoying doing things with them	3.43	0.71	3.42	0.85
The help they give you	2.45	1.02	2.72	1.01
The meaning and purpose they give your life	3.33	0.83	3.45	0.71
Being the best caretaker for them	3.02	1.11	3.00	1.02
The way they get along together	2.95	0.88	2.97	0.84
Seeing them mature and change	3.57	0.62	3.58	0.59
The way they change you for the better	3.21	0.92	2.81	1.11

Note: The full range of scores was observed for 6 of the 14 items for the healthiest group and for 7 of 14 items for the unhealthiest group. Remaining items had no scores lower than 2 (somewhat rewarding).

of (1) finding meaning and purpose in the maternal role, (2) being needed by their children, and (3) receiving help from them.

DISCUSSION

Of the psychosocial predictors of health we have examined in this study, stress was the strongest factor. The negative effect of stress on health is well known. However, the unique contribution of this investigation lies in its discovery of the centrality of the quality of experience in major social roles for women's health. Distressing *concerns* reported by women in connection with their roles were more salient to health than the *rewards* derived from role enactment, a finding similar to that of Kanner, Coyne, Schaefer, and Lazarus (1981). Using psychological symptoms as the dependent variable, "hassles" proved to be a better predictor than "uplifts" in their sample of middle-aged adults.

Quality of experience in the maternal role was an important predictor of self-rated health. In a large probability sample of urban women studied by Lopata and Barnewolt (1984), the role of mother far outweighed any other role in degree of importance; even professional women ranked the mother role first, rather than their occupational role. In the present study, women in the least healthy group—who scored higher on all the "concern" items—appeared to be more unsure of themselves as mothers, worrying more and having more arguments with their children. They also placed more emphasis on being needed by their children, and receiving help from them, than did women in the healthiest group. It is possible that their expectations of both themselves and their children were somewhat unrealistic.

Quality of experience in the wife role was also highly salient to the health of married women in the sample. Healthier women were more likely to report that sharing problems with their husbands was a rewarding aspect of the wife role, and they appeared to enjoy greater physical intimacy with their husbands than their less healthy counterparts. Scores of healthier and less healthy women were discrepant on almost all of the *concern* items; the less healthy women reported more distressing conflicts with husband about housework and children. Concerns about husband's job demands and his emotional problems appeared illustrative of the *vicarious stress* construct discussed earlier; the woman is taking on her husband's problems as her own worry. By doing so, she may help her husband to obtain some relief, but her own health may be compromised in the process.

There is some evidence supporting the latter point. In a study of middle-aged women by McKinlay, Triant, McKinlay, Brambilla, and Ferdock (1990), stress from spouse or children markedly increased the rates of negative health outcomes. Stress caused by *husband* was consistently a major factor in multivariate analyses involving five different health variables (e.g., restricted-activity days, physical symptoms). Costello (1991) found that midlife women who were dissatisfied with their relationships with their husbands were more likely to be depressed, whatever their job status or level of education and whether or not they had children at home. Conversely, in Barnett, Davidson, and Marshall's (1991) study, women who reported *rewarding* relationships with partners (or children) had *low* levels of physical symptoms. These studies again underscore the importance of examining the *quality* of experience in major life roles. Marital quality assumes increased importance in view of the likelihood that contemporary women may spend more than 40 years married (although not necessarily to the same man) (Taeuber, 1991).

Interestingly, there was a significant percentage of never-married women in the healthiest group (top quartile of scores). We know from the analyses conducted by Baruch, Barnett, and Rivers (1983) that this particular group of never-married women found their lives full and satisfying, dispelling negative stereotypes about loneliness and lower well-being. Further exploration of psychosocial variables and health indicators in other samples of never-married women is warranted. Does the single woman simply have more time to attend to self-care activities than her counterpart who has responsibilities for spouse and children? Research is lacking in this area. Since Stein's work (1981) there has been no major study of unmarried adults.

Relationships of locus of control and optimism with health in this sample were consistent with previous studies of midlife subjects by me (Thomas, 1983, 1990) and others. Midlife women who have a solid sense of hope for the future may have resolved the fabled midlife crisis, with positive consequences for their physical health (i.e., renewed vigor and vitality). Conversely, possessing robust health could influence their level of optimism regarding the future. Obviously, causal inferences cannot be drawn from the correlational data. The modest correlation between psychological well-being and health was consistent with previous studies (Okun et al., 1984). Contrary to most previous research, social network ties were not related to health in any of the analyses except for a very weak association in the zero-order correlations. The relatively weak performance of the social network variable can perhaps be understood in terms of the *costs* women incur within their intimate relationships, which mitigate against a wholly beneficial effect of social embeddedness on health. Relationships with husbands and children, as shown clearly by my findings, do provide rewards to women, but they also engender highly distressing concerns. Could some of these concerns be avoided or reduced? Do women fail to insist on reciprocity in relationships? Varvaro (1992) found that a major obstacle to women's enactment of health-protective behaviors (i.e., exercise) was *valuing of others over self.* Some women may need assistance in examining values (e.g., self-sacrifice) derived from long-entrenched patriarchy so that they claim their full, healthy personhood.

Limitations of the study include the lack of ethnic variability of the sample and the cross-sectional nature of the data. The relatively privileged status of women in this Brookline sample must also be acknowledged; results cannot be generalized to women with less education and fewer financial resources. Although secondary analysis is an excellent way to exploit the resources of data archives such as the Henry A. Murray Research Center, I was constrained by the choices made by the original research team.

As in most research on health, the amount of variance accounted for in this study was not large. Given the exclusive focus on psychosocial factors, it is not surprising that there is considerable unexplained variation in women's health. The behavioral variables already known to have robust associations with health (e.g., exercise) were not included in the Baruch and Barnett data set. Inasmuch as women have more health problems in any time frame—daily, annual, lifetime—than men do (Verbrugge, 1985b), even factors that account for a relatively small portion of the variance in health deserve closer attention by researchers and clinicians. The experiential quality of women's roles certainly appears worthy of additional examination. Jourard (1971) once wrote about "sickening roles" (i.e., stultifying jobs or marriages that were literally making people sick), and more recently Connors (1985) proposed that the sick role could be a means for women to sabotage their traditional roles. Becoming physically sick is indeed one of the few socially acceptable means of escape, even if temporary, from one's role responsibilities.

This study offers some clues regarding certain aspects of key roles that may cause women to become dispirited; inclusion of role quality measures in future health surveys appears to be warranted. Although role occupancy is customarily assessed, role quality usually is not. The sociocultural rules that influence women's role-taking and subsequent enactment of roles have been in the process of radical change for the past two decades, mandating research on cohorts of women that may differ in important respects from Baruch and Barnett's sample. Middle adulthood is a period when the cumulative effects of stress and deleterious behaviors are beginning to accrue, but women have the opportunity and sufficient time to make major attitudinal and life-style modifications that may prolong their lives and enhance the quality of their remaining years. As the life expectancy of American women continues to increase, the *quality* of the lengthened life span becomes increasingly important.

<h1 style="text-align:center">References</h1>

Adams, P., & Benson, V. (1990). Current estimates from the National Health Interview Survey, 1989. *Vital Health Statistics, 10*(176), 1–22.

Amatea, E., & Fong, M. (1991). The impact of role stressors and personal resources on the stress experience of professional women. *Psychology of Women Quarterly, 15,* 419–430.

Antonovsky, A. (1984). The sense of coherence as a determinant of health. In J. D. Matarazzo, S. M. Weiss, J. A. Herd, N. E. Miller, & S. M. Weiss (Eds.), *Behavioral health: A handbook of health enhancement and disease prevention* (pp. 114–129). New York: Wiley.

Barnett, R. C., & Baruch, G. K. (1985). Women's involvement in multiple roles and psychological distress. *Journal of Personality and Social Psychology, 49,* 135–145.

Barnett, R. C., Biener, L., & Baruch, G. K. (1987). *Gender and stress.* New York: Free Press.

Barnett, R., Davidson, H., & Marshall, N. (1991). Physical symptoms and the interplay of work and family roles. *Health Psychology, 10,* 94–101.

Barnett, R. C., Marshall, N. L., & Singer, J. D. (1992). Job experiences over time, multiple roles, and women's mental health: A longitudinal study. *Journal of Personality and Social Psychology, 62,* 634–644.

Baruch, G. K., & Barnett, R. (1986). Role quality, multiple role involvement, and psychological well-being in midlife women. *Journal of Personality and Social Psychology, 51,* 578–585.

Baruch, G., Barnett, R., & Rivers, C. (1983). *Lifeprints: New patterns of love and work for today's women.* New York: McGraw-Hill.

Berkman, L., & Syme, S. (1979). Social networks, host resistance, and mortality: A nine-year follow-up study of Alameda County residents. *American Journal of Epidemiology, 109,* 186–204.

Billings, R., & Wroten, S. (1978). Use of path analysis in industrial/organizational psychology: Criticism and suggestions. *Journal of Applied Psychology, 63,* 677–688.

Black, S., & Hill, C. (1984). The psychological well-being of women in their middle years. *Psychology of Women Quarterly, 8,* 282–292.

Caplan, G. (1981). Mastery of stress: Psychosocial aspects. *American Journal of Psychiatry, 138,* 413–420.

Coleman, L., & Antonucci, T. (1983). Impact of work on women at midlife. *Developmental Psychology, 19,* 290–294.

Connell, C., & D'Augelli, A. (1990). The contribution of personality characteristics to the relationship between social support and perceived physical health. *Health Psychology, 9,* 192–207.

Connors, D. (1985). Women's sickness: A case of secondary gains or primary losses. *Advances in Nursing Science, 7*(2), 1–16.

Costello, E. (1991). Married with children: Predictors of mental and physical health in middle-aged women. *Psychiatry, 54,* 292–305.

Cronbach, L. (1951). Coefficient alpha and the internal structure of tests. *Psychometrika, 16,* 297–334.

DeLorey, C. (1981). *Health care for midlife women.* Unpublished doctoral dissertation, Harvard University.

DeLorey, C. (1984). Health care and mid-life women. In G. Baruch & J. Brooks-Gunn (eds.), *Women in mid-life* (pp. 277–301). New York: Plenum Press.

Derogatis, L., & Coons, H. (1993). Self-report measures of stress. In L. Goldberger & S. Breznitz (Eds.), *Handbook of stress: Theoretical and clinical aspects* (2nd ed., pp. 200–233). New York: Free Press.

Duffy, M. E. (1988). Determinants of health promotion in midlife women. *Nursing Research, 37,* 358–362.

Engel, N. S. (1987). Menopausal stage, current life change, attitude toward women's roles, and perceived health status. *Nursing Research, 36,* 353–357.

Erikson, E. (1968). Generativity and ego integrity. In B. Neugarten (Ed.), *Middle age and aging.* Chicago: University of Chicago Press.

Folkman, S., Lazarus, R. S., Gruen, R. J., & DeLongis, A. (1986). Appraisal, coping, health status, and psychological symptoms. *Journal of Personality and Social Psychology, 50,* 571–579.

Franks, P., & Boisseau, V. (1980). Educational status and health. *Journal of Family Practice, 10,* 1029–1034.

George, L. K., & Landerman, R. (1984). Health and subjective well-being: A replicated secondary data analysis. *International Journal of Aging and Human Development, 19*(2), 133–156.

Givens, J. D. (1979). *Current estimates from the health interview survey.* Vital and Health Statistics: Series 10, No. 130 (DHEW Publication No. [PHS] 80-1551). Hyattsville, MD: U.S. Government Printing Office.

Gould, R. (1972). The phases of adult life: A study in developmental psychology. *American Journal of Psychiatry, 129,* 521–531.

Groër, M., Thomas, S. P., & Shoffner, D. (1992). Adolescent stress and coping: A longitudinal study. *Research in Nursing and Health, 15,* 209–217.

Heider, F. (1958). *The psychology of interpersonal relations.* New York: Wiley.

Helson, R., Elliott, T., & Leigh, J. (1990). Number and quality of roles: A longitudinal personality view. *Psychology of Women Quarterly, 14,* 83–101.

Holmes, T. H., & Rahe, R. H. (1967). The Social Readjustment Rating Scale. *Journal of Psychosomatic Research, 11,* 213–218.

Hornstein, G. (1986). The structuring of identity among mid-life women as a function of their degree of involvement in employment. *Journal of Personality, 54,* 551–575.

House, J., Landis, K., & Umberson, D. (1988). Social relationships and health. *Science, 241,* 540–544.

Hunt, S. M., McKenna, S. P., McEwen, J., Backett, E., Williams, J., & Papp, E. (1980). A quantitative approach to perceived health status: A validation study. *Journal of Epidemiology and Community Health, 34,* 281–286.

Johnston, S. A., & Ware, J. E., Jr. (1976). Income group differences in relationships among survey measures of physical and mental health. *Health Services Research, 11,* 416–429.

Jourard, S. (1971). *The transparent self.* New York: Van Nostrand.

Kanner, A., Coyne, J., Schaefer, C., & Lazarus, R. (1981). Comparison of two modes of stress measurement: Daily hassles and uplifts versus major life events. *Journal of Behavioral Medicine, 4,* 1–39.

Kennedy, J., & Comko, R. (1991). Health needs of midlife women. *Nursing Management, 22*(5), 62–66.

Kessler, R. C., & McLeod, J. D. (1984). Sex differences in vulnerability to undesirable life events. *American Sociological Review, 46,* 443–452.

Kobasa, S. C. (1979). Stressful life events, personality, and health: An inquiry into hardiness. *Journal of Personality and Social Psychology, 37,* 1–11.

Lazarus, R. S. (1991). *Emotion and adaptation.* New York: Oxford University Press.

Lempert, L. (1986). Women's health from a woman's point of view: A review of the literature. *Health Care for Women International, 7,* 255–275.

Levinson, D. (1978). *The seasons of a man's life.* New York: Ballantine Books.

Lopata, H., & Barnewolt, D. (1984). The middle years: Changes and variations in social role commitments. In G. Baruch & J. Brooks-Gunn (Eds.), *Women in mid-life* (pp. 83–108). New York: Plenum.

MacPherson, K. (1981). Menopause as disease: The social construction of a metaphor. *Advances in Nursing Science, 3,* 95–113.

Martini, C., & McDowell, I. (1976). Health status: Patient and physician judgements. *Health Services Research, 11,* 508–515.

Matthews, K. A. (1989). Are sociodemographic variables markers for psychological determinants of health? *Health Psychology, 8,* 641–648.

Matthews, K., Wing, R., Kuller, L., Meilahn, E., Kelsey, S., Costello, E., & Caggiula, A. (1990). Influences of natural menopause on psychological characteristics and symptoms of middle-aged healthy women. *Journal of Consulting and Clinical Psychology, 58,* 345–351.

McKinlay, J. B., McKinlay, S. M., & Brambilla, D. J. (1987). Health status and utilization behavior associated with menopause. *American Journal of Epidemiology, 125,* 110–121.

McKinlay, S., Triant, R., McKinlay, J., Brambilla, D., & Ferdock, M. (1990). Multiple roles for middle-aged women and their impact on health. In M. Ory & H. Warner (Eds.), *Gender, health, and longevity* (pp. 119–136). New York: Springer.

Meltzer, B., Petras, J., & Reynolds, L. (1975). *Symbolic interactionism: Genesis, varieties, and criticism.* London: Routledge & Kegan Paul.

Minkler, M. (1986). The social component of health. *American Journal of Health Promotion, 1,* 33–38.

Mossey, J., & Shapiro, E. (1982). Self-rated health: A predictor of mortality among the elderly. *American Journal of Public Health, 22,* 800–808.

Newman, M. A. (1986). *Health as expanding consciousness.* St. Louis: C. V. Mosby.

Okun, M., Stock, W., Haring, M., & Witter, R. (1984). Health and subjective well-being: A meta-analysis. *International Journal of Aging and Human Development, 19,* 111–132.

Ornstein, R., & Sobel, D. (1987). The healing brain. *Psychology Today, 21*(3), 48–52.

Pearlin, L., Lieberman, M., Menaghan, E., & Mullan, J. (1981). The stress process. *Journal of Health and Social Behavior, 22,* 337–356.

Pearlin, L., & Schooler, C. (1978). The structure of coping. *Journal of Health and Social Behavior, 19,* 2–21.

Reker, G. T., & Wong, P. T. (1983, April). *The salutary effects of personal optimism and meaningfulness on the physical and psychological well-being of the elderly.* Paper presented at the 29th annual meeting of the Western Gerontological Society, Albuquerque, NM.

Rodin, J., & Ickovics, J. R. (1990). Women's health: Review and research agenda as we approach the 21st century. *American Psychologist, 45,* 1018–1034.

Rosenberg, M. (1965). *Society and the adolescent self-image.* Princeton: Princeton University Press.

Rotter, J. B. (1954). *Social learning and clinical psychology.* Englewood Cliffs, NJ: Prentice-Hall.

Ruberman, W., Weinblatt, E., Goldberg, J., & Chaudhary, B. (1984). Psychosocial influences on mortality after myocardial infarction. *New England Journal of Medicine, 311,* 552–559.

Ryff, C. D. (1989). Happiness is everything, or is it? Explorations on the meaning of psychological well-being. *Journal of Personality and Social Psychology, 57,* 1069–1081.

Scheier, M., & Carver, C. (1985). Optimism, coping, and health: Assessment and implications of generalized outcome expectancies. *Health Psychology, 4,* 219–247.

Scheier, M., & Carver, C. (1992). Effects of optimism on psychological and physical well-being: Theoretical overview and empirical update. *Cognitive Therapy and Research, 16,* 201–228.

Scheier, M., Weintraub, J., & Carver, C. (1986). Coping with stress: Divergent strategies of optimists and pessimists. *Journal of Personality and Social Psychology, 51,* 1257–1264.

Seeman, J. (1989). Toward a model of positive health. *American Psychologist, 44,* 1099–1109.

Seeman, M., & Seeman, T. (1983). Health behavior and personal autonomy: A longitudinal study. *Journal of Health and Social Behavior, 24,* 144–160.

Selye, H. (1956). *The stress of life.* New York: McGraw Hill.

Shumaker, S., & Hill, D. R. (1991). Gender differences in social support and physical health. *Health Psychology, 10,* 102–111.

Siegel, P. M. (1971). *Prestige in the American Occupational Structure.* Unpublished doctoral dissertation, University of Chicago.

Smith, J. (1983). *The idea of health.* New York: Teachers College Press.

Stein, P. J. (1981). *Single life: Unmarried adults in social context.* New York: St. Martin's.

Steptoe, A. (1991). The links between stress and illness. *Journal of Psychosomatic Research, 35,* 633–644.

Stewart, A., & Salt, P. (1981). Life stress, life-styles, depression, and illness in adult women. *Journal of Personality and Social Psychology, 40,* 1063–1069.

Strack, S., Carver, C., & Blaney, P. (1987). Predicting successful completion of an aftercare program following treatment for alcoholism: The role of dispositional optimism. *Journal of Personality and Social Psychology, 53,* 579–584.

Strickland, B. R. (1988). Sex-related differences in health and illness. *Psychology of Women Quarterly, 12,* 381–399.

Strickland, B. R. (1989). Internal-external control expectancies: From contingency to creativity. *American Psychologist, 44,* 1–12.

Tabachnick, B., & Fidell, L. (1983). *Using multivariate statistics.* New York: Harper and Row.

Taeuber, C. (1991). *Statistical handbook on women.* Phoenix, AZ: Oryx Press.

Thomas, S. P. (1983). *The relationship between selected psychological, environmental, and behavioral variables and health status of Americans in middle adulthood.* Unpublished doctoral dissertation, University of Tennessee, Knoxville.

Thomas, S. P. (1990). Predictors of health status of mid-life women: Implications for later adulthood. *Journal of Women and Aging, 2*(1), 49–77.

Thomas, S. P., Albrecht, K., & White, P. (1984). Determinants of marital quality in dual-career couples. *Family Relations, 33,* 513–521.

Thomas, S. P., & Donnellan, M. (1993). Stress, role responsibilities, social support, and anger. In S. Thomas (Ed.), *Women and anger.* New York: Springer.

Thomas, S. P., Shoffner, D., & Groër, M. (1988). Adolescent stress factors: Implications for the nurse practitioner. *The Nurse Practitioner: The American Journal of Primary Health Care, 13*(6), 20–29.

Turner, R. H. (1990). Role change. *Annual Review of Sociology, 16,* 87–110.

Turner, R. J., & Avison, W. R. (1989). Gender and depression: Assessing exposure and vulnerability to life events in a chronically strained population. *Journal of Nervous and Mental Disease, 177,* 443–455.

U.S. Bureau of the Census (1978). A statistical portrait of women in the U.S.: 1978. *Current Population Reports,* Special Studies, Series P-23, No. 100.

U.S. Department of Labor (1990). *Employee benefits in medium and large firms 1989.* Washington, DC: U.S. Government Printing Office, Bulletin 2363.

U.S. General Accounting Office (1990). *National Institute of Health: Problems implementing policy on women in study populations.* Washington, DC: Author.

Varvaro, F. F. (1992, August). *Women's choices and values across the lifespan: Adaptation to daily hassles, obstacles in achieving cardiovascular health and fitness.* Paper presented at the Fifth International Congress on Women's Health, Copenhagen, Denmark.

Verbrugge, L. (1985a). An epidemiological profile of older women. In M. R. Haug, A. B. Ford, & M. Sheafor (Eds.), *The physical and mental health of aged women* (pp. 41–64). New York: Springer.

Verbrugge, L. (1985b). Gender and health: An update on hypotheses and evidence. *Journal of Health and Social Behavior, 26,* 156–182.

Verbrugge, L. (1990). The twain meet: Empirical explanations of sex differences in health and mortality. In M. Ory & H. Warner (Eds.), *Gender, health, and longevity* (pp. 159–199). New York: Springer.

Waldron, I., & Jacobs, J. (1989). Effects of multiple roles on women's health: Evidence from a national longitudinal study. *Women and Health, 15,* 3–19.

Ware, J. E. (1976). Scales for measuring general health perceptions. *Health Services Research, 11,* 396–415.

White, P., Mascalo, A., Thomas, S., Shoun, S. (1986). Husbands' and wives' perceptions of marital intimacy and wives' stresses in dual-career marriages. *Family Perspective, 20,* 27–35.

Wiley, J. A., & Camacho, T. C. (1980). Life-style and future health: Evidence from the Alameda County study. *Preventive Medicine, 9,* 1–21.

Witkin, G. (1991). *The female stress syndrome* (2nd ed.). New York: Newmarket Press.

Woods, N. F. (1988). Women's health. In J. J. Fitzpatrick, R. L. Taunton, & J. Q. Benoliel (Eds.), *Annual review of nursing research Vol. 6* (pp. 209–236). New York: Springer.

Woods, N. F., Lentz, M., & Mitchell, E. (1993). The new woman: Health-promoting and health-damaging behaviors. *Health Care for Women International, 14,* 389–405.

Zal, H. M. (1992). *The Sandwich Generation: Caught between growing children and aging parents.* New York: Plenum.

Zautra, A., & Hempel, A. (1984). Subjective well-being and physical health: A narrative literature review with suggestions for future research. *International Journal of Aging and Human Development, 19,* 95–110.

291

Crisis, Challenge, and Stability in the Middle Years

David A. Chiriboga

THE ROLE AND MEANING OF STRESS

Although often studied for their immediate impact on mental or physical health, stress experiences have life course implications as well. According to Gergen (1977), for example, much of what affects adult life arises from seemingly random factors, such as a traffic accident, job stress, or divorce. Similarly, in a review of developmental research conducted over the past 100 years, Baltes and Baltes (1980) proposed a multicausal framework for life-span development in which unscheduled stressors such as amputation or unemployment serve as a major source of change in people's lives.

Markers of the Life Course

That stress is a dynamic component of adult development is repeatedly demonstrated in research. One team of social scientists has gone so far as to suggest that "At the most basic level, the life course can be defined as the major life events and transitions an individual experiences between birth and death" (Schulz & Rau, 1985, p. 130).

The idea of defining the adult life course according to an individual's experience of events and transitions may seem radical, but it has been around for a long time. Nearly 20 years ago, Bernice Neugarten (1977) suggested that major life events represent markers of the passage through time. Corroborating her views, many of the events included in stress instruments cluster around particular stages of life. Going to college, starting one's first job, marriage, and the birth of a first child are more likely to occur in young adulthood than in middle age. On the other hand, the departure of the last child from the family home, retirement of a husband, and death or growing dependency of a parent are more likely during the middle years.

As an example of how knowledge of life events and transitions may help us to understand individuals or groups, let us consider one of the participants in the San Francisco–based Normative Transitions Study

(M. Fiske Lowenthal, Principal Investigator) with which I was affiliated for a number of years. Daphne Randell, the participant, was only a child when she and her family fled Nazi Germany for France and sunsequently for South America. The multiple geographic moves her family went through, as well as the devastating conditions in Europe, were not the only challenges Daphne encountered. Life in a foreign country created many new demands, including the need not only to learn a new language but also to assimilate into a new and very different culture and to adapt to a lower socioeconomic status.

As a result of all the changes and crises she had faced, Daphne not only developed a sense of herself as someone overwhelmed by life circumstances but was put seriously off schedule in many important areas of her life. She finally graduated from high school at 22, had trouble finding steady employment, and in her early 20s also assumed primary caregiving responsibilities for her ailing parents. She married at 35, quite late for someone of her birth cohort, and to a man 25 years her senior. Daphne's first and only child was born when she was 41.

In contrast to Daphne, consider the life trajectory laid out for a hypothetical (but demographically all too real) 1990s teenager who becomes pregnant and gives birth at age 14, becomes a grandmother herself at 28, and becomes a great grandmother at 42. Clearly the life course trajectories—and midlife experiences—of both individuals would be strongly influenced by the timing of each marker event or transition.

Definitional Issues

Although stress offers a potentially useful vehicle by which to further our understanding of middle age, the concept is both complex and ill-defined. What one investigator calls "stress" may be the distress and discomfort caused by a difficult situation, whereas another investigator may use the term to describe the difficult situation itself. As an example, according to Hans Selye (1982), the father of modern stress theory, stress is "the nonspecific (that is, common) result of any demand upon the body" (p. 7).

Other theorists have emphasized the external pressure or an entire process. According to the research team headed by Richard Lazarus, stress "refers to any event in which environmental demands, internal demands or both tax or exceed the adaptive resources of an individual, social system or tissue system" (Monat & Lazarus, 1985, p. 3).

Frustrated with its theoretical looseness and increasingly all-encompassing scope, some call for an abandonment of the concept of stress. However, although definitions vary, there is some agreement concerning the three basic elements that underlie the typical stress paradigm: stressors, resources that mediate the impact of stressors, and stress responses. This paradigm highlights the idea that stress is not a mechanical and preordained experience but one that works through a variety of mediators, such as cognitive appraisal, social supports, self-esteem, and coping strategies.

Another complexity in stress research is that stressors come in many sizes and shapes. Life events represent only one form of stressor. In fact, at least three different general types of stressor can be identified: micro, mezzo, and macro (Chiriboga, 1992).

Microstressors. Microstressors are the stressors of everyday life. Examples include running out of toothpaste, getting caught in a traffic jam, and finding your child in the bathroom just when you're in a rush to take a shower. Although these are by far the most commonly experienced stressors, they have received comparatively little attention and indeed are readily forgotten by those who experience them.

In one early panel investigation, Holmes and Holmes (1970) reported that the seemingly inconsequential events of daily life were associated with minor physical complaints, including the common cold. More recently, Lazarus and Folkman (1984) examined the importance of day-to-day hassles for the physical and emotional well-being of middle-aged men and women. They concluded that hassles exert a stronger influence on mental health and well-being than does exposure to the better-known life events.

Mezzostressors. Mezzostressors are situations that occur less frequently than those of the micro variety, but they generally are more memorable and recognizable as significant. Life events (Holmes & Rahe, 1967) fall into this category, as do transitions and more chronic or durable stressors. More recently, anticipated stressors and other stressors related to scheduling have been studied. Mezzostressors, especially life events, have been found to predict a variety of physical, mental, and social problems. Studies have generally reported that middle-aged and older adults experience fewer life events, but these age differences may result from a lack of age-appropriate events in many stress inventories (Chiriboga, 1992).

Macrostressors. Macrostressors impact first upon society at large and only secondarily on the individual. The threat of war, bad economic news, a flurry of near-misses in the air lanes, or a spill of environmentally hazardous materials not only make headlines but can create anxiety and a generally heightened sense of distress (Bradburn & Caplovitz, 1965; Brenner, 1985).

A STUDY OF STRESS AND CHALLENGE AT MIDLIFE

In the late 1960s, a multidisciplinary team of social and behavioral scientists in northern California began a 12-year study of how the silent majority—White and primarily lower-middle-class urban Americans—lived out their lives. The admittedly broad focus on this study was on how people adapted to changing life circumstances, and for this reason the interviews included multiple open-ended as well as structured questions dealing with stress experiences.

Sample selection was based on the premise that in order to compare the many ways in which people live out their lives, people should be matched for similarity in stage of life rather than by age. The stages chosen were those surrounding each of four expectable transitions: we sampled 52 high school seniors who at first contact were about to graduate and begin adult life; 50 newlyweds who were facing parenthood and other transitions of couplehood; 54 parents in early middle age whose youngest child was a high school senior and hence presumably about to leave home; and 60 adults in later middle age who were within two to five years of retirement. During our original contacts in 1968 and 1969, the two older groups ranged in age from 39 to 65. By the fifth and final contact in 1981, the age range was 51 to 75.

MICROSTRESSORS

As one component of the stress assessment tools, the study employed a variant of the 115-item Daily Hassles Scale (Lazarus & Folkman, 1984). Administered at the seven-year follow-up, the Normative Transitions Study approach was relatively brief: rather than 115 items, it included 11, each being a global question concerning a whole dimension of stress. For example, subjects were asked "How often are you hassled by your parents?" The Likert scale responses ranged from "1" (never) to "4" (always).

Life Course Differences

An examination of differences by life stage provides clues about the distinctive stressors of middle age (Table 11.1). By and large the retirement and empty-nest subjects proved to be less hassled than their

TABLE 11.1 ANOVA Comparisons on the 11 Hassles Indicators (seven-year follow-up)

	Friends		Parents[a]		Children[b]		Spouse[a]		Work[c]	
	Men	Women	Men	Women	Men	Women	Men	Women	Men	Women
High school	1.59	1.76	1.81	2.13	.23	1.32	.91	1.28	2.27	1.88
Newlyweds	1.64	1.77	1.67	1.59	1.55	2.09	2.05	2.18	2.45	2.95
Empty nest	1.41	1.67	1.31	1.73	1.68	2.00	1.68	1.57	2.18	1.95
Retirees	1.50	1.48	2.25	2.17	1.13	1.61	1.50	1.35	.67	1.26

	Relatives[b]		Neighbors		Health[a]		Money[b]		Social[a]		Time[b]	
	Men	Women	Men	Women	Men	Women	Men	Women	Men	Women	Men	Women
High school	1.41	1.96	1.59	1.28	1.82	1.56	2.09	2.84	1.68	1.92	2.50	2.88
Newlyweds	1.77	2.09	1.55	1.45	1.91	1.86	2.55	2.91	2.00	2.05	2.73	3.18
Empty nest	1.36	1.57	1.36	1.24	1.77	2.10	1.36	1.67	1.55	1.48	2.05	2.48
Retirees	1.42	1.39	1.50	1.48	2.21	2.09	1.29	1.22	1.33	1.61	1.42	2.04

[a]Stage difference at .05 or lower.
[b]Stage difference and gender difference at .05 or lower.
[c]Stage difference at .05 or lower; interaction effect.

younger counterparts, especially the former newlyweds. Often their reports of less-frequent hassles were quite understandable. For example, many of the oldest group had already retired by the time of the seven-year follow-up; it will come as no surprise that all others, including the younger group of middle-agers, were significantly higher in work hassles (Duncan's Multiple Range test, $p = .05$). On the other hand, the younger middle-agers ranked highest of any group on reports of being hassled by their children; this distinction was mitigated by the fact that the only significant difference was between the former high school seniors, who were the least hassled, and all others.

Given the great attention now paid in the literature to caregiver stress (Mace & Rabins, 1991), it will come as no surprise that the older middle-agers were highest in their reports of hassles with parents. On the other hand, the most hassled were not only the oldest group but the youngest as well. Both were higher than the newlywed and empty-nest stage subjects, with the latter averaging the fewest hassles (Duncan's $p = .05$). Some five years later, at the final contact, the older middle-agers remained highest in parental hassles, and the younger middle-agers remained lowest. The more burdensome aspects of parental relations thus appear to be more characteristic of later middle age, and presumably the young-old stage as well.

The distribution of hassles related to health was more in line with expectations: there was a trend ($p = .09$) for the retirement group to be most hassled by health concerns. The results suggest that these people, now approaching the young-old stage, were more likely to experience durable or chronic health concerns than any other group.

Financial hassles were also significantly lower among the two middle-aged groups when compared to the young adults. This finding may reflect not only the relatively advantaged position of middle age but also the fact that entry into retirement does not necessarily present a financial strain for men and women.

A possible mellowing out was apparent in 4 of the 11 hassle dimensions. With regard to hassles with spouse, a posteriori tests indicated that stage differences were primarily a result of the former newlyweds reporting more hassles than anyone else. The empty-nest stage fell in the middle: whereas empty nesters were more hassled by their spouses than were the youngest subjects, they were less hassled than the young marrieds (Duncan's $p = .05$). Second, the two middle-aged groups were lowest ($p = .05$) in hassles with other family members, although here the distinction existed only in comparison with the former newlyweds, who were the most hassled. The middle-aged subjects were also lowest in hassles related to social activities and time pressures. For time pressures, it was not surprising that the oldest group was significantly lower than both of the young adult groups; the younger middle-agers were lower only than the newlyweds.

Overall, the stage differences provide only partial support for the idea that the middle years are less stressful. Several exceptions were found. Compared to the young adult groups, for example, the former empty-nest group were midrange in hassles related to their spouses and work and highest in hassles with children. The oldest middle-agers were the most hassled by parents and health issues, although the latter difference existed only at a trend level. More often than not, the middle-aged were neither the lowest or highest, but merely the same as everyone else.

Gender Differences

Gender differences were found for hassles related to children, relatives, finances, and time pressures. In each area, women were more likely than men to report being hassled. These differences were usually distributed rather evenly across life stages. The one suggestion of an interaction with stage came in the area of work, where the former newlyweds, men and women, scored higher than nearly anyone else save high school men (Duncan's $p = .05$). The middle-aged women therefore appeared to be at no particular disadvantage with regard to hassles.

Stressors at the Mezzo Level
The Eventfulness of Middle Age

Coming on the scene in 1968, shortly after the introduction of the Holmes and Rahe (1967) Schedule of Recent Events (SRE), the Normative Transitions Study was one of the first to make use of the new approaches suggested by the SRE. For the data collected in 1968–1969, in-depth questions were asked in multiple areas of potential stress; on the basis of results of a content analysis, responses were then coded according to 167 life-event items. During the 5-, 7-, and 12-year follow-ups, a revision of the 42-item SRE was used that included more items and a more individually tailored approach to weighting experienced events.

In order to enhance its salience to all stages of adult life, the revised instrument included an expansion from 42 to 137 items. Desirability was assessed by asking subjects to rate each experienced item as positive or negative (although inclusion of positive items in a stress inventory might seem irrelevant, positive changes can create their own set of demands and therefore deserved consideration; Chiriboga, 1984). Subscales were developed for positive and negative events in each of 10 dimensions; an 11th dimension, school events, is not used in the present analyses:

1. Marital/dating (arguments with spouse, dating, etc.)
2. Family (more arguments than usual with children, children have problems at school, etc.)
3. Work (arguments with coworkers, promotion or demotion, etc.)
4. Legal (jail, lawsuits other than divorce, minor law violations, etc.)
5. Habits (change in routine: eating, sleeping, smoking, drinking, etc.; many of these behaviors are linked to good or bad health)
6. Internal events (not achieving an important goal, etc.)
7. Social relationships (arguments with friends, etc.)
8. Personal (e.g., discrimination, changes in religious beliefs, etc.)
9. Financial (major or minor loans, etc.)
10. Home (move to new city or within city, problems finding new homes, etc.)

Life events at first contact. Analyses of initial interview data indicated that during the past year, nearly three-fourths of the women reported events related to education, and half or more reported family, health (of themselves or others), and dating or marriage problems (Chiriboga, 1984; Fiske & Chiriboga, 1990). There were only two categories in which half or more of the men reported stress: education (for over two-thirds) and work (exactly half).

Significant differences by life stage and gender were found in recent stress experiences. Younger subjects, for example, reported over two and one-third times as many stressors as the middle-aged, and women reported more events than men. These differences corroborate results from other studies, which generally have found the younger adult generation to report more life events than the older, and women to report more events than men (e.g., Chiriboga, Catron, & Associates, 1991).

If we consider just those at earlier and later stages of middle age, we see no differences in the overall number of life events. However, differences between the middle-aged men and women were marked. Work, for example, was a major source of distress for middle-aged men; in comparison, only a fifth of the middle-aged women reported work-related stressors, even though a majority worked. Health was on top of these women's stress lists, generally not their own but that of close others. Some middle-aged women also found a variety of family relationships stressful.

Finances were a problem for the oldest group of middle-aged men; they were worrying in advance about their retirement income. Generally expecting to retire in one to five years, these men were so preoccupied with financial matters that they tended to evaluate earlier periods of their lives primarily in economic terms. Many recalled their adolescence and young adulthood as traumatized by the Great Depression, and they have felt its influence ever since. A majority said they had chosen their work (to the extent that they had a choice) with long-range financial security in mind. It is not surprising, therefore, that among this older middle-aged group civil service jobs predominated: the group included postmen, firemen, policemen, and other types of civil servants. Most either disliked their work or reported problems related to work. Interestingly, similar findings are reported by researchers at the Institute of Human Development, Berkeley; despite their more privileged socioeconomic status, middle-aged men in that study also were preoccupied with economic factors and work stress (Elder, 1974).

Longitudinal findings. Over the 12 years of study, surprisingly high levels of continuity in stress exposure were evident. In fact, when life events were correlated over time, the magnitude of the correlations approximated those reported in personality research (Fiske & Chiriboga, 1990). These findings were replicated by Zautra, Finch, Reich, & Guarnaccia (1991) with microlevel events; this suggests stressors are not necessarily independent experiences and may chain forward in time.

More central to our discussion is the question of whether persons in the middle stages of life are less likely than younger people to experience life events. To examine this question, I computed a series of repeated measures MANOVA statistics. As would be anticipated on the basis of the high correlations over time exhibited by life event scales, I found temporal differences in only two dimensions: health and family stressors had generally peaked for all respondents by the 7-year contact and had declined by the 12-year contact (Table 11.2). Gender differences remained strong across all points: women reported significantly

TABLE 11.2 Average Life Event Scores for Contacts 3–5

	High School		Newlywed		Empty Nest		Retirement	
	Men	Women	Men	Women	Men	Women	Men	Wome
Summary[a]								
Time 3	42.3	53.7	31.0	32.6	12.4	13.2	5.1	9.2
Time 4	40.3	49.9	24.6	40.7	23.5	29.7	19.0	30.8
Time 5	30.7	48.2	35.1	36.6	10.6	37.6	12.2	17.8
Habits[b]								
Time 3	2.7	3.4	0.4	4.7	2.9	1.1	0.8	2.4
Time 4	4.9	6.8	2.7	5.1	2.2	3.0	3.1	4.9
Time 5	2.2	5.2	2.1	3.6	1.6	6.6	4.1	4.2
Work[c]								
Time 3	3.1	9.6	7.2	1.9	1.9	0.0	0.2	0.0
Time 4	5.7	8.4	1.2	5.7	3.3	1.0	0.8	3.0
Time 5	3.5	4.9	5.5	2.8	0.6	2.1	0.8	0.0
Internal[a]								
Time 3	7.2	8.0	3.6	6.9	1.7	2.8	0.8	2.5
Time 4	4.4	7.5	4.4	7.6	6.1	6.1	2.5	7.6
Time 5	5.1	11.0	6.2	9.3	1.9	9.0	1.3	3.5
Marital[d]								
Time 3	6.3	9.8	3.9	7.8	0.2	2.5	1.1	0.4
Time 4	9.9	8.0	5.3	6.5	1.2	4.1	1.7	2.6
Time 5	3.2	6.8	7.1	7.4	2.1	3.2	0.5	1.2
Family[b]								
Time 3	0.6	7.3	3.8	2.1	2.4	2.3	1.0	1.6
Time 4	1.7	4.9	2.4	5.7	6.6	8.8	4.8	6.4
Time 5	3.9	5.5	6.0	6.0	3.2	7.1	1.3	4.2
Nonfamily[d]								
Time 3	7.3	4.4	2.1	3.2	1.1	0.9	0.3	0.5
Time 4	3.1	3.4	1.7	3.9	0.6	2.6	1.9	2.2
Time 5	2.2	5.6	3.8	2.0	0.8	0.6	1.3	3.7
Personal[d]								
Time 3	6.0	6.5	6.8	3.6	2.2	3.0	0.4	1.3
Time 4	5.6	4.9	5.1	3.4	2.6	1.9	4.2	3.5
Time 5	5.4	2.9	1.0	2.0	0.2	5.4	2.4	0.7
Money[a]								
Time 3	2.5	2.8	0.5	1.0	0.0	0.4	0.0	0.3
Time 4	0.6	3.2	1.3	2.4	0.0	1.4	0.0	0.3
Time 5	1.2	2.0	2.7	2.0	0.0	1.7	0.2	0.0
Home[d]								
Time 3	2.3	1.4	1.3	1.2	0.0	0.0	0.3	0.2
Time 4	1.5	1.6	0.0	0.0	0.0	0.0	0.0	0.2
Time 5	0.5	1.3	0.3	1.2	0.1	1.1	0.2	0.3

[a]Stage and gender effects ($p = .05$).
[b]Gender and time effects ($p = .05$).
[c]Stage effects and stage-gender-time interactions effects ($p = .05$).
[d]Stage effects ($p = .05$).

more negative events related to health, internal events, family events, and finances; they also scored higher on the summary measure.

By far the greatest differences, however, were found between the younger and older participants. Irrespective of contact point, the former high school seniors and sometimes the former newlyweds scored higher than the two middle-aged groups with regard to events related to work, marriage, internal events, personal, home, finances, and social events. The former high school seniors and newlyweds also reported more events on the overall or summary measure.

There was one significant interaction that indicated an interplay of time, stage, and gender. Even here, the older subjects were not the ones affected: there was simply a shifting in rank of the two younger adult groups with regard to who was highest in work stress. Men and women in the two older groups remained low to intermediate from the 5-year follow-up through to the 12-year follow-up.

The distribution of positive events. Although it is not shown in a table, in order to conserve space, the distribution of positive events was similar to that of negative events: the younger subjects generally reported more of them. A posteriori multiple-range tests indicated that the former high school students and young marrieds were significantly higher ($p = .05$) than either of the two middle-aged groups in positive events related to health, work, marriage, and social relationships and in the personal domain. With regard to home-related activities such as moving to a new home or new city, the youngest group was significantly higher than either middle-aged group, whereas the former newlyweds were higher only than the empty-nest subjects. In the family dimension, the newlyweds reported more positive events than the retired and former high school groups. The empty nesters fell in the middle for positive family events, and both middle-aged groups were midrange on financial events. It would seem, therefore, that the middle-aged respondents generally experienced fewer positive events than did the younger adults. They never reported more positive experiences than the young adults and at best were midrange on a few dimensions.

Transitions as a Catalyst for Change

Although the two middle-aged groups from the Normative Transitions Study showed little evidence of heightened exposure to either negative or positive events, certain transitions could be expected to increase stress levels at any age. Unexpected transitions such as marital separation, amputation, or sudden bereavement may, for example, lead to heightened exposure across multiple stress dimensions (Parkes, 1972; Schlossberg, 1984). The more expectable transitions, on the other hand, may lead to reductions in stress exposure. In the Normative Transitions Study, for example, empty-nest-stage subjects who had not experienced the departure of their youngest child by the five-year follow-up reported more negative events related to children ($p = .05$). Similarly, retirement-stage subjects who remained in the world of work reported significantly higher levels of work-related events ($p = .05$).

To explore the effect of unexpected transitions, I compared subjects from the Normative Transitions Study with participants in a life-span sample of men and women who at first contact had just separated from their spouses. After eliminating Normative Transitions Study subjects who were currently separated or divorced and matching for age, I compared life events across the two studies.

Analyses of the 10 negative stress measures revealed that divorcing subjects were consistently exposed to more stressors than those undergoing normative transitions (Chiriboga, Catron, & Associates, 1991). For example, separated men of all ages reported significantly higher levels of negative stress in areas related to habits, internal events, and marital or dating relationships and had higher summary scores than did men in the other study.

Of particular interest is the fact that separated men aged 40 to 65 showed the greatest differences from age peers undergoing normative transitions. These separated, middle-aged men scored higher on 8 of the 10 stress dimensions: habits, work, internal, marital/dating, non-family, personal, financial, and home. Not surprisingly, they also scored higher on the overall score.

Differences between women undergoing normative and nonnormative transitions were not as distinct. Only in areas related to internal stressors (thoughts and feelings of a distressing nature) and in marital/dating issues were the separated women as a group experiencing greater stress. Moreover, separated women in the middle years of life were not very different from middle-aged women in the Normative Transitions Study. Instead it was the separated women aged 30–39 who reported the most stressors: they were significantly higher on all but nonfamily events when contrasted with their age peers in the other study.

Somewhat surprisingly, the experience of separation was also associated with greater exposure to positive events. The separating men and women reported significantly more positive events than did adults experiencing normative transitions. For example, separated men of all ages reported more positive events having to do with marriage/dating and nonfamily relationships; the divorced men over 40 also reported more positive changes in habits, at work, and in the overall measure of positive events. And in contrast to their standing on negative events, divorcing women aged 40 and over stood out as being the most different from age peers in the normative study. They were more likely to report positive changes in work, nonfamily relationships, habits, internal events, and the marital/dating area.

Overall, the results supported the assumption that unexpected, negative transitions may usurp the usual decline in stress exposure with age. Those transitions that are more normative and expectable seem either to have no influence on stress exposure or to be linked with reductions.

Being Off Schedule as a Potential Stressor

My discussion of mezzostressors has to this point focused on life events and the stressors receiving the greatest attention in the literature, and I have also alluded to the role of transitions. Just to round out the image of stressors at the mezzolevel, I will say something about the effects of timing. That being off schedule is a source of distress was first suggested by Neugarten (1977). During the seven-year follow-up, we asked questions about nonevents, being behind and ahead of schedule, and about anticipated events. These questions were open-ended and hence required extensive content analysis and coding before data could be obtained.

Nonevents: An Example

The general procedure we followed in coding timing questions was simply to count the number of times subjects mentioned having a specific problem. Responses to one question presented challenges to the research team and I will discuss them in some detail. The specific question was "During the past eight years of your life (since [date] when you were first interviewed), have there been any events which you had expected to happen to you that didn't?"

Responses to this question were wide-ranging, and it became obvious that respondents were providing two types of answers. Some answers dealt with delays in obtaining some desired goal. In other words, although an anticipated event had not occurred, subjects assumed, implicitly or explicitly, that it still could occur. For example:

I didn't expect that none of my youngsters would be married by now. They are all getting along and not one is the slightest bit interested in getting married. [56-year-old-White male: personnel manager for small firm]

I thought I might get a job after the children left, but that was eight years ago and I still haven't! [53-year-old White woman: housewife]

The other way was to actually mention a nonevent. Examples of nonevent responses include:

I expected to get married but broke it off.

I expected to go to Harvard Law School.

The project team developed separate codes for the two types of responses: the codes assessed frequency of response as well as category of response: work, family, marital, and so forth. In all cases, only negative conditions were coded.

Timing and midlife: Some initial results. As shown in Table 11.3, ANOVA results indicated that although men and women were similar in their experience of delayed events, there was a stage effect. The former high school students were most likely to feel delayed, and the oldest group was least likely to: a multiple range test indicated that the

TABLE 11.3 Mean Scores by Gender and Life Stage
on Stressors Related to Timing

	Delayed Events	Nonevents	Behind Time	Ahead of Time	Anticipated Stressors
By gender					
Men	0.37	0.29	0.49	1.01	1.14
Women	0.55	0.22	0.59	0.69	1.17
By stage	***	**	***		***
Youngest	0.78	0.27	0.82	1.02	1.31
2nd youngest	0.44	0.49	0.72	0.88	1.65
2nd oldest	0.49	0.14	0.44	0.91	1.09
Oldest	0.13	0.13	0.17	0.61	0.61
Grand mean	0.46	0.25	0.54	0.86	1.16

Note: Higher scores indicate more potential stress.
$*p = .10. **p = .05. ***p = .01.$

only significant difference was between these two extremes. In terms of the frequency distribution, the percentage of people reporting delayed events dropped from nearly 47% among the former high school seniors to just under 11% of those in the oldest group. Overall, about 30% of the entire sample reported delays.

Twenty-seven percent of the sample reported one or more non-events, roughly the same number as reported delays. ANOVAs indicated no differences by either gender or stage of life in the reporting of nonevents. But subjects' responses to a related question differed depending on their stage: subjects were asked whether they felt they were behind time. The difference here was quite clear: the two middle-aged groups were least likely to feel behind time. As might be expected from their reports of being delayed in their experience of events, the former high school students were most likely to feel behind schedule.

No stage effect was found for feelings of being ahead of schedule, but men were more likely than women to report being ahead. A review of individual cases suggests that an underlying reason may be the competing demands placed upon women who are trying to juggle careers and family obligations. Thus, while women were no different from men in feeling behind schedule, the more positive experience of being ahead of schedule was less available to them.

Finally, in the area of anticipated stress, the two middle-aged groups once again were less likely to expect such stress. This finding paralleled results from our baseline interviews. When subjects were asked how distant they were from their most recent interesting or exciting past event, or one anticipated for the future, the two middle-aged groups stood out as being most distant in time (Lowenthal et al., 1975).

MACROSTRESSORS

Between first and last interviews, a number of sociohistorical conditions emerged, including the Vietnam War, the oil crisis of 1973, and marked fluctuations in the American economy. These conditions provided the opportunity to examine how events occurring at the societal level might influence individual lives over time. Fortunately, from its onset, the Normative Transitions Study collected data concerning how social issues of the day were affecting respondents. One instrument asked questions concerning the effect of 10 social issues and changes (e.g., changing roles of women, changes in the rights of minorities, changes in the economy and employment in the last 3 years). The structured responses ranged from 1 ("none") to 4 ("strong" effect).

Other more open-ended questions probed for the subjects' level of concern with social conditions and also asked them who they believed was responsible for problems.

At the first contact in 1969, the women far outranked men in their concern with social issues (Lowenthal et al., 1975). They also posited quite different solutions for what they perceived as negative social changes. As a group they believed that people should be more responsible and responsive to national and international problems. Those few men who were troubled by social changes tended to place responsibility squarely on the government and not on themselves. They believed the government should be more assertive in the enforcement of law and order and in the control of technology and change generally.

As the study continued over time, concern over where the country (and the world) was going increased. By the fourth contact, approximately seven years into the study, worries about social issues had doubled. Among the retirement-aged subjects, women accounted for most of the increaase in concern. But among the younger group of middle-aged parents, the increase was found among both men and women.

As might be expected, men and women in the younger and older groups varied in how much they reported being affected by social changes. The newlywed-stage women for example, were most strongly affected by the women's movement, and the newlywed men were most affected by the Vietnam War. In several areas the middle-aged groups reported greater impact from social changes than the younger. Crime in the streets is one example. The empty-nest-stage men were most likely to report being strongly affected by crime (64%), followed by empty-nest women and retirement-stage men. The Watergate incident during the Nixon presidency most affected the retirement women, with 61% reporting a strong effect, followed by retirement men and men and women in the empty-nest stage.

By the final contact, the majority in both middle-aged groups had become more worried about war; for the women, distress associated with the Vietnam War had doubled from the 7-year to the 12-year follow-up. Worry about the dangers of nuclear war and nuclear plants was high for all, but women were far more worried about such risks than the men. Despite gender differences, social issues had become of increasing concern for most of these middle-aged subjects. By and large, one can conclude that middle-aged and older persons may be more vulnerable to macrostressors than those in young adulthood.

The Most Stressful Experiences of Midlife

To this point we have focused on data collected with relatively structured instruments. We now turn to responses to more open-ended questions. At the seven-year contact, all subjects were asked about their most stressful experience of the preceding year. As shown in Table 11.4, the area that produced the greatest stressor by far was health. The empty-nest-stage men were the most likely to report greatest stress in the health arena. Recall that during the first interviews, some seven years in the past, health had not been a major concern for this group. Clearly the seven years had created some change in their life condition.

Subjects were also asked about their control over the problem and how emotionally disruptive it had been. Both middle-aged groups proved less likely to feel they had been in control of their most stressful experience than younger groups ($F = 4.64$, $p = .00$). Indeed, the majority of middle-agers felt a total lack of control: While 63.4% in the empty-nest stage and 65.1% in the retirement stage reported no control, the same was true for only 37.2% of the high school seniors and 28.6 percent of the former newlyweds. Those reporting the least control were the empty-nest males, who also were most likely to report the greatest stress in the health arena. Among these men, 71.4% reported no control.

Despite their perceived lack of control, the middle-agers were no different from younger persons in how emotionally disruptive they felt their most stressful experience had been ($F = 0.71$, $p = .55$). This is not to say that the experiences were inconsequential: 46.3% of the empty nesters and 39% of the retirees reported that the experience had been severely disruptive. This compares with 50% of the high school seniors and 58.5% of the newlyweds.

Control and severity revisited. Although differences between the younger and middle-aged subjects were apparent only in the area of control, a further analysis was suggested by Lachman's (1990) finding that perceived lack of control over stress was associated with pessimism about one's health. The question here became whether control over the most stressful experience was related to the experience's perceived severity. As shown in Table 11.5, control was not related to severity among the younger adults. Among the middle-aged, however, greater control was associated with lessened perception of stress severity. Con-

TABLE 11.4 Areas that Produced the Greatest Stress during the Preceding Year (number and percentage; 7-year follow-up)

	High School		Newlywed		Empty Nest		Retirement	
	Men	Women	Men	Women	Men	Women	Men	Women
Health	3 13.6		2 9.1		10 45.5	4 18.2	7 29.2	6 26.1
Marital	5 22.7	4 16.0	6 27.3	5 22.7	2 9.1	3 13.6	2 8.3	2 8.7
Children				3 13.6		3 13.6	1 4.2	4 17.4
Work	8 36.4	5 20.0	9 40.9	5 22.7	2 9.1	5 22.7		1 4.3
Column total	22 12.1	25 13.7	22 12.1	22 12.1	22 12.1	22 12.1	24 13.2	23 12.6

TABLE 11.5 Correlations between Control and Severity Ratings of Greatest Stressor for Groups Low and High on Stress (7-year; based on summary of 5- and 7-year data)

	All Subjects	Younger Adults	Middle-Aged
Ungrouped[a]	−.20 (165)**	−.17 (84)	−.30 (81)**
High stress	−.35 (83)***	−.27 (54)*	−.58 (29)***
Low stress	−.07 (76)	−.05 (27)	−.07 (49)

[a]Number in parentheses indicates number of subjects included in analysis.
*$p = .05$. **$p = .01$. ***$p = .001$.

trol may make a difference, apparently, but only for those in the forty-something stage of life.

Control seems to be related to perceived severity only among the middle-aged. This raises questions about which stress-moderating factors might be especially important to those in the middle years. We will explore only one possibility here: that the association between control and severity is enhanced by prior experience with stressors. Specifically, I hypothesized that (1) a history of sustained exposure to high stress conditions acts as a sensitizing factor; and (2) since middle-aged men and women have been adults for longer periods, the sensitizing nature of previous stress history should be more pronounced for that group.

To test the hypotheses, I divided the sample of younger and older middle-agers into two groups: those who reported relatively high levels of negative life events at both five- and seven-year follow-ups and those who reported relatively low levels. We then ran correlations between perceived control and severity of the most stressful experience of the past year (information collected, it should be recalled, at the seven-year follow-up) for the younger and older groups.

As shown in Table 11.5, among middle-aged persons living under circumstances of sustained high stress, lower perceived control was associated with the stress experience being reported as more severely disruptive (and vice versa). For those who were habitually low in stress exposure, no relationship was evident. These findings provide evidence that sustained stress loads may sensitize the older adult.

Similar results were evident for younger adults. Consistent with the idea that older adults would be more likely to demonstrate the sensitizing effect, however, the magnitude of the correlation between control and severity for high-stress younger people tended ($z = 1.60$, $p = .054$)

to be lower than that found among high-stress middle-agers. There is, then, confirmation of the hypothesis that the sensitizing effect of sustained stress exposure not only exists but is more pronounced in middle age. This hypothesis does not contradict past reports that because of prior experience with similar conditions, middle-aged men and women evaluate current stressors as having less impact than do younger adults (Horowitz & Wilner, 1980). The current findings simply suggest that chronically high levels of stress may exacerbate the impact of current stressors.

STRESS AND CONTINUITY

One of the more durable controversies about adult development concerns whether adult personal attributes are stable over time, evolve continuously, or even exist at all (Goldberg, 1993; Neugarten, 1969). One recurrent theme in the controversy has been that stressors affect personal development (Gergen, 1977; Ormel & Schaufeli, 1991).

The longitudinal nature of the transitions study allowed assessment of the degree to which stress exposure actually affected stability of personal functioning among the middle-aged respondents. The first step was to take negative life event scores from data collected at interview rounds conducted 5, 7, and 12 years after the initial interview and add them together. Next, the data were divided, using a median-split technique, to obtain people who scored higher and lower on negative events over a period of approximately 7 years.

After dividing the sample, we computed Pearson correlations for three types of measures often used in studies of adult development: those assessing morale (Bradburn & Caplovitz, 1965), those assessing health status (a physical health status question and a 42-item symptoms inventory based on the Cornell Medical Index; Lowenthal et al., 1975), and those assessing self-concept (all from a 70-item Adjective Rating List, including the ratio of scores on "masculine" and "feminine" items also used in Chaps. 4 and 5).

For each measure, baseline status was correlated with status at the 5-, 7-, and 12-year follow-ups. This was done separately for each of the two basic groups: those higher and lower on stress. The results (Table 11.6) suggest that although stress history may influence stability, the direction of influence is not consistent across domains of study. For the Bradburn and Caplovitz (1965) measures of well-being, the high-stress group showed higher stability coefficients for Positive Affect, and their coefficients were higher for Overall Happiness through

TABLE 11.6 Correlations between Baseline Interview Status and
Status at All Follow-up Contacts

		5th Year	7th Year	12th Year
Affect balance	High	.38**	.46**	.04
	Low	.45***	.37***	.26**
Negative affect	High	.36*	.34*	.01
	Low	.39***	.37***	.29**
Positive affect	High	.53***	.55***	.48***
	Low	.30**	.52***	.36***
Overall happiness	High	.43**	.58***	−.02
	Low	.27**	.13	.08
Psychological symptoms (total)	High	.83***	.56***	.69***
	Low	.74***	.46***	.56***
Physical health status	High	.33*	.42**	not asked
	Low	.63***	.69***	not asked
Negative self	High	.72***	.58***	.53***
	Low	.66***	.66***	.69***
Positive self	High	.81***	.71***	.52***
	Low	.66***	.61***	.67***
Assertive self	High	.48**	.47**	.58***
	Low	.76***	.72***	.76***
Hostile self	High	.71***	.64***	.50***
	Low	.64***	.61***	.63***
Masculine-feminine balance	High	.72***	.79***	.63***
	Low	.84***	.75***	.74***

Note: Bradburn and Caplovitz (1965) measures of affective well-being, measures of self-reported health status, and the self-concept. Drawn from the Longitudinal Study of Transitions. Data drawn from subjects in the early and later stages of midlife, subdivided into those with high ($N = 21$) and low ($N = 51$) stress exposure. Both sexes combined.
*$p = .10$. **$p = .05$. ***$p = .01$.

the 7th year (neither group showed any significant association between initial and 12-year contacts). Stability in the high-stress group was lower for Negative Affect and Affect Balance for the 12-year correlation, but no distinct pattern was evident during the intermediate years. A review of these results in the context of average scores revealed that the differences in stability were generally unrelated to group averages. At none of the five contacts, for example, were the high- and low-stress groups significantly different in Overall Happiness or Positive Affect. Further, no differences were found between groups on any morale measure for either the initial contact or the last two contacts.

Stress history was also related to the stability of self-reported health. Middle-agers with histories of high-stress exposure showed higher stability in psychological symptoms. Not only were they higher in stability but they were significantly higher in actual number of symptoms reported at all five contact points. In contrast, correlations over periods of five and seven years for reported physical health status were substantially higher for the low-stress group. Since further investigation revealed that the low-stress group reported better health only at the initial contact, what seems to be happening is that stress exposure is associated more with variability in health than in prolonged levels of dysfunction, as was the case for psychological symptoms.

For all measures of self-concept, the less stressed subjects demonstrated higher correlations at the 12th year, but the magnitude of correlations was often equivalent during earlier contacts. The only exception was for a summary measure of assertiveness (based on principal components analysis; Lowenthal et al., 1975) for which the correlations were consistently higher for the low-stress group at all rounds.

We may review the role of stressors for continuities in psychological status. There seems to be some evidence that prolonged exposure to stress affects the course of development, but that the effect varies by content area. With respect to the variations, it should be emphasized that the findings reported in Table 11.6 do not account for such potentially intervening variables as social supports, previous stage of development, or the possibly critical role of exposure to positive life events. Several other chapters in this book do consider such factors in detail; here the focus is more on the stressors reported in midlife and the implications of these stressors.

STRESS AND THE PREDICTION OF CHANGE

The analyses of micro-, mezzo-, and macrostressors have demonstrated that midlife is most definitely not uneventful and monotonous. Whereas younger adults reported significantly greater exposure to certain life events, hassles, and societal stressors, the midlife subjects reported greater or at least equal exposure to others. The results to this point have also suggested that stress influenced the well-being of these subjects. To further evaluate the influence of stressors, stress indices were included as predictors of change in selected personality attributes over the 12-year period of study.

Change was evaluated for three of the personal attribute measures discussed in the preceding section: the masculine-feminine balance index (Lowenthal et al., 1975), Bradburn and Caplovitz's (1965) measure of happiness, and overall number of psychological symptoms. Analyses were based on the combined sample of younger and older middle-aged subjects (N available with listwise deletion $= 64$).

Predicting Masculine-Feminine Balance

Parker and Aldwin (Chap. 4) use a developmental framework to evaluate changes over time in masculine-feminine balance scores. In order to explore the potential role of stress exposure as an additional source of change, I used a predictive model to examine this role, one that in effect pitted a stability model against the Random Change Model. The procedure I used was a hierarchical regression analysis of the 12th-year Masculine/Feminine Balance (MFB) score on several sets of predictors.

The first set of predictors included initial, or baseline, status on MFB; this set represented essentially the stability component, since the assumption was that the best predictor of status 12 years later would be initial status. The second set consisted of measures of age, gender, and education; these were included as potential controls. The following sets tapped total, summated stress scores for the first interview contact, the third interview, the fourth interview, and the fifth interview. To allow comparability over time, analyses employed only measures of the more traditional life event measures, both positive and negative, rather than daily hassles or macroevents.

Results reaffirmed the stability of self-concept indices over time but also suggested that stress events have a role to play. Initial status on MFB accounted for 50% of the variance ($R^2 = .50$, $p = .00$; Beta $= .71$, $p = .00$). Of the remaining sets, only one including stress exposure at the 7-year contact made a significant contribution, and the analyses were therefore rerun with just that additional set. The set contributed 7% of additional variance (R^2 change $= .07$, $p = .00$), with total negative stress (Beta $= -.18$; $p = .05$) and positive stress (Beta $= -.18$, $p = .05$) contributing equally. It is of interest that greater exposure to both positive and negative stress was associated with a shift toward the feminine end of the MFB scale. This suggests that stress exposure may make subjects, including men as well as women, more open to their emotional and expressive (perhaps empathetic) side.

The same equation, rerun with younger groups, produced somewhat different results. Initial levels of MFB predicted significantly ($R^2 = .41$; $p = .00$), but stress exposure did not contribute. Here then is

315

additional evidence that middle-aged men and women may be more strongly affected by stressors than persons in the young adult years— despite the fact that they often report fewer events.

Predicting Overall Happiness

To predict happiness, I followed the same approach used to predict masculine-feminine balance. The first predictive set consisted of happiness as reported at the first interview. In contrast to the strong evidence for self-concept stability, happiness 12 years into the study was unrelated to initial levels of happiness ($R^2 = .00$, $p = .93$; Beta $= -.01$, $p = .93$). Happiness during the middle years thus did not manifest any long-term developmental progression in its own right.

Nearly all the predictive measures, indeed, failed to predict happiness. The exception consisted of the summary measures of negative events reported at the 7- and 12-year contacts. The analysis was therefore rerun, including only the latter two measures as forced entries. The 7-year life events measure continued to be associated with unhappiness ($R^2 = .09$, $p = .03$; Beta at entry $= .31$, $p = .00$). With the addition of negative events reported for the year before the last interview, the overall equation accounted for 18% of the variance in happiness ($R^2 = .18$, $p = .00$; R^2 Change $= .08$, $p = .01$; Beta at entry $= .38$, $p = .01$).

Overall, the analyses suggested that happiness during the middle years was not a foregone conclusion. Whether subjects became more or less happy was associated with mediate and immediate experiences with negative events and not with initial levels of happiness. Perhaps of even greater interest was the finding that in the long run, positive life events did not play a role in the development of happiness.

Predicting Psychological Symptoms

The next analysis predicted psychological symptoms at the 12-year interview contact. The criterion was the Normative Transitions Study's adaptation of the Cornell Medical Index symptoms (see Lowenthal et al., 1975). Initial levels of symptomatology were highly predictive of symptom level 12 years later ($R^2 = .43$, $p = .00$; Beta at entry $= .65$, $p = .00$). Other than initial status, however, only one additional measure contributed to the prediction of symptoms: the summary score for negative events at the 7-year contact. Entry of the latter measure added approximately 6% to the already substantial variance accounted for

($R^2 = .49$, $p = .00$; R^2 Change $= .06$, $p = .01$; Beta at entry $= .25$, $p = .01$). As would be expected, greater exposure to negative events predicted higher levels of reported psychological symptoms some five years later.

Implications of the Prediction of Change

The three sets of predictive analyses offered support for both stability and random-change models of development. For our middle-aged subjects, masculine-feminine balance and psychological symptoms demonstrated strong autocorrelations over time. These two personal attributes therefore seem to follow more of a stability than random change model. In both instances, however, life events measures made significant but relatively small contributions to the prediction of 12-year status.

Happiness, on the other hand, seems to be an attribute that is less predictable and more readily influenced by the immediate stress context in which people find themselves. If happiness is, as the philosophers used to say, the summum bonum of life, then those interested in the well-being of middle-aged men and women would be well advised to consider their stress experiences.

Stress and growth. Although much of this chapter has been devoted to the negative implications of exposure to stress, I should point out that there is a body of literature, often in the form of anecdotal reports by clinicians, suggesting that exposure to stress may lead to personal growth and well-being. As Carl Jung (1916/1969) said, "Man needs difficulties; they are necessary for health" (p. 143).

While Jung saw personal development as associated more with youth, one set of analyses based on Normative Transitions Study data (third and fourth contact points) found evidence of positive changes, possibly indicative of growth, in our middle-aged subjects. They found that negative life events were as likely to predict positive as negative changes in a variety of indicators of well-being. For example, among the middle-aged men, greater work stress was associated with improvement in life satisfaction, a decline in psychological symptomatology, improvement in self-reported health, and an increase in the scope of activities in which the subject participated (Chiriboga & Dean, 1978). On the other hand, marital stress was generally associated with greater problems, for both middle-aged men and middle-aged women.

Discussion

This chapter has devoted considerable attention to the stress experiences of middle age. Although the presentation may border on methodological overkill, it should be kept in mind that the Normative Transitions Study is rather unique, not only in its wealth of stress instruments but also in studying men and women long enough to assess how they progressed through and out of middle age. The results of the investigation challenge at least two paradoxical ideas about middle age: that middle age is an uneventful and rather boring period, and that it is a period marked by crises and turmoil. I will address these challenges in this last section.

Middle Age as Plateau or Crisis

Consistent with the literature, middle-aged subjects were less likely than those in young adulthood to report stressors. Evidence for a reduced level of exposure was evident in the measures of timing and hassles but was most evident in data obtained from the life event questionnaire, an instrument that presents the subject with a prespecified list of conditions. Even with the event scale, however, many stressors were of equal frequency, and some were more frequent. Judging from the hassles data as well as questions dealing with the most stressful experience of the past year, health-related stressors grew in prominence during the middle years. Middle-aged men and women also seemed unusually sensitive to events occurring at the societal level—the "macro" stressors.

For all intents and purposes, then, middle age does not appear to be a time when the pace of life slows down dramatically. On the other hand, while it may not be a boring and uneventful stage of life, neither does it appear to be a time of acute crisis. There was a paucity of evidence for any midlife crisis in the lives of these middle-aged subjects. When questioned at length about their experiences, in questionnaires using both structured and open-ended formats, no subjects spontaneously made reference to anything akin to such a crisis. Indeed, other studies of these subjects suggest that at least as far as departure of the last child is concerned, the hypothesized loss is really more of a midlife gain (Krystal & Chiriboga, 1979).

The midlife crisis may be more fancy than fact, but it should be emphasized that stress definitely was not absent from the lives of these subjects. Whether it be life events, hassles, or stressors at the societal level, the middle-aged men and women in the Normative Transitions Study experienced their share. The analyses suggest that rather than some obvious and perhaps flamboyant crisis, most of the vulnerability of middle-aged men and women may result from the sustained experience of higher-than-average stress loads. One consequence of cumulative stress loads would seem to be a heightened sensitivity to current stressors.

We have already discussed an example of this heightened sensitivity. Earlier in the chapter I introduced Daphne Randell, a subject in the Normative Transitions Study. Daphne's life was marked by numerous events, including war and religious persecution, immigration, the problem of assimilating into at least two very different new homelands, marriage to a man who became in his later years a chronically sick husband, and raising a son afflicted with a potentially crippling illness. On the other hand, by the time of the first interviews, most of the acute and chronic stressors that had beset her life had diminished or ended.

Notwithstanding the changes in her life circumstances, Daphne's portrayal of her current life, not only at age 56, when she was first interviewed, but over most of her subsequent interviews, resembled that of a person suffering from major adversities. She constantly complained about problems that seemed illusory or long resolved, more akin to Don Quixote's windmills than to reality. She also scored high in depression, was higher than the average empty-nest stage woman in her reports of psychological symptoms, and could project only 7 years into the future (most women her age readily projected at least 25 years).

As exemplified by Daphne, then, some of the very real problems faced in midlife are not as dramatic as portrayed in the popular press. To paraphrase the poet T. S. Eliot, middle-agers may experience problems not with a crisis but with a whimper. This phenomenon of cumulative stress as a sensitizing agent may reach prominence during the middle years, since individuals need time to accumulate the necessary stress history. The sensitizing effect was not apparent, it should be recalled, among the younger subjects.

Concluding Thoughts

Over 40 years ago, Raymond Kuhlen (1959) hypothesized that "significant situational changes may launch a person on what amounts to a new developmental phase at almost any age of life" (p. 880). In the analyses presented in this chapter, social stressors played an important

319

role in both destabilizing personal attributes and predicting change over time. The lives of middle-aged respondents were influenced in myriad ways by these stressors, and the impact was not limited to the immediate present.

From a developmental perspective, it was encouraging to find that the lives of middle-aged subjects in the Normative Transitions Study were continuing to be affected by the world around them. Even today, some developmental researchers tend to dismiss this possibility. For example, according to Caspi (1993), "Life-course events such as military service, marriage and work can cause radical changes in the organization of the self, but receptivity to such events is the most pronounced during the transition to adulthood" (p. 364). Clearly data from the Normative Transitions Study provide evidence to dispute their contention.

Finally, a secondary objective of this review of stress in the middle years has been to provide the background necessary for understanding how and why stressors have an impact on personal functioning. In other chapters, specific situations studied by the Henry A. Murray Center researchers are described in detail. Through them all, the reader is encouraged to bear in mind that stress exposure may intrude with its own immediate and long-term consequences. As indicated by the emerging paradigms of stress reviewed earlier, the resources the individuals can bring to bear on the problem, and the way they view the problem, may be more important than stressors. And whether stress leads to growth or decline may rest ultimately on whether the experience taxes but does not exceed the individual's adaptive resources.

References

Baltes, P. B., & Baltes, M (1980). Plasticity and variability in psychological aging: Methodological and theoretical issues. In C. Guerski (Ed.), *Aging and the CNS.* Berlin: Schering.

Bradburn, N. M., & Caplovitz, D. (1965). *Reports on happiness.* Chicago: Aldine.

Brenner, M. H. (1985). Economic change and the suicide rate: A population model including loss, separation, illness, and alcohol consumption. In M. Zales (Ed.), *Stress in health and disease* (pp. 160–185). New York: Brunner/Mazel.

Caspi, A. (1993). Why maladaptive behaviors persist: Sources of continuity and change across the life course. In D. C. Funder, R. D. Parke, C. Tomlinson-Keasey, & K. Widaman (Eds.), *Studying lives through time: Personality and development* (pp. 343–376). Washington, DC: American Psychological Association.

Chiriboga, D. A. (1966). Self-Actualization in Middle-Aged Men and Women. Trial Research, Committee on Human Development, University of Chicago.

Chiriboga, D. A. (1984). Social stressors as antecedents of change. *Journal of Gerontology, 39*(4), 468–477.

Chiriboga, D. A. (1992). Paradise lost: Stress in the modern age. In M. L. Wykle, E. Kahana, & J. Kowal (Eds.), *Stress and health among the elderly* (pp. 35–73). New York: Springer.

Chiriboga, D. A., Catron, L. S., & Associates. (1992). *Divorce: Crisis, challenge or relief?* New York: New York University Press.

Chiriboga, D. A., & Dean, H. (1978). Dimensions of stress: Perspectives from a longitudinal study. *Journal of Psychosomatic Research, 22*, 47–55.

Elder, G. H., Jr. (1974). *Children of the Great Depression.* Chicago: University of Chicago Press.

Fiske, M., & Chiriboga, D. A. (1990). *Change and continuity in adult life.* San Francisco: Jossey-Bass.

Gergen, K. J. (1977). Stability, change, and change in human development. In N. Datan & H. W. Reese (Eds.), *Life span developmental psychology: Dialectical perspectives on experimental research* (pp. 136–158). New York: Academic Press.

Goldberg, Lewis R. (1993). The structure of phenotypic personality traits. *American Psychologist, 48*(1), 26–43.

Holmes, R. S., & Holmes, T. H. (1970). Short-term intrusions into the life-style routine. *Journal of Psychosomatic Research, 11*, 213–218.

Holmes T., & Rahe, R. (1967). The social readjustment rating scale. *Journal of Psychosomatic Research 11*, 213–218.

Horowitz, M. J., & Wilner, N. (1980). Life events, stress, and coping. In L. W. Poon (Ed.), *Aging in the 1980s: Psychological issues* (pp. 363–374). Washington, DC: American Psychological Association.

Jung, C. G. (1916/1969). *The structures and dynamics of the psyche.* Princeton, NJ: Princeton University Press.

Krystal, S., & Chiriboga, D. A. (1979). The empty nest process in midlife men and women. *Maturitas, 1*, 215–222.

Kuhlen, R. G. (1959). Aging and life-adjustment. In J. E. Birren (Ed.), *Handbook of Aging and the Individual* (pp. 852–897). Chicago: University of Chicago Press.

Lachman, M. (1990). When bad things happen to older people: Age differences in attributional style. *Psychology and Aging, 5*(4), 607–609.

Lazarus, R. S., & Folkman, S. (1984). *Stress, appraisal, and coping.* New York: Springer.

Lowenthal, M. F., & Chiriboga, D. A. (1972). Transition to the empty nest. *Archives of General Psychiatry, 26*, 8–14.

Lowenthal, M. F., Thurnher, M., Chiriboga, D. A., & Associates. (1975). *Four stages of life: A comparative study of men and women facing transitions.* San Francisco: Jossey-Bass.

Mace, N. L., & Rabins, P. V. (1991). *The 36-hour day* (Rev. ed.). Baltimore: Johns Hopkins University Press.

Monat, A., & Lazarus, R. S. (1985). Introduction: Stress and coping—Some current issues and controversies. In A. Monat & R. S. Lazarus (Eds.), *Stress and coping, An anthology* (2nd ed., pp. 1–12). New York: Columbia University Press.

Neugarten, B. L. (1968). Awareness of middle age. In B. L. Neugarten (Ed.), *Middle age and aging* (pp. 93–98). Chicago: University of Chicago Press.

Neugarten, B. L. (1969). Continuities and discontinuities of psychological issues into adult life. *Human Development, 12,* 121–130.

Neugarten, B. L. (1977). Personality and aging. In J. E. Birren & K. W. Schaie (Eds.), *Handbook of the Psychology of Aging* (pp. 626–649). New York: Van Nostrand Reinhold.

Ormel, J., & Schaufeli, W. B. (1991). Stability and change in psychological distress and their relationship with self-esteem and locus of control: A dynamic equilibrium model. *Journal of Personality and Social Psychology, 60*(2), 288–299.

Parkes, C. M. (1972). *Bereavement: Studies of grief in adult life.* New York: International Universities Press.

Schlossberg, N. K. (1984). *Counseling adults in transition: Linking practice with theory.* New York: Springer.

Schulz, R., & Rau, M. T. (1985). Social support through the life course. In S. Cohen & S. L. Syme (Eds.), *Social Support and Health.* Orlando, FL: Academic Press.

Selye, H. (1982). History and present status of the stress concept. In L. Goldberger & S. Breznitz (Eds.), *Handbook of Stress: Theoretical and Clinical Aspects* (pp. 7–17). New York: Free Press.

Zautra, A. J., Finch, J. F., Reich, J. W., & Guarnaccia, C. A. (1991). Predicting the everyday life events in older adults. *Journal of Personality, 59*(3), 507–538.

IV THE WORLD OF WORK

Gender, Employment, and Psychological Well-being: Historical and Life Course Perspectives

Rosalind C. Barnett

The chapters in Part 4 deal, in different ways, with the relationship between paid employment and psychological well-being. This relationship has never been seriously questioned for men; it has always been assumed that paid work is crucial to men's well-being. But it is different for women. To examine the relationship between paid employment and well-being and to consider it for both sexes, we need some background. In this overview I will provide that background, review the relevant literature, and provide a framework for understanding the contribution of Chapters 13–15.

The main theme I will be addressing is that the meaning of paid employment and of career choice in the lives of women and men has changed dramatically over time. Such changes need to be taken into account in understanding the role of employment in individual lives over time and in attempts to compare the career commitments of women and men. It is, after all, only when the career occupies a comparable place in the lives of men and women that we can meaningfully inquire into the effect of gender on the relationship between career commitment or career choice and well-being. As long as such obstacles as myths, stereotypes, social sanctions, and discrimination exist, the relationship between choice and gender will be confounded, making it impossible to draw conclusions about gender similarities or differences.

BACKGROUND

Every theory of adult male development places men's work role at the center. The centrality of paid work in theories of men's lives (Erikson, 1959; Levinson, Darrow, Klein, Levinson, & McKee, 1978; Valliant, 1977) is reflected in the descriptors Levinson et al. use to identify the "Seasons of a Man's life": "Entering the Adult World," "Settling Down," "Becoming One's Own Man" (BOOM). The markers Levinson et al. use to distinguish one season from another and to assess success at each stage are tied most strongly to events in the workplace.

For example, a man's judgment regarding his relative success or failure in meeting the goals he set for himself during the BOOM stage depends on whether "he has achieved the desired position on his 'ladder,'" whether he has been "affirmed within his occupational and social world," and whether he is "becoming a senior member of that world with all the rewards and responsibilities seniority brings" (1978, p. 191).

Further, we read, failure to achieve occupational goals results in a sense of personal failure.

> When a man experiences a developmental crisis in the late thirties, it stems from the overwhelming feeling that he cannot accomplish the tasks of Becoming One's Own Man: he cannot advance sufficiently on his chosen ladder; cannot gain the affirmation, independence and seniority he wants; cannot be his own man in the terms defined by his current life structure. (p. 191)

For women, in contrast, people assume the roles of wife and mother are the core roles. Indeed, in Erikson's seminal work, *Identity: Youth and Crisis* (1968), marriage and motherhood are considered crucial to the completion of a woman's identity.

> Young women often ask whether they can "have an identity" before they know whom they will marry and for whom they will make a home . . . something in the young woman's identity must keep itself open for the peculiarities of the man to be joined and of the children to be brought up. (p. 283)

In fact, success in the roles of wife and mother has been considered a prerequisite for women's psychological well-being. Indeed, the roles of wife and mother, although in reality quite separate and at times in conflict, are linked together as if one. Women's family roles typically have been seen as natural and as crucial for women's well-being; until recently, women who did not occupy at least one of these roles, if not both, were assumed to be immature, unfeminine, incomplete, selfish, unnatural, and deviant (Rossi, 1984; Teicholtz, 1978). Moreover, these family roles are assumed to be natural and therefore should be enacted without stress (Barnett & Baruch, 1985).

In spite of these admonitions, women did enter the paid labor force during the early twentieth century. However, dire warnings were sounded from many corners. The pursuit of intellectual activities in general and paid employment in particular were thought to damage women, making them potentially more vulnerable to a host of negative outcomes. For example, medical authorities on women maintained that the brain and the ovaries could not develop properly at the same time.

Attitudes toward women's employment moderated somewhat in the 1920s. Although it became socially acceptable for women to work, this option was allowed for only some women. In particular, work was permissible for single women, who were expected to leave the work-force as soon as they got married, or in some cases as soon as they had children. Here too was evidence of the concern that women should reserve their energies for their family roles.

Moreover, the *kinds* of work women were permitted to do were also highly restricted. Such jobs as teacher, secretary, and nurse were appropriately feminine; others were not. Thus, employment for women was at best a temporary stopgap, or at worst something to fall back on in the event of early widowhood.

This restrictiveness was also apparent in the kinds of education that were available to young women. Thus, compared to men, women faced massive intrusions of stereotypes and myths in their life options. In the context of such restrictions, any study of the impact of paid employment on women's psychological well-being would be complicated, as would the study of the impact of personality on career choice.

Women's options grew and shrank during and after World War II. It was not until the 1960s, with the advent of the Women's Movement and passage of Title IX of the Civil Rights Act of 1964, that women made more stable gains. The mass movement of women into the labor force since then has been well chronicled. Progress notwithstanding, women's options were and still are highly restricted compared to men's.

This focus on women does not imply that there were no restrictions on men's career patterns and career choices. Men did not, and still for the most part do not, have the choice of staying at home. It is expected that men will work for pay and will do so for their entire adult lives. To violate that expectation is to call into question one's masculine identity. Social norms also dictate the kinds of work men can do. The American dream of individual achievement demanded social mobility; sons were expected to do better than their fathers. Although most men do not achieve upward occupational mobility, they do move horizontally. Few men choose occupations lower in prestige than those of their fathers. Thus, the son of a doctor is less likely to choose blue-collar work than is the son of a blue-collar worker.

The social movements of the 1960s brought with them many changes that impacted on women's labor force involvement. Of particular importance, women were admitted into previously all-male professional schools. For example, the first women were admitted to the Harvard Business School in 1963, and although women had been admitted to the Harvard Medical School as early as 1945 (there were four women in the entering class of 1945), the situation for women did not improve significantly until the mid-1970s. And gender discrimination in hiring became illegal. Hence barriers to women in blue-collar and service occupations were removed. Women were now driving school buses, fighting fires, policing neighborhoods, and protecting the country.

In spite of liberalization, gender barriers still operate. For example, although more women are admitted to medical schools than ever before, the distribution of women across medical specialties is very unbalanced. There are far more female pediatricians, for example, than female neurosurgeons. And although women constitute roughly 50% of the entering classes in many prestigious law schools, we did not have a woman Supreme Court justice until 1981. As long as such discrimination exists, "career choice" has different meanings for women and men. Moreover, most women need to consider the eventual pulls of parenting on their career choices, whereas men do not.

With increased progress came increased warnings. Many prominent people, including Drs. Friedman and Rosenman of Type A fame, predicted that as women entered the paid labor force they would lose their health advantage and start dying earlier, falling victim to coronary heart disease. What has actually happened? If we look at the longitudinal data, it is clear that in America women live longer than men. In every decade since 1900, and for both Whites and non-Whites, the average female life span has lengthened more than the average male life span. For example, in 1900 the average life expectancy for men was 46 years; for women it was 48 years. At the turn of the century, White females lived, on average, two years longer than White males. By 1980, the average life expectancy was 70 years for males and 77.5 years for females. The gap between males and females had *increased* by five and a half years. These figures are not consistent with the belief that employment leads to a depletion of energy and higher risk of illness. As social roles have changed and as women have taken on increased responsibilities outside of the home, their life expectancy has actually increased.

How do the figures look if we focus only on employed women? A major study of mortality from all causes shows that among women there is no relationship between employment and mortality risk. Is it possible, however, that women are dying more than they used to from stress killers such as heart attacks, as predicted by Friedman and Rosenman? The answer is no. Age-adjusted rates of death from heart attacks show no change in the gender gap. Women have retained their health advantage.

After reviewing the available data on gender and mortality, Faye Crosby, the author of a recent book, *Juggling,* concludes: "the accumulated data . . . show not even a hint of harm to women from their expanded opportunities for playing a variety of life roles" (1990, p. 58).

Do the effects of employment show up in data on physical and mental health problems, rather than in mortality figures? No. In general, there is evidence that employed women enjoy better physical and mental health than nonemployed women. And that women with multiple roles enjoy better mental and physical health than women with fewer roles.

Overall, results from several longitudinal studies on national samples of employed middle-aged women indicate that over time, employed women report a decrease in physical health problems. In addition, there is evidence that employed and nonemployed women do not differ in incidence of coronary heart disease over a ten-year period, nor do employed women have an increased risk of mortality from all causes over an eighteen-year period. With respect to mental health, studies show employed women are less depressed than nonemployed women and report higher levels of subjective well-being.

Moreover, in what has been called the greatest revolution of the century, married women and women with children, even young children, have been flocking to the labor force. And women's work patterns have shifted in several ways. No longer are women dropping out to bear and rear their children. What had once been a bimodal distribution, with women working until they had their first child and then returning to the labor force after that their children had left home, has become a bell-shaped curve. And women increasingly are employed full-time all year in contrast to the previously prevalent part-time part-year pattern. In other words, women's and men's labor force patterns are converging.

With all these changes, echoes of the past still sound strongly. Even today, when women's role as paid employee is considered, it is almost always in the context of women's nonworkplace roles. Since the role of paid employee is assumed to be added on and thus to cause conflict, burden, and strain, women who occupy both family and workplace roles are automatically thought to be stressed. In this view, harried mothers put themselves, their marriage, and their children at risk for all kinds of problems. For example, numerous studies sought to establish an association between maternal employment and marital unhappiness and divorce. Even more studies sought a link between maternal employment and a host of negative outcomes for children (Hoffman, 1989). These included juvenile delinquency, behavior problems, and academic problems. But no such link was found.

In spite of lack of empirical support, these beliefs continue to exert inordinate pressure on many women. Employed women struggle with culturally induced guilt. Central to the traditional roles of wife and mother is the obligation to be available to meet the needs of the family, to be ready to respond whenever someone calls. In addition, wives and mothers are held, and hold themselves, responsible for the well-being of their role partners—their husbands and their children. In the traditional view, if a woman's husband is unhappy, it must be her fault. If her children have problems, she must be to blame. This assumption of responsibility is particularly strong for the role of mother. In spite of the fact that one has relatively little control over the welfare and happiness of another person, mothers are prone blame themselves whenever their children show signs of distress.

REVIEW OF THE LITERATURE

Against this background, it is not surprising that inquiries have only recently been made into the *positive* effects of women's participation in the labor force. Recent evidence indicates that the role of paid employee is both a direct and an indirect source of well-being (Barnett & Baruch, 1985). Using such indices as self-reports of physical symptoms (Coleman, Antonucci, & Adelmann, 1987; Verbrugge, 1983; Waldron & Herold, 1984) and indices of well-being (Barnett & Baruch, 1985; Merikangas, 1985), many studies show significant mental and physical health differences that favor employed women over nonemployed women. Moreover, despite the belief that the more high-powered a woman's career is, the more danger to her well-being, the advantage is greater for women in higher occupational statuses (Verbrugge, 1987). However, being employed was beneficial even to women in low-level jobs (Belle, 1982; Ferree, 1976).

The growing consensus that the employee role was typically not as stressful for women as had been assumed led researchers to expand their scope. The new villain became multiple role involvement, not employment per se. Most of the research on multiple roles and their effects on distress and well-being has focused on within-sex differences among women; men have received scant attention (Gove & Zeiss, 1987). Thus, researchers have only recently addressed the issue of gender differences in these effects.

THE SCARCITY HYPOTHESES

Underlying many of the studies exploring the relationship between the number of roles women occupy and particular role combinations and such measures as self-reported happiness or depression was the expectation that multiple roles would be associated with negative health outcomes. Roles drain energy; hence the more roles a woman occupies, the less energy she will have, the more conflict she will experience, and the more negatively her well-being will be affected.

This hypothesis, called the scarcity hypothesis, was first put forth by Goode (1960) and was extended by Coser (1974), Slater (1963), and others. It rests on two premises: (1) that individuals have a limited amount of energy; and (2) that social organizations are greedy, demanding all of an individual's allegiance. According to the scarcity model, people do not have enough energy to fulfill their role obligations; thus role strain is normal and compromises are required. Therefore the more roles one accumulates, the greater the probability that one will exhaust one's supply of time and energy and confront conflicting obligations, leading to role strain and psychological distress.

This hypothesis was developed to account for men's behavior in formal workplace organizations. When applied to women, the assumption is that family roles are greedy, demanding total allegiance and energy. Accordingly, the hypothesis is that when women assume the role of paid employee, a role that exposes them to the demands of the organization, the net effect is debilitating. The scarcity hypothesis assumes that women have limited resources with which to meet the demands of the workplace.

THE EXPANSION HYPOTHESIS

In the mid-1970s a competing hypothesis about human energy emerged: the expansion hypothesis. It focuses on the net positive gains to be had from multiple roles. The major theorists of this revisionist position (Marks, 1977; Sieber, 1964) emphasize the privileges rather than the obligations that accrue to incumbents of multiple roles. They argue that such rewards as self-esteem, recognition, prestige, and financial remuneration more than offset the costs of adding roles.

Through role bargaining, that is, delegating or eliminating onerous role obligations, men could reduce to a manageable and presumably attractive set the many demands on them associated with operating in two arenas. Thus, for men, multiple role involvement enhances well-being. Early support for this view came from the work of Gove and Tudor (1973), who suggested that men experience fewer symptoms of psychiatric dysfunction than women because they are committed simultaneously to work and family roles. Research on women supports the expansion hypothesis (Crosby, 1984; Epstein, 1988; Thoits, 1983; Verbrugge, 1982). Thoits (1983) reports a positive association between the number of roles a person (woman or man) occupies and psychological well-being. In an analysis of within-sex differences in women's physical health, Verbrugge (1982) concludes that multiple role involvement is associated with better health. In sum, the expansion hypothesis is well supported: "the more roles, the better" (p. 65) (Gove & Zeiss, 1987; Thoits, 1983).

Although the data are not all in, they overwhelmingly support the expansion view and refute the scarcity view. Women do not have to make choices in order to conserve their energy. Indeed, women who do more feel better. Women who are married and have children and are employed report better physical and mental health than their counterparts who have fewer roles. Rather than being a serious problem, for most women, working outside the home is a benefit for mental and physical health.

The next focus of research was on role combinations. Although many studies suggest that involvement in multiple roles may be beneficial, some argued that not all roles have equally positive effects. Further, the effects of the same role combinations may be different for men and women. Many researchers argue, for example, that the combination of paid worker and spouse roles has more beneficial effects for men than for women (Cleary & Mechanic, 1983; Gove & Tudor, 1973).

This issue had particular importance for women, because many believed that even if multiple roles were good for women in general, surely they could not be good for married women with children. They argued that the combination of the roles of employee, wife, and mother was particularly stressful. We can readily see in this a repetition of the myth of the fragile woman. Research once again failed to support this myth. Women who were wives and mothers and employees showed no more signs of distress than women who occupied fewer of these roles (Barnett & Marshall, 1991).

Because most of the studies on multiple role involvement and mental health were cross-sectional, it could be argued that only women with good health engaged in multiple roles: hence multiple role involvement per se was not contributing to positive health. Longitudinal data were needed. In one such longitudinal study, married women who reduced their commitment to the work force from full-time employed to homemaker over a three-year period reported a significant *increase* in distress, whereas those who increased their commitment from homemaker to full-time employed, reported a significant *decrease* in distress (Wethington & Kessler, 1989). In contrast, neither gains nor losses in parental status over the same period were related systematically to change in distress. Having a first or a subsequent child or having the last child leave the home had no impact on psychological health. Thus, increased labor force commitment was associated with improved mental health. Moreover, women who had children reported increased distress only if they *decreased* their commitment to the labor force. There is scant evidence here to support the scarcity hypothesis.

Research findings notwithstanding, there has been and still is a powerful cultural belief that impels women, especially women with young children, to cut back on or drop out of work. The weight of empirical evidence is hardly strong enough to counter the force of this belief. Thus, even today, when social attitudes are more liberal, women who undertake demanding careers and plan to have families need to have personal resilience and coping strategies that may differentiate them from their male counterparts who have the same ambitions. Surely such individual variables must have had a more profound effect on women's career choices in the past, when social support, role models, and social science data were not available.

Then and now, combining the roles of employee, husband, and father never required defying social expectations, nor was this combination of roles ever thought to be stressful. Indeed, men who occupied this role combination reported higher well-being and lower distress than men who occupied any other combination of these three major social roles (Gore & Mangione, 1983).

Over time, evidence accrued that even when as many a eight roles were considered, for both women and men, the more roles people occupied, the better their health (Thoits, 1983). As a result of these findings, interest in studying the relationship betwen multiple role involvement and health outcomes waned.

Currently the focus is on job conditions and subjective experiences on the job. It is argued that even if employment is good for women, some jobs are better than others. Early theory-building studies focused on the relationship between job conditions and physical-health outcomes in men. In particular, researchers were interested in identifying those workplace stressors and stress mitigators that were associated with coronary heart disease. Two job conditions—psychological demands and job control—emerged as critical. The combination of having many demands, which increases arousal, and little control, which blocks release, was associated with increased risk of many physical health problems, including coronary heart disease and stroke. Early success led to generalization of this two-dimensional model, referred to as the Job-Strain Model, to women, to employees in nontraditional (i.e., service sector jobs), and to mental-health outcomes. Critics have noted that had women been included in the early theory-building studies, factors other than demand and control might have been identified as especially stressful. Recent studies support this belief. For example, lack of advancement opportunities (i.e., being in a dead-end job), flexibility, and social value were more strongly related to psychological distress than were job demands or job control in a study of employed men and women (Barnett, Sayer, & Marshall, 1994). Scant attention has been paid to the effect of personality on these processes; personality may condition the relationship between job conditions and distress.

Finally, subjective experiences on the job have been related cross-sectionally and longitudinally to psychological distress for men and women (Barnett, Marshall, Raudenbush, & Brennan, 1993; Barnett, Raudenbush, Brennan, Pleck, & Marshall, 1995). Not surprisingly, people who report positive job experiences also report low psychological distress. Moreover, if job experiences deteriorate over time, distress increases, whereas if job experiences improve over time, distress decreases. What is of particular interest is that the magnitude of these relationships is virtually identical for men and women.

With few exceptions, the job stress–illness literature has not addressed the question of how personality affects these processes. One suggestion is to view personality as a stress-resistance resource, a buffer of the stress process (Kobasa, 1987). Thus, under conditions of stress, individuals with certain personality characteristics will be at lower risk for illness than individuals without those characteristics. The characteristics that have received the most research attention are control, a self-concept that reflects high self-esteem and low self-denigration, the absence of the type A behavior pattern, and hardiness. The more of each of these that one has, the less likely one is to suffer psychological or physical debilitation due to environmental stressors. Although the data are not all consistent, it does appear that these personality characteristics increase resilience to the negative mental and physical health outcomes that are associated with stressful work and family experiences (Kobasa, 1987).

Research on the job stress–illness relationship is as noteworthy for what it excludes as for what it includes. For the most part, the research is characterized by a narrow conceptualization of the factors that induce or mitigate distress outcomes and by cross-sectional ahistorical designs. The historical perspective teaches us that women's and men's relation to career and family have varied enormously. Whereas men have always been expected to operate in two arenas—work and the family—women have been largely confined to domestic pursuits. Thus women who broke out of that mold were atypical and of great interest. How did they overcome such strong social imperatives? Even today, when women's opportunities are vastly improved, women who are high achievers in traditionally male-dominated fields are still rare.

One reflection of this ahistorical bent is that almost no attention is paid either to intergenerational analyses or to intrapersonal analyses of the meaning of work over the life course. A historical perspective makes it abundantly clear that the meaning of work as well as the choice of career and the nature of career commitment have had, and perhaps still have, different meanings for men and women. Moreover, failure to address such issues and a focus on gender differences invite errors of interpretation.

Although this gender gap in meaning has probably narrowed over time, it is still present, at least with regard to blocked mobility and the added responsibilities that women with careers anticipate and actually have with regard to family. In other words, gender differences will be less pronounced between employed single men and women and more pronounced between employed married mothers and fathers.

The ahistorical bent is also reflected in the preponderance of cross-sectional studies. Even the longitudinal studies cover relatively short time periods. Yet we know that career commitments change over a lifetime, as do career choices. Similarly, job experiences that might be stressful at one point in time might not be stressful at other points in time. And job satisfaction might also vary over time and with certain life events. In other words, the maturational aspects of career commitment and career choice and their implications for psychological well-being are totally overlooked in the mainstream literature. The chapters in Part 4 use longitudinal data to address some of these issues and provide important first answers.

As noted, the issue of career choice is not addressed in the literature. For example, there are no studies that ask whether job choice or satisfaction moderates the relationship between job stress and illness. We do not know whether people who are employed in their field of choice are more resilient to distress than those who are not so employed. And we do not know how changes over time in job choice impact distress. In short, models relating job conditions to health outcomes do not consider the question of career choice or the question of the fit between person and career.

Nor are changes in career commitment over the life course studied. The intriguing finding that change over a three-year period in employment status is related to psychological health piques our curiosity about the effect of changes in career commitment over longer periods of time. Although long career interruptions are not prevalent today, or at least were not until recently, it used to be common for women to interrupt their careers for long periods to rear their children or not to begin their careers until after their children had left home.

In addition, relatively little attention is paid to the role of personality, either as directly affecting career commitment or career choice or as a stress-resistance resource. Yet we know that personality must play a role in the decision to choose certain careers and career paths over others. Moreover, we have evidence that over time, career choice can affect personality (Kohn & Schooler, 1982). Against this background, we can now turn to the studies reported in Part 4.

Overview

One of the most challenging and engrossing issues for theoreticians, practitioners, and individuals alike is to understand the process of career choice. What factors incline us toward certain careers? What factors influence our commitment to those careers? What determines whether people are satisfied with their work or are not? How do our choices affect us? Is there a relationship between career path (choices, commitments) and psychological well-being? And are there gender differences in these relationships?

The chapters in Part 4 address subsets of these questions, using longitudinal data sets available at the Murray Research Center. Tomlinson-Keasey and Gomel (Chap. 13) ask what factors lead women to seek careers in atypical, typical, or androgynous careers and how these factors differ for women who decide to be homemakers. The data they used to address these questions span a 70-year period. The 672 gifted women in the sample were first recruited when they were 11 years old (in 1922) and were studied every 5 years thereafter. Vandewater and Stewart (Chap. 14) ask about the antecedents and correlates for women of three career paths: continuous career commitments, midlife career commitments, and alternative commitments. Their data come from a sample of 171 Radcliffe College graduates of the class of 1964. Data were collected when the women were 28, 33, 37, 43, and 48 years of age. Leong and Boyle (Chap. 15) ask about the factors that are associated with midlife career changes for 300 women and 300 men who were surveyed in the 1930s, when they were in their 20s, and again in the 1950s.

Although they differ in specifics, all three chapters share a primary focus on the relationship between personality and career outcomes. In some cases, parents rated their daughters on personality traits; in others, self-reports were available, sometimes when the respondents were in early adulthood and sometimes in midlife.

Three themes emerge:

1. Situational factors need to be taken into account.
2. Career change and instability may be normative.
3. More attention needs to be paid to process rather than outcome.

Although it is a truism that early childhood factors affect later psychological development, their impact on women's career paths appears negligible. Later career choices are not merely extensions of early manifestations of such traits as social responsibility, achievement motivation, and academic capabilities. Nor did parents' educational attainments or early family losses (through death or divorce) determine later choices, at least not in Tomlinson-Keasey and Gomel's sample of intellectually gifted women (Chap. 13). Women who at age 48 were in occupations classified as typical, atypical, or androgynous and women who became homemakers did not differ on these early childhood indicators.

The failure to find such linkages may be interpreted variously. Perhaps it reflects the restriction of range due to the homogeneity of the sample. (The same point is relevant to the failure to find a substantial relationship between academic propensities or academic preferences and career direction.) One might expect, therefore, to find stronger relationships in a more heterogeneous sample. Another possibility is that events in the larger socioeconomic environment of the time swamped the effects of early personality and family stability.

These young women grew up in the 1920s, a period of marked liberalization of attitudes toward women. They came to adulthood during the Depression (i.e., in 1929 they would have been roughly 18 years of age), when opportunities for women and men were constricted by the failed economy. With few jobs to be had, women were passed over to make room for male breadwinners. At that time, women who pursued atypical careers, more specifically careers in such male-dominated fields as medicine and law, were perhaps more exposed than other women to the backlash of the times.

Because the economic opportunities for women had changed drastically during their formative years, it is not surprising that their occupational goals when they had just reached adulthood were the most important predictors of later career directions. Perhaps in more stable economic periods, early family stability and early personality might have had a greater impact on later choices.

These women undoubtedly knew how hard it would be to pursue atypical careers, but they decided on that course anyway. They may therefore have been more highly selected than contemporary women who make such choices because of such personality factors as perseverance. It is also important to remember that the data collection period ended in 1959, before the advent of the Women's Movement. Thus, these atypical women had neither the social support nor the institutional opportunities available to later cohorts.

*

The failure to find an association between early personality and later career choice may also reflect the changing nature of career commitments. As suggested by Leong and Boyle, change of career choice, not stability, may be normative. Indeed, men's career paths are not nearly as linear as is often assumed (Treiman, 1985). Hence, there may have been a stronger relationship between early personality and the typicality/atypicality of choices at some period in the women's lives before they were 48. Because of antifeminist feelings and barriers to success in atypical fields, it is conceivable that many women who had selected atypical careers may have dropped out, leaving behind those who were more successful or had a higher tolerance for misogyny. Alternatively, those whose personalities best fit with the dominant culture or those whose personalities were malleable may have remained, whereas the misfits and less compliant personalities may have left. Through such a reciprocal process, personality may predict stability of choice over time rather than choice at one point in time.

Selective retention might account for the higher work satisfaction of the 48-year-old atypicals compared to that of the other employed women. Such a process of adaptation might also account for the higher satisfaction homemakers report with community activities. Women for whom such activities were not so rewarding might have moved out of the home and into some form of career by the age of 48. In other words, they might have become the midlife career commitment group illuminated by Vandewater and Stewart (Chap. 14).

The historical period in which the Tomlinson-Keasey and Gomel (Chap. 13) data were collected may also account for the failure to find an association between the husband's involvement with child care and any of the outcome variables. Indeed, it is surprising that in the 1950s husbands did enough child care even to permit analysis of that variable. Undoubtedly the problem of restriction of range precluded finding any meaningful relationships.

The women studied by Vandewater and Stewart came to maturity in a vastly different sociocultural period. They graduated from Radcliffe College in 1964, the early years of the Women's Movement. (In 1963, Betty Friedan published her landmark book, *The Feminine Mystique*.) Whereas only the midlife career commitment group reported that they were affected by the Women's Movement, the weight of the evidence indicates that all 171 women in this study were affected by the changing attitudes toward women and work. In particular, the majority of the women were continuously in the paid labor force and held high-prestige jobs. Even though the college culture may have publicly endorsed women's roles as wife and mother, privately female undergraduates were clearly responding to a different message.

Recognizing that career commitments change over time, Vandewater and Stewart classified the women on the basis of the similarity or difference between their career comitments at ages 28 and 43. The groups thus comprised the continuous career commitment, the midlife career commitment, and the alternative commitments groups; they were compared on the basis of demographic data as well as self-reported well-being assessed at age 48.

In contrast to the finding that atypicals were unlikely to be married (Chap. 13), Vandewater and Stewart reported no differences among the three groups in the age at which they first married. The continuous career commitment women in the Vandewater and Stewart study, many of whom undoubtedly would have been classified as atypicals by Tomlinson-Keasey and Gomel, as well as the other two groups, all married at about age 23. Apparently by the 1960s it was no longer necessary to forego marriage in order to pursue a serious lifelong commitment to a high-prestige job, again reflecting the changing cultural attitudes toward women. This liberalization may have attenuated the linkage between early personality and career choice.

Consistent with findings from more recent cohorts, there were no differences among the three groups of women on any of the well-being indicators assessed when the women were 33, 37, 43, or 48 years of age. Recall that although there were differences in the kinds of work they did and in the number of hours per week they worked, almost 90% of the women were employed. In fact, at age 43, even the alternative commitment women, those who worked significantly fewer hours than the other two groups, were employed on average 31 hours per week, which is considered full-time by some researchers. Much literature indicates that employment per se (i.e., at least half-time employment) confers a mental health benefit to women, and these women all seem to have benefited equally.

The finding that the women in the three groups differed in self-reported personality at age 43 could be seen as supporting a selection process, or as reflecting adaptation over time, or both. For example, the continuous career commitment and midlife career commitment groups were both higher than the alternative commitment group on dominance, sociability, self-acceptance, and independence. The alternative commitment group was higher than the other two groups on communality and internality. It is as plausible that women were attracted to their particular career patterns because of these traits as that they developed these traits in response to the demands of their chosen career path.

Such a process of reciprocal adaptation might underlie some of the findings of Leong and Boyle (Chap. 15). Focusing on change, they found that in 1930, 37% of the men but only 15% of the women held jobs that were congruent with their interests. Twenty years later the figures were 44% for the men but only 19% for the women. Here, too, socioeconomic factors rather than gender might account for this large difference. In the 1950s, there were far more opportunities in the workplace for men than for women. World War II was over, women were encouraged to leave the workplace and stay at home, and importantly, the Women's Movement had not yet surfaced. Thus, the job situations faced by men and women were vastly different. Under these circumstances, men had many more opportunities to match their vocational interests to their job choices than women did.

Conclusion

The hypothesis that personality affects the choice of role commitments has not received much support. Indeed, these studies raise important questions that need to be addressed before we will make significant progress in understanding the relationship of personality to career choice and commitment. These questions include: (1) How should we conceptualize interactions between personality and context? (2) How should we conceptualize the process of change over time in choices and commitments during changing times? (3) How should we conceptualize the reciprocal effects of personality and job choice? In order to make progress we need to generate longitudinal data sets that incorporate both personality and contextual variables, thereby enabling comparative longitudinal analyses and analyses of cohort effects.

References

Barnett, R. C. (1992). Multiple roles, gender, and psychological distress. In L. Goldberger & S. Breznitz (Eds.), *Handbook of stress* (pp. 427–445). New York: Free Press.

Barnett, R. C., & Baruch, G. K. (1985). Women's involvement in multiple roles and psychological distress. *Journal of Personality and Social Psychology, 49,* 135–145.

Barnett, R. C., & Marshall, N. L. (1991). The relationship between women's work and family roles and their subjective well-being and psychological distress. In M. Frankenhaeuser, U. Lundberg, & M. Chesney (Eds.), *Women, work, and health: Stress and opportunies* (pp. 111–136). New York: Plenum.

Barnett, R. C., Marshall, N. L., Raudenbush, S., & Brennan, R. (1993). Gender and the relationship between job experiences and psychological distress: A study of dual-earner couples. *Journal of Personality and Social Psychology, 65*(5), 794–806.

Barnett, R. C., Raudenbush, S. W., Brennan, R. T., Pleck, J. H., & Marshall, N. L. (1995). Change in job and marital experience and change in psychological distress: A longitudinal study of dual-earner couples. *Journal of Personality and Social Psychology, 69,* 839–850.

Barnett, R. C., Sayer, A., & Marshall, N. L. (1994). *Gender, job rewards, job concerns, and psychological distress: A study of dual-earner couples.* (Working Paper). Wellesley, MA: Center for Research on Women, Wellesley College.

Belle, D. (Eds.), (1982). *Lives in stress: Women and depression.* Beverly Hills: Sage.

Cleary, P., & Mechanic, D. (1983). Sex differences in psychological distress among married people. *Journal of Health and Social Behavior, 24,* 111–121.

Coleman, L., Antonucci, T., & Adelmann, P. (1987). Role involvement, gender, and well-being. In F. J. Crosby (Ed.), *Spouse, parent, worker: On gender and multiple roles.* New Haven: Yale University Press.

Coser, L. (with R. Coser). (1974). *Greedy institutions.* New York: Free Press.

Crosby, F. (1984). Job satisfaction and domestic life. In M. D. Lee & R. N. Kanungo (Eds.), *Management of work and personal life.* New York: Praeger.

Crosby, F. (1990). *Juggling.* New York: Free Press.

Epstein, C. F. (1988). *Deceptive distinctions: Sex, gender, and the social order.* New Haven, CT: Yale University Press.

Erikson, E. (1968). *Identity: Youth and crisis.* New York: Norton.

Ferree, M. (1976). The confused American housewife. *Psychology Today, 10,* 76–80.

Goode, W. (1960). A theory of strain. *American Sociological Review, 25,* 483–496.

Gore, S., & Mangione, T. W. (1983). Social roles, sex roles, and psychological distress: Additive and interactive models of sex differences. *Journal of Health and Social Behavior, 24,* 300–312.

Gove, W. R., & Tudor, J. (1973). Adult sex roles and mental illness. *American Journal of Sociology, 78,* 812–835.

Gove, W. R., & Zeiss, C. (1987). Multiple roles and happiness. In F. J. Crosby (Ed.), *Spouse, parent, worker: On gender and multiple roles.* New Haven: Yale University Press.

Hoffman, L. W. (1989). Effects of maternal employment in the two-parent family. *American Psychologist, 44,* 283–292.

Kobasa, S. C. O. (1987). Stress responses and personality. In R. C. Barnett, L. Biener, & K. Baruch (Eds.), *Gender and Stress.* New York: Free Press.

Kohn, M. L., & Schooler, C. (1982). Job conditions and personality: A longitudinal assessment of their reciprocal effects. *American Journal of Sociology, 87,* 1257–1286.

Levinson, D. J., Darrow, C. N., Klein, E. B., Levinson, M. H., & McKee, B. (1978). *The seasons of a man's life.* New York: Ballantine.

Marks, S. R. (1977). Multiple roles and role strain: Some notes on human energy, time, and commitment. *American Sociological Review, 41,* 921–936.

Merikangas, K. (1985). *Sex differences in depression.* Paper presented at Murray Center (Radcliffe College) Conference: Mental Health in Social Context, Cambridge, MA.

Rossi, A. (1984). Gender and parenthood. *American Sociological Review, 49,* 1–19.

Sieber, S. D. (1974). Toward a theory of role accumulation. *American Sociological Review, 39,* 567–578.

Slater, P. (1963). On social regression. *American Sociological Review, 28,* 339–364.

Teicholtz, J. G. (1978). *Psychological correlates of voluntary childlessness in married women.* Paper presented at the meeting of the Eastern Psychological Association, Boston.

Thoits, P. (1983). Multiple identities and psychological well-being. *American Sociological Review, 48,* 174–187.

Treiman, D. (1985). The work histories of women and men: What we know and what we need to find out. In A. Rossi (Ed.), *Gender and the life course* (pp. 213–231). New York: Aldine.

Vaillant, G. E. (1977). *Adaptation to life.* Boston: Little, Brown.

Verbrugge, L. M. (1982). Women's social roles and health. In P. Berman and E. Ramey (Eds.), *Women: A developmental perspective.* Publication No. 82-2298. Washington, DC: U.S. Government Printing Office.

Verbrugge, L. M. (1983). *Pressures, satisifactions, and the link to physical health of young women.* Paper presented at the meeting of the American Psychological Association, Anaheim, CA.

Verbrugge, L. M. (1986). *Sex differences in physical health: Making good sense of empirical results.* Paper presented at the meeting of the Society of Behavioral Medicine, San Francisco.

Verbrugge, L. M. (1987). Role responsibilities, role burdens, and physical health. In F. Crosby (Ed.), *Spouse, parent, worker: On gender and multiple roles.* New Haven: Yale University Press.

Waldron, I., & Herold, J. (1984). *Employment attitudes toward employment, and women's health.* Paper presented at the meeting of the Society of Behavioral Medicine, Philadelphia.

Wethington, E., & Kessler, R. C. (1989). Employment, parental responsibility, and psychological distress: A longitudinal study of married women. *Journal of Family Issues, 10*(4), 527–546.

THIRTEEN

Antecedent Life Events and Consequences for Homemakers and Women Employed in Atypical, Typical, and Androgynous Professions

Carol Tomlinson-Keasey and Jessica N. Gomel

During the 1970s, the women's movement gradually entered the national consciousness, in part because nightly television features focused on a variety of feminine causes. These highly visible effects were accompanied by a more subtle, disciplined reconsideration of women's lives that emerged in academic circles in the 1970s and 1980s. Women's issues and women's lives were subjected to the empirical scrutiny of researchers from many disciplines (Baruch & Brooks-Gunn, 1984; Betz & Fitzgerald, 1987; Chodorow, 1978; Epstein, 1981; Giele, 1982a; Helson, 1967; Hennig & Jardim; 1977). Textbooks, theories, and anthologies focusing on women's development followed quickly (Aisenberg & Harrington, 1988; Baruch, Biener, & Barnett, 1987; Brown and Kerns, 1985; Gilligan, Lyons, & Hanmer, 1990; Grossman & Chester, 1990; Gustafson & Magnusson, 1991; Heilbrun, 1988; McGuigan, 1980; Rivers, Barnett, & Baruch, 1979; Williams, 1987).

Three landmark studies presented compellingly the differing circumstances that surround a woman's adult development. Gilligan (1982) argued that

> the most pressing items on the agenda for research on adult development are studies that would delineate *in women's own terms* the experience of their adult life . . . As we have listened for centuries to the voices of men and the theories of development that their experience informs, so we have begun more recently to notice not only the silence of women but the difficulty in hearing what they say when they speak. (p. 112)

Helson, Mitchell, and Moane (1984) discussed the social clock that ticked away the scheduled events of a woman's life. Tangri (1975) and her colleagues (Tangri & Jenkins, 1986) followed women she described as role innovators. A common thread of these studies, and the hundreds of studies they spawned, was that the occupational themes that dominated theories of men's development (Levinson, 1978; Vaillant, 1977) must yield to theories that examined the psychological importance of relationships and that noted the cultural obstacles that impeded women's achievements.

Well after the more obvious legal barriers to women's achievement had been eliminated, a variety of cultural, personal, and pragmatic obstacles remained as invisible but effective deterrents to women's occupational achievements, especially in male-dominated fields (American Association of University Women, 1991; Morrison, White, & Velsor, 1987). Still, the number of women in the labor force continued to soar, and more women began seeking entry into professions that had been the province of men.

The flood of women in the labor market provided a stark reality to relate to the abstract issues and theories appearing in professional journals. In 1950, almost 90% of married women with preschool children stayed home (Hayghe, 1986). During the 1970s, women's participation in the labor force increased dramatically, spurred by economic factors and no-fault divorce settlements (Rexroat & Shehan, 1984). By 1988, over half of the women with preschool children were working (Matthews & Rodin, 1989), prompting questions about the special characteristics or experiences that induced women to join the labor force. In this chapter we attempt to answer that question, but pose it in a more differentiated fashion. Specifically, we would like to know what factors led women to seek careers in atypical, typical, or androgynous careers and how these differed for women who decided to be homemakers. Given the difficulties that women encountered as they pursued a career, especially in atypical professions, we wanted to know how women felt about their work experience and what satisfaction they reaped from their lives.

To answer these questions, we needed four kinds of information. We needed accurate data on the psychological makeup of girls and in-depth chronicles of their interaction with their families. We needed detailed information on their goals and aspirations as they progressed through adolescence into their adult years. We needed to be able to identify empirically women who embarked on careers considered atypical and those who pursued careers in more traditional feminine roles. Finally, we needed to assess the satisfaction these women expressed with their adult lives. With these sorts of data, we would be able to identify personal traits, elements of the family of origin, and significant experiences that shaped these women's career decisions. In addition, we could assess the impact that their career decisions had on their adult lives.

The Terman Study of the Life Cycle offers this variegated information through the life span. Beginning in 1922, Lewis M. Terman of Stanford University recruited 672 eleven-year-old girls into his study of gifted individuals. The study followed these girls through their adolescent and college years into their productive adult careers and continues today. The 70 years of data collection covers most of the life-span and allows researchers to ask questions about both the antecedents of career choices and the consequences of those decisions. The Terman Study, then, offers a singular opportunity to examine the experiences of women who entered college in the late 1920s and reached midlife in the 1950s.

The Terman women made career decisions in a culture that differed dramatically from the culture of the 1990s. The obstacles to a professional career were daunting (see Helson, Elliott, & Leigh, 1989), and women who entered professions encountered conspicuous cultural pressure and obvious legal impediments (Kessler-Harris, 1982). Not only was the social zeitgeist such that women were not expected or encouraged to pursue a profession (Rossi, 1965) but the economic climate of the country precluded any fair consideration for positions that would deprive a male of a job (Chester & Grossman, 1990; Matthaei, 1983; Milkman, 1979). Despite these impediments, two-thirds of the Terman women graduated from college, and 279 of the 672 pursued postgraduate studies. These women, then, were educationally prepared for career positions, but few pursued them.

To understand the movement of women into the labor force, we examined (1) factors that helped the Terman women succeed in their career choices, and (2) the personal consequences of their decision to launch careers in atypical, typical, or adrogynous areas.

We assume that the factors enabling women to surmount the hurdles of the 1930s will be germane to studies of women in the 1990s who are trying to break through the glass ceiling. Additionally, contemporary women might well profit from understanding the consequences of career decisions to an earlier cohort of women.

Factors that might predict women's career direction include personality characteristics (Helson, Elliott, & Leigh, 1989), family of origin variables (Halpern-Felsher, Tomlinson-Keasey, & Huntley, 1992; Hennig & Jardim, 1977), the timing of career involvement (Super, 1957), and personal aspirations and planfulness (Clausen, 1986; Stewart, 1980). In this chapter we will focus on (1) personal traits that were evident in the young girls and adolescents, (2) characteristics of the family of origin, (3) academic capabilities, and (4) occupational aspirations. These areas were selected because they are theoretically important predictors of career direction and because Terman and his collaborators collected data relevant to the area.

Women's career decisions certainly alter other aspects of their lives (Betz, 1984; Cooney & Uhlenberg, 1989; Harmon, 1989; Perrucci, 1970; Stewart, 1980). As more and more women have entered the labor market, the number of women who are single, childless, or who have children late in life has increased dramatically (Gerson, 1985). But career decisions have ramifications beyond decisions about childbearing. Gove and Tudor (1973) presented epidemiological evidence that the traditional feminine role "makes women sick" (Bernard, 1972, p. 53). Their data set off a psychological controversy that shows no signs of abating (Barnett & Marshall, 1991; Killien, 1991; Kotler & Wingard, 1989; Rodin & Ickovics, 1990; Helson & Picano, 1990; Rosenfeld, 1992). In examining the impact of career decisions of the Terman women's lives, we included outcome variables that would address these issues whenever appropriate data existed.

We were able to identify a variety of achievement variables such as income, work history, and stature in the field that might well have been altered by early career decisions. We also evaluated the effects of women's personal lives and examined the woman's marital status, marital history, number of children, and the success of her husband. Because they fit with Terman's research questions, there are continuing data evaluating the Terman women's mental and physical health. These provide important information about the long-term effects of trying to succeed in a chilly climate. Finally, we were able to compare the women in the four groups on a variety of indices of life satisfaction. The Terman women looked back over their lives in 1972, 1982, and 1986 and offered a set of interesting observations about the fulfillment of their intellectual potential, whether they would alter their lives if they had another chance, and the kind of satisfaction they derived from their lives.

METHOD

Sample

Between the years 1922 and 1928, Terman identified 672 girls who scored in the top percentile on an intelligence test. The girls were approximately 11 when they were first tapped to participate in the study. In general, these preadolescents came from White, middle-class homes and lived in the Bay Area or the larger Los Angeles basin in California. Since 1922, the women have been studied approximately every five years, with the latest data collection occurring in 1992. Perhaps it is not surprising, given that the study spans 70 years and each subject has been asked thousands of questions (Sears, 1984), that few subjects have complete data records. Occasionally the parents of the subject would fail to return an entire questionnaire. More often, sporadic questions would not be answered. Sometimes, families lived too far away to be included in an interview or assessment. Of course, as the decades passed, some of the women died and some were lost to the study. To be included in the analysis, a woman must have completed at least 70% of the items selected for our analyses. These criteria were imposed to minimize the data that would be missing in our analyses. The final sample included 450 women, who had a mean response rate to the items used in the study of 86.9%. Missing values in each group were then replaced with each group's mean value.

Occupational Categories

Our initial goal was to identify variables in a girl's personality, her family of origin, or her early experiences that predicted her adult decision to pursue a career and foreshadowed the nature of that career. Our second goal was to examine the life outcomes of women who were homemakers or pursued careers in atypical, typical, or androgynous professions. Did that choice enhance or diminish a woman's life? The first step in accomplishing these goals was to categorize the women in the Terman study into appropriate occupational groups.

The *Classified Index of Occupations and Industries* for the 1950 Census (U.S. Bureau of the Census, 1950a) was used to classify the occupations listed on the 1959 Terman questionnaire. The *Classified Index* listed general occupational categories found in the Census, followed by the specific jobs included in each category. For the most part, the Terman categories exactly matched those of the Census.

After the Terman occupations were classified, labor force statistics were used to determine whether the women had entered an atypical, typical, or androgynous profession. Labor force statistics were taken from the 1950 U.S. Census of the Population (U.S. Bureau of the Census, 1952), the U. S. Statistical Abstracts (U.S. Bureau of the Census, 1950b), and Current Population Reports (U.S. Bureau of the Census, 1986). Using these different sources, we were able to determine that the percentage of women employed in the different occupations never varied by more than 2 percent.

Labor statistics from 1950 were used, although we coded the women's occupations from their 1959 questionnaires. In leaving this gap we recognized that women who listed atypical occupations in 1959 had fought their way into atypical professions during the previous decade.

The women's occupations listed on the 1959 questionnaire were coded to reflect four occupational categories: (1) Atypical professions: women comprising less than 33% of the employees in these occupations. Examples included medical doctors, lawyers and judges, and university professors. (2) Typical professions: women accounting for more than 66% of the employees in these professions. Examples included nurses, grade school teachers, and clerical/secretarial workers. (3) Androgynous professions: women constituting between 34% and 65% of the labor force. Examples included music/dance teachers and telephone/telegraph operators. (4) Homemakers: women who were not employed outside the home.

Table 13.1 gives the percentage of women workers out of the total number of workers in the general population for each of the Terman occupations and the number of Terman women in the occupation in 1959. Occasionally an occupation listed on the Terman questionnaire seemed to overlap multiple Census occupations. In these cases, the average proportion across the Census occupations is reported.

Using these strategies, we categorized the Terman women as follows: 84 in atypical professions, 34 in androgynous professions, 144 in typical professions, and 188 homemakers. Of the 262 Terman women employed outside the home, over half were employed in typical professions, approximately 32% were employed in atypical professions, and fewer than 15% were employed in androgynous professions.

Selecting Predictor and Outcome Variables

From the thousands of variables available for the Terman women, we initially selected over 700 variables, either as predictors of career

TABLE 13.1 Women in Certain Occupations (general population in 1950; Terman Women in 1959)

Occupation	Women (%)	Terman Women (N)
Teacher or researcher—college level	23	19
Teacher at junior college or below; public school administrator	75	60
Writer—journalist, editor, reporter, advertising agent, background researcher, reviewer, radio & TV	32	7
Writer—fiction, essays, poetry, drama	39	3
Social welfare—probation officer, administrator	69	10
Librarian	89	12
Applied arts—ceramist, fashion artist, interior decorator, advertising artist, cartoonist	42	3
Theatre arts—actor, entertainer, dancer, singer	46	2
Economist, statistician	32	4
Accountant	15	9
Clinical psychologist, guidance counselor, school psychologist, Juvenile Court psychiatrist	32	4
Medicine (researcher, teacher), psychiatrist	6	3
Lawyer	4	3
Artist—painter, sculptor, illustrator	38	1
Nurse (RN)	98	4
Music teacher, dance teacher, accompanist	59	6
Laboratory technician or assistant	40	1
Public relations person, personnel director	31	4
Scientist, natural	14	1
Secretary, stenographer, bookkeeper, office manager, clerical, machine operator, typist, receptionist	76	58
Sales clerk	24	4
Buyer (department store or other retail business)	25	3
Realtor	14	5
Investor (buying/selling real estate, stocks)	10	2
Executive or administrator in business (e.g., dress shop)	27	14
Housewife—not employed outside the home	76	188
Student	32	3
Miscellaneous professions	27	8
Miscellaneous business	27	8
Miscellaneous public and personal service	82	1

Note: There were three "miscellaneous" Terman categories in which several different occupations were grouped together and classified under one title, i.e., "Miscellaneous Professions," "Miscellaneous Business," and "Miscellaneous Public and Personal Service." In each case, the percentages of women workers from the general population in 1950 for each of the occupations in these categories were averaged to determine whether the category represented atypical, typical, or androgynous occupations.

direction or as indicators of meaningful life outcomes. These variables were divided generally into two broad categories. Information gathered up to 1940 was examined for predictors of career direction; information that was collected after 1940 was more concerned with the quality of a woman's life as a function of the occupational and role decisions she had made. The year 1940 was chosen to separate the predictors from the outcomes, because in 1940 the women were approximately 30 years old and typically had made the transition from their families of origin to their adult families. Occasionally items were included as predictors that spanned many years. One such item was IQ, which was measured on three occasions, in 1922, 1940, and 1950. Similarly, years of education and a subject's marriage and divorce history were not tabulated until the 1950s, but these items covered earlier time periods. Some of the items included as predictors were gathered retrospectively in 1950. These items were included as predictors because they covered the earliest years of the subject's life.

Our initial identification of 700 relevant variables was designed to cast a wide conceptual net. As the first step toward culling these variables, we deleted all variables that had not been answered by at least 60% of the women. We then examined the variability of the remaining items. If little or no variance existed, the items were dropped from the study. Two examples were items asking about drug abuse and arrests among the women. Virtually none of the women reported any drug abuse and only two of the 672 women were ever arrested (Terman & Oden, 1947). Through these procedures, we reduced the number of variables of interest to 370.

A third step in culling the variables was a factor analysis that identified items that did not fit with any of the dimensions being examined. Two such items were "importance of sports before age 12" and "mechanical ingenuity." Although both of these items could be conceptually relevant to a woman pursuing an occupation, the factor analysis indicated that they did not add appreciably to any of the dimensions being considered.[1]

When all of these strategies had been applied to the remaining 370 items, we retained 117 predictor variables, which were grouped into 13 dimensions of interest and 109 life outcome variables that represented 19 dimensions. In addition, we retained 5 individual variables in the predictor analysis and 3 individual variables in the outcome analysis.

Predicting Career Direction

The factor analysis of the 122 predictor variables suggested 13 dimensions that might be used to predict women's adult career decisions. These 13 dimensions were turned into scales by calculating a mean of the equally weighted, standardized items ($M = 50$, $SD = 10$) comprising each dimension. The scales that were constructed are listed below, along with the number of items comprising each scale, the sense of the items, and the Cronbach's alpha.

Childhood personality characteristics. Three of the scales tapped particular personality characteristics of the girls as 11- and 17-year-olds. In 1922 and 1928, parents and teachers rated the child on 25 personality traits, including such characteristics as conscientiousness, sensitivity, physical energy, sense of humor, and desire to know. Ratings were made on a 13-point scale, with higher numbers meaning a greater amount of the possessed trait. These particular groupings of characteristics might well predict which women would pursue atypical occupations. Such personality characteristics have proved useful in a variety of predictive analyses over the life span (Block, 1971; Friedman, Tucker, Tomlinson-Keasey, Schwartz, Wingard, & Criqui, 1993; Tomlinson-Keasey & Little, 1990).

1. Social Responsibility (trait ratings for freedom from vanity, sympathy/tenderness, conscientiousness, generosity/unselfishness, and sensitivity; alpha = .73)
2. Sociability (social ability in childhood/adolescence, trait ratings for popularity, amount of physical energy, physical health, sense of humor, cheerfulness, fondness of groups, permanency of moods; alpha = .68
3. Achievement Motivation (trait rating for desire to know, originality, general intelligence, self-confidence, leadership, appreciation of beauty; alpha = .74)

Academic Capabilities. Three scales measured the child's academic skills and propensities. Given that many of the professions listed as atypical required graduate study and years of preparation, academic skills might well be a factor, even among a sample of women who were identified as intellectually gifted.

4. Academic Propensity (facility in math, persistence in math/science, trait ratings for willpower, desire to excel, common sense, truthfulness, prudence/forethought; alpha = .70)
5. Academic Preferences (liking for arts, science, math, English, practical subjects; alpha = .50)
6. IQ scored as indicated on three tests (Stanford-Binet 1922, Concept Mastery 1940, Concept Mastery 1950; alpha = .67)

Family of origin. Whenever possible, objective indices of the family of origin were coded. One of these scales assessed social status through the father's occupation in 1922 and the highest school grade completed by both parents. A second scale examined the stability of the home environment by noting information on death and divorce history of the parents. Similar indicators of the atmosphere in the home environment have been correlated with a subjects' ahievement (Dornbusch, Ritter, Leiderman, Roberts, & Fraleigh, 1987; Thompson, Alexander, & Entwisle, 1988).

7. Parental Education (highest school grade completed by father, highest school grade completed by mother, father's occupation in 1922; alpha = .69)
8. Parental Loss (age range of subject at death of father, age range of subject at death of mother, whom subject lived with after death/divorce; alpha = .52)

Occupational aspirations. Aspirations are ultimately altered by a variety of factors, ranging from happiness in chosen roles to physical health. Five scales were included that measured variables that might influence occupational goals and aspirations. In 1940, when the women were in their late 20s, they were asked about their ultimate occupational goals and their roles as wives and mothers. In addition, they were asked whether they had made definite occupational choices and whether these choices were being fulfilled. As part of an assessment of the obstacles they had encountered, they were asked about disappointments, good fortune, and profound life influences. Because of the era in which these women came of age, it was hypothesized that the subjects' happiness and involvement with their marriages would moderate the types of occupational goals they held and pursued. Therefore, items assessing marital status and happiness were included in this category. Finally, a person's mental and physical health alter aspirations in profound ways (Terman & Oden, 1947). Hence items assessing health might well predict a subject's commitment to an atypical career.

9. Occupational Goals (age at marriage, ultimate occupational goals as indicated in 1940, ultimate life goals as indicated in 1940, life goals regarding wife/motherhood as indicated in 1940; alpha = .74)
10. Occupational Choice (occupational preferences, have chosen life work, occupation chosen or drifted into, definite choice in life work, received as much schooling as wanted, early occupational choice fulfilled; alpha = .50)
11. Profound influences in Life (sources of profound influence in life, sources of disappointments, sources of good fortune, alpha = .54)
12. Marital Happiness (ratings of marital happiness of subject, regret marriage, sexually well mated, would marry same person again, index of marital happiness, contemplation of divorce/separation, happiness of marriage; items alpha = .85)
13. Health (rating of general health, illnesses and their aftereffects, causes and seriousness of nervousness/worries, ratings on general adjustment, how adjustment difficulties were handled physical factors affecting personality; alpha = .71)

The literature on achievement indicates that these 13 dimensions might well predict career choice and direction (DeBaryshe, Patterson, & Capaldi, 1993; Fehrmann, Keith, & Reimers, 1987; Forehand, Long, Brody, & Fauber, 1986; Kimball, 1989; Matyas, 1984; Mednick, Baker, Reznick, & Hocevar, 1990; Rathunde & Csikszentmihalyi, 1991; White, 1986). The following individual items were also included in the discriminant analysis of the predictor variables: the number of children a woman had by 1940, the number of deaths in her family by 1940, her cumulative education, her admiration for her father, and marked friction in her family of origin. Each of these was considered theoretically important enough to be considered separately in an analysis (Csikszentmihalyi, Rathunde, & Whalen, 1993; Kurdek & Sinclair, 1988; Thompson et al., 1988).

The number of children often determined a woman's ability to pursue any of her occupational goals. Although one of the Terman women had eight children and enjoyed a successful career as a medical doctor, she was certainly atypical on many dimensions.

Some of the Terman women curtailed their aspirations when a sig-

TABLE 13.2 Significant Mean Differences among Predictor Variables

Variable	Atypical	Androgynous	Typical	Homemaker	F
	($n = 84$)	($n = 34$)	($n = 144$)	($n = 188$)	
Occupational goals	53.85^{xz}	51.25^{y}	50.37^{xz}	47.77^{xyz}	14.68***
Number of family deaths	51.14^{x}	45.63^{xy}	49.06	51.00^{y}	3.64**
Occupational choice	50.88	51.03	50.39	49.12	3.20*
IQ	51.70^{x}	52.75^{y}	50.02	48.72^{xy}	4.58**
Cumulative education	53.86^{xyz}	47.94^{x}	49.67^{y}	48.90^{z}	5.62***
Sociability	50.32	50.05	48.72^{x}	50.83^{x}	4.05**

Note: Shared superscripts identify means for each variable that are significantly different from each other. For example, when occupational goals are examined, homemaker's goals are significantly different from those of each of the other three groups. In addition, women in the typical and atypical groups differed significantly on occupational goals.
*$p < .05$, **$p < .01$, ***$p < .001$.

nificant relative died. In some instances, the death in the family increased the financial difficulties in the family and limited the woman's ability to pursue her goals. In other cases, Terman women had to step into caretaking voids created by untimely deaths in their families.

Cumulative years of education becomes an important variable because many of the atypical professions require longer periods of education. In the tight financial circumstances created by the Depression, women often had to forego the education they desired.

Several studies suggest that fathers play a particular role in demystifying career goals for women and in providing women with the self-confidence that they might need to succeed, especially in atypical professions (Halpern-Felsher, Tomlinson-Keasey, & Huntley, 1992; Hennig & Jardim, 1977). For this reason we wanted to focus on the woman's admiration for her father and on the friction in the family of origin.

To summarize, our efforts to predict career direction for the Terman women focused on 440 women. We identified 13 scales and 5 individual variables that the literature suggests moderate achievement and career success. For all of these scales, the mean score was standardized at 50, with a standard deviation of 10.

The first analysis to be undertaken was an analysis of variance examining the different predictors for the four occupational groups (see Table 13.2). Not surprisingly, the women in atypical professions had the highest level of occupational goals and had achieved the highest educational levels. The homemakers had the lowest level of occupational goals, despite the fact that their educational levels differed significantly only from those women pursuing atypical professions. Remember that in this sample, two-thirds of the women earned a college degree. Although all of the children in this sample were identified as gifted, the women in atypical professions received higher scores on the cumulative intelligence measures. The homemakers had not maintained the same high level of intellectual superiority. The only personality measure that predicted career direction was sociability. Women in typical professions received significantly lower scores on this dimension than homemakers.

We have examined the analyses of variance that differentiated significantly among the four occupational groups. It is perhaps as telling to consider those scales which did not differentiate among the occupational groups. Except for sociability, none of the personality characteristics measured during childhood and adolescence predicted career direction. Neither the academic propensities nor the academic preferences substantially influenced career direction. Marital happiness, health, and a variety of influences, both positive and negative, did not predict the woman's career direction.

The second anlysis conducted using the predictor scales was a discriminate function analysis. To assess what factors distinguished between women who pursued atypical professions and the other three groups, we included the 13 predictor scales and 5 individual variables in a discriminant function analysis with equal prior probabilities.

All of the predictor variables were submitted to a stepwise discriminant analysis, needing an F value of at least 4.00 to be considered significant. Table 13.3 lists the predictor dimensions that were significant. As can be seen, Occupational goals had the largest F value (Wilks's Lambda $= .91$, $F = 14.67$, $df = 3, 446$). The two other significant predictor dimensions to be entered were Occupational choice (Wilks's Lambda $= .88$, $F = 9.61$, $df = 6, 890$) and Sociability (Wilks's Lambda $= .86$, $F = 7.82$, $df = 9, 1080$).

The analysis produced two significant discriminant functions ($\chi^2 = 68.34$ $df = 9$, $p < .001$ and $\chi^2 = 10.69$, $df = 4$, $p < .05$). The standardized coefficients for each of the significant variables on the discriminant functions, as well as the group centroids, are listed in Table 13.3. Based on the group centroids, the first discriminant function serves primarily to differentiate the homemakers from the other three groups, and particularly from women in atypical professions, who had the highest oc-

TABLE 13.3 Discriminant Analysis of Predictor Variables; Variables Entered, Standardized Coefficients, and Group Centroids

Step	Variable	F to enter	Wilks's Lambda	F (df) (approx.)	Standardized Coefficients	
					Discriminant Function 1	Discriminant Function 2
1	Occupational goals	14.67	0.91	14.67 (3, 446)	−0.91	0.29
2	Occupational choice	4.73	0.88	9.61 (6, 890)	−0.50	−0.11
3	Sociability	4.20	0.86	7.82 (9, 1080)	0.25	0.93

Group Centroids

Group	Discriminant Function 1	Discriminant Function 2	Percentage Correctly Classified
Homemakers	0.40	0.07	57.4
Typical careers	−0.14	−0.21	24.3
Androgynous careers	−0.25	0.04	2.9
Atypical careers	−0.56	0.19	56.0

Note: Overall jackknifed classification hit rate: 42.4%.

cupational goals and made deliberate occupational choices to pursue careers in male-dominated professions. The second discrimination function distinguishes women in typical careers from women in atypical careers and focuses primarily on sociability.

Despite their significance, these three predictor dimensions did not predict occupational group very accurately. Although 57% of the homemakers and 56% of the women in atypical professions were classified correctly, only 24% of the women in typical professions and 3% of the women in androgynous professions were classified correctly. The overall classification rate of 42.4% suggests that the predictor dimensions we identified were not the only factors shaping these women's career directions.

In this cohort of women, childhood personality characteristics did not predict career direction. A third of the Terman women spent significant amounts of time during their adult lives in volunteer efforts (Terman & Oden, 1947). Such positions welcomed women who were active, persistent, problem oriented, and decisive (Reinharz, 1984). Equally likely is an explanation that focuses on the serendipitous factors that molded women's careers for this cohort (Clausen, 1986). If a husband had not materialized by the end of college, many of the Terman women went on to graduate school. If their husbands were not able to support them, they sought a job to contribute to the family finances. If their husband's death or a divorce left these women single, they entered the workforce. Their educational preparation and their life circumstances were more critical than their personality traits or their academic preferences (Angrist & Almquist, 1975).

Similarly, the family-of-origin variables failed to discriminate among the four groups of women. Parental education and the number of deaths in the family could be coded objectively from the Terman data, but they really did not convey much about the achievement cues that existed for an individual woman. Two other indices—friction in the family and admiration for the father—were retrospective ratings by the women. These variables did not differentiate between the four groups of women.

The occupational aspirations of these young women, as reflected in their occupational goals and their cumulative education, did predict the later career achievements of the Terman women. The women in atypical careers differed significantly from the homemakers on these indices.

Occupational Choice and Life Outcomes

Our second purpose was to examine the ways in which career choice enhanced or diminished these women's lives. To do this, we examined the broad categories of occupational achievements, various facets of life satisfaction, physical and mental health during the midlife and retirement periods, and support from the husbands.

Proceeding as we did with the predictor dimensions, we evaluated hundreds of midlife variables that might be influenced by the woman's occupational direction. A factor analysis was the final step in the process. The factor analysis identified 19 dimensions of adult life, represented by 109 items, that might be altered, both positively and negatively, by women's career choices. As with the predictor variables, we included 3 single variables that we considered theoretically important enough to warrant separate investigation.

Occupational Achievement. The broad area of occupational achievement was assessed by five dimensions.

1. Work Pattern (This set of 17 items assessed the subject's work pattern over the course of her life. Information regarding employment status was assessed by work pattern from 1941–1972 (6 items), work output ages 51–60 (2 items), work history indices spanning the years from 1940 to 1970 (8 items) and work plan (1 item). Subjects who pursued a full-time career throughout these years received the highest scores; alpha = .95)

2. Occupational Achievement (Seven items assessing occupational achievement included the subjects' mean income, their rating on a professional or casual employment dimension, their occupation in 1946–1949, their satisfaction with their occupational achievement, the percentage of time they spent on paid work, their income in 1970, and any unused training they had received; alpha = .84)

3. Educational achievements that affected occupational accomplishments (these 2 items evaluated the influence of education on the woman's occupational accomplishments. The first item indicated whether or not occupational accomplishments were facilitated by education; the second indicated whether or not such accomplishments were hindered by lack of an education; alpha = .57)

4. Personality traits that affected occupational accomplishments (The 5 items included in this dimension asked the subjects

whether their occupational accomplishments were facilitated by their social adjustment, personality, and mental stability and whether occupational accomplishments were hindered by poor social adjustment or personality traits; alpha = .61)
5. Health factors that changed occupational accomplishments (2 items indicating whether occupational accomplishments were facilitated by excellent health or hindered because of poor health; alpha = .50)

Personal Traits in Midlife. Another broad category of midlife functioning involved personal traits that were exhibited or altered during the adult years. The relationship between career involvement and personal attributes, especially among adult women, continues to intrigue psychologists (Helson & Wink, 1992). Career involvement is seen by some as altering adult personality characteristics (Baruch et al., 1987). Others argue that as early as college, personal traits forecast later career involvement (Zuckerman, 1985). We examined personal characteristics and asked how these characteristics related to occupational achievement. Five dimensions emerged from the factor analysis that assessed individual traits in midlife.

6. Persistence (The 6 items in this scale assessed persistence, integration, and work habits as factors contributing positively to adult life; alpha = .70)
7. Ambitiousness (Eight items assessed the subject's ambitiousness in a variety of spheres during the 30s and 40s; alpha = .75)
8. Change in Ambitions (Three items in this dimension assessed the subject's change in ambitions during midlife; alpha = .77)
9. Interpersonal Characteristics (Self-ratings on 5 items—happiness, self-confidence, sociability, feelings of inferiority, and sensitivity—were included in this dimension; alpha = .70)
10. Personality Characteristics (These 6 items assessed emotional adjustment, the existence of mental difficulty, and self-ratings on moodiness, impulsiveness, emotionality, conforming to authority, and congeniality; alpha = .62)

Satisfaction. A third broad category of interest was the subject's satisfaction with all the nuances of her life. One can imagine that career success would bring personal satisfaction, but that career satisfaction might not generalize into the family sphere. A factor analysis of the outcome variables suggested seven dimensions of satisfaction during the adult years.

11. Overall Satisfaction (The three items in this scale measured joy in living, general life satisfaction, composite satisfaction score: occupational success, family life, friendships, cultural life, service to society; alpha = .75)
12. Intellectual Satisfaction (Two items, including subjects' assessments of whether or not they had lived up to their intellectual abilities and their responses to the question, Does life offer sufficient outlets for your mental abilities? alpha = .51)
13. Family Satisfaction (Six items assessing satisfaction with marriage, children, and family life; alpha = .79)
14. Work Satisfaction (Three items measuring satisfaction with work, the recognition received from work, and income; alpha = .77)
15. Satisfaction with Community Activities (Five items including satisfaction with community activities, service to society, community service, and volunteer activities; alpha = .73)
16. Satisfaction with Cultural Life (Two items measuring satisfaction with cultural life; alpha = .90)
17. Satisfaction with Friendships (Two items measuring satisfaction with friendships; alpha = .89)

Two other dimensions were identified by the factor analysis. One included a variety of health items, and the final dimension measured the husband's responsibility for child care.

18. Physical Health (Five items rating health during the adult years, reporting changes in physical health, and assessing the amount of energy and vitality; alpha = .66)
19. Husbands's Responsibility for Child Care (Two items measuring the husband's responsibility for child care when the children were young and when they were adolescents; alpha = .70)

It is important to remember that alpha levels of a particular dimension can be quite low and still be part of a scale that is predictive. This is especially true when items in the dimension represent different facets of that dimension. An example from our study concerns the dimension of intellectual satisfaction, which had an alpha of .51. Women might well respond quite positively to one item, indicating they had lived up to their intellectual abilities, but not endorse a second item, that life offered sufficient outlets for their mental abilities. Similarly, our index of parental loss included the age of the father's death and the age of the mother's death. These two variables are not necessarily correlated but might well have an influence on career aspirations and direction.

As with the predictor dimensions, there were three individual items that did not fit with any of the 19 dimensions mentioned, but that were considered important enough to be included in the analysis as individual items. There were (1) the husband's cumulative education, (2) the huband's earned income in 1950, and (3) a woman's feeling that she had achieved occupationally because of chance factors. The husband is of interest because many women, especially in this cohort, derived their identity from their husband's success (Tomlinson-Keasey, 1990). If this is the case, life satisfaction and long-term evaluation of a life might well be predicted by the husband's success, regardless of the woman's career pattern. Hence, both the husband's educational achievements and his income were included in the analysis.

Other investigators have discussed the role of serendipity in many of the women's career decisions (Bateson, 1989); Helson, Elliott, & Leigh, 1989; Terman & Oden, 1947; Tomlinson-Keasey, 1990). An item that assessed chance factors in each woman's life might shed light on this factor.

The 19 outcome dimensions and the 3 individual outcome items listed above were included in a multivariate analysis of variance in which the four occupational groups were the independent variables. The overall MANOVA was significant (Wilks's lambda = .228, F Rao = 12.34 [66, 1270], $p < .0001$). Pairwise multivariate comparisons were calculated using Hotelling's T^2 to assess which groups were different from each other on the entire set of outcome variables (Stevens, 1986).

As indicated in Table 13.4, when all 22 of the outcome dimensions were considered, the women in each of the four occupational groupings differed significantly from the women in each of the other occupational groupings, with one exception. The women in atypical occupations did not differ from women in androgynous occupations.

Univariate analyses of the 22 dimensions helped pinpoint the areas of significant differences (see Table 13.5). Tukey tests were used for the univariate comparisons, as this procedure helps control for Type I errors (Stevens, 1986). Not surprisingly, the dimensions assessing occupational achievement showed that women employed in atypical occupations received the highest scores on all four of the occupational

TABLE 13.4 MANOVA of Outcome Variables
(pairwise multivariate comparisons)

Group	Hotelling's T^2	F (df)
Atypical vs. typical	105.18	4.33*** (22, 205)
Atypical vs. androgynous	41.38	1.54 (22, 95)
Atypical vs. homemakers	696.39	29.19*** (22, 249)
Typical vs. androgynous	86.88	3.47* (22, 155)
Homemakers vs. typical	809.74	34.46*** (22, 309)
Homemakers vs. androgynous	334.90	13.77*** (22, 199)

*$p < .05.$ ***$p < .001.$

achievement dimensions. On three of these four dimensions, the homemakers received the lowest scores. Of interest in these dimensions is the assessment of chance factors that contributed to occupational achievement. Even women in atypical occupations, who had worked hard at educating themselves for their careers, attributed their success to chance factors.

In sharp contrast to the focus on chance factors, the personal dimensions that were significant highlighted the effort that women put into their careers. Persistence and ambition were qualities that were noticeably absent from the homemakers' assessments, and they reported minimal changes in their ambitions through adulthood. Women employed in both typical and atypical professions became more ambitious as they moved up the career ladder.

Of the 7 dimensions of satisfaction that were included among the outcomes, 4 differentiated among the occupational groups. The women in atypical professions reported the highest levels of intellectual satisfaction and satisfaction with their work. They reported the lowest levels of family satisfaction. The opposite pattern was found with women who were homemakers. They reported the lowest levels of intellectual and work satisfaction but had the highest levels of family satisfaction. The homemakers also reported a high level of satisfaction surrounding their community activities. Homemakers in the Terman study participated in many volunteer organizations and often were highly valued in these organizations and recognized for their contributions. It is interesting that women who pursued occupations in feminine fields reported high levels of satisfaction in three of the four areas. These results suggest that occupations that employed a high percentage of women were somehow able to accommodate the woman's family

TABLE 13.5 Significant Mean Differences among Outcome Variables

Variable	Atypical	Androgynous	Typical	Homemaker	F
Work pattern	55.87^x	54.93^y	54.90^z	42.73^{xyz}	309.83***
Occupational achievement	56.67^x	54.12^y	53.11^{xz}	43.90^{xyz}	185.45***
Occupational achievement due to education	51.51	45.78^x	50.85^x	49.44	4.70**
Occupational achievement due to chance factors	53.73^{xy}	51.17	49.92^x	48.19^y	6.34***
Persistence	51.52^x	52.80^y	49.88	48.91^{xy}	5.87***
Ambitiousness	50.77	50.76	50.92^x	48.81^x	4.22**
Change in ambitions	49.79	47.15^x	52.03^{xy}	49.06^y	5.20***
Overall satisfaction	48.84	47.14	50.93	50.32	2.70*
Intellectual satisfaction	51.95^x	50.61	50.88^y	48.35^{xy}	4.86**
Family satisfaction	46.12^{wx}	46.76^{yz}	50.59^{wy}	52.10^{xz}	18.86***
Work satisfaction	53.94^x	53.36^y	51.45^z	46.52^{xyz}	23.96***
Satisfaction with community activities	49.08	47.48^x	49.49	51.26^x	4.37**
Husband's education	54.66^{xyz}	47.69^x	50.52^y	47.94^z	10.03***
Husband's earned income	52.30^x	47.87^y	45.79^{xz}	52.58^{yz}	16.19***

Note: Shared superscripts identify means for each variable that are significantly different from each other. For example, when we examined the work pattern variable, homemakers were significantly different from all other groups.

$*p < .05$; $**p < .01$; $***p < .001$

and social needs in ways that were not possible in either the atypical or androgynous occupations.

The spousal dimensions allowed us to examine the woman in relation to her husband. Since many of the women in atypical professions had advanced degrees, it is not surprising that their husbands were very highly educated. One might expect that these men would be successful financially. Notice, however, that the homemakers were also married to very successful wage earners.

As with the predictor dimensions, it is instructive to consider those dimensions which did not differentiate between the four occupational groups. Personal variables other than those associated with persistence and ambition did not differentiate among the groups. Regardless of career direction, the Terman women were similar on dimensions that assessed personal traits, physical health, and interpersonal skills. Of passing interest is the fact that a husband's involvement with child care was not a differentiating factor for these four occupational groups, despite the differing career responsibilities of their wives.

CONCLUSIONS

Predicting career directions and identifying women who sought a profession in an typical, atypical, or androgynous profession proved to be extremely difficult. We looked for clues to later career direction in particular personality characteristics, in indices of the support and stability of the family of origin, in the young girl's academic propensities and preferences, and in the aspirations of these young, gifted women. The occupational goals the women indicated when they had just reached adulthood were the most important predictor of later career direction.

Although women today report career goals when they are in college (Machung, 1989; Regan & Roland, 1982), they often cannot take the further steps of planning for their careers in distinct and discreet steps (Locke, Shaw, Saari, & Latham, 1981). The relationships that form the core of their lives make pursuing specific career goals difficult (Gilligan, 1982). Their lives, rather than following an optimum career sequence, are characterized by several viable options, all of which call for improvising as the life course unfolds (Bateson, 1989; Giele, 1982b).

The Terman women who decided to pursue lives as homemakers and who pursued atypical professions made salient choices as they proceeded from adolescence into their adult careers. Still, predicting which women would follow each path proved problematic. We can conclude that the Terman women who chose these very different life paths had a range of personal characteristics, and that their career choices were based on interpersonal factors and environmental contingencies. For this cohort at least, serendipitous events that occurred as the women moved through college and young adulthood seemed to determine whether they would pursue a career and the nature of that career.

When these women were adults, the life paths that they selected impacted on their lives in significant ways. At midlife, the homemakers were easily differentiated from the women who pursued an atypical profession. The homemakers had few occupational achievements but indicated high levels of satisfaction with their family and their social spheres. In most cases, these women married well and enjoyed full and productive lives contributing to their families and communities.

The women who pursued atypical professions achieved significant occupational success. As adults they reported a persistence and ambition that distinguished them from women who had not pursued a career. They also reaped satisfaction in intellectual and occupational arenas. As with contemporary working women, their occupational success was correlated with remaining single, not having children, or having small families (Gerson, 1985; Helson, Elliott, & Leigh, 1989). It is not surprising, then, that the Terman women in atypical professions reported much lower levels of family satisfaction and had little time for the social outlets that other women pursued.

The women classified in the androgynous occupational role had lives that were similar to those of the women working in atypical fields when it came to the satisfaction dimensions. They enjoyed their work and garnered meaningful intellectual benefits from their career, but they had less time for family life and socializing. These women had the lowest levels of education among the four occupational groups, and they married men with similar educational levels. Reading between the lines, one might conclude that these women entered the labor force to help their families financially. Once employed, their intelligence served them well and they rose quickly in their positions. Notice that they received the highest scores in persistence of any of the occupational groups and that, despite their persistence, they still believed their careers were shaped by unpredictable events.

An interesting group of women, who deserve close attention, are those women who pursued occupations in fields typically designated at feminine. These were the school teachers, nurses, and clerical workers from this era. The data suggest that these women enjoyed the best of both worlds. Their lives brought them intellectual satisfaction and they felt fulfilled by their work. In addition, they reported high levels of satisfaction with their families and were close to the mean in their satisfaction with community activities. For them, occupational achievement was less a function of chance factors, probably because their sights were set on careers in feminine fields.

The Terman women had the cognitive skills to achieve at any occupation. That so few of them chose to pursue atypical occupations is perhaps not surprising, given the cultural context in which they lived. Like women in other studies (Gerson, 1985; Helson, Elliott, & Leigh, 1989), those who decided to use their talents in male-dominated professions and careers felt actualized intellectually but sacrificed some of the more traditional family roles. Women who pursued more typical professions achieved an enviable balance in their lives, perhaps because their career choice minimized the obstacles to their success.

In noting the differences between the four groups of Terman women, it is important to mention that cultural norms change (Mellinger & Erdwins, 1985; Ross, Mirowsky, & Huber, 1983). A bright young woman who became a librarian in 1958 and suffered the stigma of being a spinster might become a lawyer today and feel much more at ease in the culture (Helson, Elliott, & Leigh, 1989). Despite the changes in norms and the elimination of legal impediments, women currently pursuing professions report that social and family lives continue to compete with career achievements (Benditt, 1992; Hochschild, 1989). Women in male-dominated professions fight subtle obstacles and assumptions rather than the explicit sexism of the 1930s and 1940s (Benditt, 1992).

The task for researchers studying midlife is to suggest a paradigm that encompasses the different arenas of life that women value. Linear models with clearly delineated steps of development deny the multiplicity of paths that women might pursue and their interrelationship (Giele, 1982b). Lindberg's (1955) poetic description provides the literary essence of the paradigm which must be developed.

> For to be a woman is to have interests and duties raying out in all directions from the central mother-core, like spokes from the hub of a wheel. The pattern of our lives is essentially circular. We must be open to all points of the compass; husband, children, friends, home, community;

stretched out, exposed, sensitive like a spider's web to each breeze that blows, to each call that comes. How difficult for us, then, to achieve a balance in the midst of these contradictory tensions, and yet how necessary for the proper functioning of our lives. (p. 28)

ACKNOWLEDGMENTS

This chapter was made possible by an intramural research grant from the University of California-Riverside as well as support from the John D. and Catherine T. MacArthur Foundation Research Network on Successful Midlife Development. We owe a special debt to Robert Sears, Albert Hastorf, and Eleanor Walker of Stanford University for helping us gain access to the data from the Terman Study of the Life Cycle

NOTES

1. Details of the factor analyses are available from Jessica Gomel, Psychology Department, University of California, Riverside, Riverside, CA 92521.

REFERENCES

Aisenberg, N., & Harrington, M. (1988). *Women of academe: Outsiders in the sacred grove.* Amherst, MA: University of Massachusetts Press.

Angrist, S. S., & Almquist, E. (1975). *Careers and contingencies: How college women juggle with gender.* New York: Dunellen.

American Association of University Women, (1991). *Shortchanging girls, short-changing America.* Washington, DC: AAUW Education Foundation.

Barnett, R. C., & Marshall, N. L. (1991). The relationship between women's work and family roles and subjective well-being and psychological distress. In M. Frankenhaeuser, U. Lundberg, & M. Chesney (Eds.), *Women, work and Stress.* New York: Plenum.

Baruch, G. K., Biener, L., & Barnett, R. C. (1987). Women and gender in research on work and family stress. *American Psychologist, 42,* 130–136.

Baruch, G. K., & Brooks-Gunn, J. (1984). *Women in midlife.* New York: Plenum.

Bateson, M. C. (1989). *Compsing a life.* New York: Plume.

Benditt, J. (1992). Women in science. *Science, 255,* 1365–1388.

Bernard, J. (1972). *The future of marriage.* New York: World Time.

Betz, N. E. (1984). A study of career patterns of college graduates. *Journal of Vocational Behavior, 24,* 249–264.

Betz, N. E., & Fitzgerald, L. E. (1987). *The career psychology of women.* New York: Academic Press.

Block, J. (1971). *Lives through time.* Berkeley, CA: Bancroft Books.

Brown, J. K., & Kerns, V. (1985). *In her prime: A new view of middle-aged women.* South Hadley, MA: Bergin & Garvey.

Chester, N. L., & Grossman, H. Y. (1990). Introduction: Learning about women and their work through their own accounts. In H. Y. Grossman & N. L. Chester (Eds.), *The experience and meaning of work in women's lives* (pp. 1–9). Hillsdale, NJ: Lawrence Erlbaum.

Chodorow, N. (1978). *The reproduction of mothering: Psychoanalysis and the sociology of gender.* Berkeley, CA: University of California Press.

Clausen, J. A. (1986). Early adult choices and the life course. *Zeitschrift für Sozialisationsforschung, 6,* 313–320.

Cooney, T. M., & Uhlenberg, P. (1989). Family-building patterns of professional women—a comparison of lawyers, physicians, and postsecondary teachers. *Journal of Marriage and the Family, 51,* 749–758.

Csikszentmihalyi, M., Rathunde, K., & Whalen, S. (1993). *Talented teenagers: A longitudinal study of their development.* New York: Cambridge University Press.

DeBaryshe, B. D., Patterson, G. R., & Capaldi, D. (1993). *A performance model for academic achievement in early adolescent boys. Developmental Psychology, 29,* 795–804.

Dornbusch, S. W., Ritter, P. L., Leiderman, P. H., Roberts, D. F., & Fraleigh, M. J. (1987). The relation of parenting style to adolescent school performance. *Child Development, 58,* 1244–1257.

Elder, G. H. (1985). *Life course dynamics: Trajectories and transitions, 1968–1980.* Ithaca, NY: Cornell University Press.

Epstein, C. F. (1981). *Women in law.* New York: Basic Books.

Fehrmann, P. G., Keith, T. Z., & Reimers, T. M. (1987). Home influences on school learning: Direct and indirect effects of parental involvement on high school grades. *Journal of Educational Research, 80,* 330-337.

Forehand, R., Long, N., Brody, G. H., & Fauber, R. (1986). Home predictors of young adolescents' school behavior and academic performance. *Child Development, 57,* 1528–1533.

Friedman, H. S., Tucker, J., Tomlinson-Keasey, C., Schwartz, J. E., Wingard, D. L., & Criqui, M. H.(1993). Does childhood personality predict longevity? *Journal of Personality and Social Psychology, 65,* 176–185.

Gerson, K. (1985). *Hard Choices: How women decide about work, career, and motherhood.* Berkeley, CA: University of California Press.

Giele, J. Z. (1982a). Women in adulthood: Unanswered questions. In J. Z. Giele (Ed.), *Women in the middle years* (pp. 1–35). New York: Wiley.

Giele, J. Z. (1982b). Women's work and family roles. In J. Z. Giele (Ed.), *Women in the middle years* (pp. 115–150). New York: Wiley.

Gilligan, C. (1982). Adult development and women's development: Arrangements for a marriage. In J. Z. Giele (Ed.), *Women in the middle years* (pp. 89–114). New York: Wiley.

Gilligan, C., Lyons, N. P., & Hanmer, T. J. (1990). *Making connections.* Cambridge, MA: Harvard University Press.

Gove, W. R., & Tudor, J. (1973). Adult sex roles and mental illness. *American Journal of Sociology, 78,* 812–835.

Grossman, H. Y., & Chester, N. L. (1990). *The experience and meaning of work in women's lives.* Hillsdale, NJ: Lawrence Erlbaum.

Gustafson, S. R., & Magnusson, D. (1991). *Female life careers: A pattern approach.* Hillsdale, NJ: Lawrence Erlbaum.

Halpern-Felsher, B. L., Tomlinson-Keasey, C., & Huntley, L. (1992, August), *Environmental influences on adolescents' self-perceptions and academic achievement.* Paper presented at the meeting of the American Psychological Assocation. Washington, D.C.

Harmon, L. W. (1989). Longitudinal changes in women's career aspirations—developmental or historical. *Journal of Vocational Behavior, 35,* 46–63.

Hayghe, H. (1986). Rise in mothers' labor force activity includes those with infants. *Monthly Labor Review, 109,* 43–45.

Heilbrun, C. (1988). *Writing a woman's life.* New York: Norton.

Helson, R. (1967). Personality characteristics and developmental history of creative college women. *Genetic Psychology Monographs, 76,* 205–256.

Helson, R., Elliott, T., & Leigh, J. (1989). Adolescent personality and women's work patterns. In D. Stern & D. Eichorn (Eds.), *Adolescence and work: Influences of social structure, labor markets, and culture* (pp. 259–289). Hillsdale, NJ: Lawrence Erlbaum.

Helson, R., Mitchell, V., & Moane, G. (1984). Personality and patterns of adherence and non-adherence to the social clock. *Journal of Personality and Social Psychology, 53,* 176–186.

Helson, R., & Picano, J. (1990). Is the traditional role bad for women? *Journal of Personality and Social Psychology, 59,* 311–320.

Helson, R., & Wink, P. (1992). Personality change in women from the early 40s to the early 50s. *Psychology and Aging, 7,* 46–55.

Hennig, M., & Jardim, A. (1977). *The managerial woman.* Garden City, NY: Anchor Press.

Hochschild, A. (1989). *The second shift: Working parents and the revolution at home.* New York: Viking Press.

Kessler-Harris, A. (1982). *Out to work: A history of wage-earning women int he United States.* New York: Oxford University Press.

Killien, M. (1991, April). *Integrating work and family: Women's health outcomes.* Paper presented at Society for Research in Child Development, Seattle, WA.

Kimball, M. M. (1989). A new perspective on women's math achievement. *Psychological Bulletin, 105,* 198–214.

Kotler, L. P., & Wingard, D. L. (1989). The effect of occupational, marital, and parental roles on mortality: The Alameda County study. *American Journal of Public Health, 79,* 607–611.

Kurdek, L. A., & Sinclair, R. J. (1988). Relationship of eighth graders' family structure, gender, and family environment with academic performance and school behavior. *Journal of Educational Psychology, 80,* 90–94.

Levinson, D. J. (1978) *Seasons of a man's life.* New York: Knopf.

Lindberg, A. M. (1955). *Gift from the sea.* New York: Vintage Books.

Locke, E. A., Shaw, K. A., Saari, L. M., & Latham, G. P. (1981). Goal setting and task performance: 1969–1980. *Psychological Bulletin, 90,* 125–152.

Machung, A. (1989). Talking career, thinking jobs: Gender differences in career and family expectations of Berkeley seniors. *Feminist Studies, 15,* 35–58.

Matthaei, J. (1983). *An economic history of women in America: Women's work, the sexual division of labor, and the development of capitalism.* New York: Schocken.

Matthews, K. A., & Rodin, J. (1989). Women's changing work roles. *American Psychologist, 44,* 1389–1393.

Matyas, M. L. (1984). Factors affecting female achievement and interest in science and in scientific careers. In J. B. Kahle (Eds.), *Women in science.* Philadelphia, PA: Falmer Press.

McGuigan, D. G. (1980). Exploring women's lives: An introduction. In D. G. McGuigan (Ed.), *Women's lives: New theory, research, and policy* (pp. i–xii). Ann Arbor, MI: University of Michigan, Center for Continuing Education of Women.

Mednick, B. R., Baker, R. L., Reznick, C., & Hocevar, D. (1990). Long-term effects of divorce on adolescent academic achievement. *Journal of Divorce, 13,* 69–88.

Mellinger, J. C., & Erdwins, C. J. (1985). Personality correlates of age and life role in adult women. *Psychology of Women Quarterly, 9,* 503–514.

Milkman, R. (1979). Women's work and the economic crisis: Some lessons from the Great Depression. In N. F. Cott & E. H. Pleck (Eds.), *A heritage of her own* (pp. 507–541). New York: Simon & Schuster.

Morrison, A. M., White, R. P., & Velsor, E. V. (1987). *Breaking the glass ceiling.* New York: Addison-Wesley.

Perrucci, C. C. (1970). Minority status and the pursuit of professional careers: Women in science and engineering. *Social Forces, 49,* 245–258.

Rathunde, K., & Csikszentmihalyi, M. (1991). Adolescent happiness and family interaction. In K. McCartney & K. Pillemer (Eds.), *Parent-child relations throughout life* (pp. 143–162). Hillsdale, NJ: Lawrence Erlbaum.

Regan, M. C., & Roland, H. E. (1982). University students: A change in expectations and aspirations over the decade. *Sociology of Education, 55,* 223–228.

Reinharz, S. (1984). Women as competent community builders: The other side of the coin. In A. U. Rickel, M. Gerrard, & I. Iscoe (Eds.), *Social and psychological problems of women: Prevention and crisis Intervention* (pp. 19–44). New York: Hemisphere.

Rexroat, C., & Shehan, C. (1984). Expected versus actual work roles of women. *American Sociological Review, 49,* 349–358.

Rivers, C., Barnett, R., & Baruch, G. (1979). *Beyond sugar and spice: How women grow, learn, and thrive.* New York: G. P. Putnam.

Rodin, J., & Ickovics, J. R. (1990). Women's health: Review and research agenda as we approach the 21st century. *American Psychologist, 45,* 1018–1034.

Rosenfeld, J. A. (1992). Maternal work outside the home and its effect on women and their families. *Journal of the American Medical Women's Association, 47,* 47–53.

Ross, C. E., Mirowsky, J., & Huber, J. (1983). Dividing work, sharing work, and in-between: Marriage patterns and depression. *American Sociological Review, 39,* 809–823.

Rossi, A. S. (1965). Barriers to the career choice of engineering, medicine, or science among American women. In J. A. Mattfeld & C. G. Van Aken (Eds.), Women and the scientific professions. Cambridge, MA: MIT Press.

Sears, R. R. (1984). The Terman gifted children study. In S. A. Mednick, M. Harway, & K. M. Finello (Eds.), *Handbook of longitudinal research* (Vol. 1. pp. 398–414). New York: Praeger.

Stevens, J. (1986). *Applied multivariate statistics for the social sciences.* Hillsdale, NJ: Lawrence Erlbaum.

Stewart, A. (1980). Personality and situation in the prediction of women's life patterns. *Psychology of Women Quarterly, 5,* 195–206.

Super, D. E. (1957). The psychology of careers. New York: Harper & Row.

Tangri, S. S. (1975). Determinants of occupational role innovation among college women. In M. T. S. Mednick, S. S. Tangri, & L. W. Hoffman (Eds.), *Women and Achievement: Social and motivational analyses.* New York: Wiley.

Tangri, S. S., & Jenkins, S. (1986). Stability and change in role innovation and life plans. *Sex Roles, 14,* 647–662.

Terman, L. M., & Oden, M. H. (1947). *Genetic studies of genius: Vol. 4. The gifted child grows up.* Stanford, CA: Stanford University Press.

Thompson, M. S., Alexander, K. L., & Entwisle, D. R. (1988). Household composition, parental expectations, and school achievement. *Social Forces, 67,* 424–451.

Tomlinson-Keasey, C. (1990). The working lives of Terman's gifted women. In H. Y. Grossman and N. L. Chester (Eds.), *The experience and meaning of work in women's lives* (pp. 213–240). Hillsdale, NJ: Lawrence Erlbaum.

Tomlinson-Keasey, C., & Little, T. D. (1990). Predicting educational attainment, occupational achievement, intellectual skills, and personal adjustment among gifted men and women. *Journal of Educational Psychology, 82,* 442–455.

U.S. Bureau of the Census (1950a). *Classified index of occupations and industries: 1950 Census of the population.* Washington, DC: U. S. Government Printing Office.

U.S. Bureau of the Census (1950b). *Statistical abstract of the United States: 1950 (71st ed).* Washington, DC: U. S. Government Printing Office.

U.S. Bureau of the Census (1952). *1950 Census of the popoulation.* Washington, DC: U. S. Government Printing Office.

U.S. Bureau of the Census (1986). *Current population reports. Special Studies. Women in the American Economy.* Washington, DC: U. S. Government Printing Office.

Vaillant, G. E. (1977). *Adaptation to Life.* Boston, MA: Little, Brown.

White, J. (1986). *Girls into science and technology: The story of a project.* London: Routledge & Kegan Paul.

Williams, J. H. (1987). *Psychology of Women: Behavior in a biosocial context.* New York: Norton.

Zuckerman, D. M. (1985). Confidence and aspirations: Self-esteem and self-concepts as predictors of students' life goals. *Journal of Personality, 53,* 543–560.

FOURTEEN

Women's Career Commitment Patterns and Personality Development

Elizabeth A. Vandewater and Abigail J. Stewart

In this chapter we explore the personality implications of three different career commitment patterns in a sample of women who attended college in the early 1960s. Traditionally, most personality theorists have assumed that career commitments are consequential for men's personality and well-being but not for women's (Gergen, 1990; see also Erikson, 1964, 1968; Gould, 1978; Levinson, 1978; Vaillant, 1977). A parallel but reverse assumption has often been made about relational lives, that they are consequential for women's personality but not for men's (Chodorow, 1978; Gilligan, 1982; Miller, 1986). Given the strong and changing social pressures affecting men's and women's occupational and relational lives, we suspect that, at least now, both assumptions are unwarranted. The career and relational commitments of different groups of women and men vary in the depth and pervasiveness of their meanings and consequences. Moreover, the significance of commitments for any group changes as sex role values change (Stewart & Healy, 1989).

By focusing on a single, relatively homogeneous cohort of women, we can be quite precise in our understanding of the sex role pressures they encountered in the course of their early and later adult lives. This group of women attended Radcliffe College in the early 1960s; we know that on the whole they were privileged in terms of their race (White), social class origin (largely middle and upper class), and certainly their educations. We know, too, that young women who attended Radcliffe at that time were educated to become wives of successful men and mothers of successful children. It was expected that these domestic roles would be their careers. However, with the onset of the modern women's movement and the affirmative action laws of the late 1960s and early 1970s, these women faced new ideas about women's roles in their early adulthood, as well as new opportunities to pursue occupational careers of their own. Some of them entered such careers soon after college and remained in them for the next 25 years. Others eschewed occupational careers and pursued other commitments (at home, in volunteer and avocational spheres, etc.). Still others made career commitments for the first time in their thirties and early forties. By differentiating the cohort into women with different career commitment patterns, we hope to observe the connections between occupational commitments, identity, and personality in these women at midlife.

Linking Personality and Career Commitments

Those theorists of personality development who have considered the implications of career commitment for men have focused on men whose work involves considerable training and is highly valued socially (high-status and well-paid; Gould, 1978; Levinson, 1978; Vaillant, 1977). These theorists, like Erikson (1964, 1968, 1982), have generally assumed that men's self-conceptions and identity development include a strong vocational or occupational component, and also that men's occupational involvements are consequential for their mental health and well-being in later adult life.

However, those theorists previously mentioned and others who have explored women's personality development have made somewhat different assumptions about women. First, Erikson (1968) suggested that women's identity formation might take place later than men's, in part because relational ties (or "intimacy" in his words) may play a more central role in shaping the course of women's personality development. Similarly, a variety of researchers have suggested that women's identities may not be so exclusively bound up in their work lives as men's are (Ackerman, 1990; Helson, 1992; Hornstein, 1986; Moen & Smith, 1986). Finally, although many researchers have reported that women's employment is often a source of well-being and mental health (Baruch, Barnett, & Rivers, 1983; Crosby, 1987), others have found that employed and unemployed women do not differ in terms of mental health (Stewart & Vandewater, 1993).

One reason for these conflicting results may be that different kinds of employment have different consequences for different groups of women. Recent studies of women's personality development support the notion that different groups of women experience their work lives differently (Gerson, 1985; Josselson, 1987). A number of researchers have reported that women who pursued careers in the 1950s and 1960s and were successful in them were higher in a variety of instrumental, assertive characteristics than women who didn't (Baruch, 1967). Helson, in her ongoing study of Mills college graduates a few years older than the Radcliffe women, found that occupationally committed women even in college were unusually high in assertiveness and independence (Helson, Mitchell, & Moane, 1984). Similarly, studies of women with primary commitments in the relational rather than occupational sphere have suggested that these women are particularly responsive to others (Helson et al., 1984), and are often high in self-control and self-sacrifice (Helson & Picano, 1990).

Personality Development of Women with Different Career Commitment Patterns

Our purpose here is mainly exploratory. Because of assumptions about the primacy of familial relationships for women's personalities, there is relatively little research that specifically examines women's work commitments and personality. However, on the basis of the personality theory reviewed above, as well as previous findings and our expectation that within-gender career commitment differences may be important, we suspect that different career commitment patterns will be differentially related to personality characteristics in midlife. Since career commitments were not obligatory for women in this sample, nor were they socially disapproved to the extent they were for previous samples, women who pursued high-level careers probably share certain midlife personality characteristics—unusually high levels of assertive, independent qualities. Similarly, women who pursued other commitments (avocations, relationships, volunteer careers) probably also share midlife personality characteristics—responsiveness to others, self-control, and self-sacrifice. Finally, women who pursued high-level careers, but only later in adulthood, when the climate of social approval for them had warmed considerably, may have some of the midlife personality characteristics of both groups. In addition, it seems that for this cohort, a woman's identity would be tied to her work life only if she were committed to her career; other aspects of a woman's life, including relationships, but not limited to them, would also be important sources of identity for all women. Therefore, we suspect that there will be no connection between career commitment and well-being for this sample. We will examine a variety of indicators of well-being and personality in considering the relationships between career commitments and personality development.

METHOD

Sample

We used longitudinal data from a sample of 171 women who graduated from Radcliffe College in 1964 (Stewart, 1975, 1978, 1980). The data used for this study were collected from the women in 1974 at age 31, in 1986 at age 43, and in 1991 at age 48. At each wave, the women were asked basic demographic questions and a number of open-ended questions about their lives and were administered standardized measures of well-being and personality.

Career Commitment

Creating our career commitment groups involved a two-step process. For the first step we used a scoring system adapted from Helson and her colleagues (Helson et al., 1984; Helson & Moane, 1987). They introduced the notion of "occupational clocks," defined by the timetable of commitment to and advancement in a career. Using their scoring system, we judged all of the women to be either on a career track, on a job track, or not in the paid labor force at both age 28 and age 43. This coding focuses mainly on whether the work has *opportunity for advancement* for the worker. That is, the focus is on whether the work has a ladder of advancement associated with it within which the woman could advance and reap the rewards of higher status positions in her field. A "career" was defined as involving work with status potential, demanding lengthy training, and with considerable opportunity for advancement in it. Examples of people in careers are lawyers, executives, doctors, academicians, and those artists and freelance writers who are publicly recognized and successful. A "job" was defined as relatively lower paying, lower status work that was easy to move in and out of and, most importantly, provided little opportunity for advancement. Jobs, therefore, were ladderless—there was no hierarchy within which the woman could keep advancing. Examples of people in jobs are secretaries and elementary or secondary school teachers.

Using this coding, we then categorized each participant into one of three career commitment groups based on the woman's career/job commitments early and later in life. These three groups reflect the women's career commitment patterns from age 28 to age 43 and encompass: (1) *women with continuous career commitment patterns* (those who were on career tracks at both age 28 and 43; $N = 68$); (2) *women with midlife career commitment patterns* (those who were not on a career track by age 28 but were on a career track by age 43; $N = 36$); and (3) *women with alternative commitment patterns* (those who were not on career tracks at age 28 or age 43; $N = 67$). (We have labeled this group as "alternative" because it is important to acknowledge that although in this paper we are focusing on career commitments, many of these women have made life commitments other than career commitments.)

Observer Report of Midlife Personality Characteristics: The California Adult Q-set (CAQ)

The 1986 wave of the questionnaire data (when the women were 43 years old) was Q-sorted using the California Adult Q-set (CAQ; Block 1961). At that time, participants completed 39 pages of questionnaires which involved open-ended questions in combination with closed-ended items and scales. These provided a rich and differentiated impression of each individual woman's life to that point. Block and Hann (1971) and Helson (1992) have shown that Q-sorts based on questionnaire files such as these provide extremely useful summaries of observers' impressions of personality.

The CAQ consists of 100 items assessing various aspects of personality. Each sorter is asked to judge, from all available data, the salience of each of the 100 items for a particular participant's personality. Each item is placed on a forced, normal distribution scale ranging from 1 (extremely uncharacteristic or negatively salient) to 9 (extremely characteristic or positively salient). For this study, at least three sorters sorted each file and then a composite sort was created from these three sorts, using the mean scale placement of each item as the new composite item placement. Acceptable alpha coefficients for composite sorts range from .57 and above (Wink, 1991). The alpha coefficients for these participants ranged from .60 to .91, with a mean of .77.

Self-Report of Midlife Personality Characteristics: The California Psychological Inventory (CPI)

The California Psychological Inventory (CPI) was administered to these women when they were 48 years old, in 1991. The inventory contains 462 items to be answered "true" or "false" according to whether the respondent found them to be descriptive of self or nondescriptive. Internal consistencies for the various scales were computed on a sample of 400 college students (200 female, 200 male) randomly drawn from archival samples; they were acceptably high. The intention of the CPI (Gough, 1987) is to assess the kind of everyday interpersonal themes in behavior that may be called "folk concepts." Folk concepts refer to human attributes or qualities such as dominance, sense of responsibility, and self-control that all people everywhere recognize and denominate in their languages. The 20 folk scales generated by the CPI are clustered into four groupings. The first cluster of seven scales (dominance, status potential, sociability, social presence, self-acceptance, independence, and empathy) pertains to different aspects of *interpersonal style;* the second cluster of seven scales (responsibility, socialization, self-control, good impression, communality, well-being, and tolerance) pertains to *normative orientations and values,* with each scale assessing a particular facet of normative or prescriptive social rules. The third cluster of three scales (achievement via conformance, achievement via independence, and intellectual efficiency) pertains to the *intellective-cognitive* domain. Finally, the fourth cluster of three scales assesses *broadly stylistic aspects of behavior,* including psychological-mindedness, flexibility, and masculine/feminine role modalities.

In addition to the folk scales, there are three bipolar structural scales called vectors. These were empirically derived from the correlational structure of the test and are used to define a personological taxonomy (Gough, 1987, 1989). Vector 1, or *internality,* is a scale of interpersonal orientation. Persons scoring high on internality are generally inwardly oriented, moderate, modest, and reserved in manner and can be reluctant to initiate decisive social action. Persons scoring lower generally have an external or outward interpersonal orientation and are more likely to be outgoing and confident and to have social poise and presence. Vector 2, or *norm-favoring,* describes an individual's normative preferences. Persons scoring high are generally conscientious, self-disciplined, conventional, dependable, and controlled. Vector 3, or *realization,* describes the individual's sense of self-actualization. Persons scoring high on vector 3 feel themselves to be capable, able to cope with the stresses of life, and reasonably fulfilled or actualized (Gough, 1987, 1989; Lanning & Gough, 1991).

Well-being

Well-being was measured in this sample at several times and in a variety of ways. At age 33, the women were administered a variety of standardized measures of well-being, including a modified version of the Cornell Medical Index (Abramson, 1966), and the Zung self-rating depression (1965) and anxiety scales (1971). At age 43 they were again administered the Zung (1965, 1971) depression and anxiety scales, as well as the Profile of Mood States (POMS; McNair, Lorr, & Doppleman, 1971) and the Symptom Check List (SCL; Gurin, Veroff, & Feld, 1960). All of the measures have been validated on large samples, are widely used in research, and possess more than adequate psychometric characteristics.

The Cornell Medical Index (Abramson, 1966; collected at age 33) asks participants to indicate chronic or persistent health problems, major operations, and major and minor illnesses over the past year. The modified medical questionnaire contained 117 items, each rated on a four-point scale, and results in a total illness score (Stewart & Salt, 1981).

The Zung self-rating anxiety (1965) and depression (1971) scales (collected at ages 33 and 43) ask participants to rate both physical and emotional symptoms associated with anxiety (such as feeling nervous or panicky and having shaking hands) or depression (such as loss of appetite, feeling downhearted and blue, and being constipated) on a four-point scale ranging from "never" to "nearly all the time." Anxiety and depression scores are created for each participant by averaging their answers on the 15 and 20 items making up each scale.

The Profile of Mood States (POMS; McNair, Lorr, & Doppleman, 1971), collected at age 43, is an instrument designed to measure subjective moods and feelings of intermediate duration. The POMS contains 66 items that the participants are asked to rate on a five-point scale ranging from "not at all" to "extremely." The POMS includes six subscales: tension-anxiety, depression-dejection, anger-hostility, fatigue-inertia, vigor-activity, and confusion-bewilderment. In addition, a total mood disturbance score can be obtained by summing the negative affect scores and then subtracting the vigor score from that total.

The Symptom Check List (SCL; Gurin, Veroff, & Feld, 1960), collected at age 43, is often used to assess the quality of subjective adjustment for adults (Baruch et al., 1983) and indicates how much participants are bothered by symptoms associated with anxiety and other indicators of ill-being. The 48-item checklist includes three scales, which are labeled anxiety, immobilization, and physical health (Veroff, Douvan, & Kulka, 1981).

In addition, there is a well-being scale embedded in the interpersonal style cluster of the CPI, collected at age 48. On this scale, low scorers tend to be worrying, complaining, and dissatisfied, while high scorers tend to be optimistic about their own prospects and feel in good physical and emotional health (Helson et al., 1984).

Analysis Plan

One-way ANOVAs were conducted to assess differences on all personality and well-being measures among the three commitment pattern groups. Post hoc *t* tests were used to identify significant differences between any two of the three groups. Unless otherwise noted, we will only discuss significant group differences. Thus, if a particular group comparison is not discussed, the differences between the two groups were not significant.

PRELIMINARY FINDINGS
Differences in Family Background

In order to consider some possible familial antecedents of these women's differing career commitment patterns, we examined variables based on the women's family of origin (see Table 14.1). Although father's occupational status, education, and work patterns did not differentiate the groups of women, these same variables in terms of their mothers, did. The mothers of the women with continuous career commitments were more highly educated (they were more likely to have attained a college degree) than the mothers of the women with midlife career commitments (who were more likely to have had some college but not to have attained a college degree), though not more than the mothers of the women with alternative commitments. On the other hand, the mothers of the women with continuous career commitments were more likely to have worked at all, and they had worked significantly more throughout their lives than the mothers of the women with alternative commitment patterns. Interestingly, although there was no difference among the groups in their birth order in their families, both the women with midlife career commitments and the women with alternative commitments came from larger families ($M = 3.26$ and $M = 3.03$ children, respectively) than the women with continuous career commitments ($M = 2.46$; $F = 4.06$, $df = 2$, $p < .05$). Taken together, these findings suggest that it was not social class per se that affected these women's adult career commitment patterns but rather their mothers' education and career commitments.

Differences in Midlife Outcomes

By age 43, the three groups of women had cumulated differences in their lives in ways that make intuitive sense, and can be taken as validation that the groups of women are qualitatively different from each other in ways one would expect (see Table 14.2). By age 43, women with midlife career commitments and those with continuous career commitments were more educated and had higher status jobs and higher personal incomes than those with alternative commitments. Although no group of women were more likely to engage in volunteer work than any other group, women with midlife career commitments and those with alternative commitments spent more hours per week in volunteer activities (about 8 hours per week) than women with continuous career commitments (who spent about 2 hours a week in them; $F = 3.41$, $df = 2$, $p < .05$). In addition, both women with midlife career commitments and women with alternative commitments were significantly younger when they began their first job (about age 21) than those with continuous career commitments (about age 24). Both women with midlife career commitments and those who were continuously career committed worked significantly more years between graduation from college and midlife (an average of about 18 years) than women with alternative commitments, who worked an average of about 12 years ($F = 13.99$, $df = 2$, $p < .001$). In addition, both of the career-committed groups worked more of those years full-time (an average of about 11 years) than women with alternative commitments (an average of about 4 years of full-time work; $F = 21.03$, $df = 2$, $p < .001$). Interestingly, there was no difference among the three groups in the amount of time they engaged in part-time work (they all averaged about three years), but both of the career-committed groups were much less likely to have spent the time between college and midlife unemployed (an average of about 3 years) than women with alternative commitments, who were unemployed for an average of 12 years ($F = 24.76$, $df = 2$, $p < .001$). By the time they were 43, women with continuous career commitments worked more hours per week (about 50) than women with alternative commitments (who worked about 30 hours per week) and tended to work more than women with midlife career commitments (who worked about 42 hours per week; $F = 12.27$, $df = 2$, $p < .001$).

In terms of family, there was no difference among the three groups

TABLE 14.1 Differences in Family Background among Women with Different Career Commitment Patterns

Family of Origin	Continuous Career Commitment	Midlife Career Commitment	Alternative Commitment	Significance of Differences
Father's highest educational attainment[a]	2.84 (50)	2.84 (25)	2.59 (59)	ns
Father's occupational status[b]	5.95 (49)	6.20 (25)	6.03 (59)	ns
Father ever unemployed[c]	(N = 31)	(N = 19)	(N = 42)	ns
Yes	39%	26%	33%	
No	61%	74%	67%	
Mother's highest educational attainment	2.30[e] (50)	1.65[f] (24)	1.87 (56)	$F = 3.33^{\star}$
Mother ever employed?	(N = 50)	(N = 25)	(N = 59)	$\chi^2 = 5.526t$
Yes	80%	64%	59%	
No	20%	36%	40%	
Mother's occupational status	5.32 (31)	4.78 (18)	5.17 (36)	ns

Mother's work pattern[d]	(N = 49)	(N = 24)	(N = 57)	
Never worked	16%	17%	32%	F = 4.32*
Worked until marriage	8%	25%	19%	
Worked until had children	12%	17%	12%	
Worked after children were in high school or college	33%	25%	21%	
Always worked	31%	17%	16%	

Note: Numbers in parentheses indicate the *N* associated with each mean.

[a] Both father's and mother's highest education attainment were rated on a scale where 0 = high school or less; 1 = some college; 2 = college (4 year) degree; 3 = master's degree; 4 = doctoral-level degree. Doctoral-level degrees include academic degrees (e.g., Ph.D.'s) as well as doctoral-level professional degrees (e.g., M.D., J.D.).

[b] Both father's and mother's occupational status were rated on a scale after Hollingshead and Redlich (1956) where 1 = unskilled; 2 = semiskilled; 3 = skilled; 4 = sales/clerical; 5 = administrative; 6 = minor professional (e.g., high school teacher, social worker); 7 = major professional (e.g., doctor, lawyer, college professor, executive).

[c] Column percentages add up to 100. Thus the first column indicates the percentage of women with continuous career commitments whose fathers were ever unemployed or were never unemployed.

[d] Although percentages were reported for ease of interpretation, analyses were conducted on a scale for mother's work pattern where 1 = never worked; 2 = worked until marriage; 3 = worked until had children; 4 = worked after children were in high school or college; 5 = always worked.

†*t* = *p* < .10. **p* < .05.

TABLE 14.2 Differences in Midlife Outcomes among Women with Different Career Commitment Patterns

Outcomes at Age 43	Continuous Career Commitment	Midlife Career Commitment	Alternative Commitment	Significance of Differences
Highest educational attainment[a]	(N = 45)	(N = 25)	(N = 60)	F = 60.30***
College degree (4-year)	2%	12%	50%	
Master's degree	11%	40%	42%	
Doctoral-level degree	87%	48%	8%	
Occupational status[b]	(N = 32)	(N = 15)	(N = 33)	F = 61.16***
White collar	6%	6%	67%	
Minor professional	10%	47%	33%	
Major professional	84%	47%		
Personal income[c]	(N = 32)	(N = 19)	(N = 43)	F = 43.99***
None			26%	
<$5,000	3%	11%	14%	
$5,000–19,999	23%	16%	42%	
$20,000–29,999	23%	5%	16%	
$30,000–39,999	19%	32%	2%	
$40,000–49,999	16%	15%		
>$50,000	39%	21%		
Average age at first job	24[e] (42)	21[f] (19)	22[f] (38)	F = 9.43**

Ever married by age 43?	$(N = 51)$	$(N = 27)$	$(N = 64)$	ns
Yes	90%	89%	94%	
No	10%	11%	6%	
Divorced by age 43 if married?	$(N = 47)$	$(N = 24)$	$(N = 59)$	$\chi^2 = 10.51^\star$
Yes	30%	54%	19%	
No	70%	46%	81%	
Age first became a mother[d]	30[f] (38)	28 (26)	27[e] (49)	$F = 3.96^\star$
Had children by age 43?	$(N = 66)$	$(N = 35)$	$(N = 66)$	$\chi^2 = 9.96^{\star\star}$
Yes	70%	89%	89%	
No	30%	11%	11%	
Number of children at age 43	1.3[f] (32)	2.0 (20)	2.4[e] (46)	$F = 5.73^{\star\star}$

Note: Although percentages are reported for ease of interpretation, analyses were conducted on scales for all variables with an F test of significance. Numbers in parentheses indicate the N associated with each mean.

[a] For each set of outcomes, the column percentages add up to 100. Thus the first column indicates the percentage of women with continuous career commitment who fell into each of the educational brackets, and so forth, at age 43. Highest educational attainment was rated on a scale where 1 = college degree (4-year); 2 = master's degree; 3 = doctoral-level degree. Doctoral-level degrees include academic degrees (e.g., Ph.D.'s) as well as doctoral-level professional degrees (e.g., M.D., J.D.).

[b] Occupational status was rated on a scale after Hollingshead and Redlich (1956), where 1 = white-collar (e.g., clerical, sales, and administrative); 2 = minor professional (e.g., high school teacher, social worker); 3 = major professional (e.g., doctor, lawyer, college professor, executive).

[c] Income was rated on a scale where 1 = none; 2 = <$5,000; 3 = $5,000–19,999; 4 = $20,000–29,999; 5 = $30,000–39,999; 6 = $40,000–49,999; 7 = >$50,000.

[d] Age first became a mother includes becoming a mother to stepchildren by marriage, as well as giving birth.

[e] Means significantly different from [f]. Not different from other [e] or no superscript.

[f] Means significantly different from [e]. Not different from other [f] or no superscript.

$\star\, p < .05.\ \star\star\, p < .01.\ \star\star\star\, p < .001.$

in the age at which they first married (they all got married at around age 23), or indeed in whether they had ever married by midlife; but those with alternative commitments were significantly younger when they first became mothers (at around age 27) than women with continuous career commitments (who first became mothers at age 30, on average). Interestingly, women with midlife career commitments were more likely to have divorced by their midforties than those with alternative commitments. There were significant differences among the groups both in how likely they were to have had children by age 43 and in how many children they had by that time. The women with alternative commitments were significantly more likely to have had children by age 43, and had more of them (an average of a little more than two children), than women with continuous career commitments (who had an average of one child). In addition, women with midlife career commitments were more likely to have had children by age 43 and to have more of them (they had two children on average) than women with continuous career commitments.

Results
Well-being

There were no significant differences among the three groups of women on any standardized well-being measure at any age or on the CPI well-being scale. Thus, no particular group seems to be suffering more than any of the others or to feel less satisfied because of their career commitment patterns.

Midlife Personality Correlates of Commitment: Observer Reports

Analyses showed that out of 100 items on the Q-sort, there were significant differences among the women on 43 of those items, more than eight times the number of differences one would expect by chance. This large number of differences among the career commitment groups confirms the impression on the basis of midlife outcomes that they were qualitatively different. In this case, their personalities were perceived as quite different by observers.

When interpreting these findings, it is important to remember that the scale of the ratings ranges from 1 (not at all descriptive of the person) to 9 (very descriptive of the person). Thus, although the differences in the mean placement of items were significantly different from each other as noted, they are often on the same end of the rating scale.

If, for example, one notes the means for the item "deceitful and manipulative," it is clear that the mean item placements for all three groups of women are on the low end of the scale; thus all three groups were seen as not deceitful and manipulative, and the women with continuous career commitments were only rated as being less likely to be *not* manipulative. Another example is the item "productive." This is rated at the high end of the scale for all groups, with means ranging from 8.42 for women with continuous commitments to 7.07 for women with alternative commitments. This indicates that *all* of the women were seen as productive, but that women with alternative commitments were seen as relatively less productive than women with continuous commitments.

The Q-sort item analyses indicated that the women with midlife career commitments seemed to live in both worlds. They were sometimes perceived as like those with continuous career commitments and sometimes like those with alternative commitments; but those with continuous career commitments and those with alternative commitments were never seen as like each other. Table 14.3 indicates how women with continuous career commitments and those with midlife career commitments were seen as similar to each other and different from women with alternative commitments.

In comparison with the women with alternative commitments, both women with midlife career commitments and those with continuous career commitments were rated as being more productive, as valuing intellectual matters more highly, having a higher intellectual capacity, being more assertive, being more nonconforming, having a higher personal aspiration level, valuing independence more, seeing to the heart of important problems more, giving up less easily when things got hard, delaying or avoiding action less, being less uncomfortable with uncertainty, having less conservative values, being self-defeating, and having a more rapid personal tempo. They were also less aesthetically reactive. On three items there were significant differences among all three groups: The women with continuous career commitments were seen as the most power oriented, the least genuinely submissive, and behaving least femininely; the women with midlife career commitment were rated in the middle for these items, and the women with alternative commitments were rated at the other extreme.

Table 14.4 indicates how women with midlife career commitments and those with alternative commitments were seen as similar to each other and different from women with continuous career commitments.

TABLE 14.3 Observer Report (CAQ) Personality Differences among
Women with Different Career Commitment Patterns

CAQ Items	Continuous Career Commitment (N = 33)	Midlife Career Commitment (N = 20)	Alternative Commitment (N = 46)	Significance of Differences
Productive	8.42[a]	8.15[a]	7.07[b]	$F = 10.29$***
Values intellectual matters highly	8.49[a]	8.10[a]	7.15[b]	$F = 12.91$***
High intellectual capacity	8.46[a]	8.15[a]	7.39[b]	$F = 14.40$***
Assertive	7.06[a]	6.15[a]	3.98[b]	$F = 27.58$***
Nonconforming	6.06[a]	5.20[a]	3.70[b]	$F = 15.55$***
High personal aspirations	8.18[a]	7.70[a]	5.15[b]	$F = 44.40$***
Power oriented	7.12[a]	5.45[b]	3.57[c]	$F = 35.74$***
Values independence	8.30[a]	8.05[a]	6.37[b]	$F = 20.09$***
Sees to heart of problems	6.36[a]	6.25[a]	5.28[b]	$F = 10.80$***
Gives up easily	2.12[a]	2.20[a]	3.48[b]	$F = 10.22$***
Delays or avoids action	1.82[a]	2.30[a]	3.67[b]	$F = 10.81$***
Uncomfortable with uncertainty	3.58[a]	3.45[a]	4.69[b]	$F = 6.46$**
Genuinely submissive	1.42[a]	2.10[b]	4.37[c]	$F = 37.64$***
Conservative values	3.27[a]	3.10[a]	4.74[b]	$F = 6.96$**
Self-defeating	2.42a	2.40[a]	3.59[b]	$F = 6.82$**
Rapid personal tempo	6.12[a]	6.10[a]	4.85[b]	$F = 9.22$***
Aesthetically reactive	6.24[a]	5.95[a]	7.39[b]	$F = 10.24$***
Behaves femininely	3.73[a]	4.95[b]	6.67[c]	$F = 32.57$***

Note: CAQ = California Adult Q-set.
[a] Means significantly different from [b] and [c]. Not significantly different from other [a].
[b] Means significantly different from [a] and [c]. Not significantly different from other [b].
[c] Means significantly different from [a] and [b]. Not significantly different from other [c].
* $p < .05$. ** $p < .01$. *** $p < .001$.

TABLE 14.4 Observer Report (CAQ) Personality Differences among Women with Different Career Commitment Patterns

CAQ Items	Continuous Career Commitment (N = 33)	Midlife Career Commitment (N = 20)	Alternative Commitment (N = 46)	Significance of Differences
Behaves givingly	6.06[a]	7.70[b]	7.74[b]	$F = 11.25$***
Feels guilty	4.27[a]	5.35[b]	5.44[b]	$F = 5.509$**
Takes pride in objectivity	7.00[a]	5.75[b]	5.11[b]	$F = 14.16$***
Skeptical	6.70[a]	5.70[b]	4.95[b]	$F = 9.81$***
Protective of others	5.00[a]	6.80[b]	6.52[b]	$F = 10.81$***
Warm	6.52[a]	7.60[b]	7.48[b]	$F = 3.62$*
Avoids close relationships	4.33[a]	3.00[b]	3.07[b]	$F = 4.06$*
Self-indulgent	5.03[a]	3.85[b]	4.08[b]	$F = 3.26$*
Concerned with philosophical matters	4.76[a]	6.05[b]	5.91[b]	$F = 3.61$*
Arouses nurturance in others	3.57[a]	4.65[b]	5.07[b]	$F = 15.13$***
Self-dramatizing	2.33[a]	3.15[b]	3.39[b]	$F = 6.53$**
Moody	4.70[a]	5.55[b]	5.59[b]	$F = 3.28$*

Note: CAQ = California Adult Q-set.
[a] Means significantly different from [b] but not from other [a].
[b] Means significantly different from [a] but not from other [b].
* $p < .05$. ** $p < .01$. *** $p < .001$.

In comparison with the women with continuous career commitments, both women with midlife career commitments and those with alternative commitments were rated as behaving more givingly toward others, feeling more guilty, taking less pride in objectivity, being less skeptical, more protective of important others in their life, warmer, less likely to avoid close relationships, less self-indulgent, more concerned with philosophical matters, more likely to arouse nurturance in others, more self-dramatizing, more moody, and less emotionally bland.

Finally, Table 14.5 indicates how women with continuous career commitments and women with alternative commitments were seen as different from each other. In comparison with women with alternative commitments, women with continuous career commitments were rated as having a more clear-cut personality, less likely to daydream, more likely to compare themselves to others, more likely to express hostility directly, less introspective, less maladaptive under stress, more manipulative, less moralistic, enjoying sensuous experiences less, pushing and stretching limits more, and less likely to seek reassurance from others for their actions.

The coding of our career commitment groups was based on all available data, and thus some women's career commitments were based on the 1986 data if there were no data before this time. In principle, since observer judgments on the CAQ were also based on 1986 data, our findings might simply be an indication that the observers held shared stereotypes about women on particular career patterns. In order to rule out this possibility, we ran the same analyses removing the women whose career commitment codes were based solely on 1986 data because they had no data before this time. This left us with a reduced N ($N = 26$ for continuous career commitments; $N = 14$ for midlife career commitments; $N = 28$ for alternative commitments). The results of this analysis were virtually the same as the analysis with the larger N. All 43 items except "expresses hostility directly" revealed the same differences between the groups. In addition, the significance of seven items (maladaptive under stress, feels guilty, has warmth, avoids close relationships, is self-indulgent, arouses nurturance in others, and concerned with philosophical matters) dropped to the trend level ($p < .10$), but this is to be expected due to the much reduced N. The consistency in these results allows us to have confidence in the differences observers saw between these groups of women: the observers were capturing some qualitative distinctions among them. The results based on the self-report data also bore this out.

TABLE 14.5 Observer Report (CAQ) Personality Differences among Women with Different Career Commitment Patterns

CAQ Items	Continuous Career Commitment ($N = 33$)	Midlife Career Commitment ($N = 20$)	Alternative Commitment ($N = 46$)	Significance of Differences
Has clear-cut personality	6.54[a]	5.90	5.54[b]	$F = 3.37$*
Daydreams	4.30[a]	4.60	5.11[b]	$F = 3.74$*
Emotionally bland	4.18[b]	3.10[a]	3.37[a]	$F = 3.99$*
Compares self to others	5.24[a]	4.75	4.61[b]	$F = 3.65$*
Expresses hostility directly	5.12[a]	4.40	4.09[b]	$F = 4.84$**
Introspective	5.24[a]	6.05	6.33[b]	$F = 4.88$**
Maladaptive under stress	2.61[a]	3.25	3.61[b]	$F = 3.93$*
Deceitful, manipulative	2.18[a]	1.70	1.54[b]	$F = 5.31$**
Moralistic	4.46[a]	4.70	5.59[b]	$F = 6.04$**
Enjoys sensuous experiences	5.94[a]	6.05	6.63[b]	$F = 3.34$*
Pushes and stretches limits	3.51[a]	2.90	2.41[b]	$F = 6.40$**
Seeks reassurance	4.30[a]	4.95	5.98[b]	$F = 10.08$***

Note: CAQ = California Adult Q-set.
[a] Means significantly different from other [b] but not from other [a] and no superscript.
[b] Means significantly different from other [a] but not from other [b] and no superscript.
* $p < .05$. ** $p < .01$. *** $p < .001$.

Midlife Personality Correlates of Commitment: Self-Report

Of the 20 scales making up the four clusters on the CPI, one-way ANOVAs revealed that 6 produced significant differences, 2 produced trends, and 2 out of 3 vector scores were significantly different from each other. This large number of differences confirms the observer reports and indicates that not only do others see these groups of women differently but they also see themselves differently (See Table 14.6).

When interpreting the differences among these groups' scores on the CPI, it should be noted that this sample taken as a whole has significantly elevated scores on 19 out of the 20 folk scales and all 3 of the vectors. That is, the scale means for all but the masculinity-femininity scale are significantly different from the scale means obtained from the CPI normative population (Gough, 1987). This means that taken as a whole, the sample has a very positive personality profile and feel quite good about themselves and where they are. As with the Q-sort differences, it is important to remember that the significant differences between the groups are relative to each other, and do not indicate that any group is doing poorly.

In the interpersonal style cluster, women with midlife career commitments and women with continuous career commitments scored significantly higher on dominance than women with alternative commitments. The group of women with midlife career commitments also scored significantly higher on independence than women with alternative commitments. In addition, there was a trend for women with midlife career commitments to score higher on sociability—which indicates responsiveness to what others do and think as well as interpersonal obligations—than women with alternative commitments. Finally, there was a trend for women with midlife career commitments to score higher on self-acceptance than those with alternative commitments, which is associated with self-confidence and self-esteem (Gough, 1987).

In the normative orientations and values cluster, women with midlife career commitments scored higher on tolerance than either women with continuous career commitments or those with alternative commitments; there was also a trend for women who became career committed to score higher on communality than those with alternative commitments. High scores on tolerance indicate attitudes of open-mindedness, clear and insightful thinking, and fair-mindedness. Communality indicates societal conventionality, and high scorers are generally reasonable, organized, and stable (Gough, 1987).

In the intellective-cognitive cluster, women with midlife career commitments scored higher on two of the three scales making up this cluster than women with alternative commitments: achievement via conformance and intellectual efficiency. They also tended to score higher on intellectual efficiency than women with continuous career commitments. High scorers on achievement via conformance are described as having a strong desire to do well and as liking to have things clearly structured and defined. Intellectual efficiency assesses the effective use of intelligence through confidence, perseverance, and sensible, positive attitudes (Gough, 1987).

In terms of the fourth cluster of scales describing broadly stylistic aspects of behavior, the women who became career committed later scored significantly higher on psychological-mindedness than women with alternative commitments, indicating a more objective and fair-minded view of others (Gough, 1987).

In terms of the vector scores, women with alternative commitments scored higher on internality (vector 1) than either women who became committed to a career later or women with continuous career commitments. In addition, women with midlife career commitments scored significantly higher on self-realization (vector 3) than women with alternative commitments.

Discussion

These analyses show a decided connection between different life paths and personality characteristics. The three groups of women with different career commitment patterns are qualitatively different from each other in both the eyes of observers and their own eyes. On the Q-sort, the women with continuous career commitments and the women with alternative commitments were clearly seen as quite different from each other, while the women with midlife career commitments were seen as having characteristics of both of the other groups. The women with continuous career commitments and midlife career commitments were seen as more productive, intellectually oriented, assertive, and independent than the women with alternative commitments. However, the women with alternative career commitments and those with midlife career commitments were seen as being warmer, behaving more givingly, and being more concerned with philosophical matters. In addition, in comparison with each other, the women with

Table 14.6 Self-report (CPI) Personality Differences among Women with Different Career Commitment Patterns

CPI Scales	Continuous Career Commitment ($N = 37$)	Midlife Career Commitment ($N = 21$)	Alternative Commitment ($N = 55$)	Significance of Differences
Cluster 1: interpersonal style				
Dominance	63.52[a]	67.27[a]	57.55[b]	$F = 8.14$***
Status potential	58.79	61.14	59.66	ns
Sociability	52.74	56.72[c]	51.77[d]	$F = 2.37t$
Social presence	54.76	55.61	51.57	ns
Self-acceptance	57.34	59.07[c]	54.33[d]	$F = 2.62t$
Independence	59.12	62.92[a]	57.26[b]	$F = 3.77$*
Empathy	55.89	60.41	56.67	ns
Cluster 2: normative values				
Responsibility	58.03	60.11	57.91	ns
Socialization	53.10	53.84	53.58	ns
Self-control	54.66	55.94	56.56	ns
Good impression	52.43	53.17	53.65	ns
Communality	51.94	54.39[c]	50.24[d]	$F = 2.59t$
Well-being	53.87	55.63	53.38	ns
Tolerance	57.99[a]	61.61[e]	58.10[d]	$F = 3.13$*

Cluster 3: intellective-cognitive				
Achievement via conformance	57.32	58.70[a]	55.10[b]	$F = 3.73$*
Achievement via independence	62.17	63.40	61.60	ns
Intellectual efficiency	58.37[c]	61.32[f]	57.61[b]	$F = 3.42$*
Cluster 4: stylistic aspects of behavior				
Psychological-mindedness	61.93	64.23[a]	58.87[b]	$F = 6.65$**
Flexibility	55.16	58.46	57.70	ns
Masculinity/Femininity	47.40	49.24	50.23	ns
Vector 1: internality	42.83[a]	41.28[a]	49.56[b]	$F = 6.58$**
Vector 2: norm favoring	51.26	52.52	50.71	ns
Vector 3: realization of potential	58.14	63.06[a]	57.83[b]	$F = 3.49$*

Note: CPI = California Psychological Inventory.

[a] Means significantly different from [b], [c], [d], and [e], but not from other [a], [f], and no superscript.

[b] Means significantly different from [a], [c], [d], and [f], but not from other [b], [e], and no superscript.

[c] Means significantly from [a], [b], [d], and [f], but not from other [c], [e], or no superscript.

[d] Means significantly different from [a], [b], [c], and [e], but not from other [d], [f], and no superscript.

[e] Means significantly different from [a], [d], and [f], but not from other [e], [b], [c], and no superscript.

[f] Means significantly different from [b], [c], and [e], but not from other [f], [a], [d], and no superscript.

$t = p < .10.$ *$p < .05.$ **$p < .01.$

alternative commitments were seen as more introspective, while the women with continuous career commitments were seen as having a more clear-cut personality.

When we examine the differences on the Q-sort ratings, some items stand out because they were rated at opposite ends of the scale for different groups (as opposed to being significantly different from each other but still at the same end of the scale). These items are assertive, nonconforming, power oriented, behaves in a feminine manner, and arouses nurturance in others. Women with continuous career commitments were seen as being characterized by assertiveness, nonconformity, and power orientation. These same items were seen as uncharacteristic of women with alternative commitments. The reverse is true for the other two items. Women with alternative commitments were seen as being characterized as behaving in a feminine manner and arousing nurturance in others, while these same items were seen as uncharacteristic of women with continuous commitments.

These findings were broadly replicated on the CPI; women with continuous career commitments and those with midlife career commitments scored higher on dominance and lower on internality than women with alternative commitments. The interpretation of the difference among the groups on vector 1 is particularly important to the overall picture of results. Gough (1990) describes scores on vector 1 as "addressed to the interpersonal continuum. Low scores refer to engagement in the interpersonal milieu, affective response to the rewards and punishments of the social nexus, and externality of behavior. High scores refer to detachment, libidinization of the private, inner world, and feelings of internality" (p. 43). Overall, the results on the CPI can be taken to mean that these two groups of women—in comparison to women with alternative commitments—were relatively more confident, assertive, and dominant. As a group, women with continuous career commitments and women with midlife career commitments were relatively more engaged in the external world, were more task oriented, and were more responsive to the demands and rewards of the social milieu around them.

However, on the CPI, it is women with midlife career commitments and women with alternative commitments who stand out as being different from each other. Women with continuous career commitments actually scored in the middle of the other two groups on 17 out of the 23 scales. And although the pair comparison did not show significant differences, it is the women with *midlife career commitments* who scored highest on dominance and lowest on internality. Women with midlife career commitments also scored higher on independence, tolerance, achievement via conformance, intellectual efficiency, psychological mindedness, and self-realization than women with alternative commitments. In addition, they tended to score higher on sociability, self-acceptance, and communality than women with alternative commitments; they scored higher on tolerance and intellectual efficiency than women with continuous career commitments. This means that in contrast to women with midlife career commitments (and somewhat in contrast to the women with continuous career commitments), women with alternative commitments were less assertive and task oriented and more likely to seek support from others. Yet they were also more likely to retreat into their own personal world. As a group, they were less likely to be responsive to the demands and rewards of the social world, and perhaps because they tend to see themselves as not quite fitting in, they had a preference for staying in the background in social situations.

All three groups of women were actively engaged in the social world and connected to the people around them. However, they seemed to be interpersonally connected in different ways. Women with continuous career commitments and those with midlife career commitments combined achievement strivings and task orientation with engagement in their social world. They were active in their interpersonal milieu and both attended to and used the feedback that the people around them conveyed. They enjoyed their social world, felt a part of it, and were actively engaged in it. However, they did not rely on the people in their social world for reassurance about themselves or their self-confidence. The women with alternative commitments, on the other hand, were engaged in their social world in a different way. They tended to feel a bit different from others and needed their personal space, but they enjoyed the connections they had with other people and looked to these connections for nurturance and reassurance about who they were. And in turn, they provided warmth and protection for the people with whom they were connected.

We have said that the women with midlife career commitments seemed to live in both worlds, combining characteristics of the other two groups. In general, this seems to be true, and could be true because they have pursued both of the paths of the other groups. They combined the external engagement, intellectual orientation, and achievement strivings of the women with continuous career commitments with the more philosophically oriented, interpersonal, and relationally connected stance of the women with alternative commitments. Interestingly, they scored high on the scales of the CPI that indicate an interest in conforming with prescribed norms and values. It may be that these women conformed to both the old sex role standards that they were raised with and the newer sex role standards that developed later in their lives. If it is true that this type of conformity is a need or a value of theirs, it may explain why they also scored higher on self-realization. This CPI vector score indicates fulfillment and actualization of one's potential. Thus, with their changing commitments, these women have fulfilled their need to be on track with regard to societal sex role values.

It is important to note that both career opportunities for women and sex role values changed drastically from the time these women went to college (the early 1960s) to the time they became young adults (the late 1960s and early 1970s). Because of the interaction between these social events and their ages at the time, they were truly a "transitional cohort" (Stewart & Vandewater, 1993). It was while they were in college that the civil rights movement grew. And it was while they were making adult commitments to careers and interpersonal lives that the contemporary women's movement really gained steam, and affirmative action laws went into effect, with an accompanying increase in the presence of women in fields and professions dominated by White men. The different groups of women dealt with this dramatic social change in different ways.

It is important to remember that there were virtually no differences among these women in terms of their well-being. This suggests that no particular group of women was more or less happy with or because of their career commitment patterns. These findings are important because they indicate that at least for this cohort of highly educated women, feelings of well-being on both physiological and emotional levels were not necessarily related to career commitment patterns. Both the findings on standardized measures of well-being and life satisfaction and qualitative information from individual files show the richness and enjoyment that each group of women found in their way of life. They are different, to be sure, and there are ups and downs for women in each group, but no group seems to feel particularly disturbed by the life paths they have taken. Reviews of their files, along with the Q-sort and CPI findings, help to give a more complete picture of their lives.

Women with Continuous Career Commitments

Taken together, the findings on the Q-sort and CPI and the individual file information indicate that by their late 40s, women with continuous career commitments were confident, assertive, dominant, and task oriented. They felt engaged in the external world and were seen by others as having a highly intellectual orientation and high personal standards and ambitions. Observers saw them as highly productive, able to see to the heart of important problems, and as having a clearcut personality. They were also seen as less introspective and less interested in philosophical or spiritual matters.

These women pursued relatively stable and high-level careers after college; they went almost immediately to graduate school in law, medicine, or the physical or social sciences. Although they were just as likely to marry as the other two groups, and all of the groups married at about the same time, these women had fewer children, and they had them later, than the other two groups. Their lives were full, busy, and dedicated to work, research, and family. Most of these women entered graduate school before the affirmative action laws of the early 1970s came into effect; thus they chose career paths in which they were neither encouraged by society (or Radcliffe either) nor had easy access to, and they stuck with them. These women, though actively engaged in (and clearly enjoying their engagement in) their social world, did not accept the tenet of their upbringing that women should be nurturant of others at the expense of self-nurturance. As a group, these women have a no-nonsense, task-oriented approach to life. They seemed to take the world as it was (or ignore it as it was with respect to attitudes about women) and simply carved out their own niche, whether they were welcomed into that niche by society or not.

They have found enormous satisfaction in their work and the lives they have built around it and in their families. In telling us of their future goals at age 43, their dedication to both work and family is evident. One woman wrote: "Get some really innovative research done and published. Make sure my kids have no drug problems and get through adolescence with a minimum of trauma. Get elected to the National Academy." Another wrote: "Make major gains in understanding the biological problems that interest me. Experience the richness that is my present life." Another woman told us: "I am bursting with projects and feel able to do them. Would like to spend all my time at it. Still happily married. Proud of how my children are turning out after all."

It is clear that they experience their present lives as rich and rewarding. These women are the scientists, lawyers, and doctors of their cohort. They are passionately dedicated to their work and just as passionately dedicated to the well-being of their families. The joy and excitement they find in their work is evident in their recounting of the high points in their lives. The high points they describe are full of theses and books completed, grants received, and research breakthroughs. One woman wrote: "I love deciphering documents. . . . I love solving problems in my research. Also finding the right way to state conclusions and marshal evidence."[1]

Women with Alternative Commitments

In their late 40s, women with alternative commitments reported that they felt somewhat different from others, internally oriented and unassuming. They were seen by others as warm and giving, concerned with philosophical and spiritual matters, aesthetically reactive, and introspective. They were also seen by others as seeking reassurance and arousing nurturance in others and having a somewhat complicated or hard-to-read personality. They reported that they felt comfortable in seeking support from others around them, that they had a hard time seeing projects through to completion, and that they found it difficult to work in situations with strict rules and expectations. They had an underlying feeling of being different or not fitting in, while at the same time engaging with others and enjoying and deriving reassurance from this engagement. They were private people and reported that they preferred to keep somewhat in the background in social situations.

These women did not buck the system in terms of marriage and family, quite the opposite in fact. These were the women who embraced the social roles for women of their upbringing. They married successful husbands and had children almost immediately after college. These women accepted wholeheartedly the message of their upbringing that women were to be, above all, nurturant and giving. They were dedicated to their roles as nurturers—of their husbands, their own children, and the world in general. One woman wrote, "My whole life became my kids once I had them—they were my career, my activity, etc. All my decisions were pretty much centered on them." It is also clear that they have derived tremendous enjoyment from their ability to nurture. Nevertheless, these women were also the idealists, the dreamers, and the adventurers of the cohort. One striking thing about them is that fully one-third of them have traveled extensively outside of the United States, living abroad for periods ranging from 1 year to 25 years (in contrast to less than 10% of the women in the other two groups). Many of them have taught abroad, particularly with the Peace Corps, and many of those who taught in the United States worked with underprivileged or special-needs children. They were a politically aware and active group of women; they had worked for either environmental concerns or the Great Society concerns of the 60s, such as poverty and education.

In terms of work, the women with alternative commitments have pursued roles and careers more traditionally acceptable for women. For the most part, they were either teachers or homemakers. There were also artists, librarians, nurses, writers, administrators, social workers, real estate agents, editors, and technicians among their numbers. Their work lives are particularly interesting because many of them seem to be still searching for a fulfilling career.

Their spiritual and philosophical interests are evident in their statements about the high points of their lives, as well as their future goals. One woman wrote "[I'm] always 'doing' something—[I'm] never bored with life—there is so much to learn and experience—[I] enjoy simple pleasures—nature, beauty, music." Another woman told us that her future goals were to "Make really beautiful and satisfying works of art. Learn some new stuff and continue to grow and be physically active. Expand my mental and spiritual repertoire/horizons." Yet another woman wrote: "Stay in touch with my sexuality and explore the spiritual aspects of the universe."

That they are introspective and internally oriented is also evident in their quotes. One woman, displaying her penchant for staying in the social background, told us: "I guess I see myself as an observer first and foremost." Another woman, displaying the introspectiveness characteristic of her group, wrote: "I hope to deepen my relationship with my lover, to resolve some of my intimacy issues so that I can be emotionally more available more often. I would wish to be able to see more clearly what is really important to me so that I can set priorities."

Women with Midlife Career Commitments

Women with midlife career commitments met their late 40s with feelings of confidence in themselves, assertiveness, self-sufficiency, and resourcefulness. They reported that they were able to accept others as they are, were functioning well intellectually, and felt a sense of self-realization or attainment of personal goals. For these women, there also seemed to be an underlying interest in fitting into society; they felt that they were similar to others, enjoyed being with other people, and had a strong drive to do well in areas where tasks and expectations were clearly defined. In addition, they were seen by others as warm and giving but also as feeling guilty, as being self-dramatizing and a little moody.

These women began life after college by embracing the roles for women that they had been raised in; they entered into marriage and motherhood very early on. They began as homemakers, teachers, and librarians but turned to a career commitment by the time they were in their early 40s. They often stayed home when their children were young and turned to a high-level career as they grew older, although this was not exclusively the case. They seem to have come to their later career commitment through different paths. For some women, their careers grew out of interests that they had had in college, which developed into a career over the course of their adult life. Some women, after taking a hiatus from the paid labor force to stay home with their children, decided that it was time to get back to the careers they had left. As one woman wrote: "I had taken time off to be with my children when they were young—it was time to get back to my field." Still others had a major shift in interest and decided to pursue that interest. For example, one of the women wrote: "[At age 36 I] realized I'd always wanted to be a doctor. Husband encouraged me. Prepared, applied, went to med school. Graduate next year. Never happier!"

The women's movement was very important to these women as a group. They were significantly more likely to endorse it as personally meaningful than were the other two groups.[2] For some of them, the women's movement probably came along at a time when they were floundering in their engagement of the traditional role for women. The women's movement allowed them to pursue high-level careers they would not have otherwise pursued. For example, many of these women acquired their advanced degrees between 1973 and 1976. One woman, commenting on the influences in her life, wrote: "[The] women's movement taught me that I could be a doer and not a helper and opened lots of institutional doors." Another woman explicitly stated that the women's movement was responsible for her career change: "Women's movement and political activism of the 60s led me to law school." The women's movement also seemed to play a part in the self-development and self-understanding of these women. One woman wrote: "Going through the women's movement and gaining, through

404

it, an understanding of my struggles with self-esteem, marriage, career, etc." Yet another woman told us: "The whole body of feminist litera- ture . . . reshaped sense of self and possibilities, sense of who I am and how important we are (women, teachers, mothers). I feel very good about self now—not possible 10 years ago or without feminist books and community." Thus, these women entered adulthood with an ac- ceptance of the notion that women should be nurturant of others but then often found this nurturance to be at the expense of their own self-realization and fulfillment.

These women were more likely to have been divorced by midlife than the other two groups. A complete change of career and lifestyle subsequent to divorce (either at their own or their husband's initiative) is a common story among these women. When telling us of the high points in her life, one woman wrote: "Having the courage to pull out of dead-end marriage and seek full-time employment . . . receiving post-doctoral fellowship to do fascinating research."

It seems that the road along the way to their change has been a bit rocky, at least for some. Changes in themselves and their lives due to the influence of the women's movement, divorce, or other factors led them to renegotiate their social roles and their own performance of those roles. They struggled with their new role and their older ones as well. One woman summed this up perfectly when telling of the high points in her life, saying: "Going to graduate school . . . I only wish it weren't complicated by husband's job difficulties . . . I'd like a chance to concentrate on myself . . . it's hard in middle age when there are so many other demands."

Regardless of whether the path to change was rocky or smooth, how- ever, these women loved the change, and the sense of accomplishment and pride they felt in making and completing the career change success- fully is evident in their telling of their high points. One woman wrote: "Law school graduation. I did it by myself, for myself; I finished it and I did well." Another woman told us that a high point in her life was "Starting own law practice and having it succeed, in a very over-lawyered city." Another told us: "Finishing my Ph.D. after a seven-year period was wonderful. My dissertation research was satisfying and the finished product one for which I felt considerable pride." They obviously enjoyed their new roles and the return to school that most of their career turns meant. For example, one woman told us that her high points were "Birth of my children—I loved the process of giving life. Studying—ac- quainting myself with new ideas was a wonderful adventure."

These women, like the alternative women, displayed a somewhat philosophical and spiritual inclination in the comments in their files. Telling us of her future goals, one woman wrote: "Meditate deeply, do work well, give good guidance to my children and find great peace and contentment from within." Another told us: "I would set my life on a path toward greater integration and less fragmentation, . . . more creativity, less 'sophistication,' and more inner-directedness."

Connections between Life Paths and Personality

When thinking about the personality differences among the three groups of women, we were struck by the interiority of women with alternative commitments (the abundance of their interest both in internal processes and interpersonal life), the exteriority of women with continuous career commitments (their external, task-oriented, no-nonsense approach to life), and the combination of these two dimensions in women with midlife career commitments. There are a number of possible explanations for these findings. One explanation is that the women who never made career commitments were always more interested in interior life, were spiritually and philosophically oriented to begin with; and this type of woman would find it extremely hard to cope with the demands of male-dominated, fast-track careers. These careers often demand a kind of nonemotional, extraverted stance, and because of the pervasiveness of institutional sexism, these fields are particularly hard on women if they do not or cannot meet these standards. We would apply this interpretation the same way for the other two groups: they were to begin with these types of people (extraverted or a combination), which allowed them to make career commitments early and later, respectively.

Another interesting possibility is that there is a developmental component to the personality differences we found among these women which is related to their career commitment patterns. It is possible that for the women who made early career commitments and continued them into midlife, a focus on feelings, interior life, and interpersonal relationships was simply not feasible if they were to continue their career commitments with no consequences for their well-being. This interpretation would mean that being continuously career committed shaped and helped to develop the exteriority that we saw in them at midlife. For the alternative women, then, not being career committed early or later would mean that the women could develop complex and absorbing interior and interpersonal lives, because their life pattern did not demand an external stance of them. For the women with midlife career commitments, however, not having a career early would allow them to develop the focus on internal life; becoming career committed later would demand that they develop some of the exteriority that we also saw in them. Because we only have measures of their personality at midlife, it is impossible to know which of these interpretations is correct.

However, there are clues in other work that there may be some developmental component to the findings we have reported. As previously noted, Kohn and Schooler (1978, 1982) have longitudinal evidence that men's job conditions actually do affect their personalities in adulthood. Ravenna Helson and her colleagues (Helson et al., 1984) found that women who graduated from college in 1958 and 1960 and who made lasting commitments to marriage and children increased on the responsibility, self-control, and tolerance scales of the CPI by midlife. They concluded that "Increased responsibility, tolerance and nurturance can be seen as effective adaptations to the roles of wife and mother" (p. 1085). In addition, they found no differences at age 22 between women who made career commitments later and women who did not on the CPI scales of independence, dominance, or intellectual efficiency. Moreover, Helson and Picano (1990) found that between the ages of 21 and 43, women who were in the paid labor force increased on both the independence and dominance scales of the CPI, whereas those women who were homemakers did not. These findings, along with ours, lend support to the interpretation that the commitments we make in life help to shape and determine our personality.

FUTURE DIRECTIONS

These findings suggest a very real connection between life paths or experiences and personality characteristics. In fact, all three of these groups of women seem to have characteristics commensurate with their different life experiences and life paths. In this chapter we focused solely on women's career commitment patterns. Clearly, career commitments are not the only kind of commitments that people make throughout their lives; nor are they made in a vacuum, independent of the other commitments people already have, or plan to have, in their lives. In later analyses, we plan to examine the different patterns of other kinds of commitments that women make (i.e., relational, interpersonal, and avocational) and how these commitments may also be related to women's personality development. In addition, we plan to examine the interaction of all of these various kinds of commitment, their interplay, and their effect on women's lives. This last piece of work, though a complex and difficult undertaking, is crucial if we are to come to a better understanding of the connections between people's lives and their personality development.

ACKNOWLEDGMENTS

Our research was conducted with support from Boston University Graduate School, National Science Foundation Visiting Professorships for Women, the Society for the Psychological Study of Social Issues, and the University of Michigan Rackham Graduate School, as well as the MacArthur Foundation Network for Research on Successful Mid-life Development, and Radcliffe Research Support and Midlife Program Grants from the Henry A. Murray Research Center. We are grateful to the participants in the study for their generous contributions of time over the past eighteen years, to Ravenna Helson, Joan Ostrove, and Brent Roberts for comments on earlier drafts of this chapter, and to David Winter, Bill Peterson, Paul Wink, Lauren Duncan, Wendy Welsh, Linda Demo-Dannenberg, and Thomas Popoff for their helpful comments and untiring assistance.

NOTES

1. We are grateful to Ravenna Helson for her insightful comments about this particular group of women.

2. The women were asked to rate the women's movement (along with a number of other sociohistorical events ranging from the Depression to Three Mile Island) on a scale where 1 = little personally meaningful; 2 = somewhat personally meaningful; 3 = very personally meaningful. In addition, they were given space to write if it was particularly personally meaningful with regard to all other events; and thus 4 = particularly personally meaningful. Results showed that $M = 3.21$ for women with midlife career commitments; $M = 2.88$ for women with continuous career commitments; $M = 2.40$ for women with alternative commitments; $F = 5.22$, $df = 2$, $p < .01$.

REFERENCES

Abramson, J. H. (1966). The Cornell Medical Index as an epidemiological tool. *American Journal of Public Health, 56,* 287–298.

Ackerman, R. J. (1990). Career developments and transitions of middle-aged women. *Psychology of Women Quarterly, 14,* 513–530.

Baruch, R. (1967). The achievement motive in women: Implications for career development. *Journal of Personality and Social Psychology, 5,* 260–267.

Baruch, G., Barnett, R., & Rivers, C. (1983). *Lifeprints: New patterns of love and work for today's women.* New York: McGraw Hill.

Block, J. (1961). *The Q-sort method in personality assessment and psychiatric research.* Springfield, IL: Charles C. Thomas.

Block, J., & Hann, N. (1971). *Lives through time.* Berkeley, CA: Bancroft Books.

Chodorow, N. (1978). *The reproduction of mothering.* Berkeley: University of California Press.

Crosby, F. (Ed.). (1987). *Spouse, parent, worker: On gender and multiple roles.* New Haven, CT: Yale University Press.

Erikson, E. (1964). *Insight and responsibility.* New York: W. W. Norton.

Erikson, E. (1968). *Identity, youth, and crisis.* New York: W. W. Norton.

Erikson, E. (1982). *The life cycle completed.* New York: W. W. Norton.

Gergen, M. (1990). Finished at 40: Women's development within the patriarchy. *Psychology of Women Quarterly, 14,* 471–493.

Gerson, K. (1985). *Hard choices: How women decide about work, career, and motherhood.* Berkeley: University of California Press.

Gilligan, C. (1982). *In a different voice.* Cambridge: Harvard University Press.

Gough, H. G. (1987). *California Psychological Inventory Administrator's Guide.* Palo Alto, CA: Consulting Psychologists Press.

Gough, H. G. (1989). The California Psychological Inventory. In C. S. Newmark (Ed.), *Major psychological assessment instruments* (Vol. 2, pp. 67–98). Boston: Allyn and Bacon.

Gough, H. G. (1990). The California Psychological Inventory. In C. E. Watkins and V. L. Campbell (Eds.), *Testing in counseling practice* (pp. 37–62). Hillsdale, NJ: Erlbaum.

Gould, R. L. (1978). *Transformations: Growth and change in adult life.* New York: Simon & Schuster.

Gurin, G., Veroff, J., & Feld, S. C. (1960). *American view their mental health.* New York: Basic Books.

Helson, R. (1992). Women's difficult times and the rewriting of the life story. *Psychology of Women Quarterly, 16,* 331–347.

Helson, R., Mitchell, V., & Moane, G. (1984). Personality and patterns of adherence and non-adherence to the social clock. *Journal of Personality and Social Psychology, 46,* 1079–1096.

Helson, R., & Moane, G. (1987). Personality change in women from college to midlife. *Journal of Personality and Social Psychology, 53,* 176–186.

Helson, R., & Picano, J. (1990). Is the traditional role bad for women? *Journal of Personality and Social Psychology, 59,* 311–320.

Hollingshead, A., & Redlich, C. (1956). Social class and mental illness: A community study. New York: Wiley.

Hornstein, G. A. (1986). The structuring of identity among midlife women as a function of their degree of involvement in employment. *Journal of Personality, 54,* 551–575.

Josselson, R. (1987). *Finding herself: Pathways to identity development in women.* San Francisco: Jossey-Bass.

Kohn, M. L., & Schooler, C. (1978). The reciprocal effects of the substantive complexity of work and intellectual flexibility: A longitudinal assessment. *American Journal of Sociology, 85,* 66–94.

Kohn, M. L., & Schooler, C. (1982). Job conditions and personality: A longitudinal assessment of their reciprocal effects. *American Journal of Sociology, 87,* 1257–1286.

Lanning, K., & Gough, H. G. (1991). Shared variance in the California Psychological Inventory and the California Q-set. *Journal of Personality and Social Psychology, 60,* 596–606.

Levinson, D. (1978). *The seasons of a man's life.* New York: Ballantine Books.

McNair, D. M., Lorr, M., & Doppleman, L. F. (1971). *Profile of Mood States.* San Diego: Educational and Industrial Testing Service.

Miller, J. B. (1986). *Toward a new psychology of women.* Boston: Beacon Press.

Moen, P., & Smith, K. R. (1986). Women at work: Commitment and behavior over the life course. *Sociological Forum, 1,* 450–475.

Stewart, A. J. (1975). *Longitudinal prediction from personality to life outcomes among college-educated women.* Unpublished doctoral dissertation, Harvard University.

Stewart, A. J. (1978). A longitudinal study of coping styles of self-defining and socially defined women. *Journal of Consulting and Clinical Psychology, 46,* 1079–1084.

Stewart, A. J. (1980). Personality and situation in the prediction of women's life patterns. *Psychology of Women Quarterly, 5,* 195–206.

Stewart, A. J., & Healy, J. M., Jr. (1989). Linking individual development and social changes. *American Psychologist, 44,* 30–42.

Stewart, A. J., & Salt, P. (1981). Life-stress, lifestyles, depression, and illness in adult women. *Journal of Personality and Social Psychology, 40,* 1063–1069.

Stewart, A. J., & Vandewater, E. A. (1993). Career and family clocks in a transitional cohort. In K. Hulbert & D. Schuster (Eds.), *Women's lives through time: Educated American women of the twentieth century* (pp. 235–258). San Francisco: Jossey-Bass.

Vaillant, G. (1977). *Adaptation to life.* Boston: Little, Brown.

Veroff, J., Douvan, E., & Kulka, R. (1981). *The inner American: A self-portrait from 1957 to 1976.* New York: Basic Books.

Wink, P. (1991). Self and object-directedness in adult women. *Journal of Personality, 59,* 769–791.

Zung, W. W. K. (1965). A self-rating depression scale. *Archives of General Psychiatry, 12,* 63–70.

Zung, W. W. K. (1971). A rating instrument for anxiety disorders. *Psychosomatics, 12,* 371–379.

An Individual Differences Approach to Midlife Career Adjustment: An Exploratory Study

Frederick T. L. Leong and Kristin A. Boyle

Freud's often-quoted reply to the question of the indicators of mental health illustrates the centrality of work as a major dimension in the arena of human development. Few would argue with Freud about the importance of "the ability to love and to work" as crucial dimensions of psychosocial maturity. Problems with work are of great interest to vocational psychologists, and yet this area of psychology, with a few exceptions, is generally lacking in longitudinal studies of career development (Herr & Cramer, 1988).

One area that has generated a considerable amount of research interest in the last two decades is the notion of a midlife crisis and its impact on an individual's career development (Herr & Cramer, 1988). This area also suffers from a lack of longitudinal emphasis. The majority of existing studies on midlife career adjustment have been cross-sectional in design (Clausen, 1981). While it is recognized that designing and executing longitudinal studies can be very costly, the availability of longitudinal data sets at the Henry Murray Research Center at Radcliffe College and other archives argues against the building of our career development theories on mainly cross-section data. In this chapter we use the E. L. Kelly Longitudinal Study data set at the Murray Research Center to examine the predictors of midlife career adjustment.

MIDLIFE CAREER ADJUSTMENT

Midlife career adjustment can be conceptualized in a number of ways. Indeed, job stress, job dissatisfaction, burnout, midlife crises that lead to midcareer change, and reentry into the job market for homemakers have all been examined as indicators of midlife career adjustment in the popular press (Lofquist & Dawis, 1984). At the broadest level, we will concern ourselves with the explication of midlife crises that lead to career change. According to Campbell and Heffernan (1983), "mid-life crises refers to the questioning of values, attitudes, life-styles, and generally a re-assessment of personal goals during the

411

midyears 35–55. As a result of this re-assessment, many people have undergone significant changes especially in their vocational behavior. Jobs that were once satisfying no longer seem to be attractive. Generally, the crisis is understood to be a period of restlessness in personal life and career status" (p. 225).

Thus, one operationalization of midlife career adjustment is job stability. Those individuals who hold their jobs for a considerable length of time are generally considered well-adjusted when compared with those individuals who hold many different jobs in that same period of time. However, in recognition of the potential lateral and vertical movement of individuals across jobs but within similar types of occupations, career consistency will also be examined. That is, occupation choices that differ greatly at midlife from those at initial entry into the marketplace (e.g., a lawyer who becomes a truck driver) may also indicate a midlife crisis.

We used job satisfaction as an additional operationalization of midlife career adjustment for two reasons. First, from a theoretical standpoint, career or work adjustment exists when the worker is satisfied with the work situation. For example, in their Theory of Work Adjustment (TWA), Lofquist and Dawis (1984) advocate work satisfaction as the primary indicator of work adjustment. Second, the restlessness experienced by those undergoing a midlife crisis—with respect to values, attitudes, lifestyles, and goals—may not be directly reflected in their vocational behavior. In other words, job stability and career consistency may not be sensitive enough to reflect the construct of career adjustment, in that environmental events (e.g., the lack of alternative jobs for which the individual is qualified) may prevent the individual from translating cognition and emotion into behavior.

Midlife Career Change and Development

Conceptual underpinnings. Based in part on a growth of interest in gerontology and adult development within the field of psychology, the development of theoretical underpinnings of career change has been a response to changing demographics and the greying of America. For instance, Britton (1970) estimated that about one-half of the U.S. labor force was over 45. In addition, both Kelleher (1973) and Saben (1967) reported that 40 percent of job changers were over 35 years old. In short, the middle-aged and the elderly constitute a substantial portion of the career or job changers. In fact, career change is so common among the middle-aged that the majority of the studies on second careers have focused on what has now come to be referred to as the "mid-life career change" (Thomas, 1975; Work in America Institute, 1978).

The development of the aging perspective or adult development focus within psychology has also provided a theoretical orientation from which to examine aspects of career change (see Gould, 1972; Levinson, Darrow, Klein, Levinson, & McKee, 1974; Vaillant & MacArthur, 1972, for examples). See also excellent reviews of the coming of age of adult development as a field in its own right (e.g., Fozard & Popkin, 1978; Rhodes, 1983).

Empirical evidence. The development of empirical research on career change, on the other hand, has been less promising than the development of the theoretical underpinnings. In reviewing the literature on midlife career adjustment and midlife career change, one is struck by the scarcity of research studies. Holland, Magoon, and Spokane (1981), in their review of the literature, observed that "interest in mid-career change has become strong, but this interest has not been associated with an equally strong research interest" (p. 290). In a 1973 ERIC bibliography on career education, there were only two references pertaining to career change. This is true even of the dozen or so career counseling or career development texts in the market. One noteworthy exception is Herr and Cramer (1979), which provides a compelling argument about why so little attention has been paid to adult career development.

> Until fairly recently, anyone interested in career guidance might well have wondered if there is a career life after adolescence. Early work in career development and behavior focused on factors and processes leading to the initial choice of an occupation and rarely addressed adult career development. Further, researchers and theorists were grounded in the specialties of child and adolescent psychology and ignored that portion of the career life span subsequent to exploration and initial choice. (p. 233)

Other contributing factors include the reality that most researchers and theorists have been based in universities, where access to college and high school samples for study (not people in middle age) was most convenient and expedient. In addition, funding for research on career development processes was often provided by organizations that preferred research about high school and college students, such as Holland's programmatic research at the American College Testing (ACT) program and Krumboltz's recent research with the Educational Testing Service (ETS).

Fortunately, some correction to these problems is under way in the field of career change. Although not extensive, empirical studies of midlife career changers are beginning to emerge in the career development literature (Bartol, 1981; Fretz & Leong, 1982; Garbin & Stover, 1978; Swanson, 1992). Even so, these studies are not entirely systematic and often treat very complex problems in rather superficial ways. Goldstein (1974) has pointed out the ways in which some of these studies "emphasize the ignorance about the characteristics of our second-career population and about the relationship of particular methods to various required behaviors. As long as all behaviors, individuals, and jobs are treated as part of one large package, the picture will remain ambiguous" (p. 208).

The available literature about midlife career change typically addresses one of two major questions. First, a recurring debate about the midlife career crisis concerns whether it is an unavoidable developmental stage or a personal experience that is by no means universal (Farrell & Rosenberg, 1981; Levinson, 1978). Second, various studies have been conducted to discover what motivates individuals to make major career changes at midlife (Herr & Cramer, 1988). Some of these focus on the environment as the source of motivation for midlife career problems (Hall & Associates, 1986), while others focus on the individual (Osherson, 1980). Unsurprisingly, a number of earlier studies sought primarily to describe the phenomenon of interest.

What do these studies on adult development tell us about midlife career development? Levinson et al. (1974), in a four-year study of the lives of 40 middle-aged men, found that their subjects shared common concerns such as anxiety over aging and death, a questioning of the basis of their lives, and a need to be affirmed by society through success in their careers. The men also underwent a common experience of taking stock of their lives, of realizing and accepting the disparity between their early goals and their present achievements. Finally, around age 45, they entered a new stage of stability and began to emphasize those things in their lives that were fulfilling and became reconciled to those that were not. (See Brim, 1976, for a similar stage model.)

Horrocks and Mussman (1970) examined responses to a questionnaire from over 1000 teachers and other employees of a school district and discovered that individuals in their early forties shared a general feeling of dissatisfaction with life and exhibited a marked drop in self-concept which revived again in the late forties, whereas Thomas's investigation (Bischof, 1969) uncovered a trough of "boredom" in the lives of his subjects between the ages of 40 and 50. These men expressed a longing for a change in their lives but were fearful of the consequences of such a change to others close to them.

Gould (1972) questioned 524 male and female subjects aged 19 to 60 in order to determine their attitude toward life at various ages. He found that those aged 35–43 characteristically asked themselves questions such as, "Have I done the right thing? Is there time to change?" Among those aged 44–50, however, he found more acceptance of life as it is, a resignation to reality. In a related study, Henry (1961) examined a group of 45 male executives for evidence of changes in attitudes, values, and self-concept with age. For the group in their thirties, success was found to be all-important. Thus, identity lay in the company, and inner feelings and personal desires tended to be denied when they conflicted with the organization. The older group, in their forties, however, questioned company policy and wondered about the value of success. They doubted their choice of career and were inclined to wish they had chosen work that focused more on interpersonal relations. This latter group demonstrated the greatest conflicts in values. The executives in their fifties usually resolved value conflicts in favor of personal needs rather than company requirements. They tended to be contemplative and to see themselves as a guide for others.

Entine (1977) provided a similar but broader taxonomy of why individuals make midcareer changes by examining whether reasons were internal or external and whether problems were unanticipated or anticipated (Herr & Cramer, 1979). Sinick (1975) examined 26 possible motivations for causes of career shifts, including, for example, original aspirations not met by career, purpose of first career accomplished, inadequate outlet for creativity, desire to implement avocational interests, work pressures and deadlines too demanding, personality conflicts with supervisor or coworkers, and so forth. As with most theoretical models, there are considerable overlaps between the taxonomies formulated by the different models. They reveal, however, the amazing complexity of the career change phenomenon. Herr and Cramer (1979), in presenting a typology of "corporate drop-outs," hinted at this complexity: "Adults are indeed experienced-based. Changes result mainly from life experiences, and thus there may never be a uniform adult career psychology. In just a small sample of corporate 'drop-out' career-shifters, Thomas et al. (1976) [Thomas, Mlea, Robbins, & Harvey, 1976] uncovered a large number of diverse reasons for career change" (pp. 236–237). Clearly, the reasons are multiply determined. Brim (1976, cited by Herr & Cramer, 1988) hypothesized that midlife career change is a function of an aspiration-achievement gap:

> The aspirations in life that men set for themselves are primarily expressed through the institution of work. Over the course of the working life, from entry to the mid-life period, it is likely that although aspirations may be adjusted downward on occasion, one usually believes there is enough time left for the desired level of achievement to be reached in future years. But during mid-life most American males must adjust their career aspirations of earlier years downward to fit current reality. A man may be told that he has risen as high as he can go in his place of work; that his present position must be accepted by him as the achievement level for his lifetime (Brim, 1976, p. 3).

This same aspiration-achievement gap for many men at midlife is echoed by Hall (1986), who identified a common set of themes in the midcareer experience: "perceived constriction of career opportunity, organizational maturity (slow growth, no growth, or decline), ambiguity and uncertainty about one's future career role, midcareer change experienced as disjunctive and individualized, . . . shift in balance from work roles to personal roles, increased connectedness between career transitions and life events" (p. 128).

Similarly, Hurrell, McLaney, and Murphy (1990) examined the stresses experienced by 6,000 postal workers in early, middle, or late career stages. They found that underuse of abilities was more strongly related to job dissatisfaction and somatic complaints for the midcareer workers than for the early and late career workers.

Williams and Savickas (1990) examined the career concerns of workers at midlife in order to assess career continuity and change. The career concerns generated by 136 workers presented six factors, three of which closely matched those presented by Super (1957), that is, keeping up with new developments, struggling to hold on, and shifting focus. One factor was concerned with "preparing for retirement," which was also consistent with Super's developmental model but inconsistent with career maintenance. Neither the "continuing education" nor the "questioning future direction and goals" matched Super's description of midlife career development and appeared to support some of the findings mentioned earlier about the unique adjustment problems encountered by individuals at midlife.

On the other hand, some studies have found that midlife career crises are by no means universal. For example, Clausen (1981), in his study of the occupational careers of men at midlife from the classic Oakland Growth Study and the Guidance Study (see Elder, 1983), found that the majority of the men were quite successful occupationally and quite satisfied with their jobs. Roughly 60% of the men in Clausen's study (1981) had achieved occupational positions that were higher than those of their fathers. However, social class and personality differences were found to be significant moderators of occupational attainment and work adjustment. In a separate study, Kohn and Schooler (1983) also found that social class significantly influenced the occupational attainment and work orientation of men.

Taken together, these studies seem to reveal a pattern whereby *some* individuals in middle age experience some kind of transition in their adjustment to work. Some of the developmental tasks confronting these individuals included reexamination of values, career direction, and accomplishments. Individuals within this transition are then particularly vulnerable to changing careers because of frustrations and dissatisfactions. They are not abnormal or maladjusted individuals but are faced with a new level of challenge with respect to their work. As shown in these studies, this pattern of midlife transition problems was found across different samples and different occupational groups, attesting to the generality of the phenomenon, at least for some men. We do not know, however, whether these patterns reflect ongoing dissatisfaction or whether they emerge in middle age. Only longitudinal data will address this issue.

What the literature on midlife career development does suggest is that individual differences play a significant role in determining whether a person experiences career adjustment difficulties in midlife. Different authors have identified various personality differences (i.e., individual differences) as significant moderators of these difficulties (e.g., Clausen, 1981; Kohn & Schooler, 1983). Clausen (1981) found that certain items in the Block personality Q-sort, which were administered during adolescence, significantly differentiated the men that were high from those that were low in their occupational success at midlife. These personality items were primarily concerned with intellectual capacity/interest and what Clausen (1981) has referred to as items indexing the "Protestant ethic" (e.g., ambitious, productive, dependable, and not self-indulgent). Indeed, Kohn and Schooler (1983) have demonstrated that there is a complex and reciprocal relationship between personality and job characteristics underlying individuals' work adjustment. In their analysis of the relationships between social stratification and occupational attainment, Kohn and Schooler (1983) concluded that "much of the variation in the men's values and orientations results from idiosyncratic personal experience, unrelated to the positions men occupy in the general social structure" (p. 32). Therefore, the examination of how salient individual differences account for midlife career adjustment problems seems to be the most fruitful avenue to pursue in the present study.

Gender issues. Traditionally, research focusing on midlife career development and change has tended to ignore the experiences of women. Furthermore, if women are included in a mixed sample of workers, little attention is given to the fact that the kinds of career patterns and changes characteristic of women present another level of complexity. Thus, what little is known about women's work adjustment is often contradictory (see Betz & Fitzgerald, 1987).

Such complexities stem from the quite different experiences of men and women in the work environment. For example, employment patterns differ for the two genders. At least in the past, women's lives tended to be organized around events in the family life cycle, so that unlike those of their male counterparts, their careers were often interrupted and then resumed or terminated (James, 1989). Super (1957), in his Career Pattern Study, for example, formulated the following classification system of different career patterns among women: stable homemaking career, conventional career, stable working career, double-track career, interrupted career, unstable career, and multitrial career.

Not only do women interrupt careers to take care of children, but they may also do so when they find themselves being passed over for advances by less-experienced men (Gerson, 1985). That is, sex discrimination affects the career advancement of women (Swanson & Tokar, 1991), and thus their career development and change patterns. This tendency may be particularly exacerbated for women employed in occupations traditionally dominated by males (James, 1989). Betz and Fitzgerald (1987) made the following observation about women's work adjustment: "In most objective senses, employed women as a group are less successful than employed men. They make considerably less money and are concentrated on the lower end of the organizational hierarchy. Often, they must cope with the attitudinal bias of coworkers, superiors, and subordinates, which creates barriers to their organizational achievement." (p. 185).

Moreover, women's reasons for working may differ from those of males and thus differentially impact the frequency and pattern of career changes for men and women. In particular, in the past women may have been more constrained than their male counterparts from seeking jobs that fulfilled interpersonal needs or mastery needs rather than monetary needs.

Finally, the lack of longitudinal studies of women's career development adds another layer of complexity to this picture. Specifically, because of the broad social revolution in expectations and norms for women's behavior (work and nonwork) that has occurred relatively recently, as well as slower, more gradual changes that have impacted cohorts of women differentially (i.e., younger women may have experienced the effects of such changes more dramatically than their older counterparts), longitudinal studies are sorely needed to allow researchers to pinpoint change due to developmental effects alone (Stewart, Lykes, & LaFrance, 1982). That is, as compared to those of men, the experiences of women in the workplace have undergone such rapid change that the examination of career development and change from initial entry to midlife necessitates longitudinal research.

Given both the importance of gender differences in the experience and meaning of work and the contrast in social change experienced by the two genders, we will examine the results for men and women separately.

Personality Theories and Career Development

Previous research, although not longitudinal or focused on the midlife stage, has already demonstrated a significant relationship between personality factors and career interests and adjustment (Kohn & Schooler, 1983; Osipow, 1983). We will use personality variables as the operationalization of individual differences in accounting for variations in midlife career adjustment. Within the field of vocational psychology, Holland's theory of careers is certainly one of the most widely used and researched today. In one estimate, Holland's theoretical constructs have been tested in over 450 studies (Weinrach & Srebalus,

1990). As a person-environmental theory, Holland's model focuses on types of people and their fit with different types of work environment (Walsh & Holland, 1992). Holland believes that most people can be classified as one of six basic personality types (realistic, investigative, artistic, social, enterprising, or conventional), and that a person's vocational interests reflect this typology. Research using Holland's theory has found that his personality typology is significantly correlated to other personality models. For example, Costa, McCrae, and Holland (1984), in using the NEO Personality Inventory (NEO-PI) on a community-based sample of adults, found that vocational personality patterns as measured by Holland's model were significantly and differentially related to the Extraversion and Openness dimension but not the Neuroticism dimension. In a more recent study, Goh and Leong (1993) found that Holland's theory of vocational personality types was significantly related to Eysenck's model of personality. They found that Eysenck's Psychoticism scale was significantly predictive of interests in Realistic (positively) and Social (negatively) type occupations, while Eysenck's Extraversion scale was much more associated with Holland's Enterprising than Social type. Interestingly, they also found that Holland's construct of Differentiation (i.e., having a more highly differentiated interest profile) was significantly predicted by Eysenck's Neuroticism (positively) and Extraversion (negatively) scales.

According to Holland's model, there are also six kinds of environments that accompany the six personality types. They are also realistic, investigative, artistic, social, enterprising, and conventional. Holland contends that "people search for environments that will let them exercise their skills and abilities, express their attitudes and values, and take on agreeable problems and roles" (Holland, cited in Weinrach & Srebalus, 1990). This means that people prefer their environmental types and their personality types to match. Finally, Holland's theory proposes that people's behavior, vocational success, stability, and satisfaction are determined by the interaction between their personality and their environment. This leads into Holland's concept of congruence.

Congruence is high when people's environment is identical or similar to their personality type. When this happens, people should exhibit more satisfaction than when their person-environment types are incongruent. For example, Wiggins, Lederer, Salkowe, and Rys (1983) tested 247 teachers to determine whether job satisfaction was greater for those whose area of specialty (environment) matched their personality type as measured by Holland's Vocational Preference Inventory. The results of this study did support Holland's theory. Thus, teachers who were classified as artistic reported greater job satisfaction if they taught an artistic subject, like English, than if they taught something conventional, like Economics.

The concept of congruence has been the focus of a great deal of the research within Holland's theory. Previous researchers have found congruence to be a good predictor of a number of variables. Specifically, in a review, Spokane (1985) examined 63 studies that used congruence as a variable. Among the variables found to be related to congruence were career stability, satisfaction, achievement in the workplace, and vocational maturity. Of particular interest to many researchers is the relationship between congruence and job satisfaction, which was well supported in the Spokane review (1985). Of the 63 studies reviewed, 17 tested the relationships between person-environment congruence and job satisfaction. Spokane (1985) found that 11 of the studies provided support for Holland's theory, indicating that person-environment congruence is predictive of job satisfaction. Four of the studies had mixed results, and only 2 studies showed a negative relationship between congruence and job satisfaction. Hence, past research gives strong support for Holland's theory. In addition to the support provided by Spokane, a more recent review of vocational research by Fitzgerald and Rounds (1989) listed 2 more studies supporting Holland's theory. Another recent review (Meier, 1991) also found studies that supported Holland's proposition about the positive relationship between congruence and job satisfaction.

Thus, the evidence supporting Holland's theories appears to be quite strong. However, the support is by no means universal. As mentioned earlier, the review by Spokane (1985) did list six studies in which either a mixed relationship was found between congruence and job satisfaction or no significant relationship was found. Although much of the research reviewed indicates that there is a positive relationship between Holland's person-environment congruence and job satisfaction, the fact that some mixed results and some negative results have been found suggests that further research is needed. For example, Heesacker, Howe, and Elliott (1988) found that Holland's model was not predictive of job satisfaction for a group of clothing factory workers. Also, Mazen (1989) found that women and minorities may be congruent in their occupational preferences and not their actual occupational choices because of employment barriers. The question becomes when and with whom does Holland's model of career choice and job satisfaction not work?

Holland's model is primarily a trait-and-factor theory that ignores developmental contructs such as age. Very little of the research on the relationship between congruence and job satisfaction has considered age or developmental level as a variable. The primary focus has been on testing congruence in educational environments and work environments, assuming that age or developmental level has little or no impact on the relationship between congruence and job satisfaction. Whereas some of Holland and Gottfredson's (1981) criticisms of developmental models of career choice are valid, the validity of Holland's model across developmental stages should still be examined. This is particularly important given that many of the studies supporting Holland's model have been conducted on college samples and young adult samples.

Indeed, there is a significant body of literature to suggest that something special occurs in the career experiences of men at midlife (Campbell & Heffernan, 1983; Entine, 1977; Murphy & Burck, 1976). One of our purposes is to test the validity of Holland's theory along a specific section of the developmental continuum, specifically midlife. If Holland's theory is valid, then congruence for men and women would be as predictive of job satisfaction at midlife as it is for other age groups. If the model does not hold for men and women at midlife, the results would suggest that development level may serve as a moderating, if not limiting, factor in Holland's model. This aspect of the study is also theoretically significant because it seeks to test the predictive ability of Holland's theory for midlife career adjustment. Such a test or developmental extension is very important, since much of the supporting research for Holland's theories and similar ones has been based primarily on college students and has tended not to use a longitudinal design.

PURPOSE

The purpose of this exploratory study is to use the E. L. Kelly Longitudinal Study data set at the Murray Research Center to identify major personality and individual differences variables that predict midlife career adjustment. These variables, if proved to be longitudinally predictive of midlife career problems, may become important markers for differentiating persons who are likely to encounter significant difficulties at midlife from others that are successful at midlife development as measured by job satisfaction, job stability, and career consistency.

The significance of this study is that it will be a *longitudinal* study of the predictors of midlife career adjustment; much of existing knowledge is based on cross-sectional studies. However, it should be acknowledged that although the data set is longitudinal, it is vulnerable to cohort and period effects.

We will also test an individual-differences approach to midlife adjustment rather than assume that a midlife crisis is an inevitable developmental outcome. We hope that the study will identify the individual differences markers that predict successful or unsuccessful midlife adjustment in the career sphere. Using the theoretical framework of Lofquist and Dawis's (1984) Theory of Work Adjustment, we will determine those personality and individual differences variables, such as values, that are significantly predictive of midlife career adjustment. The personality variables to be tested as predictors of midlife career adjustment include Holland's personality model of career choice and adjustment and the Bernreuter Personality Inventory (BPI). Also included is the Personality Rating Scale (PRS) developed by Kelly (1940). One of our primary theses is that individual differences, in the form of measured personality differences and values, will be significantly predictive of different career adjustment outcomes at midlife.

METHOD

Data set

The Kelly data set provides an invaluable opportunity to address this problem because of several of its major features. First, it is one of a few longitudinal data sets that collected data on career development. Second, it collected data on a large sample ($N = 600$) with well-established psychological measures of personality and individual differences. Third, it includes the Strong Vocational Interest Inventory (SVII), which is the best established and most widely used measure of career development (Campbell, 1971). Finally, it collected data from the sample at Time 2 during the midlife period of these individuals.

Sample

The sample consists of 300 engaged couples in their early 20s ($N = 600$) who were enlisted during 1935–1938 to participate in a longitudinal study of marital compatability (Kelly, 1955). The original plan was for a 7-year study beginning with a comprehensive battery of tests and annual follow-up questionnaires. The disruption of civilian activities due to the World War II and other factors resulted instead in a

20-year follow-up study of this sample during 1953–1954, when the participants were in their 40s. The follow-up consisted of retesting on five of the seven psychological tests and detailed questions about their marriages.

Instruments and Variables

The independent variables or predictors come from three of the instruments administered to the sample at Time 1 (1935–1938). The first instrument is the 36-item Personality Rating Scale (PRS) developed by Kelly (1940). The second instrument, the Bernreuter Personality Inventory (BPI), is used to provide an estimate of an individual's Neurotic Tendency, Self-Sufficiency, Introversion-Extraversion, Dominance, Self-Confidence, and Sociability. The third instrument, the Allport-Vernon Scale of Values (AV), is used to provide an estimate of an individuals' values along the following dimensions: Theoretical, Economic, Aesthetic, Social, Political, and Religious.

Two of the scales on the Bernreuter Personality Inventory (BPI) have been labeled in a counterintuitive fashion. For example, whereas a high score on the BPI Neurotic Tendency scale indicates a higher level of emotional instability, a high score on the BPI Sociability scale represents a high level of an asocial and solitary tendency. To avoid confusion and to make all the scales consistent in direction and meaning, we will refer to the counterintuitive scales as the Lack of Sociability (BPI Sociability) and the Lack of Self-Confidence (BPI Self-Confidence) scales.

It should be noted that while the original Personality Rating Scale (PAS; Kelly, 1940) consisted of 36 items, the version of the PRS in the public-access data tape consisted of only 10 items. However, we were able to derive composite scales from these 10 items using Conley's (1985) factor analyses of the 36-item version. More details about the PRS composites are presented in the Results section.

The dependent variables or criteria consist of several items related to job outcomes, such as job satisfaction. Another dependent variable comes from a recoding of the Strong Vocational Interest Inventory (SVII). The occupational interest scales of the SVII were recoded according to Holland's (1985) theoretical typology of vocational types (i.e., Realistic, Investigative, Artistic, Social, Enterprising, and Conventional). Two undergraduate research assistants were trained to do the recoding. Checked at the beginning and the end of the coding process, the interrater reliability ranged from .57 for the second code to .95 for the first code. Holland's (1985) theory of vocational choices is based on a person-environment interaction model with optimal fit producing the best outcomes. Descriptions of the six types of work personalities and work environments can be found in Holland (1985, pp. 19–23). By applying a commonly used coding procedure (Gottfredson, Holland, and Ogawa, 1982), one can estimate individuals' dominant types from their high-scoring occupational interest scales on the SVII. Indeed, Holland's theoretical model has been incorporated into the current version of the Strong Interest Inventory (Campbell & Holland, 1972). Although the Strong in the current data set does not have the Holland variables available, they were created by recoding using the dictionary of Holland occupational codes (Gottfredson, Holland, & Ogawa, 1982).

This recoding allowed us to use the vocational model developed by Holland (1985), which has extensive empirical support (Brown & Brooks, 1990). An individual's current occupation (at Times 1 and 2) was also coded according to the Holland typology. The coding of a participant's occupational interests and occupational choice (at Times 1 and 2) enabled us to create a new variable, congruence. According to Holland (1985), individuals that selected occupations that are congruent with their vocational type are more likely to be productive and satisfied with their jobs than noncongruent individuals: "For example, Realistic types flourish in Realistic environments because such an environment provides the opportunity and rewards a Realistic type's needs. Incongruence occurs when a type lives in an environment that provides opportunities and rewards foreign to the person's preferences and abilities" (p. 5). There is considerable evidence supporting the positive relationship between congruence and job satisfaction across a variety of studies (Spokane, 1985).

An individual's Holland codes were then used in two different ways. First, congruence was used as an independent variable to predict job satisfaction and similar criterion variables. Second, the Holland codes for the individual's job at Time 1 and at Time 2 were cross-tabulated to identify those who remained consistent across time in their careers (e.g., Realistic in 1930s and 1950s) as contrasted with those who were inconsistent (e.g., changed from Realistic in 1930s to Social in 1950s). For example, one man who was coded as career-consistent was a salesman in the 1930s (Enterprising) and manager of sales in the 1950s (Enterprising). Another man who was coded as career inconsistent was a bookstore manager in the 1930s (Enterprising) and became a statistician in the 1950s (Investigative). An example of a career-inconsistent woman was subject no. 120, who was a dance instructor in the 1930s

(Artistic) and who became a salesperson in a dress store in the 1950s (Enterprising). This construct of career consistency became another operationalization of midlife career adjustment.

It should be noted that neither the dependent variables of interest—job stability, job satisfaction, and career consistency—nor the information needed to calculate congruency scores were always available for all the respondents. Thus, analyses were often conducted with fewer than 300 men and 300 women. Sample sizes for specific analyses are discernible from the associated degrees of freedom delineated in the text and tables or from the notes below the relevant tables.

Results

Descriptive statistics and correlations for the dependent variables of interest are presented in Table 15.1 for each gender. One operationalization of midlife career adjustment was individuals' evaluation of their occupation, or job satisfaction. Although the data collected from the sample at Time 2 yielded two potential items measuring job satisfaction, satisfaction with present work and satisfaction with type of work held longest, we used only the latter in our analyses. In general, the two variables were not highly intercorrelated ($r_{male} = .48$, $p < .001$; $r_{female} = .09$, *ns*), and satisfaction with the type of work held longest

TABLE 15.1 Descriptive Statistics and Correlations for Dependent Variables

Variable	1	2	3	4	M_m	SD_m	M_f	SD_f
1. Number of years in present type of work		0.78	0.10	0.12	4.05	2.21	2.01	2.11
2. Number of years in type of work held longest	0.86		0.08	0.22	4.63	1.87	1.91	1.68
3. Satisfaction with present work	0.07	0.00		0.48	1.37	0.72	1.28	0.62
4. Satisfaction with type of work held longest	−.10	−.07	0.09		1.42	0.81	1.45	0.89

Note. Correlations for males are above the diagonal, while correlations for the females are below the diagonal. For males, *n* ranges from 135 to 170 because of missing data. For females, *n* ranges from 66 to 154 because of missing data. For the job satisfaction items, higher scores indicate lower levels of job satisfaction.

captured the longitudinal aspect of midlife career adjustment better than satisfaction with present work. It should be noted that higher scores on this variable indicate lower levels of job satisfaction.

Job stability was a second operationalization of midlife career adjustment. Again, the data yielded two potential items—number of years in present type of work and number of years in type of work held longest. As explained above, we selected the second variable because of its relevance to stability over time. In this case, however, the two items were highly intercorrelated ($r_{male} = .78$, $p < .001$; $r_{female} = .86$, $p < .001$), suggesting that the two items would have yielded similar results.

Because the Allport-Vernon Scale of Values and the Bernreuter Personality Inventory are scale-level items, the item-level traits of the graphic Personality Rating Scale (PRS) were assembled into three scales: PRS Neuroticism, PRS Social Extraversion, and PRS Impulse Control. In addition to a conceptual analysis, the structure of these scales is based on a series of factor analyses conducted by Conley (1985) on this data set using all 36 traits. The resulting composites are presented in Table 15.2.

For males, four items that loaded from $-.18$ to $-.83$ on the first factor were selected to create a composite reflecting Neuroticism. These traits are numbered, 3, 6, 8, and 9 in Table 15.2. To create a composite reflecting Social Extraversion, four items that loaded from .26 to $-.66$

TABLE 15.2 Factor Loadings for Traits

Trait	Males			Females		
	I	II	III	I	II	III
1. Energetic	.20	.40	.38	.08	.53	.24
2. Intelligent	−.15	.01	.25	−.02	.11	.63
3. Pleasant voice	−.19	.01	−.05	−.27	.13	.06
4. Fastidious	.07	.06	.07	−.04	−.10	−.06
5. Wide interests	−.13	.26	.14	−.05	.28	.63
6. Conventional	−.18	−.02	.09	−.34	−.29	−.03
7. Quiet	−.42	−.66	.12	−.52	−.60	−.04
8. Rarely angered	−.83	−.02	.14	−.69	.11	.06
9. Modest	−.42	−.43	.29	−.77	−.03	−.15
10. Dependable	−.23	.06	.83	−.57	−.12	.47

on the second factor were selected. These traits are numbered 1, 5, 7, and 9 in Table 15.2. Three items that loaded from .25 to .83 on the third factor were selected to create a composite reflecting Impulse Control. These traits are numbered 1, 2, and 10 in Table 15.2. The remaining trait in Table 15.2 did not load very highly on any of the three factors.

Slightly different composites were formed for females. The first factor, Neuroticism, comprises the traits numbered 3 and 6–10 in Table 15.2. Their factor loadings ranged from −.27 to −.77. The traits numbered 1 and 7 in Table 15.2 loaded .53 and −.60, respectively, on Social Extraversion. The third factor, Impulse Control, comprises the traits numbered 2, 5, and 10 in Table 15.2, with factor loadings ranging from .47 to .63. As with the factor analysis for the males, the remaining trait in Table 15.2 did not load very highly on any factor.

As suggested by one of the reviewers of this chapter, we sought to identify the level of unique variance attributable to each of the three sets of independent scale measures (i.e., the PRS, AV, and BPI) in a series of hierarchical multiple regression analyses. All measures other than the target measures were entered first into a regression analysis, with the target measures entered last. The difference in the amount of variance accounted for from the first step to the second step was then tested for significance at the traditional alpha level ($p = .05$). The very conservative nature of these procedures thus identified the measures that possessed explanatory value. These results are reported in Table 15.3.

To identify the set(s) of personality and values variables most predictive of job stability, we used this procedure six times. That is, each set of predictors—the PRS composites, the AV scores, and the BPI dimensions—was in turn identified as the target measure and tested for significance for both genders separately. For males, only the PRS significantly accounted for a unique portion, about 6%, of the variance in the dependent variable ($F_{(3,128)} = 3.06$, $F_{crit} = 2.68$). The BPI, however, was the only significant predictor of the number of years females held a type of work longest, uniquely explaining 10% of the variance ($F_{(6,138)} = 2.57$, $F_{crit} = 2.16$).

We then used the same analytical approach for satisfaction with type of work held longest. Although none of the sets of variables predicted a unique portion of the variance significantly in the dependent variable for men, the PRS uniquely predicted 8% of the variance in job satisfaction for women ($F_{(3,145)} = 4.87$, $F_{crit} = 2.67$).

TABLE 15.3 Hierarchical Multiple Regression Analyses of the PRS, AV, and BPI

DV	Gender	Set	F	df	F_{crit}	Set R^2	Overall R^2
Number of years in type of work held longest	M	PRS	3.06	3,128	2.68	.06	.19
		AV	1.06	6,128	2.18	.04	.19
		BPI	0.88	6,128	2.18	.03	.19
	F	PRS	1.06	3,138	2.67	.02	.16
		AV	1.04	6,138	2.16	.04	.16
		BPI	2.57	6,138	2.16	.10	.16
Satisfaction with type of work held longest	M	PRS	2.54	3,157	2.67	.04	.16
		AV	1.91	6,157	2.16	.06	.16
		BPI	1.34	6,157	2.16	.04	.16
	F	PRS	4.87	3,145	2.67	.08	.14
		AV	1.30	6,145	2.16	.04	.14
		BPI	0.67	6,145	2.16	.02	.14

Note. For job satisfaction item, higher scores indicate lower levels of job satisfaction. PRS = Personality Rating Scale Composites. AV = Allport-Vernon Scale of Values. BPI = Bernreuter Personality Inventory. DV = Dependent variable.

Having looked for the set of variables (i.e., BPI, PRS, AV) most predictive of our dependent variables, we next investigated the specific scales that may have predicted job stability and job satisfaction. Simultaneous multiple regression analysis, in which all predictor variables are entered simultaneously, was used to identify the extent to which the personality and values variables were jointly predictive of midlife career adjustment. We conducted regression analyses to determine if the number of years holding the type of work held longest and satisfaction with the type of work held longest could be predicted by three graphic Personality Ratings Scale (PRS) composites, the Allport-Vernon Scale of Values (AV), and the Bernreuter Personality Inventory (BPI). We conducted separate analyses for males and females. Table 15.4 contains these results.

Job stability, the number of years holding the type of work held longest, was first regressed on the three sets of predictor variables. For males, the combined sets of variables accounted for 19% of the variance

TABLE 15.4 Simultaneous Multiple Regression Analyses of the PRS, AV, and BPI

DV	Gender	F	df	p	R^2	Significant IV	t	p
Number of years in type of work held longest	M	2.04	15 128	.02	.19	BPI Sociability	1.97	.05
	F	1.71	15 138	.05	.16	BPI Neurotic Tendency	2.61	.01
						BPI Self-Confidence	-2.17	.03
Satisfaction with type of work held longest	M	2.03	15 157	.02	.16	AV Economic	-2.12	.04
						PRS Impulse Control	2.08	.04
						AV Aesthetic	-2.14	.03
						AV Social	-1.87	.06
						PRS Social Extraversion	-1.76	.08
	F	1.63	15 145	.07	.14	PRS Neuroticism	2.18	.03
						PRS Social Extraversion	-2.80	.01

Note. For job satisfaction item, higher scores indicate lower levels of job satisfaction. PRS = Personality Rating Scale Composites. AV = Allport-Vernon Scale of Values. BPI = Bernreuter Personality Inventory. DV = Dependent variable.

in the dependent variable ($F_{(15,128)} = 2.03$, $p = .02$). BPI Lack of Sociability, however, was the only item to emerge as a significant predictor of job stability ($t = 1.97$, $p = .05$). Although the 15 predictors were somewhat intercorrelated, in only a few cases did the correlations exceed .40, suggesting the multicollinearity was not a limiting factor.

The overall set of variables also significantly predicted number of years holding the type of work held longest for females ($F_{(15,138)} = 1.71$, $p = .05$), jointly accounting for 16% of the variance. Two items from the BPI, Neurotic Tendency and Lack of Self-Confidence, significantly contributed to the prediction of stability for women ($t = 2.61$, $p = .01$; $t = -2.17$, $p = .03$). The tendency for the predictor variables to be intercorrelated was somewhat less for women, rarely exceeding .30.

Satisfaction with type of work held longest (job satisfaction) was then regressed on the identical set of independent variables. These items accounted for 16% of the variance in satisfaction for men ($F_{(15,157)}$ = 2.03, p = .02). The Economic (t = -2.12, p = .04) and Aesthetic (t = -2.14, p = .03) dimensions of the AV were significant predictors of the dependent variable, as was Impulse Control (t = 2.08, p = .04) from the PRS.

For females, the combined set of predictors did not significantly predict job satisfaction, jointly accounting for 14% of the variance ($F_{(15,145)}$ = 1.63, p = .07). At the item level, however, PRS Social Extraversion (t = -2.80, p = .01) and PRS Neuroticism (t = 2.18, p = .03) emerged as significant predictors of the dependent variable for females.

In addition to personality and values variables, Holland's construct of congruence was used to predict midlife career adjustment. To calculate congruence, we first determined each respondent's occupational interests and occupational choice. Using a Dictionary of Holland Occupational Codes (Gottfredson, Holland, & Ogawa, 1982), each of the 44 occupational interests that comprise the Strong Vocational Interest Blank was assigned a primary code: Realistic, Investigative, Artistic, Social, Enterprising, or Conventional. For each code, the subject's responses to the occupations that comprised that code were averaged to yield a mean score. The highest of the six mean scores was considered the individual's dominant occupational interest. Then the individual's current occupation was coded according to the same six-category typology using the Dictionary of Holland Occupational Codes.

We computed congruence by calculating the similarity between subjects' occupational interests and choices. Specifically, we constructed a hexagon and assigned each side one of the six codes in the following order: R I A S E C. Interests and choices falling on the same side received a score of 4, those on sides touching one another received a score of 3, those separated by one side received a score of 2, and those on sides directly opposite one another received a score of 1. In this manner, we created two congruence scores for each respondent: one from occupational interests and choice at Time 1 and one from the same variables at Time 2.

Both job stability (number of years holding type of work held longest) and job satisfaction (satisfaction with type of work held longest) were regressed on congruence at Time 1 and Time 2 for both males and females, yielding eight separate regression analyses. Although congruence at Time 2 accounted for 3% of the variance in job stability for women, no other significant results were found.

TABLE 15.5 Dominant Occupational Interest by Occupational Choice for
Males at Time 1

Occupational	Dominant Occupational Interest						
Choice	R	I	A	S	E	C	RowTot
Realistic	18	5	12	2	12	0	49 23.1%
Investigative	4	4	5	0	4	1	18 8.5%
Artistic	1	0	3	0	0	0	4 1.9%
Social	1	1	5	0	3	2	12 5.7%
Enterprising	5	3	14	13	37	5	77 36.3%
Conventional	1	0	12	3	20	16	52 24.5%
ColTot	30	13	51	18	76	24	
	14.2%	6.1%	24.1%	8.5%	35.8%	11.3%	

Note. RowTot = Row totals and percentages. ColTot = Column totals and percentages.

To explore further the relationship between congruence and job stability and between congruence and job satisfaction, we constructed cross-tabulation tables examining dominant occupation interest and occupation choice. As indicated in Table 15.5, only 37% of the men at Time 1 held jobs congruent with their dominant interest. Whereas this sample possessed predominantly Enterprising (35.8%) and Artistic (24.1%) interests, they worked in Enterprising (36.3%), Conventional (24.5%), and Realistic (23.1%) jobs. Fifteen percent of the women at Time 1 worked in jobs congruent with their interests: a majority expressed Artistic interests (65.6%) but most worked in Conventional (48.3%) or Enterprising (24.9%) environments. These results are presented in Table 15.6.

By Time 2, 44% of the males possessed congruent occupational interests and choices. As indicated by Table 15.7, the males still held strong Enterprising interests (41.3%) and worked in Enterprising (36.2%) and Realistic (22.4%) jobs. Congruence increased from Time 1 to Time 2 for females as well. Whereas this sample expressed predominantly Artistic (48.1%) and Social (21.4%) interests, most held Social jobs (72.3%). These results are presented in Table 15.8.

On the basis of these results, we constructed cross-tabulation tables examining occupational choice at Time 1 and Time 2 to examine the construct of career consistency. Persons who stayed in the same Holland type across time (e.g., Social in 1930s and Social in 1950s) were classified as career consistent, whereas those who changed across time

TABLE 15.6 Dominant Occupational Interest by Occupational Choice for
Females at Time 1

Occupational	Dominant Occupational Interest						
Choice	R	I	A	S	E	C	RowTot
Realistic	18	5	12	2	12	0	49 23.1%
Investigative	0	0	2	0	1	1	4 1.9%
Artistic	0	0	6	1	0	0	7 3.3%
Social	3	0	30	4	0	1	38 18.2%
Enterprising	0	2	37	13	0	0	52 24.9%
Conventional	3	1	58	10	8	21	101 43.3%
ColTot	6	3	137	29	10	24	
	2.9%	1.4%	65.6%	13.9%	4.8%	11.5%	

Note. RowTot = Row totals and percentages. ColTot = Column totals and percentages.

TABLE 15.7 Dominant Occupational Interest by Occupational Choice for
Males at Time 2

Occupational	Dominant Occupational Interest						
Choice	R	I	A	S	E	C	RowTot
Realistic	20	5	1	0	15	3	44 22.4%
Investigative	6	8	2	5	7	3	31 15.8%
Artistic	1	0	0	1	0	0	2 1.0%
Social	2	2	5	11	8	4	32 16.3%
Enterprising	7	0	12	5	44	3	71 36.2%
Conventional	3	1	0	2	7	3	16 8.2%
ColTot	39	16	20	24	81	16	
	19.9%	8.2%	10.2%	12.2%	41.3%	8.2%	

Note. RowTot = Row totals and percentages. ColTot = Column totals and percentages.

(e.g., Realistic at Time 1 and Artistic at Time 2) were considered career
inconsistent. As indicated in Table 15.9, 43% of the men held jobs at
Time 1 that were consistent with those at Time 2 within Holland's
classification scheme. That is, both occupations could be classified similarly according to the Holland typology. Over time, the males left Conventional positions (28.4% at Time 1 to 10.1% at Time 2) and moved
to Enterprising (33.1% at Time 1 to 37.8% at Time 2) and Realistic
(23.6% at Time 1 to 25.7% at Time 2) positions. According to Table

TABLE 15.8 Dominant Occupational Interest by Occupational Choice for Females at Time 2

Occupational Choice	Dominant Occupational Interest						RowTot	
	R	I	A	S	E	C		
Realistic	1	0	3	1	0	1	6	2.9%
Investigative	0	0	0	1	0	0	1	0.5%
Artistic	0	1	1	1	0	0	3	1.5%
Social	11	6	76	30	15	11	149	72.3%
Enterprising	1	1	13	6	4	1	26	12.6%
Conventional	1	0	6	5	4	5	21	10.2%
ColTot	14	8	99	44	23	18		
	6.8%	3.9%	48.1%	21.4%	11.2%	8.7%		

Note. RowTot = Row totals and percentages. ColTot = Column totals and percentages.

TABLE 15.9 Occupational Choice for Males at Time 1 by Time 2

Occupational Choice	Dominant Occupational Interest						RowTot	
	R	I	A	S	E	C		
Realistic	19	2	0	5	7	2	35	23.6%
Investigative	4	6	0	0	2	0	12	8.1%
Artistic	0	0	0	1	0	0	1	0.7%
Social	2	2	1	3	1	0	9	6.1%
Enterprising	9	3	1	5	27	4	49	33.1%
Conventional	4	5	0	5	19	9	42	28.4%
ColTot	38	18	2	19	56	15		
	25.7%	12.2%	1.4%	12.8%	37.8%	10.1%		

Note. RowTot = Row totals and percentages. ColTot = Column totals and percentages.

15.10, only 28% of the women held jobs at Time 1 that were consistent with those at Time 2. In general, the females exchanged Enterprising (22.6% at Time 1 to 13.8% at Time 2) and Conventional (49.7% at Time 1 to 11.9% at Time 2) positions for Social positions (19.5% at Time 1 to 69.2% at Time 2).

We used discriminant analysis to identify the personality and values variables that were predictive of career consistency. As with the multiple regression analyses, a simultaneous procedure was used. The sample proportions were specified as prior probabilities. Again, we did sep-

TABLE 15.10 Occupational Choice for Females at Time 1 and Time 2

Occupational	Dominant Occupational Interest						
Choice	R	I	A	S	E	C	RowTot
Realistic	0	0	1	4	0	0	5 3.1%
Investigative	0	0	0	2	0	0	2 1.3%
Artistic	0	0	0	3	3	0	6 3.8%
Social	2	0	0	22	5	2	31 19.5%
Enterprising	0	1	2	26	6	1	36 22.6%
Conven-							
tional	2	0	0	53	8	16	79 49.7%
ColTot	4	1	3	110	22	19	
	2.5%	0.6%	1.9%	69.2%	13.8%	11.9%	

Note. RowTot = Row totals and percentages. ColTot = Column totals and percentages.

TABLE 15.11 Discriminant Analyses of the PRS, AV, and BPI

Gender	χ^2	df	p	CanCorr^2	Wilks
M	14.80	15	.47	.10	.90
F	32.27	15	.01	.20	.80

Note. CanCorr^2 = (Canonical Correlation)^2. PRS = Personality Rating Scale Composites. AV = Allport-Vernon Scale of Values. BPI = Bernreuter Personality Inventory

arate analyses for males and females. The results are reported in Table 15.11.

The discriminant function was not significant ($\chi_{15}^2 = 14.80$, $p = .47$) for the males, with only 10% of the variance in the dependent variable accounted for by this model. Interestingly, the combined sets of variables were significant discriminators for women ($\chi_{15}^2 = 32.27$, $p = .01$), accounting for 20% of the variance in consistency. The 76% classification accuracy of the function was only slightly more predictive than the maximum chance criterion, or the percentage correctly classified if all observations were placed in the group with greater probability of occurrence (in this case, 72%).

Following the analytical strategy advanced for job stability and job satisfaction, we conducted a series of nested discriminant analyses to identify the level of unique variance attributable to each of the three sets of independent scale measures. All measures other than the target measures were entered first into a discriminant analysis, with the target measures entered last. Since the difference between chi-squares is itself distributed as a chi-square, and the model introduced in the first step is nested within the fuller model introduced at the second step, the difference between the steps in chi-squares was subjected to a significance test. In this way, we could identify the set(s) of personality and values variables most predictive of career consistency.

As indicated in Table 15.12, none of the sets of variables significantly predicted a unique portion of the variance in the dependent variable for men. Such a finding is not surprising, however, given the fact that the overall function was not significant. Two sets of predictors, the PRS composites and the BPI, significantly accounted for a unique portion of the variance in consistency for females, with 8% and 11% variance of the dependent variable explained, respectively ($\chi_3^2 = 13.17$, $\chi^2_{crit} = 7.82$; $\chi_6^2 = 18.18$, $\chi^2_{crit} = 12.59$). Whereas the classification accuracy of the overall function without the PRS dropped from 76% to 63% (thus indicating the importance of the set for predictive purposes), the same index for the overall function without the BPI decreased only to 73%.

Recent research (Vandewater & Stewart, 1993) has suggested that occupational status may be an important component of midlife career adjustment. That is, the relationships of personality, values, and congruence with job stability, job satisfaction, and career consistency for those subjects employed in jobs may be different for those engaged in careers.

Therefore, using the Dictionary of Holland Occupational Codes (Gottfredson et al., 1982), each subject's occupation was coded in terms of General Educational Development (GED) and Specific Voca-

TABLE 15.12 Nested Discriminant Analyses of the PRS, AV, and BPI

Gender	Set	χ^2	df	χ_{crit}	Set CanCorr²	Overall CanCorr²
M	PRS	1.51	3	7.82	.01	.10
	AV	6.30	6	12.59	.04	.10
	BPI	4.52	6	12.59	.03	.10
F	PRS	13.17	3	7.82	.08	.20
	AV	5.39	6	12.59	.04	.20
	BPI	18.18	6	12.59	.11	.20

Note. CanCorr² = (Canonical Correlation)². PRS = Personality Rating Scale Composites. AV = Allport-Vernon Scale of Values. BPI = Bernreuter Personality Inventory

TABLE 15.13 Correlations of GED and SVP with Dependent
Variables by Gender at Time 1 and Time 2

Variable	GED	GED2	SVP	SVP2
Job stability M	−.14	.02	−.17	−.09
Job satisfaction M	−.16	−.07	−.14	.01
Career consistency M	−.06	.03	.02	.02
Job stability F	−.07	.10	−.07	.21
Job satisfaction F	.00	.04	.01	−.01
Career consistency F	−.26	−.04	−.13	−.05

Note. M = measures collected from males. F = measures collected from females.
2 = measures collected at Time 2. For males, *n* ranges from 95 to 138 because of
missing data. For females, *n* ranges from 113 to 153 because of missing data. For
the job satisfaction item, higher scores indicate lower levels of job satisfaction.

tional Preparation (SVP) at Time 1 and Time 2. The GED ratings reflect the general educational development typically required to enter
or perform well in an occupation, ranging from 1 (some elementary
school required for commonsense understanding) to 6 (college required for logic and abstract thinking). The SVP ratings reflect the
training time required by an occupation, ranging from 1 (short demon-
stration only) to 9 (over 10 years). High GED and SVP ratings would
provide evidence of having a career, whereas low ratings would provide
evidence of holding a job.

Although restrictive sample sizes did not permit using occupational
status as a moderating variable, GED and SVP at Times 1 and 2 were
correlated with the dependent variables of interest for exploratory purposes. As indicated by Table 15.13, there were no significant correlations for males at Time 1 or Time 2. For females, GED was intercorrelated with career consistency ($r = -.26$, $p < .001$) at Time 1, and SVP
was intercorrelated with job stability ($r = .21$, $p = .01$) at Time 2.

DISCUSSION

In general, we found that individual differences such as personality
traits and values are significant predictors of various midlife career adjustment. In discussing the significant predictors of midlife career adjustment, it seems best to focus on men and women separately. As in
the Results section, the findings are organized by the dependent variable of interest.

Results for Men

Job Stability. When we tested the predictive value of the different sets of variables, the hierarchical regression results indicated that the Personality Rating Scale (PRS) was the only set that significantly predicted the number of years holding the type of work held longest. The combined set of personality and values predictors in the simultaneous regression accounted for a significant amount of the variance (19%) of job stability. An examination of the univariate relationships, however, highlighted the Lack of Sociability Scale from the Bernreuter Personality Inventory as the only significant predictor of the dependent variable. That highly asocial and solitary men would stay longer at their jobs makes sense intuitively. Similarly, in his investigation of occupational mobility and personality, Clausen (1981) found that mobile men exceeded their nonmobile peers from comparable backgrounds in personal effectiveness as measured in the junior high school years. This result suggests that it may be quite typical for sociable individuals to change jobs regularly, while those who are less sociable may stay at their jobs much longer. Perhaps the lack of sociability of the latter restricts their personal and professional networks, thereby efficiently filtering out information about promising opportunities at other jobs. Furthermore, those employees that are less sociable may stay longer at their jobs because they lack social skills and do not do well at interviews when new positions become available. Alternatively, people who are highly sociable and gregarious may have larger personal and professional networks and have good interviewing skills and therefore may indeed change jobs more frequently. Interestingly, lack of sociability, and not social extraversion, was the significant predictor of job stability, suggesting that these two dimensions may have differential relationships to job attitudes and outcomes.

Job Satisfaction. Although none of the sets of variables was uniquely predictive of satisfaction with type of work held longest, the combined set of personality and values predictors in the simultaneous regression accounted for a significant portion of the variance of the second criterion (16%). Individuals with higher values on the Economic and Aesthetic dimensions on the Allport-Vernon Scale of Values were more satisfied with their jobs. In other words, those subjects who tended to be practical, goal-oriented, and interested in business careers (Economic), or who were concerned with beauty, harmony, and finding fulfillment in artistic experiences (Aesthetic), tended to express more satisfaction with their jobs.

Additionally, employees exhibiting lower scores on the PRS Impulse Control composite (indicating less control of their impulses) were more satisfied with their jobs. Hence, the picture that emerges is that individuals who have less control of their impulses and who possess Economic and Aesthetic values are the ones most likely to be satisfied with their jobs and their careers at midlife. This picture seems intuitive except for the low impulse control. Future research to follow up on this counterintuitive relationship between low impulse control and job satisfaction seems warranted. Perhaps the low-impulse-control variable is tapping into a trait such as risk-taking behavior and sensation-seeking tendencies. Future research could examine whether individuals with (1) lower impulse control or (2) higher risk-taking or sensation-seeking tendencies are generally more satisifed with their jobs than those who are not.

Interestingly, although the pattern of results obtained for job stability indicate that individuals who lack sociability (as indicated by the BPI Lack of Sociability scale) may remain in their work environment for a long time, the pattern of results obtained for job satisfaction indicates that these same individuals are unlikely to be satisfied with their jobs. That is, the evidence that BPI Lack of Sociability predicted job stability, whereas PRS Impulse Control and AV Economic and Aesthetic predicted job satisfaction, suggests that job stability and job satisfaction may not have a simple and direct relationship. In other words, although both criteria may function as valid indicators of midlife career adjustment, they may be tapping different aspects of this multidimensional construct. Overall, however, these findings demonstrate the criticality to work adjustment of the social and interpersonal adjustment.

Surprisingly, Holland's concept of congruence was not predictive of either job stability or job satisfaction. These results run counter to numerous studies (Spokane, 1985) that have found that congruence significantly predicts job satisfaction. Admittedly, none of these other studies has actually used a longitudinal design spanning a 20-year time period. It is possible that Holland's model of congruence and job satisfaction, a personality model, does not work very well further along the developmental continuum, especially at midlife. Indeed, there is some evidence to support this interpretation. For example, Leong, Rosenberg, and Chervinko (1991), in a study of vocational adjustment, found that Holland's concepts of congruence, consistency, and differentiation were not predictive of job satisfaction for a group of men at midlife. On the other hand, it should be noted that the current study used a very crude operationalization of Holland's construct of congruence, in that Holland's theoretical model was not integrated into the Strong Interest Inventory until 1972 and the current data set was based on the 1935 version of the Strong Vocational Interest Blank. Thus, future research will have to determine more definitely if Holland's model works for men at midlife.

Congruence. In general, men tended to possess more congruence between their measured interests and their actual occupations (37% at Time 1 and 44% at Time 2) than women (15% at Time 1 and 20% at Time 2) did. However, both groups became more congruent over time. In fact, it appears that individuals' occupational interests and choices converge as they grow older and accrue experience in the world of work, regardless of gender. Perhaps individuals not prepared for a particular occupation may try out a succession of job for fit until they find one job, or a set of jobs, that is sufficiently rewarding (Clausen, 1981). Across time, men tended to nurture a high and consistent interest in Enterprising careers. As time progressed, men tended to leave Conventional jobs and enter Enterprising and Realistic positions. However, it is difficult to discern from the current data what accounts for this migration over time into more traditionally masculine jobs (i.e., Enterprising and Realistic types).

Career Consistency. Recall that we measured career consistency as the movement or lack of movement in occupations across time using the Holland Classification for Occupations. In other words, individuals who at Time 1 were in Realistic occupations and stayed within Realistic occupations at Time 2, some 20 years later, were considered career consistent. Those who changed from Realistic to Artistic occupations, however, we classified as career inconsistent.

In both the overall discriminant function analyses and the nested discriminant function analyses, the predictors (the BPI, the PRS, and the AV) did not significantly discriminate between those men whose occupations were classified similarly from Time 1 to Time 2 and those who occupations were classified dissimilarly.

Exploratory analyses revealed that the GED and SVP indices, this study's operationalization of occupational status, were not significantly correlated to job stability, job satisfaction, or career consistency for men. While the correlations were statistically not significant ($r = .01$, to $r = -.17$), this may have resulted from the small sample size (n ranging from 95 to 138). Although there were no significant relationships between general educational development or specific vocational preparation and the dependent variables of interest, other studies suggest that occupational status may be an important moderator of job stability, job satisfaction, and career consistency. Future research should thus examine the relationships between predictors and dependent variables separately for those subjects holding jobs and those having careers (or any other subgroups who are likely to differ in their beliefs about the psychological meaning of work).

Results for Women

It should be noted that overall, there were just as many significant predictors for the midlife career adjustment of women as for men. However, while there were some overlap, many of the variables that significantly predicted job stability, job satisfaction, and career consistency for women were not the variables that did so for men. This finding further supports the contention that women's career choice, work behavior, and work adjustment may be influenced by a separate set of variables, or the same set of variables in a qualitatively different manner (see Betz & Fitzgerald, 1987), than those for men.

Job Stability. Although the independent variables in concert did account for a significant portion of the variance (16%) in the criterion, the BPI was the only set that uniquely predicted job stability for women. Not surprisingly, then, the Neurotic Tendency scale and the Lack of Self-Confidence scale emerged from the BPI as significant predictors of job stability at the univariate level. More specifically, women scoring high on the Neurotic Tendency scale tended to remain longer in their main type of work. This finding for females, in conjunction with the inverse relationship between sociability and job stability for males, again reinforces the connection between emotional stability and career adjustment at midlife.

In addition to neuroticism, self-confidence was also a significant predictor of job stability. In this case, however, more self-confidence was associated with a longer tenure in the job. It is possible that emotionally unstable women—that is, those high in neurotic tendencies— remained in their jobs for a longer period of time because, like the asocial men, they were afraid that they would not be succeed in other opportunities. Indeed, there may be a maladaptive component to job stability, such that individuals may remain in a position not because of their satisfaction with it but rather because of the fear that accompanies change and new opportunities. Interestingly, however, although one would expect that women who lack self-confidence would show a relationship to job stability similar to that of women who are very neurotic, the opposite relationship was found. Instead, women with low levels of self-confidence tended *not* to invest many years in their jobs. James (1989) found that many women left their jobs and did not pursue certain careers for a variety of reasons, including the lack of self-confidence regarding completion of necessary education and the ability to gain advancement on the job, expectations of low pay, and the demands of motherhood and children. Several of the reasons highlighted in James's study as well as the current one reaffirm the importance of the career self-efficacy contruct in women's career development (Betz & Fitzgerald, 1987).

Overall, the evidence suggests that job stability or job tenure is a rather complicated outcome, in that there may be a multitude of reasons for remaining in or leaving a position. Indeed, the conflicting pattern of results for neuroticism and job stability in contrast with self-confidence and job stability only serves to highlight such an interpretation.

Job Satisfaction. According to the series of hierarchical regressions conducted, the PRS was the only set of variables that uniquely predicted job satisfaction for women. Not surprisingly, then, the PRS Neuroticism and the PRS Social Extraversion composites emerged as the significant predictors of the criterion at the univariate level.

While the results presented earlier delineated a positive relationship between the BPI Neurotic Tendency scale and job stability, the current findings indicate a negative relationship between the PRS Neuroticism composite and job satisfaction, in that women scoring higher on the composite tend to be less satisfied with their jobs. Given the almost nonexistent relationship between the BPI Neurotic Tendency scale and the PRS Neuroticism composite ($r = .01$), this further supports our earlier interpretation that more neurotic women tend to remain in their jobs even though they may not be particularly satisfied with them.

Additionally, females having more social extraversion exhibited greater job satisfaction. In particular, a significant component of job satisfaction seems to be related to the social or interpersonal domain, although the highly interpersonal nature of work is often overlooked in many studies of job satisfaction (Cranny, Smith, & Stone, 1992). Indeed, a multifaceted model of job satisfaction advocated by Smith, Kendall, and Hulin (1969) contains two facets that pertain to the social or interpersonal dimension—satisfaction with coworkers and supervision. Thus, it is not surprising that women who are gregarious and outgoing are more satisfied with their jobs. We would speculate that the workplace probably served as a major source of social stimulation for these women.

Congruence. As noted earlier, although men tended to have more congruence between their measured interests and their actual occupations than women, both genders displayed more congruence as time progressed (i.e., at Time 2 as compared to Time 1). Across time, the women tended to leave Conventional and Enterprising jobs and enter predominantly Social professions. Like men, women tended to migrate into more sex-role traditional positions (i.e., jobs classified as Social positions, such as teachers and nurses). Again, we have no way of determining the potential causes for this change over time.

Career Consistency. The combined set of predictor variables (the BPI, the PRS, and the AV) significantly discriminated between those women whose occupations were classified similarly at Time 1 and Time 2 and those whose occupations were not. In fact, the combined set of variables accounted for 20% of the variance in career consistency. Moreover, the PRS and the BPI each significantly predicted a unique portion of the variance in the dependent variable for women.

Finally, in our exploratory analysis of the effects of occupational status on midlife career adjustment, GED was correlated with career consistency at Time 1, but SVP was correlated with job stability at Time 2. Those females that had higher general educational development at Time 1 tended to hold positions in the 1930s and in the 1950s that were classified similarly according to the Holland typology. Similarly, higher specific vocational preparation scores at Time 2 tended to accompany higher job stability. Those females engaged in careers may not have enjoyed the same opportunities and mobility in general as their male counterparts.

Summary

In general, a number of the significant relationships that were discovered between the personality and values variables and job stability, job satisfaction, and career consistency were straightforward and unsurprising. For example, women who were more socially extraverted tended to be more satisfied with their jobs. However, other results were somewhat puzzling and are therefore open to several possible explanations. When in doubt about the causal mechanisms under operation, we allowed a combination of parsimony and our knowledge of the instrumentation as well as the predominant work conditions of the 1930s and 1950s to guide our interpretations. For example, we believed that men who lacked sociability and women who possessed neurotic tendencies remained in their positions for longer periods of time as a result of anxiety and fears about change and new opportunities. This should be tested with more recent instruments and a different cohort.

Overall, some general patterns emerged that are of interest to career counselors. First, the personality variables (the BPI and the PRS) tended to function better as predictors of midlife work adjustment than did the values variables (the AV). Furthermore, the sets of variables that were predictive of men's and job stability, job satisfaction, and career consistency were different from those predictive for women, thus supporting the contention that men and women undergo differential career experiences and adjustment processes (Betz & Fitzgerald, 1987). Finally, the pattern of results obtained indicates that the social and interpersonal domain (as evidenced by the BPI Sociability and Self-Confidence scales and the PRS Social Extraversion composite) is a critical factor in midlife career adjustment. More detailed analyses of these general patterns would provide useful information to career counselors about midlife career adjustment.

We operationalized career adjustment as job stability (staying at the same job for a long time), job satisfaction, and career consistency (not changing from one career to another). Some difficulties we encountered can be traced to these criterion variables of midlife career adjustment. Specifically, the variables that were available in the current data set may have been too global in nature. Midlife career adjustment may indeed be such a multifaceted and multidimensional construct that the global job satisfaction and job stability (number of years in which individuals held their longest job) measures may not have captured the complexity of the phenomenon we have attempted to study (see Cranny, Smith, & Stone, 1992). Indeed, persons may remain in or leave a job or career for a variety of reasons, including those "pull or push" factors outlined by Haug and Sussman (1970). Whereas job stability may represent a negative event for upwardly mobile individuals who aspire to advance beyond the level of their job, it may represent a positive event for a working-class individual who places a high value on job security. For example, in an examination of men's occupational histories, Clausen (1981) notes that older, middle-class males who were not upwardly mobile—that is, they remained in jobs they had obtained nearly a decade earlier—expressed greater dissatisfaction with their careers. Thus, just as many of our results linked positive and negative characteristics with job stability, it would not be too far-fetched to assume that there may be both positive and negative career changes at midlife, as well as positive and negative reasons for job stability or career consistency.

Research on midlife career adjustment will not improve until more specific criterion variables can be identified (e.g., investigation of facet satisfaction and reasons for job stability and career consistency similar to the ones outlined by Campbell & Cellini, 1981). For example, Neuroticism as a personality variable would be expected to be more associated with coworker and supervision facets of job satisfaction. Ambigious results will continue to be generated if midlife career change is viewed as either mainly a positive event or mainly a negative event.

In general, our results suggest that personality or trait variables such as those on the Personality Rating Scale, the Allport-Vernon Scale of Values, and the Bernreuter Personality Inventory are quite valuable in predicting job stability and job satisfaction. The value of personality models in predicting work behavior has gone through cycles in which such models have either been discarded as worthless or resurrected as valuable explanatory models for selection and career counseling. Nevertheless, our results do provide some patterns that are consistent with previous studies of work and personality (Brown & Brooks, 1990) and personality and adjustment in later life (Conley, 1985). They also delineate potential avenues for future exploration.

The failure of Holland's model (i.e., congruence) to predict job stability and job satisfaction was surprising. Yet because it is a personality-based model, most assessments of it have not incorporated a developmental component and have tended to rely on college student samples. Indeed, one major implication of the current negative findings for Holland's mode is that we need to test the validity of personality-based models of career adjustment along the developmental continuum to determine the relative contributions of each theoretical framework for understanding vocational adjustment. It is true that the imposition of Holland's occupational classification model on a very old interest inventory is methodologically weak. Despite this methodological weakness, it is still important to begin to assess the relative strengths of both personality and developmental conceptualizations of vocational adjustment. Our study is one of few longitudinal tests of Holland's personality-based model of career choice and adjustment. We clearly need more, given the complexity of the undertaking.

There are some serious limitations to this study that should be noted. Although the study began with a sample of 300 men and 300 women, the sample sizes dropped significantly as specific variables were examined. Sometimes we conducted analyses with relatively small samples of 160 men and 60 or 70 women. Often, such small samples are not capable of capturing constructs or effects that are not initially robust in the social sciences. In fact, the smaller sample size for women was quite problematic. This in turn points to the more limited generalizability of the results for women than for men.

Second, personality instrumentation in the 1930s was not as sophisticated as that which is currently available. Furthermore, recall that the construct of congruence that initiates from the Holland model was not predictive of job satisfaction. This may also be a measurement problem, in that the Strong Vocational Interest Blank was used and the Holland model was superimposed upon a very old instrument. Future research will have to determine if Holland's model, as assessed by a more up-to-date instrument, would be predictive of job satisfaction twenty years later.

These limitations notwithstanding, our study is one of few longitudinal approaches to the prediction of midlife career adjustment (e.g., Clausen, 1981). In an attempt to demonstrate the utility of an individual differences approach to midlife career adjustment, we have demonstrated that personality traits and values are predictive of job stability, job satisfaction, and career consistency for both men and women nearly twenty years later. Like Kohn and Schooler (1983), we have found that personality differences do play a significant and complex role in the work adjustment process. To the extent that our goal is to maximize the potential of individuals to love and to work across the life span, we need further research into the complex interactions and influence of individual differences, developmental processes, and organizational dynamics in midlife career adjustment.

REFERENCES

Allport, G., Vernon, P., & Lindsey, G. (1960). *Study of values* (3rd ed). Boston: Houghton Mifflin.

Baltes, P. B., Reese, H. W., & Lipsitt, L. P. (1980). Life-span developmental psychology, *Annual Review of Psychology, 31,* 65–110.

Bartol, K. M. (1981). Vocational behavior and career development, 1980: A Review. *Journal of Vocational Behavior, 19,* 123–162.

Betz, N. E., & Fitzgerald, L. E. (1987). *The career psychology of women.* New York: Academic Press.

Birren, J. E. (1960). Psychological aspects of aging. *Annual Review of Psychology, 11,* 161–198.

Birren, J. E., Cunningham, W. R., & Yamamoto, K. (1983). Psychology of adult development and aging. *Annual Review of Psychology, 34,* 543–575.

Bischof, L. J. (1969). *Adult psychology.* New York: Harper & Row.

Botwinick, J. (1970). Geropsychology. *Annual Review of Psychology, 21,* 239–272.

Brim, O. G., Jr. (1976). Theories of the male mid-life crisis. *Counseling Psychologist, 6,* 2–9.

Britton, J. O. (1970). Training and counseling of the older worker. *Journal of Employment Counseling, 7,* 137–141.

Brown, D., & Brooks, L. (1990). *Career choice and development* (2nd ed). San Francisco: Jossey-Bass.

Campbell, D. (1971). *Handbook for the Strong Vocational Interest Blank.* Stanford, CA: Stanford University Press.

Campbell, D., & Holland, J. L. (1972). A merger in vocational interest research: Applying Holland's theory to Strong's data. *Journal of Vocational Behavior, 2,* 353–376.

Campbell, R. E., & Cellini, J. V. (1981). A diagnostic taxonomy for adult career problems. *Journal of Vocational Behavior, 19,* 175–190.

Campbell, R. E., and Heffernan, J. M. (1983). Adult vocational behavior. In W. Bruce Walsh and Samuel Osipow (Eds.), *Handbook of Vocational Psychology,* (Vol. 1, pp. 223–260). Hillsdale, NJ: Lawrence Erlbaum Associates.

Chown, S. M., & Heron, A. (1965). Psychological aspects of aging in man. *Annual Review of Psychology, 16,* 417–450.

Clausen, J. A. (1981). Men's occupational careers in the middle years. In D. H. Eichorn, J. A. Clausen, N. Haan, M. P. Honzik, & P. H. Mussen (Eds.), *Present and past in middle life.* New York: Academic Press.

Conley, J. J. (1985). A personality theory of adulthood and aging. In R. Hogan & W. H. Jones (Eds.), *Perspectives in Personality: A research annual. Volume 1. Annual Review.* Greenwich, CT: JAI Press.

Costa, P. T., & McCrae, R. R. (1985). *The NEO Personality Inventory Manual.* Odessa, FL: Psychological Assessment Resources.

Costa, P. T., McCrae, R. R., & Holland, J. L. (1984). Personality and vocational interests in an adult sample. *Journal of Applied Psychology, 69,* 390–400.

Cranny, C. J., Smith, P. C., & Stone, E. F. (1992). *Job satisfaction: How people feel about their jobs and how it affects their performance.* New York: Lexington Books.

Elder, G. H., Jr. (1983). Social history and life experience. In D. H. Eichorn, J. A. Clausen, N. Haan, M. P. Honzik, & P. H. Mussen (Eds.), *Present and past in middle life.* New York: Academic Press.

Entine, A. (1977). Counseling for midlife and beyond. *Vocational Guidance Quarterly, 25,* 332–336.

Farrell, M. P., & Rosenberg, S. D. (1981). *Men at midlife.* Boston: Auburn House.

Fitzgerald, L. E., & Rounds, J. B. (1989). Vocational behavior, 1988: A critical analysis. *Journal of Vocational Behavior, 35,* 105–163.

Fozard, J. L., & Popkin, S. J. (1978). Optimizing adult development. *American Psychologist, 33,* 975–989.

Fretz, B. R., & Leong, F. T. L. (1982). Vocational behavior and career development, 1981: A Review. *Journal of Vocational Behavior, 21,* 123–163.

Gandz, J., & Murray, V. V. (1980). The experience of workplace politics. *Academy of Management Journal, 23,* 237–251.

Garbin, A. P., & Stover, R. G. (1978). Vocational behavior and career development, 1977: A review. *Journal of Vocational Behavior, 17,* 125–170.

Gerson, K. (1985). *Hard choices: How women decide about work, career, and motherhood.* Berkeley: University of California Press.

Goh, D. S., & Leong, F. T. L. (1993). The relationship between Holland's theory of vocational interest and Eysenck's model of personality. *Personality and Individual Differences, 15,* 555–562.

Goldstein, I. L. (1974). *Training: Program development and evaluation.* Monterey, CA: Brooks/Cole.

Gottfredson, G. D., Holland, J. L., and Ogawa, D. K. (1982). *Dictionary of Holland occupational codes.* Palo Alto, CA: Consulting Psychologists Press.

Gould, R. (1972). The phases of adult life: A study in developmental psychology. *American Journal of Psychiatry, 5,* 521–531.

Gross, E. (1975). Patterns of organizational and occupational socialization. *Vocational Guidance Quarterly, 24,* 140–149.

Hall, D. T. (1986). Breaking career routines: Midcareer choice and identity development. In Hall, D. T., and Associates (Eds.), *Career development in organizations* (pp. 120–159). San Francisco: Jossey-Bass.

Hall, D. T., and Associates (Ed.), (1986). *Career development in organizations.* San Francisco: Jossey-Bass.

Haug, M. R., & Sussman, M. B. (1970). The second career-variant of a sociological concept. In H. L. Sheppard (Ed.), *Toward an Industrial Gerontology: An Introduction to a New Field of Applied Research and Service.* Cambridge, MA: Schenkman.

Heesacker, M., Howe, L. A., & Elliott, T. R. (1988). Does the Holland Code predict job satisfaction and productivity in clothing factory workers? *Journal of Counseling Psychology, 35,* 144–148.

Henry, W. E. (1961). Conflict, age, and the executive. *Business Topics, 9,* 15–25.

Herr, E. L., & Cramer, S. H. (1979). *Career guidance through the life span.* Boston: Little, Brown.

Herr, E. L., and Cramer, S. H. (1988). *Career guidance and counseling through the life span.* (3rd ed.). Glenview, IL: Scott, Foresman.

Holland, J. L. (1985). *Making vocational choices: A theory of vocational personalities and work environments.* (2nd ed.). Englewood Cliffs, NJ: Prentice-Hall.

Holland, J. L., & Gottfredson, G. D. (1981). Using a typology of persons and environments to explain careers: Some extensions and clarifications. In D. H. Montross & C. J. Shinkman (Eds.), *Career development in the 1980's: Theory and practice* (pp. 5–27). Springfield, IL: Charles C. Thomas.

Holland, J. L., Magoon, T. M., & Spokane, A. R. (1981). Counseling psychology: Career interventions, research, and theory. *Annual Review of Psychology, 32,* 279–305.

Horrocks, J. E., & Mussman, M. C. (1970). Middlescence: Age-related stress periods during adult years. *Genetic Psychology Monographs, 82,* 119–159.

Hurrell, J. J., McLaney, M. A., & Murphy, L. R. (1990). The middle years: Career stage differences. *Prevention in Human Services, 8,* 179–203.

James, J. B. (1989). *Women's employment patterns, occupational attitudes, and psychological well-being at midlife.* Unpublished doctoral dissertation, Boston University, Boston, MA.

Kelleher, C. H. (1973). Second careers—a growing trend. *Industrial Gerontology,* Spring, 1–8.

Kelly, E. L. (1940). A 36-trait personality rating scale. *Journal of Psychology, 9,* 97–102.

Kelly, E. L. (1955). Consistency of the adult personality. *American Psychologist, 10,* 659–681.

Kohn, M. L., & Schooler, C. (1983). *Work and personality: An inquiry into the impact of social stratification.* Norwood, NJ: Ablex.

Leong, F. T. L., Rosenberg, S. D., & Chervinko, S. (1991). Assessing the validity of Holland's model of careers for men at midlife. Unpublished manuscript.

Levinson, D. J. (1978). *The seasons of a man's life.* New York: Ballantine.

Levinson, D. J., Darrow, C., Klein, E. Levinson, M., & McKee, B. (1974). The psychological development of men in early adulthood and the mid-life transition. In D. F. Hicks, A. Thomas, & M. Roff (Eds.), *Life history research in psychopathology* (Vol. 3). Minneapolis: University of Minnesota Press.

Locke, E. A. (1976). The nature & causes of job satisfaction. In M. Dunnett (Ed.), *Handbook of industrial and organizational psychology.* Chicago: Rand McNally.

Lofquist, L. H., & Dawis, R. V. (1984). Research on work adjustment and satisfaction: Implications for career counseling. In S. D. Brown & R. L. Lent (Eds.),

Handbook of counseling psychology (pp. 216–237). New York: John Wiley and Sons.

Mazen, A. M. (1989). Testing an integration of Vroom's instrumentality theory and Holland's typology on working women. *Journal of Vocational Behavior, 35,* 327–341.

Meier, S. T. (1991). Vocational behavior, 1989–1990: Vocational Choice, Decision-Making, Career Development Interventions, and Assessment. *Journal of Vocational Behavior, 39,* 131–181.

Murphy, P. P., & Burck, H. D. (1976). Career development of men at mid-life. *Journal of Vocational Behavior, 9,* 337–343.

Neugarten, B. L. (1976). Adaptation and the life cycle. *Counseling Psychologist, 6,* 16–20.

Osherson, S. D. (1980). *Holding on or letting go: Men and career change at mid-life.* New York: Free Press.

Osipow, S. H. (1983). *Theories of career development.* (3rd ed.). Englewood Cliffs, NJ: Prentice-Hall.

Rabinowitz, S., & Hall, D. T. (1981). Changing correlates of job involvement in three career stages. *Journal of Vocational Behavior, 18,* 138–144.

Rhodes, S. R. (1983). Age-related differences in work attitudes and behavior: A review and conceptual analysis. *Psychological Bulletin, 93,* 328–367.

Saben, S. (1967). Occupational mobility of employed workers. *Monthly Labor Review,* June.

Schaie, K. W., & Gribbin, K. (1975). Adult development and aging. *Annual Review of Psychology, 26,* 65–96.

Schaie, K. W., & Willis, S. L. (1979). Life-span development: Implications for education. In *Review of Research in Education,* Volume 6. Washington, D.C. American Educational Research Association.

Schein, E. H. (1976). Career development: Theoretical and practical issues for organizations. In *Career Planning and Development: Management Development,* Series No. 12. Geneva: International Labour Office.

Schlossberg, N. K. (1981). A model for analyzing human adaptation to transition. *Counseling Psychologist, 9,* 2–18.

Sinick, D. (1975). *Counseling older persons: Careers, retirement, dying.* Ann Arbor, MI: Eric Clearinghouse on Counseling and Personnel Services.

Smith, P. C., Kendall, L. M., & Hulin, C. L. (1969). *The measurement of satisfaction in work and retirement: A strategy for the study of attitudes.* Chicago: Rand McNally.

Spokane, A. R. (1985). A review of research on person-environment congruence in Holland's theory of careers (Monograph). *Journal of Vocational Behavior, 26,* 306–343.

Stewart, A. J., Lykes, M. B., & LaFrance, M. (1982). Educated women's career patterns: Separating social and developmental changes. *Journal of Social Issues, 38,* 97–117.

Super, D. E. (1957). *The psychology of careers.* New York: Harper and Brothers.

Super, D. E. (1980). A life-span: Life-space approach to career development. *Journal of Vocational Behavior, 16,* 282–298.

Swanson, J. L. (1992). Vocational behavior, 1989–1991: Life-span career development and reciprocal interaction of work and nonwork. *Journal of Vocational Behavior, 41,* 101–161.

Swanson, J. L., & Tokar, D. M. (1991). Development and initial validation of the Careers Barriers Inventory. *Journal of Vocational Behavior, 39,* 344–361.

Thomas, L. E. (1975). Why study mid-life career change. *Vocational Guidance Quarterly, 24,* 37–40.

Thomas, L. E., Mlea, R. L., Robbins, R. I., & Harvey, D. W. (1976). Corporate drop-outs: A preliminary typology. *Vocational Guidance Quarterly, 24,* 220–228.

Thurnher, M. (1974). Goals, values, and life-evaluations at the pre-retirement stage. *Journal of Gerontology, 29,* 85–96.

Tiedeman, D., & Ohara, R. (1963). *Career development: Choice and adjustment.* Princeton: College Entrance Examination Board.

Vaillant, G. E. (1977). *Adaptation to life.* Boston: Little, Brown.

Vaillant, G. E., & MacArthur, C. C. (1972). Natural history of male psychological health: The adult life cycle from 18–50. *Seminars in Psychiatry,* November.

Vandewater, E. A., & Stewart, A. J. (1993). Changes in women's career commitments and personality development. Unpublished manuscript.

Walsh, W. B., & Holland, J. L. (1992). A theory of personality types and work environments. In W. B. Walsh, K. H. Craik, & R. H. Price (Eds.), *Person-environment psychology: Models and perspectives* (pp. 35–69). Hillsdale, NJ: Lawrence Erlbaum Associates.

Weinrach, S. G., & Srebalus, D. J. (1990). Holland's theory of careers. In Duane Brown and Linda Brooks, *Career choice and development: Applying contemporary theory to practice* (pp. 37–67). San Francisco: Jossey-Bass.

Wiggins, J. D., Lederer, D. A., Salkowe, A., & Rys, G. (1983). Job satisfaction related to tested congruence and differentiation. *Journal of Vocational Behavior, 23,* 112–121.

Williams, C. P., & Savickas, M. L. (1990). Developmental tasks of career maintenance. *Journal of Vocational Behavior, 36,* 166–175.

Work in American Institute Studies in Productivity. (1978). *Mid-Career Perspectives: The Middle-Aged and Older Population.* Scarsdale, NY: Work in America Institute.

APPENDIX: Data Sets Used for Midlife Research Program Studies

Principal Investigator	Data Set	Design	Description
Atchley, R.	*Impact of Retirement on Aging and Adaptation, 1975–1977*	Longitudinal	Age, retirement, income, marital status, and health factors related to satisfaction and leisure in later life for men and women.
		$N = 1,000+$	Computer data generated from precoded questionnaires given in 4 waves (1 & 2 available).
Baruch, G. K., & Barnett, R. C.	*Women in the Middle Years, 1980*	Field Study	Psychological well-being in women (35–55) and its relation to age, income, education, health, work, and family status.
		$N = 238$	Computer data and structured interviews available.
Center for the Study of Aging and Human Development at Duke University	*Second Duke Longitudinal Study, 1968–1976*	Longitudinal & Cross-sectional	Psychological, social, and biomedical changes that characterize middle and later life in 10 age-sex cohorts.
		$N = 347$	Computer data available for all 4 waves.
Davidoff, I., & Platt, M.	*Two Generations of College-Educated Women: The Postparental Phase of the Life Cycle, 1957–1979*	Longitudinal	Education, work, family relationships, and self-concept related to adaptation and coping in women in the postparental phase.
		$N = 25$	Computer and interview data available for 2 waves; TATs in wave 2 assessment.

APPENDIX: *continued*

Principal Investigator	Data Set	Design	Description
Fiske, M., Thurnher, M., & Chiriboga, D.	*Longitudinal Study of Transitions in Four Stages of Life, 1968–1977*	Longitudinal	Commonalities and differences in coping processes at four different types of transitions in the life cycle.
		$N = 216$	Computer data, structured instruments, and lengthy opened-ended interviews from 5 waves available.
Jackson, J.	*National Survey of Black Americans, 1979–1980*	Survey	Development of appropriate theoretical and empirical approach to concepts, measures, and methods in the study of Black Americans.
		$N = 2,107$	Computer data available from extensive questionnaire.
Kelly, E. L.	*Kelly Longitudinal Study, 1935–1955*	Longitudinal	Marital compatibility and other aspects of married life, such as fertility, across a 20-year period.
		$N = 500+$	Computer and questionnaire data available from waves 1 and 2.
Connolly, J.	*Follow-up of the Kelly Longitudinal Study, 1979–1981*		Relationship between (inter/intra) personality characteristics and marriage compatibility over a 40-year period.
		$N = 393$	Questionnaire data available.

Sears, R., Maccoby, E., & Levin, H.*	Patterns of Child Rearing, 1952–1958	Longitudinal		Mothers' child-rearing practices and values. Children were 5–6 years of age at wave 1; 12–13 years at wave 2.
			N = 379+	Computer and interview data available for waves 1 and 2.
McClelland, D. C.	Follow-Up of Patterns of Child Rearing Subjects, 1978			Follow-up of the children at 30–31 years addressing their child-rearing practices and influences on their lives.
			N = 118	Computer data, interviews, and TATs available.
McClelland, D. C., & Franz, C.	Life Patterns Project: 1987–1988 Follow-Up of Patterns of Childrearing, 1987–1988			Follow-up of the children at 40–41 years focusing on predictors of four types of adjustment: social and work accomplishment and psychological and physical health.
			N = 89	Computer, interviews, TATs, and questionnaire data available.
Stewart, A. J.	Longitudinal Study of the Life Patterns of College-Educated Women, 1960–1986	Longitudinal		Effects of personality and situation on life outcomes of college-educated women.
			N = 100–244	Computer data for all waves; TATs for 1964; interviews and open-ended questions for 1974, 1976, and 1979 follow-ups available.

APPENDIX: *continued*

Principal Investigator	Data Set	Design	Description
Tangri, S.	*Longitudinal Study of Career Development in College-Educated Women, 1967–1981*	Longitudinal	Background, personality, and college experience characteristics of women entering fields dominated by men and those choosing careers more typical of women.
		$N = 100–200$	Computer data for all 3 waves; questionnaires from 1970 and projective stories from 1967 available.
Terman, L., Sears, R., Cronbach, L., & Sears, P.	*Terman Life Cycle Study of Children with High Ability, 1922–1986*	Longitudinal	Multiple measures of developmental issues; comparisons between a group of children with IQs of 135 or more and groups of children typical of the general population; conducted from 1922 to 1986.
		$N = 1,000+$	Computer and raw data, including original instruments, available for 12 waves.

*More follow-ups available

Hiroko Akiyama is assistant research scientist in the Life Course Development Program of the Institute for Social Research, University of Michigan. Her research interests focus on gender, culture, social relations, and health.

Carolyn M. Aldwin is associate professor in the Department of Human and Community Development, University of California, Davis. Her research is in the area of stress and coping in adulthood. She is author of *Stress, Coping, and Development: An Integrative Approach* (1994).

Toni Antonucci is program director in the Life Course Development Program of the Institute for Social Research, University of Michigan, and professor of psychology, also at Michigan. Her research focuses on social relations across the life span, including mother-infant attachment; multigenerational studies of the elderly; and comparative studies of social relations across the life span in the United States and Japan.

Rosalind C. Barnett is a senior scholar-in-residence at the Murray Research Center, Radcliffe College. She is co-author of *She Works / He Works: How Two-Income Families Are Happier, Healthier, and Better Off* (1996), *Lifeprints: New Patterns of Love and Work for Today's Women* (1985), and *Beyond Sugar and Spice* (1979); and is co-editor of *Gender and Stress* (1987).

Kristin A. Boyle is assistant professor in the Industrial / Organizational Psychology program of the Georgia Institute of Technology. Her research activities focus on self-regulation in organizational contexts, including goal setting and job satisfaction.

David A. Chiriboga is professor and chair of the Department of Health Promotion and Gerontology, School of Allied Health Sciences, as well as associate director of the Center on Aging, at the University of Texas Medical Branch, Galveston. He is the author, with Marjorie Fiske Lowenthal and Majda Thurnher, of *Four Stages of Life* (1974); with Marjorie Fiske, of *Change and Continuity in Adult Life* (1990); and, with Linda Catron and others, of *Divorce: Crisis, Challenge, or Relief?* (1991).

Anne Colby is director of the Murray Research Center, Radcliffe College. She is co-author, with William Damon, of *Some Do Care: Contemporary Lives of Moral Commitment* (1992); and co-editor, with Richard Jessor and Richard Shweder, of *Ethnography and Human Development: Context and Meaning in Social Inquiry* (1996).

Laura Gillespie DeHaan is assistant professor in the Department of Child Development and Family Science, North Dakota State University. Her research is in the area of adolescent identity development.

Carol E. Franz is research psychologist at the Institute of Human Development, University of California, Berkeley. She conducts research in the area of midlife development. She is co-editor, with Abigail Stewart, of *Women Creating Lives: Identities, Resilience, and Resistance* (1994).

Jessica Gomel is an evaluation and training consultant at Health and Education Research Services, Riverside, California.

Ravenna Helson is research psychologist at the Institute of Personality and Social Research, and adjunct professor in the Department of Psychology, University of California, Berkeley. She is director of the Mills Longitudinal Study, which she began in 1957. Her research is on personality and adult development in the social world.

Gabriela Heilbrun works in the field of child development and family studies, with an emphasis on the elderly. She is currently studying the quality of care in institutions—in particular, nursing homes for the aged.

Jacquelyn Boone James is assistant director of the Murray Research Center, Radcliffe College. Her work is in the area of gender and archival analysis.

Margie E. Lachman is professor of psychology and director of the Life-Span Developmental Psychology Laboratory, Brandeis University. She is the editor of *Planning and Control Processes Across the Life Span* (1993) and conducts research on cognition, personality, and the sense of control in adulthood and old age.

Frederick T. L. Leong is associate professor of psychology in the Counseling and Industrial/Organization programs, Ohio State University. His research is in the areas of vocational and cross-cultural psychology. He is the editor of *Womanpower: Managing in Times of Demographic Turbulence* (1992), with Uma Sekaran; *Career Development and Vocational Behavior of Racial and Ethnic Minorities* (1995); and *The Psychology Research Handbook: A Primer for Graduate Students and Research Assistants* (1996).

Corinne J. Lewkowicz is assistant research child psychologist at McLean Hospital, Belmont, Massachusetts, and research associate at the Harvard University Medical School. Her research interests focus on the development of gender stereotypes in deaf children and on adolescent psychopathology.

Shelley M. MacDermid is associate professor and head of the Graduate Program in the Department of Child Development and Family Studies, Purdue University. Her chapter in this volume was the 1995 winner of the Feldman Award from the Groves Conference on Marriage and Family.

Rebecca A. Parker is migrant education consultant to the State of California. She conducts research on adult psychosocial development.

Elizabeth L. Paul is assistant professor in the Psychology Department, Trenton State

College. Her research focuses on interpersonal relationships in adolescence and adulthood.

Ilene C. Siegler is associate professor of medical psychology in the Department of Psychiatry and Behavioral Sciences, and associate professor of psychology in Social and Health Sciences, Duke University. She is also adjunct associate professor of epidemiology in the School of Public Health, University of North Carolina, Chapel Hill. She is director of the Alumni Heart Study at North Carolina and conducts research at the Duke University Behavioral Medicine Research Center on developmental health psychology.

Abigail J. Stewart is professor of psychology and women's studies and director of the Institute for Research on Women and Gender, University of Michigan. She is co-editor, with Carol Franz, of *Women Creating Lives* (1994); with Anne Herrmann, of *Theorizing Feminism* (1994); and with Donna Stanton, of *Feminisms in the Academy* (1995).

Sandra P. Thomas is professor in the College of Nursing and Director of the Ph.D. Program in Nursing, University of Tennessee, Knoxville. She is author of *Women and Anger* (1993), and co-author, with Cheryl Jefferson, of *Use Your Anger* (1996).

Carol Tomlinson-Keasey is professor of psychology and vice provost for academic planning and personnel, University of California, Davis. Her research focuses on the adult lives of women and the way achievement and development during adulthood are defined.

Elizabeth A. Vandewater is assistant professor, St. Lawrence University. Her research is in the area of women's adult development and well-being.

identity of, 128–29; multiple roles for, 326–27, 332–36; and need for power, 132

The Wizard of Oz (Baum), 33–34

women: adult development of, 38–39, 48, 345–48, 368–69, 376–77; affiliation need of, 122–35; coping strategies of, 245; expectations for, 149, 326, 347; family values of, 89, 94–95; femininity of, 70, 75–76; gender identity of, 68, 111; generativity of, 210–14, 236; and health status, 257–91; masculinity of, 70–71, 75–76, 85, 88–89, 100–101; mastery by, 115; motivation of, 56–57; personality changes reported by, 26, 30–31; power need of, 121–35; prime of life for, 28; and social change, 308; and social relationships, 28–29, 151–54, 266–67; and stress, 265–66, 309–11; and timing issues, 307, 345–46; unexpected events for, 304–5; well-being of, 184–99. *See also* homemakers; mothers; wives; women's roles; working women

women's movement: influence by, 102, 308, 339, 345, 375, 404–5; rating of, 408n2; and women's work, 327, 338

women's roles: assumptions about, 213–14, 232, 326–27, 376; as caregivers, 160, 194, 356; changes in, 26, 29, 345–48; complexity of, 153–55, 163–64, 210–12, 265, 330, 368–69; as coworkers, 160–61; discontinuity of, 210, 235; dissatisfaction with, 264; expansion hypothesis on, 332–36; generativity in context of, 210–12; and health status, 257–58, 263–64, 274–76, 278–79, 328–29; influences on, 128, 404; measures of, 217–23, 235–36, 272–73; path analysis of, 225–29; scarcity hypothesis on, 331–32; sick/sickening type of, 285; and sociohistorical context, 49–50, 148–49, 339–40, 354–55,

368; subjective experience of, 257–58; traditional versus nontraditional, 34, 128, 157. *See also* mothers; parental roles; spousal role; wives; working women

work. *See* career orientation; employment; professions

working class, 27, 36. See also *Transitions in Four Stages of Life* study (TS)

working women: academic abilities of, 353–54; analysis of, 349–52; attitudes toward, 327–30, 333; career adjustment of, 441–43; career commitment of, 375–410; career consistency of, 443; career orientation of, 9, 94–95, 337–41, 347–48, 353–59; childhood personality characteristics of, 353; and children's development, 150; congruence of job/interests for, 443; differential experiences of, 376–77; discrimination against, 327–28, 368, 418–19, 422; family background of, 354, 382, 384–85, 388; generativity of, 162–63, 207–40; goals of, 346–47; health status of, 268–69, 275–76; increased number of, 76, 149, 329–30, 346–48; job satisfaction of, 422, 442–43; job stability of, 441–42; and life outcomes, 360–66; measures of role as, 217–23, 225; motivations of, 152–53, 354–55, 419; obstacles for, 335–36, 346–47; occupational categories for, 327, 349–51; occupational predictors for, 356–59; path analysis of roles of, 225–29; positive factors for, 330–36; power of, 211; predictor and outcome variables for, 350, 352; prestige of, 223, 225, 233–34, 269, 276; and social norms, 76, 333, 337–39, 368; and social roles, 76, 149, 263–65; and sociohistorical context, 339–40, 354–55, 368; stress for, 301, 334; well-being of, 325–43. *See also* career adjustment; career

DATE DUE